Handbook on European Nuclear Law

Energy and Environmental Law and Policy Series

VOLUME 39

Editor

General Editor: Professor Kurt Deketelaere, Professor of Law, University of Leuven, Belgium; Honorary Professor of Law, University of Dundee, UK; Honorary Chief of Staff, Flemish Government; Secretary-General, League of European Research Universities (LERU), Belgium. Kurt's CV – see www.kurtdeketelaere/en/kurt.

Introduction

Environmental protection and energy efficiency/security are important societal challenges. In order to tackle them, policy and legal frameworks are developed at national, regional and global level. Through study and best practices development, the challenges will prove to be solvable.

Contents/Subjects

Environment/Nature/Energy/Climate.

Objective

The aim of this series is to publish works of excellent quality that focus on the study of energy and environmental policy. Through this series the editors:

- contribute to the improvement of the quality of energy/environmental law and policy in general and environmental quality and energy efficiency in particular; increase the access to environmental and energy information for academics, non-governmental organizations, government institutions, and business; and
- facilitate cooperation between academic and non-academic communities in the field of energy and environmental law and policy throughout the world.

Readership

Academics and practitioners in environmental and energy matters.

The titles published in this series are listed at the end of this volume.

Handbook on European Nuclear Law

Competences of the Euratom Community under the Euratom Treaty

Rasa Engstedt

Wolters Kluwer

Published by:
Kluwer Law International B.V.
PO Box 316
2400 AH Alphen aan den Rijn
The Netherlands
E-mail: international-sales@wolterskluwer.com
Website: lrus.wolterskluwer.com

Sold and distributed by:
Wolters Kluwer Legal & Regulatory U.S.
7201 McKinney Circle
Frederick, MD 21704
United States of America
Email: customer.service@wolterskluwer.com

ISBN 978-94-035-2830-4

e-Book: ISBN 978-94-035-2831-1
web-PDF: ISBN 978-94-035-2832-8

Table of Contents

Preface

The Euratom Treaty was adopted more than sixty years ago. While the EEC has evolved through decades into the legal entity of the EU, the Euratom Community and the substantive law contained in the Euratom Treaty has never been amended. Hence, the stagnation of primary substantive law is a key legal feature that distinguishes the Euratom Treaty from the EU Treaties. Recurring legal discussions of the potentially obsolete nature of the Euratom Treaty is indicative of the need for the Handbook on European Nuclear Law to facilitate this discussion.

The main part of the Handbook consists of ten chapters mirroring the structure of the Euratom Treaty and examines the scope and content, the exercise and the case-law of the Euratom Communities competences in the field of: Promotion of Research (Chapter 1), Dissemination of Information (Chapter 2), Health and Safety (Chapter 3), Investments (Chapter 4), Joint Undertakings (Chapter 5), Supplies (Chapter 6), Safeguards (Chapter 7), Property Ownership (Chapter 8), the Nuclear Common Market (Chapter 9) and External Relations (Chapter 10).

After that, the classification of the Euratom Community's competences is proposed. The scope, content and the level of detail of the Euratom Community's competences under the Euratom Treaty show that these competences can be classified based on the legislative amendment procedure and on the level of regulatory detail. The evaluation of exercise of the Euratom Community's competences show that these competences can be classified based on quantitative elements of exercise, and based on whether secondary legal acts exercise the Euratom Community's competences in accordance with the wording of the Euratom Treaty. The competences can also be classified based on how active the CJEU has been in defining and delimiting the Euratom Community's competences.

Finally, the evaluation of the stagnation of the Euratom Treaty is provided. This study has identified the risks of generalisation when evaluating the relevance or obsoleteness of the provisions of the Euratom Treaty and the need for a systematic approach when evaluating the effects of stagnation of the Euratom Treaty on the acquis of the Euratom Community.

List of Abbreviations

ALARA	Acronym for optimisation principle ('as low as reasonably achievable')
BSS	Basic Safety Standards
CJEU	Court of Justice of the European Union
CPPNM	Convention on Physical Protection of Nuclear Materials, Facilities and Transports
E(E)C	European (Economic) Community
ECURIE	European Community Urgent Radiological Information Exchange
EEC	European Economic Community
EP	European Parliament
ESA	Euratom Supply Agency
ESARDA	European Safeguards Research and Development Association
EU	European Union
Euratom/EAEC	European Atomic Energy Community
IAEA	International Atomic Energy Agency
ITER	International Thermonuclear Experimental Reactor
JRC	Joint Research Centre
NPT	Treaty on the Non-Proliferation of Nuclear Weapons
OECD/NEA	Organisation for Economic Co-operation and Development/Nuclear Energy Agency
PINC	Nuclear Illustrative Programme
TEU	Treaty on European Union
TFEU	Treaty on the Functioning of the European Union

Acknowledgements

This book is dedicated to my family. I am lucky to have hard-working, ambitious, and loving people surrounding me. I am very greatful for that.

Brussels, Autumn of 2020
Rasa Engstedt

CHAPTER I
Introduction

The Euratom Treaty was drafted more than sixty years ago at a time when knowledge about and the economic prospects of nuclear energy were very different from today. This introductory chapter establishes the objectives and the structure of this study, presents the historical aspects on the origin of the Euratom Treaty and identifies its stagnant features.

A ORIGIN AND STAGNATION OF THE EURATOM TREATY

The historical aspects of the origin of the Euratom Treaty constitute important background information that helps one to understand the origin of the competences of the Euratom Community. From a policy perspective, the nuclear industry has gone through several phases.[1] The first phase was from the 1950s through to the Chernobyl accident in 1986, during which period law was an instrument for the promotion of the peaceful use of nuclear power. The second phase started with the Chernobyl nuclear accident in 1986 and was characterised by the use of law as a source of constraint amid renewed concerns about safety. The third phase started around 2006[2] and involved a focus on the cautious rebalancing of elements of constraint and promotion. This ongoing phase is the so-called nuclear renaissance or nuclear new build.[3] Each of these

1. P. D. Cameron identifies three phases of the nuclear industry. *See* P. D. Cameron, 'The Revival of Nuclear Power: An Analysis of the Legal Implications', (2007) 19/1 *Journal of Environmental Law*, p. 2. However, one could argue that the Fukushima Daiichi nuclear accident in 2011 triggered a new phase in which the nuclear industry began to focus once again on the safety of nuclear installations.
2. The start of the nuclear renaissance in the EU may be associated with the Commission of the European Communities, Green Paper: A European Strategy for Sustainable, Competitive and Secure Energy, COM (2006) 105 final, 8.3.2006, p. 9, where the Commission stated that '[t]he EU can play a useful role in ensuring that all costs, advantages and drawbacks of nuclear power are identified for a well-informed, objective and transparent debate'.
3. The term 'nuclear new build' is used, e.g., in the OECD/NEA publication 'Nuclear New Build: Insights into Financing and Project Management', No 7195, Paris: OECD/NEA, 2015. On the

phases has had some impact on the *acquis communautaire* of the Euratom Community. Understanding the origin of the Euratom Treaty facilitates understanding the origin of the Euratom Community's competences. When considering the historical aspects of the Euratom, the main focus is on the early stages of the Euratom Community and the adoption of the Euratom Treaty.

In the early stages of the communities, nuclear energy was regarded as being a sort of panacea for the pressing economic problems of 'the Six',[4] and as having the potential to spur economic growth for the still young and fragile European Community.[5] Spaak and Monnet started with the sectoral integration of nuclear energy because this was viewed as less ambitious than seeking to establish a general common market or customs union, and therefore less likely to fail.[6] Integration in the nuclear field would have not entailed the assimilation of national nuclear industries into a supranational one – national nuclear industries were to remain independent while being governed by a common supranational authority in the fields covered by the Euratom Treaty.[7]

The negotiations and creation of the Euratom Community also reflected a wider contemporary international phenomenon: universal optimism about the commercial and scientific applications of nuclear energy. The shift away from coal as the primary source of energy in the Western European economy exacerbated European anxieties

---

challenges and opportunities in the 'nuclear new build' phase, *see inter alia*: I. M. Drupady, 'Emerging Nuclear Vendors in the Newcomer Export Market: Strategic Considerations', (2019) 12 *Journal of World Energy Law and Business*, pp. 4–20; F. P. Lucet, 'Conditions and Possibilities for Financing New Nuclear Power Plants', (2019) 12 *Journal of World Energy Law and Business*, pp. 21–35; I. Wood and R. Broom, 'Newcomer Countries, Welcome to the 'Nuclear Club' but Before You Join, Plan Ahead and Take Example from Those Before You; Issues Relating to Construction Contracts in Countries Developing New Build Nuclear Power Plants', (2019) 12 *Journal of World Energy Law and Business*, pp. 89–107. The role of nuclear energy in combating climate change has been highlighted during this phase, *see, inter alia*: International Energy Agency, *Nuclear Power in a Clean Energy System*, Paris: IEA, May 2019; Intergovernmental Panel on Climate Change, *Global Warming of 1.5 °C: An IPCC Special Report on the Impacts of Global Warming of 1.5 °C Above Pre-industrial Levels and Related Global Greenhouse Gas Emission Pathways, in the Context of Strengthening the Global Response to the Threat of Climate Change, Sustainable Development, and Efforts to Eradicate Poverty*, IPCC: in Press, 2019; and T. Bruckner, I. A. Bashmakov, Y. Mulugetta, H. Chum, A. de la Vega Navarro, J. Edmonds, A. Faaij, B. Fungtammasan, A. Garg, E. Hertwich, D. Honnery, D. Infield, M. Kainuma, S. Khennas, S. Kim, H. B. Nimir, K. Riahi, N. Strachan, R. Wiser, and X. Zhang, '2014: Energy Systems', in O. Edenhofer, R. Pichs-Madruga, Y. Sokona, E. Farahani, S. Kadner, K. Seyboth, A. Adler, I. Baum, S. Brunner, P. Eickemeier, B. Kriemann, J. Savolainen, S. Schlömer, C. von Stechow, T. Zwickel and J. C. Minx (eds), *Climate Change 2014: Mitigation of Climate Change. Contribution of Working Group III to the Fifth Assessment Report of the Intergovernmental Panel on Climate Change*, United Kingdom and New York: Cambridge University Press, 2014; V. Knapp and D. Pevec, 'Promises and Limitations of Nuclear Fission Energy in Combating Climate Change', (2018) 120 *Energy Policy*, pp. 94–99.

4. The Inner Six, or simply 'the Six', were the six founding Member States of the European Communities: Belgium, France, Italy, Luxembourg, the Netherlands, and West Germany.
5. I. Cenevska, *The European Atomic Energy Community in the European Union Context: The 'Outsider' Within*, Leiden: Brill Nijhoff, 2016, p. 20.
6. J. Monnet, *Mémoires*, Paris: Fayard, 1976; S. Wolf 'Euratom Before the Court: A Political Theory of Legal Non-Integration', (2011) 15/10 *European Integration Online Papers*, p. 4.
7. J. G. Polach, *Euratom: Its Background, Issues and Economic Implications*, Dobbs Ferry, NY: Oceana Publications Inc., 1964, p. 28.

about the dangers of dependence on Middle East oil. The political goal of furthering European integration through the device of a nuclear energy community thus proved attractive.[8] The European Communities Treaty and the Euratom Treaty were signed at the same time in Rome on 25 March 1957 and entered into force on 1 January 1958, following ratification by the national parliaments. Together with the European Coal and Steel Community Treaty,[9] these Treaties formed the legal basis by means of which the Member States moved from the traditional international cooperation and relinquished part of their sovereignty to common institutions in the areas of coal and steel production, nuclear energy and the economy.[10] Being the basis and the starting point of the process of European integration, the Euratom Treaty is often overlooked in the history and operation of the European Union (EU). However, its tactical pairing with the European Economic Community was the crucial factor in initially persuading a sceptical French government to engage with European integration and eventually convincing it of the merits of so doing. In due course, Euratom was to be overshadowed by its sister proposal for the creation of a 'common market'. At the time, in 1955 and early 1956, however, it was widely believed in many quarters that the Euratom Community proposal held the greatest promise of success, as the negotiations over the European Economic Community (EEC) were faltering.[11] Some conclude that in the final analysis, the Euratom Treaty was effectively 'gutted',[12] that it became clear that the civil nuclear energy was still in its commercial infancy, and the economic predictions for nuclear energy were somehow unrealistic, and that the Euratom Community was justified largely by the expedient of political argument and by its role in contributing to a united Europe.[13]

The historical reasons for creating the Euratom Community and the promotional aspects of the Euratom Treaty also left behind certain legislative traces.[14] In order to create a new industrial sector and focus on establishing a legal basis for cooperation between the Euratom Community, companies and the Member States, as well as

8. A. Moravcsik, *The Choice for Europe: Social Purpose and State Power from Messina to Maastricht*, Ithaca, NY: Cornell University Press, 1998, pp. 119–120.
9. Treaty establishing the European Coal and Steel Community. No longer in force, date of end of validity was 23 July 2002.
10. European Commission, '50 Years of the Euratom Treaty', Memo/07/118, 26 March 2007 Brussels, p. 1.
11. European Parliament Directorate-General for Research/ M. O'Driscoll and G. Lake, The European Parliament and the Euratom Treaty: past, present and future, Energy Research Series, Working Paper ENER 114 EN, European Parliament L-2929 Luxembourg, p. 1.
12. *See* J. G. Polach, *Euratom: Its Background, Issues and Economic Implications*, Dobbs Ferry, NY: Oceana Publications Inc., 1964, p. 39; and A. Moravcsik, *The Choice for Europe: Social Purpose and State Power from Messina to Maastricht*, Ithaca, NY: Cornell University Press, 1998, p. 120.
13. A. Kramish, *The Peaceful Atom in Foreign Policy*, New York: Harper & Row/Council on Foreign Relations, 1963, pp. 233–234.
14. The promotion of research and dissemination of information is regulated in great detail and takes up twenty-six articles of the Euratom Treaty. By way of comparison, provisions on the health and safety of workers take up ten articles and the common market for nuclear energy takes up six articles.

coordination inside the Euratom Community,[15] the Euratom Treaty gave broad legislative powers to the institutions. However, some authors implied the Treaty lacked the typical features of a framework Treaty and did not lay down a comprehensive institutional and normative framework.[16]

Some researchers maintain that the Euratom Treaty was from the outset an outlier within the context of the EU and regard the fact that it has lasted for such a long time as a remarkable achievement.[17] This view of the Euratom Treaty is widespread, largely due to the specificity of the area of regulation and the fact that while the EEC has evolved through decades into the legal entity of the EU, the Euratom Community and the substantive law contained in the Euratom Treaty has never been amended. The Euratom Treaty therefore holds a special status.[18] It has undergone revision around the margins, in terms of taking account of institutional changes in the EU, such as notable accession rounds and the establishment of various EU institutions, but its substantive provisions have never undergone amendment.[19] Hence, the nuclear law remains the only European energy law field that is regulated by a separate primary legal act and falls primarily under the competences of the Euratom Community, and not the EU. Given the complexity of the process required to revise the Euratom Treaty, for which unanimity among all Member States is required,[20] it seems unlikely that the Euratom Treaty will change in the near future. It is its concrete application in the field that matters.[21]

15. I. Cenevska, *The European Atomic Energy Community in the European Union Context: The 'Outsider' Within*, Leiden: Brill Nijhoff, 2016, pp. 26–27.
16. H. Steiger, 'An Evaluation of Legal Development on a Regional Basis: The Search for European Unity', (1961) 22 *Ohio State Law Journal*, p. 505.
17. I. Cenevska, *The European Atomic Energy Community in the European Union Context: The 'Outsider' Within*, Leiden: Brill Nijhoff, 2016, p. 3.
18. R. J. Heffron, *Deconstructing Energy Law and Policy: The Case of Nuclear Energy*, Edinburgh: Edinburgh University Press, 2015, p. 2; J. Handrlica, 'Nuclear Law Revisited as an Academic Discipline', (2019) 12 *Journal of World Energy Law and Business*, p. 57; R. J. Heffron and K. Talus, 'The Development of Energy Law in the 21st Century: A Paradigm Shift?', (2016) 9 *Journal of World Energy Law and Business*, p. 191.
19. R. Kobia, 'The EU and Non-proliferation: Need for a Quantum Leap', (2008) 81 *Nuclear Law Bulletin*, p. 37; and W. Kilb, 'The European Atomic Energy Community and Its Primary and Secondary Law', in Legal Affairs of the OECD Nuclear Energy Agency (ed.) *International Nuclear Law: History, Evolution and Outlook, 10th Anniversary of the International School of Nuclear Law*, Paris: OECD, 2010, p. 44; on the stagnation of the Euratom Treaty *see, inter alia*, I. Cenevska, *The European Atomic Energy Community in the European Union Context: The 'Outsider' Within*, Leiden: Brill Nijhoff, 2016; and T F. Cusack, 'A Tale of Two Treaties', (2003) 40 *Common Market Law Review*, p. 121.
20. Under Article 106a of the Euratom Treaty, an ordinary amendment procedure of the Euratom Treaty is established in Article 48(2) to (5) of the Treaty on European Union.
21. W. Kilb, 'The Nuclear Safeguards Regime of Euratom: A Regional Cornerstone of the Verification of Non-Proliferation Obligations in the European Union', in J. L. Black-Branch and D. Fleck (eds), *Nuclear Non-Proliferation in International Law, Volume II: Verification and Compliance*, The Hague: Asser Press, 2016, p. 151.

Stagnation of primary substantive law is a key legal feature that distinguishes the Euratom Treaty from the EU Treaties.[22] Concern as to the stagnation of the Euratom Treaty was expressed by some Member States in Declaration No. 54 of the Lisbon Treaty.[23] It was noted that the Treaty establishing the European Atomic Energy Community needed to be brought up to date. Therefore Germany, Ireland, Hungary, Austria and Sweden supported the idea of a Conference of the Representatives of the Governments of the Member States, to be convened as soon as possible. However, only a few Member States have signed the declaration, and twenty-two have, at least for the moment, chosen not to address this issue, which is politically sensitive because it divides EU Member States into two camps by reference to whether they support or do not support the use of nuclear energy. Due to the need for consensus in decision-making mentioned above, the political sensitivity of the issue, the existence of a number of conflicting interests and also due to the fact that the Euratom Treaty does not impose any obligation on the Member States to use nuclear energy, it appears unlikely that the substantive law it contains will be subject to a major reform in the short or mid-term.[24] Some authors consider that some of the provisions of the Euratom Treaty have not been implemented and are therefore obsolete,[25] implying not only stagnation of the provisions of the Euratom Treaty but also of the legal framework of the Euratom Community.

The fact that certain provisions might not be implemented does not diminish the Commission's legal right to start implementing these seemingly obsolete provisions at any time. Discussion of the potentially obsolete nature of some of the provisions of the

22. J. Handrlica analyses the stagnation of the Euratom Treaty by defining the Euratom Community as static or flexible, depending on how competences have been used. *See* J. Handrlica, 'The Splendid Durability of the Provisional: A Tribute to Euratom', (2018) 14/14 *Croatian Yearbook of European Law & Policy*.
23. Declaration No 54 by the Federal Republic of Germany, Ireland, the Republic of Hungary, the Republic of Austria and the Kingdom of Sweden, Consolidated versions of the Treaty on European Union and the Treaty on the Functioning of the European Union, OJ C 83 of 30 March 2010, p. 356.
24. W. Kilb, 'The European Atomic Energy Community and Its Primary and Secondary Law', in Legal Affairs of the OECD Nuclear Energy Agency (ed.), *International Nuclear Law: History, Evolution and Outlook, 10th Anniversary of the International School of Nuclear Law*, Paris: OECD, 2010, p. 85; J. Handrlica, 'The Splendid Durability of the Provisional: A Tribute to Euratom', (2018) 14/14 *Croatian Yearbook of European Law & Policy*, p. 173; C. True, 'The Euratom Community Treaty´s Prospects at the Start of the New Millennium' (2006) 1/1 *International Journal of Nuclear Law*, p. 247. For analysis of nuclear energy policy and nuclear integration and cooperation in Europe, *see* P. M. Barnes and B. Leverkusen, *The Politics of Nuclear Energy in the European Union. Framing the Discourse: Actors, Positions and Dynamics*, Opladen, Berlin and Toronto: Budrich Publishers, 2018, p. 292; and J. Handrlica, 'The Politics of Nuclear Energy in the European Union. Framing the Discourse: Actors, Positions and Dynamics', (2019) 37/4 *Journal of Energy & Natural Resources Law*, pp. 438-442.
25. Some authors argue that, for example, in the field of supplies, the Euratom Treaty was drafted to cope with scarcity of supply, but in practice the main problem turned out to be oversupply. Due to that, regulation concerning equal access to source of supply, stockpiles and right of option became obsolete. *See* A. Bouquet, 'How Current Are Euratom Provisions on Nuclear Supply and Ownership in View of the European Union's Enlargement?', (2001) 68 *Nuclear Law Bulletin*, p. 11. For the Euratom Treaty being obsolete, *see also* T. Erhag, 'Är kärnavfall ett bekymmer för EU eller medlemsstaterna? – om kärnavfallsfrågan och principen om nationellt ansvar i EG-fördraget och Euratomfördraget', (2007) 7/1 *CERGU Working Papers Series*.

Euratom Treaty is indicative of the need for systematic analysis and evaluation of the competences conferred under the Euratom Treaty in order to evaluate the implications of its stagnation on the entirety of the *acquis* of the Euratom Community. The perception that such stagnation might exist in the primary legal act of the Euratom Community should not per se be interpreted as implying the stagnation of the Euratom Community's *acquis* in its entirety.

B OBJECTIVES OF THIS STUDY

Competence means an ability or a capacity of a natural, legal person or institution to do something that is legally binding or has some legally valid effect.[26] Some authors describe competence as having a hypothetical possibility to change legal position by performing a special kind of act; and exercise of a competence as bringing about an intended change in legal position by performing a competence-exercising act.[27] The idea of competence is also related to the idea of legal validity. If a person or a body does not have a competence to do something, then that person or body cannot make a legally valid decision on the matter in question.[28] The issue of defining and delimiting competences is complex. The Court of Justice of the European Union (CJEU) does not provide a one-size-fits-all definition of what constitutes the delimitation of competences, as it has established different doctrines that vary by reference to the sector involved and sometimes even within the same sector.[29] This implies that competences differ and the methods and approaches suitable for the analysis of some competences cannot be applied to others. The case-law of the CJEU shows that the specificity of the field concerned, and the substantive law related to each competence require an individual approach.

Since the signing of the Lisbon Treaty, the EU's competences have been a high profile and much-researched subject.[30] However, comparatively little research has been carried out in relation to competences under the Euratom Treaty, and the available legal research mostly focuses on reconciling the Euratom Treaty's provisions with those of the EU Treaties.[31] The Euratom Community is sometimes considered to

26. G. Conway, *EU Law*, London and New York: Routledge, 2015, p. 259.
27. T. Spaak 'Norms That Confer Competence' (2003) 16/1 *Ratio Juris*, p. 91.
28. T. Spaak 'Norms That Confer Competence' (2003) 16/1 *Ratio Juris*, pp. 91–92.
29. C. Timmermans, 'ECJ Doctrines on Competences', pp. 155–159, in L. Azoulai (ed.), *The Question of Competence in the European Union*, Oxford: Oxford University Press, 2014.
30. Examples of such research include L. Azoulai (ed.), *The Question of Competence in the European Union*, Oxford: Oxford University Press, 2014; G. Conway, 'Conflicts of Competence Norms in EU Law and the Legal Reasoning of the ECJ', (2010) 11/9 *German Law Journal*; R. Schutze, 'Lisbon and the Federal Order of Competences: A Prospective Analysis', (2008) 33/5 *European Law Review*, pp. 709–722; S. Prechal, 'Competence Creep and General Principles of Law', (2010) 3/1 *Review of European Administrative Law*, pp. 5–22; A. Dashwood, 'The Limits of European Community Powers', (1996) 21/2 *European Law Review*, pp. 113–128.
31. I. Cenevska, *The European Atomic Energy Community in the European Union Context: The 'Outsider' Within*, Leiden: Brill Nijhoff, 2016; and A. Södersten, 'The EU and Nuclear Safety: Challenges Old and New', (2012) 10 *SIEPS European Policy Analysis*.

be *terra incognita* for scholars of EU law.[32] Although the stagnation of primary law is the main feature of the Euratom Treaty, its provisions were expressly confirmed by the Treaty of Lisbon and, therefore, the Euratom Treaty cannot be considered to be an outdated or antiquated Treaty that has no practical applicability.[33] The parties to the Lisbon Treaty considered it necessary for the provisions of the Euratom Treaty to continue to have full legal effect.[34] The substantive law of the Euratom Treaty does not form part of the provisions of the Lisbon Treaty. The Euratom Treaty is a primary legal act that stands on its own, creating an odd construction under European Law, where the main institutions are shared between the EU and the Euratom Community and different policies are closely interlinked.[35]

The Euratom Community and its competences under the Euratom Treaty are the focus of this study. As competence implies a capacity to regulate, and regulation itself may be understood as one of the outcomes of this capacity, the overarching objective of this study is to analyse the way in which the stagnation of the primary law of the Euratom Community has affected its *acquis*. For this purpose, it is necessary to analyse, characterise and categorise the Euratom Community's competences in relation to the Euratom Treaty's areas of regulation. This general objective may be subdivided into three more specific objectives. First, to analyse the scope, content and exercise of the competences under the Euratom Community, and the CJEU's case-law on it, by reference to the way in which these competences are drafted under the Euratom Treaty. Second, using a systematic comparative analysis an objective is to evaluate how the Euratom Community's competences under the Euratom Treaty differ from each other, depending on the area of regulation. Third, based on these different features of competences, to propose a systematisation of the Euratom Community's competences. This will reveal how the stagnation of the Euratom Treaty has affected the *acquis* of the Euratom Community.

This study accordingly focuses on the legal analysis[36] Euratom Community's competences and covers the Euratom Treaty, secondary legislation derived from it and CJEU's case-law in this field. Only the secondary legislation currently in force is addressed, and historical aspects are excluded from the scope of the study. Furthermore, only the case-law of the CJEU that specifically addresses provisions of the Euratom Treaty in confirming or defining the Euratom Community's competences fall under the scope of the study. Due to the ambit of the study, the analysis mainly focuses on the Euratom Community's vertical competences. The Euratom Community's horizontal competences are wider than the scope of this study because they are regulated

32. J. Handrlica, 'The Splendid Durability of the Provisional: A Tribute to Euratom', (2018) 14/14 *Croatian Yearbook of European Law & Policy*, p. 164; and A. Södersten, 'The EU and Nuclear Safety: Challenges Old and New', (2012) 10 *SIEPS European Policy Analysis*, p. 1.
33. Commission Decision (EU) 2017/2112 of 6 March 2017 on the measure/aid scheme/State aid SA.38454 – 2015/C (ex 2015/N) which Hungary is planning to implement for supporting the development of two new nuclear reactors at Paks II nuclear power station (notified under document C(2017) 1486), OJ L 317, 1.12.2017, recital 292, p. 104.
34. *See* Protocol No 2 to the Treaty of Lisbon.
35. L. Krämer, *EU Environmental Law*, London: Sweet & Maxwell, 2011, p. 381.
36. Policy aspects regarding the role of nuclear energy in the clean energy transition are excluded from the scope of this study.

both by the Euratom Treaty and by the EU Treaties.[37] They are accordingly only analysed in the context of vertical competences where this appears relevant in the light of the objectives of this study. The methodology of the study is qualitative research based on a descriptive, analytical and comparative approach.

To achieve the first objective, a comprehensive analysis of the areas regulated by the Euratom Treaty is needed. In this context, the specific features of the Euratom Treaty are identified to analyse whether and how the specificity of a stagnant Euratom Treaty has influenced the Euratom Community's competences. Achieving the second objective and showing that these competences differ from one another calls for comparative legal analysis. In other words, there is a need to analyse and evaluate the competences in a manner applicable to all the Euratom Community's competences. To achieve the third objective and to propose a systematisation of the Euratom Community's competences, the common features of these competences are used with a view to group them.

C STRUCTURE OF THIS STUDY

The study consists of two overarching chapters (II. Evaluation of Competences under the Euratom Treaty; III. General Aspects of the Euratom Community's Competences), which provide a general overview of the Euratom Community's competences; and an analysis of specific Euratom Community competences, which is divided into ten constituent chapters (from 1 Promotion of Research to 10 External Relations). In addition, there is also an introduction and conclusions.

The Chapter II on the evaluation of competences under the Euratom Treaty has two main objectives. First, it embarks upon a process of comparative evaluation and seeks to determine whether there are any similarities between the origins of the EU's competences and those of the Euratom Community. It analyses whether certain aspects of competence under EU law are applicable to the Euratom Treaty – the concept of lack of competence, the concept of common interest, the shift in approach under Article 3(6) TEU, the classification of competences under the TFEU and the principle of subsidiarity. Second, it identifies the methodology used to analyse and evaluate the specific competences of the Euratom Community under the Euratom Treaty.

The Chapter III on general aspects of the Euratom Community's competences identifies objectives and tasks of the Euratom Community, as these are essential to evaluate the scope of a competence. This chapter also addresses certain general aspects of the Euratom Community's horizontal competences, i.e., the connection between the Euratom Treaty and the EU Treaties via Article 106a of the Euratom Treaty, the limited competences of the European Parliament (EP) under the Euratom Treaty, and the role of the Council, the Commission and the CJEU in the Euratom Community. Furthermore, the methodology for the evaluation of competences established in the introductory Chapter II Section C of this study is utilised to provide an analysis of the Euratom

37. Article 106a of the Euratom Treaty makes articles of the Treaty on European Union (TEU) and Treaty on the Functioning of the European Union (TFEU) applicable to the Euratom Community.

Community's competences in respect of the military application of nuclear energy and its competences under Article 203[38] of the Euratom Treaty.

The methodology set out in Chapter II Section C is used to analyse and evaluate the Euratom Community's fields of competence under Title II of the Euratom Treaty.[39] This analysis seeks to identify common elements (features) in competences that permit their classification into certain groups. Consequently, the Euratom Community's competences are analysed based on their scope and content, the exercise of these competences under the Euratom Treaty in the shape of secondary legal acts and on the CJEU's case-law. The latter analysis evaluates the Euratom Community's competences in respect of the following areas: the promotion of research in the Euratom Community under Chapter 1 of the Euratom Treaty (Articles 4 to 11); the dissemination of information under Chapter 2 of the Euratom Treaty (Articles 12 to 29); ensuring the health and safety of the general public and workers from the hazardous effects of ionising radiation under Chapter 3 of the Euratom Treaty (Articles 30 to 39); the promotion of investment in nuclear energy in Europe under Chapter 4 of the Euratom Treaty (Articles 40 to 44); the establishment of Joint Undertakings in the Euratom Community under Chapter 5 of the Euratom Treaty (Articles 45 to 51); the creation of the Euratom Community's common supply policy and the creation of the Euratom Supply Agency under Chapter 6 of the Euratom Treaty (Articles 52 to 76); the establishment of the exclusive nuclear safeguards system in the Euratom Community under Chapter 7 of the Euratom Treaty (Articles 77 to 85); the canalisation of the exclusive ownership of all fissile materials provided to the Euratom Community under Chapter 8 of the Euratom Treaty (Articles 86 to 91); the creation of the nuclear common market under Chapter 9 of the Euratom Treaty (Articles 92 to 100); and the establishment and maintenance of the Euratom Community's external relations under Chapter 10 of the Euratom Treaty (Articles 101 to 106).

The concluding chapter of this study has two different functions. First, it proposes classifications of the Euratom Community's competences, based on their features – regulation under the Euratom Treaty; the way in which they are exercised in the secondary legal acts; and on how active the CJEU has been in delimiting them. Second, based on these classifications, it discusses the manner in which the stagnation of the Euratom Treaty has affected the *acquis* of the Euratom Community.

---

38. Article 203 of the Euratom Treaty provides that where action proves necessary to attain one of the objectives of the Euratom Community and the Euratom Treaty does not provide the necessary powers to do so, the Council shall, acting unanimously on a proposal from the Commission and after consulting the EP, take the appropriate measures.
39. Under Title II of the Euratom Treaty, the Contracting Parties established the ten main areas of the Euratom Community's competences. *See also* J. Handrlica, 'The Splendid Durability of the Provisional: A Tribute to Euratom', (2018) 14/14 *Croatian Yearbook of European Law & Policy*, p. 162.

CHAPTER II

Evaluation of Competences under the Euratom Treaty

While each field of competence requires an individual approach, the question of whether there are certain structural aspects that all competences share should be answered. This chapter assesses the relevance of certain key issues concerning competences under EU law to the evaluation and analysis of competences under the Euratom Treaty. For this purpose, both the origin and the concept of a competence are analysed. The chapter also offers a method by which to analyse and evaluate competences under the Euratom Treaty in order to ensure a basis for comparative analysis and the identification of common features of these competences.

There has been scant legal research on the analysis and evaluation of competences under the Euratom Treaty, but the competences of the EU have been broadly analysed, especially during the last few decades. Therefore, an overview of EU law doctrines is set out below with a view to finding parallels between the origin and concept of EU competences and the origin and concept of Euratom Community competences. However, the concept of competence is a complex issue,[40] and this chapter confines itself to analysing those aspects of EU law concerning competences that raise the questions that need to be raised in order to analyse a competence in a certain area of regulation. In other words, EU law on competences is investigated only in order to facilitate the elaboration of the method to be followed to analyse and evaluate competences under the Euratom Treaty.

40. Due to the fact that the CJEU has not developed a real doctrine, in the sense of a self-standing, systematically ordered construct, on the issue of competences and the division of competences between the EU and its Member States, it should not be called a doctrine, but different approaches to the issue of competence. Furthermore, as these approaches vary not only between different sectors of regulation, but also within one and the same sector, the usefulness of EU competence approaches to the delimitation of competences under the Euratom Treaty seems to lie in posing relevant questions in relation to the latter. *See* C. Timmermans, 'ECJ Doctrines on Competences', in L. Azoulai (ed.), *The Question of Competence in the European Union*, Oxford: Oxford University Press, 2014, pp. 155–159.

A ORIGIN OF COMPETENCE

There has always been a certain ambiguity about defining the limits of the competences of the European Communities. Some contend that the law governing European integration has from the outset dealt mainly with 'the matter of defining spheres of competence and power relationships'.[41] Until the end of the 1990s astonishingly little research had been carried out in respect of the system of the communities' competences,[42] but the Member States have become increasingly alert to the issue of defining EU competences over time, especially from the Treaty of Maastricht in 1992 onwards.[43] Despite that, defining competences under EU law has always been problematic, notwithstanding the inclusion of the principle of conferred powers in the Treaty of Maastricht.[44] Some authors state that the concept of competence originates from the ultimate purpose of all three Communities (the European Coal and Steel Community, the Euratom Community and the European Economic Community), which is to create a common market. However, as national rules may be viewed as obstacles to free movement or a possible source of distortion of competition, it may be difficult to define the precise scope of EU competences.[45] The objectives of this study necessitate analysis of whether a 'common market goal' or 'ever-closer Union goal' applies to the Euratom Community in the same way as it does to the EU. In other words, the question is whether the goal of creating a common market may be understood as an element of the origins of the Euratom Community's competences.

Article 1 of the Euratom Treaty establishes that it is the task of the Euratom Community to contribute to the raising of the standard of living in the Member States and to the development of relations with other countries by creating the conditions necessary for the speedy establishment and growth of nuclear industries. One of the measures for establishing nuclear industries in Europe was the creation of a nuclear common market,[46] which would facilitate the movement of nuclear goods and services between different national nuclear installations. Therefore, one of the purposes of the Euratom Community was to promote the use and development of civil nuclear energy[47] by creating a common market for it. Some scholars imply that the Euratom Community

41. P. Pescatore, *The Law of Integration: Emergence of a New Phenomenon in International Relations, Based on the Experience of the European Communities*, Leiden: Sijthoof, 1974, p. 26.
42. A. von Bogdandy and J. Bast, 'The Federal Order of Competences', in A. von Bogdandy and J. Bast (eds), *Principles of European Constitutional Law*, Oxford: Hart Publishing, 2011, p. 276.
43. G. Conway, *EU Law*, London and New York: Routledge 2015, p. 257.
44. G. Conway, 'Conflicts of Competence Norms in EU Law and the Legal Reasoning of the ECJ', (2010) 11/9 *German Law Journal*, p. 966.
45. G. Conway, *EU Law*, London and New York: Routledge 2015, pp. 258–259.
46. Article 2(g) of the Euratom Treaty states that the Community shall 'ensure wide commercial outlets and access to the best technical facilities by the creation of a common market in specialised materials and equipment, by the free movement of capital for investment in the field of nuclear energy and by freedom of employment for specialists within the Community'. *See also* Chapter 9 of the Euratom Treaty and Chapter 9 of this study for the nuclear common market.
47. D. D. Smith, 'The European Atomic Energy Community (Euratom): The Limits of Supranationalism', (1970) 1 *California Western International Law Journal*, p. 53; P. M. Barnes, 'Nuclear Safety for Nuclear Electricity – The Search for a Solid Legal Basis for Nuclear Safety in an Enlarged European Union', (2003) 45 *Managerial Law*, p. 134.

may be regarded as a promotional enterprise.[48] Consequently, the 'common market goal' inherent in EU law is also an important aspect of the origin of the Euratom Community's competences.

B CONCEPT OF COMPETENCE

As the origin of competence lies within EU and the Euratom Community, it is reasonable to start the analysis with a comparative approach to the concept of competence. This section discusses a few key aspects of the treatment of this concept under EU law in relation to its treatment under the Euratom Treaty, focusing on the following five aspects of competence under EU law and whether they apply to the Euratom Treaty: lack of competence; the concept of common interest; the shift in approach under Article 3(6) TEU; the classification of competences under Articles 2–6 TFEU; and the principle of subsidiarity in Article 5 TEU.

The term 'competence' was originally enshrined in Article 173 of the EEC Treaty (now Article 263 TFEU).[49] Article 263 TFEU states that the CJEU shall 'have jurisdiction in actions brought by a Member State, the EP, the Council or the Commission on grounds of lack of competence, infringement of an essential procedural requirement, infringement of the Treaties or of any rule relating to their application, or misuse of powers'. The wording 'on grounds of lack of competence' refers in this context both to the question of jurisdiction (the scope of a competence to act) and to the question of powers (the means and instruments of a competence to act).[50] In other words, lack of competence under the EU Treaties can be based on the fact that an institution has acted in a field that it does not have competence over or on the fact that an institution has acted beyond the powers it was delegated in the field that it has competence in. This implies that issues concerning lack of competence may originate from the content (lack of scope) or from the method (lack of means and instruments). The question here is whether the Euratom Treaty defines competence in the same manner. Title III, Chapter 2, Section 4 of the Euratom Treaty regulates the competences of the CJEU under the Euratom Treaty. Before the amendments introduced by the Lisbon Treaty, Article 146 of the Euratom Treaty[51] conferred on the Court the task of reviewing the legality of acts of the Council and the Commission other than recommendations or opinions and granted, for this purpose, jurisdiction in actions brought by a Member State, the Council or the Commission on grounds of lack of competence, infringement of an essential procedural requirement, infringement of the Euratom Treaty or of any rule of law relating to its application, or misuse of powers. Comparative analysis of Article 263 TFEU and Article 146 of the Euratom Treaty reveals they are very similar both in

48. L. Scheinmann, 'Euratom: Nuclear Integration in Europe', (1967) 563 *International Conciliation*, p. 56; P. Mathijsen, 'Some Legal Aspects of Euratom', (1965–1966) 3 *Common Market Law Review*, p. 330.
49. L. Azoulai, 'Introduction: The Question of Competence', in L. Azoulai (ed.), *The Question of Competence in the European Union*, Oxford: Oxford University Press, 2014, p. 2.
50. L. Azoulai, 'Introduction: The Question of Competence', in L. Azoulai (ed.), *The Question of Competence in the European Union*, Oxford: Oxford University Press, 2014, p. 2.
51. No longer in force.

wording and in content. This means that the concept of 'lack of competence' and the origin of 'lack of competence' was in the Euratom Treaty from its adoption and the establishment of the Euratom Community. Article 146 of the Euratom Treaty was repealed by the Lisbon Treaty[52] and replaced with a reference to specific articles of the TFEU in Article 106a of the Euratom Treaty. Under Article 106a(1) of the Euratom Treaty, Articles 246 to 270 TFEU are applicable to the Euratom Treaty, which means that Article 263 TFEU is applicable too. The fact that the wording of Article 146 of the Euratom Treaty was very similar to that of Article 263 TFEU implies that 'lack of competence' should be applicable under the Euratom Treaty in the same way as under the EU Treaties, and that the origin of the concept of competence and the analysis of the 'lack of competence' originated from the EEC Treaties and the Euratom Treaty simultaneously. Analysis of the competence, or lack of it, under the Euratom Treaty should therefore cover aspects of scope and instruments.

In relation to EU competences, in addition to the functional understanding of competences, the structural conception of integration[53] and the concept of 'common interest' of the EU must also be taken into account. For example, in respect of the common commercial policy, particular interests of the Member States must endeavour to adapt to each other to defend the common interests of the EU.[54] This implies that integration requires a common interest of the EU and that it is not possible to defend a common interest unless the EU has a competence in that field. Therefore, it is reasonable to assume that, on the one hand, a common interest may be considered to be a source of competences, and, on the other hand, that an interest may be regarded as common when particular interests of different Member States must adapt to each other for a purpose promoted by the EU. A common interest may be justified either by a need to present a 'unified system' to the outside world,[55] for example, in respect of external relations; or due to the need to ensure the effectiveness of the objectives of the EU in the internal domain of competences. This rationale of the effectiveness of the EU Treaties and ultimately of the legal integration process has been essential in the approach to the competence problem in all areas and throughout different periods of European integration.[56]

Regarding the Euratom Treaty, the analyses should start with an assessment of whether the concept of common interest has played any significant role in relation to the issue of competences under the Euratom Treaty. Furthermore, it is also necessary to assess whether the rationale of an increased effectiveness and integration, which has been a cornerstone in the development of the competences of the EU, has had any impact on the Euratom Community's competences.

52. Article 5 of Protocol No 2, Treaty of Lisbon Amending the Treaty on European Union and the Treaty Establishing the European Community, (2007/C 306/01).
53. L. Azoulai, 'Introduction: The Question of Competence', in L. Azoulai (ed.), *The Question of Competence in the European Union*, Oxford: Oxford University Press, 2014, p. 5.
54. Opinion of the Court of 11 November 1975, 1/75, ECLI:EU:C:1975:145, p. 1363.
55. Opinion of Advocate General Tesauro of 13 November 1997, *Hermès International v FHT Marketing Choice*, C-53/96, ECLI:EU:C:1997:539.
56. *See* P. Craig, 'Competence and Member State Autonomy: Causality, Consequence and Legitimacy', in H.-W. Micklitz and B. De Witte (eds), *The European Court of Justice and the Autonomy of the Member States*, Antwerp: Intersentia, 2012, p. 11.

It has been established that stagnation is the main feature of the Euratom Treaty, meaning that practically no integration took place in the Euratom Community, in comparison to the continuous development that took place in the context of the European Communities and, later, the EU. Nevertheless, the lack of different periods of integration should not automatically exclude the possibility of a common interest being the ground for the Euratom Community's competences.

The preamble of the Euratom Treaty states that the establishers of the Euratom Community recognised that nuclear energy represents an essential resource for the development and were convinced that only a joint effort undertaken without delay could offer the prospect of achievements commensurate with the creative capacities of their countries. This, together with the historical background given above, allows one to conclude that the Euratom Community was created on the strength of a common interest, on the part of the Member States, in combining their forces to establish a nuclear energy sector that would contribute to raising standards of living in the Member States.[57] Another common interest that arises from the preamble is the need for common safety conditions in order to eliminate hazards to the life and health of the public that can be caused by the negative effects of ionising radiation and securing the same level of protection throughout the Euratom Community.[58] The concept of a common interest generally requires a certain sacrifice on the part of the Member States or adaption of their needs to those of the Community. Therefore, the issue of whether the adaptation of national freedom of actions to the needs of the Community have been functioning under the Euratom Treaty in the same way as under the EU Treaties should be analysed. Without embarking on a deeper analysis of the substantive law contained in the Euratom Treaty so early in this study, some articles should still be mentioned here, as they play a significant role in defining the existence of a 'common interest' under the Euratom Treaty. Article 30 of the Euratom Treaty states that basic standards shall be laid down within the Community for the protection of the health of workers and the general public against the dangers arising from ionising radiation. This means that protection against the dangers arising from ionising radiation is an interest of the Euratom Community and Member State have to adopt appropriate national provisions to ensure compliance with Euratom Community's basic standards and take the necessary measures with regard to teaching, education and vocational training.[59] Article 37 of the Euratom Treaty establishes that each Member State shall provide the Commission with general data relating to any plan for the disposal of radioactive waste in order for the Commission to determine whether the implementation of such plan is liable to result in the radioactive contamination of the water, soil or airspace of another Member State. This article prioritises the common interest in preventing radioactive contamination in the territory of the Euratom Community above each Member State's right to make a national decision on the radioactive waste disposal facilities without supranational interference. Article 52(1) of the Euratom Treaty establishes the Euratom

57. Article1 of the Euratom Treaty.
58. The Preamble of the Euratom Treaty states that the Member States are anxious to create the conditions of safety necessary to eliminate hazards to the life and health of the public.
59. Article 33(1) of the Euratom Treaty.

Community's common policy on security of supply, and states that the supply of ores, source materials and special fissile materials shall be ensured by means of a common supply policy, based on the principle of equal access to sources of supply. This means that no Member State of the Euratom Community owns its supply of ores, source materials and special fissile materials – it is owned and administered by the Nuclear Supply Agency[60] in order to protect the common interest of security of supply of the Euratom Community. These examples are indicative of the theme of prioritisation of the Euratom Community's needs above the interests of individual Member States that runs through the Euratom Treaty. Consequently, the concept of 'common interest' is also relevant to analysis of the Euratom Community's competences under the Euratom Treaty.

The introduction of Article 3(6) TEU was one of the biggest shifts from the original concept of broad EU competences, where the fact that the EU could act was taken for granted and only the exercise, not the existence, of EU competence was disputed.[61] This provision states that the EU shall pursue its objectives by appropriate means commensurate with the competences which are conferred upon it in the Treaties. This meant that the EU's objectives were no longer the main source for delimiting its powers and legal instruments.[62] Instead, its objectives became subject to the competences listed in the EU Treaties.[63] This change of direction on the interpretation of the relationship between the competences of the EU and the objectives of the EU established in the EU Treaties is also starting to be reflected in the CJEU's case-law. In one of its cases, the CJEU stated that "in view of that significant development of primary law, the question of distribution of competences of the European Union and the Member States must be examined on the basis of the Treaty now in force".[64] The relevance of this shift to Euratom Community law should be analysed here, starting with a discussion of the relationship between Article 3 TEU and the Euratom Treaty. Article 106a of the Euratom Treaty, which is a connecting 'bridge' between the Euratom Treaty and the EU Treaties, does not refer to Article 3 TEU in the list of articles of the EU Treaties that apply to the Euratom Treaty. The shift in the interpretation of the relationship between the objectives and the established competencies cannot, therefore, be directly applicable to the Euratom Treaty. Second, the question of whether the shift could indirectly influence the interpretation of provisions of the Euratom Treaty – implying that the Euratom Treaty should not be read in the light of its objectives but rather its objectives should be subject to actual competences – should be analysed. There are no legal obstacles that prevent EU law from indirectly influencing the interpretation of provisions of the Euratom Treaty, especially keeping in mind that the

60. Articles 53 to 56 of the Euratom Treaty.
61. L. Azoulai, 'Introduction: The Question of Competence', in L Azoulai (ed.), *The Question of Competence in the European Union*, Oxford: Oxford University Press, 2014, p. 7.
62. J. Larik, *Worldly Ambitions: Foreign policy objectives in European Constitutional Law*, Florence: EUI, 2013, pp. 201 and 205.
63. L. Azoulai, 'Introduction: The Question of Competence', in L. Azoulai (ed.), *The Question of Competence in the European Union*, Oxford: Oxford University Press, 2014, pp. 11–12.
64. Judgment of 18 July 2013, *Daiichi Sankyo and Sanofi-Aventis Deutschland*, C-414/11, ECLI: EU:C:2013:520, paragraph 48.

EU and the Euratom Community share the same institutions.[65] However, the historical aspects of the Euratom Community play a significant role in this context. First, unlike the EU Treaties, the Euratom Treaty has never undergone an expansion of competences, or what is sometimes referred to as 'competence creep', in which the application of general principles of law has, in the case of the EU Treaties, led to an extension of EU competences.[66] Second, the competences laid down in the Euratom Treaty, which was established for the purpose of governance over a specific energy sector, have been subject to judicial scrutiny more rarely than those laid down under the EU Treaties. Consequently, the possible change in interpretation of competences in relation to objectives, which limits the legal weight of those objectives, does not seem to be as relevant in relation to the Euratom Treaty as is the case in respect of the EU Treaties. This implies that objectives still play a significant role in defining the Euratom Community's competences.

The ongoing integration and development of the EU prompted discussion on the effectiveness of the regulation of competences, and the European Council meeting in Laeken on 14 and 15 December 2001 provided significant impetus to increase the momentum of the EU's integration.[67] The Laeken Declaration identified the divisions between different types of competence and the definition of competence in the EU as areas in which improvements were needed. The declaration covered issues of balance (sufficient but not excessive assumption of competence on the part of the EU); transparency as to divisions between different types of competence; the possible need to reorganise the EU's competences; and a need for a control mechanism that would prevent creeping expansion of the EU's competences. When referring to issues concerning divisions between different types of competence, the Laeken Declaration focused explicitly on the EU's competences and not on those of the Euratom Community, implying that the issues listed above were either viewed as not being relevant to the Euratom Community or that the drafters simply forgot to include them. The reasons behind it are unclear, but the statement is explicit: the regulation of division of competences was to be transformed only within the EU. In the Lisbon Treaty, a clear attempt has been made to divide all the competences into certain categories: exclusive competences,[68] shared competences[69] and complementary competences.[70] Some researchers argue that one of the reasons the Lisbon Treaty introduced these different categories was to enhance clarity and thus safeguard the competences that rest with the Member States, particularly by defining competences that are not exclusive.[71] There

65. *See also* Chapter III Section B on general aspects of the Euratom Community's horizontal/institutional competences.
66. *See* S. Prechal, 'Competence Creep and General Principles of Law', (2010) 3/1 *Review of European Administrative Law*, pp. 5–22.
67. Laeken Declaration of December 15, 2001 on the Future of the European Union, DOC/01/18. It should be noted that paragraph 59 of the Presidency Conclusion of the European Council meeting in Laeken makes reference to the high level of nuclear safety in the EU, but not in the context of competences.
68. Article 3 TFEU.
69. Article 4 TFEU.
70. Article 6 TFEU.
71. G. Conway, *EU Law*, London and New York: Routledge, 2015, p. 266.

are, however, more sceptical points of view on how much clarity these changes have actually brought, which argue that instead of three clear-cut competences, the Lisbon Treaty gave us three official as well as a number of 'unofficial' types of competence, none of which stands out as having clearly defined contours.[72] Relying on Articles 2 to 6 TFEU to understand the competences available in particular areas might be difficult. The reason for this is not only that in many policy areas there is a complex relationship between the space occupied by the Member States and that occupied by the Union,[73] but also, and primarily, because the scope of EU competence is itself a space for interaction between EU and national powers.[74]

The Euratom Community has not, however, followed the EU's lead in clarifying the regulation of competences in the manner set out in Articles 2 to 6 TFEU. The areas of Euratom competences are neither set out in a specific list, nor have distinct types of competence been specified. Article 106a of the Euratom Treaty does not mention Articles 2 to 6 TFEU, which implies that there is no direct linkage in the Euratom Treaty between the categories of competences established in the TFEU and the competences established under the Euratom Treaty. Some authors argue that this could mean that all the competences established by the Euratom Treaty are shared competences, implying that the Euratom Community's powers regarding nuclear integration are less imposing and are complementary in character rather than exclusive.[75] Other authors have sought to categorise the Euratom Community's competences as exclusive or shared.[76] The CJEU has mentioned certain competences as being shared between the Community and the Member States, namely, in the field of radiation protection and emergency planning and response.[77] The lack of classification of competences under the Euratom Treaty also means that evaluation of the nature and type of any given competence has to be done on a case-by-case basis. This standpoint is also confirmed by the fact that despite the structured categories of competences under the EU Treaties, the CJEU's case-law reveals that there is no one-size-fits-all solution in respect of competences.[78] Consequently, as the Lisbon Treaty did not reform the competences under the Euratom

72. R. Schütze, 'Lisbon and the Federal Order of Competences: A Prospective Analysis', (2008) 33/5 *European Law Review*, pp. 709–722 at 721.
73. S. Weatherill, 'The Constitutional Context of (Ever-Wider) Policy-Making', in E. Jones, A. Menon, and S. Weatherill (eds), *The Oxford Handbook of the European Union*, Oxford: Oxford University Press, 2012, pp. 572-573.
74. L. Azoulai, 'Introduction: The Question of Competence', in L Azoulai (ed.), *The Question of Competence in the European Union*, Oxford: Oxford University Press, 2014, p. 13.
75. I. Cenevska, *The European Atomic Energy Community in the European Union Context: The 'Outsider' Within*, Leiden: Brill Nijhoff, 2016, p. 28; L. Scheinmann, 'Euratom: Nuclear Integration in Europe', (1967) 563 *International Conciliation*, p. 57.
76. A. Södersten has concluded that the Euratom Community has exclusive powers in the areas of supply, ownership, dissemination of information and safeguards; that some competences under the Euratom Treaty are shared; and that in some areas the Euratom Community only coordinates or supplements Member States' action (e.g., the area of investment). *See* A. Södersten, *Euratom at the Crossroads*, Cheltenham, Northampton: Edward Elgar Publishing Limited, 2018, pp. 228–229.
77. Judgment of 10 December 2002, *Commission v Council*, C-29/99, ECLI:EU:C:2002:734, paragraph 72.
78. C. Timmermans, 'ECJ Doctrines on Competences', in L. Azoulai (ed.), *The Question of Competence in the European Union*, Oxford: Oxford University Press, 2014, pp. 155–159.

Treaty, the Euratom Community's competences cannot be 'labelled' by reference to the TFEU system: they should instead be analysed and evaluated on the basis of their origin, content and exercise, and in the light of the relevant case-law.

The principle of subsidiarity is also of importance to the concept of competence. The Lisbon Treaty introduced a new Article 5 in the TEU on the principle of conferral and the principles of subsidiarity and proportionality. This article provides that the limits of EU competences are governed by the principle of conferral, and the use of EU competences is governed by the principles of subsidiarity and proportionality. The main function of the subsidiarity principle is to deal with the division of fields of competences between the EU and its Member States and to ensure that the EU stays within the bounds of its conferred competences.[79] Subsidiarity may be monitored by means of two procedural tests of competence that are available in the post-Lisbon era. The first of these is set out in Article 5 TEU and comprises a safeguard vested with the national parliaments that enables them to warn the Commission of potential infringements of the subsidiarity principle. The second lies in the obligation imposed on the Commission to include subsidiarity and proportionality assessments when carrying out an impact assessment in the pre-legislative phase.[80] Article 5 TEU establishes a clear, although somewhat theoretical, line between the limits (existence) of a competence through the principle of conferral and its use (exercise), which is governed by the principles of subsidiarity and proportionality. In other words, analysis of an EU competence must include two main aspects: analysis of the competence's limits (the nature of the competence and whether it is exclusive or shared with the Member States) and analysis of the exercise of a certain competence (the doctrine of pre-emption, the subsidiarity and proportionality principles). As established above, for a long time it was simply assumed that the EU could act, and the existence of an EU competence was not disputed, with the focus being purely on the exercise of the competence.[81] Some authors argue that even after the attempt to clarify the regulation of competences in the Lisbon Treaty, the question of the exercise of competences remains far more significant than that of limits, implying that the EU will probably remain primarily concerned not with the question of who holds a competence, but rather with how to exercise it, irrespective of who holds or who exercises it.[82]

The principle of subsidiarity comes into focus on this point. The subsidiarity principle under EU law may be interpreted as a guarantee of Member States' right to

79. R. Schütze, *From Dual to Cooperative Federalism: The Changing Structure of European Law*, Oxford: Oxford University Press, 2009, p. 247.
80. X. Groussat and S. Bogojević, 'Subsidiarity as a Procedural Safeguard of Federalism', in L. Azoulai (ed.), *The Question of Competence in the European Union*, Oxford: Oxford University Press, 2014, pp. 234–235. For further discussion of subsidiarity in relation to the Commission's impact assessments, *see* COM (2002) 278 final, Action Plan 'Simplifying and improving the regulatory environment'; A. Meuwese and P. Popelier, 'Legal Implications of Better Regulation: A Special Issue', (2011) 17 *European Public Law*, p. 456; Report from the Commission on Subsidiarity and Proportionality COM (2012) 373 final.
81. L. Azoulai, 'Introduction: The Question of Competence', in L Azoulai (ed.), *The Question of Competence in the European Union*, Oxford: Oxford University Press, 2014, pp. 1, 7.
82. *See* F.-X. Millet, 'The Respect for National Constitutional Identity in the European Legal Space: An Approach to Federalism as Constitutionalism', in L. Azoulai (ed.), *The Question of Competence in the European Union*, Oxford: Oxford University Press, 2014, p. 254.

autonomous action.[83] It may also be understood as fundamentally addressing the vertical distribution of competences, meaning that it does not aim at vesting powers in the Member States, but is a flexible tool that regulates the exercise of certain EU competences to ensure the efficiency of certain political action.[84] The issue of whether the principle of subsidiarity is applicable to the Euratom Treaty should be analysed here.

Article 5 TEU is not mentioned in Article 106a of the Euratom Treaty as being applicable to the Euratom Treaty. In addition, the preamble of the Protocol on the application of the principles of subsidiarity and proportionality notes that the provisions of the protocol will be annexed to the TEU and TFEU, but does not mention the Euratom Treaty. Accordingly, the principles of subsidiarity and proportionality do not seem to apply with regard to the Euratom Treaty. Nonetheless, the line that the principle of subsidiarity draws between the limits of a competence and its exercise can be used as one of the methods to analyse and evaluate competences under the Euratom Treaty. Under the Euratom Treaty, the national parliaments do not need to be consulted when a new legislative act is proposed. Hence the Euratom Treaty does not lay down any formal obligation for the Commission to carry out the subsidiarity and proportionality assessment in the pre-legislative phase. Nevertheless, the Commission's practice is inconsistent in relation to the subsidiarity and proportionality clause in the impact assessment of new legislative proposals under the Euratom Treaty. In the impact assessment carried out in respect of the most recent amendment of Directive 2009/71/Euratom on nuclear safety,[85] the Commission did make such an assessment.[86] It also carried out a subsidiarity evaluation in the impact assessment concerning Directive 2011/70/Euratom[87] and stated that the development of an EU legislative framework in relation to spent fuel and radioactive waste management is in line with the subsidiarity principle, in particular, since it provides added value compared to national and international approaches without any undue or excessive interference with national competences.[88] The Commission's practice implies either that it does not draw an artificial distinction between the EU Treaties and the Euratom Treaty in terms

83. For example, G. A. Bermann, 'Taking Subsidiarity Seriously: Federalism in the European Community and the United States', (1994) 94 *Colombia Law Review*; X. Groussat and S. Bogojević, 'Subsidiarity as a Procedural Safeguard of Federalism', in L. Azoulai (ed.), *The Question of Competence in the European Union*, Oxford: Oxford University Press, 2014.
84. F.-X. Millet, 'The Respect for National Constitutional Identity in the European Legal Space: An Approach to Federalism as Constitutionalism', in L. Azoulai (ed.), *The Question of Competence in the European Union*, Oxford: Oxford University Press, 2014, p. 262.
85. Council Directive 2014/87/Euratom of 8 July 2014 amending Directive 2009/71/Euratom establishing a Community framework for the nuclear safety of nuclear installations, OJ L 219, 25.72014, pp. 42–52.
86. Commission Staff Working Document, Impact Assessment Accompanying the document Proposal for a Council Directive amending Directive 2009/71/Euratom establishing a Community framework for the nuclear safety of nuclear installations, SWD (2013) 423 final, p. 26.
87. Council Directive 2011/70/Euratom of 19 July 2011 establishing a Community framework for the responsible and safe management of spent fuel and radioactive waste, OJ L 199, 2.8.2011, pp. 48–56.
88. Commission Staff Working Document Accompanying document to the revised proposal for a Council Directive on the management of spent fuel and radioactive waste (Euratom), SEC (2010) 1289 final.

of application of the procedural requirements during the pre-legislative phase or that it has given limited consideration to the fact that the EU Treaties and the Euratom Treaty might differ on the principle of subsidiarity. The latter seems more likely, as in another impact assessment, this time concerning Directive 2013/59/Euratom (hereinafter the 'BSS Directive'),[89] the Commission concluded that 'the exclusive nature of the Euratom Community's legislative powers under Articles 30 and 31 of the Euratom Treaty does not require, in principle, the application of the principle of subsidiarity'.[90] These three directives share the same legal basis - Article 31 of the Euratom Treaty. Therefore, different interpretations of the applicability of the subsidiarity principle are a sign of inconsistency. In the impact assessment in respect of the BSS Directive the Commission also indicated its view that the competences under Article 30 and 31 of the Euratom Treaty are exclusive,[91] while the scope of the subsidiarity principle is limited to only the shared competences.[92]

C METHOD OF ANALYSIS AND EVALUATION OF COMPETENCES UNDER THE EURATOM TREATY

The overarching objective of this study is to evaluate, characterise and categorise the Euratom Community's competences, in the light of the stagnation of the provisions of the Euratom Treaty. As noted in the introductory part of this study, attaining this objective entails defining the method to be used to analyse and evaluate each field of competence under Title II of the Euratom Treaty. The method for the legal analysis of the Euratom Community competences presented below is based on a comparative analysis between EU law and the Euratom Treaty set out in the previous section in the context of analysing the concept of competence. The objective of this analysis method is to provide a framework and structure for the evaluation of the scope and limits of specific substantive Euratom Community competences under the Euratom Treaty.

On the basis of the systematic analysis of the concept of competence set out in the preceding section, one might conclude that any competence, regardless of the substantive provisions in the primary legal act, consists of two main elements - scope and

89. Council Directive 2013/59/Euratom of 5 December 2013 laying down basic safety standards for protection against the dangers arising from exposure to ionising radiation, and repealing Directives 89/618/Euratom, 90/641/Euratom, 96/29/Euratom, 97/43/Euratom and 2003/122/Euratom, OJ L 13, 17.1.2014, pp. 1-73.
90. Commission Staff Working Document, Executive Summary of the Impact Assessment Accompanying the document Council Directive laying down basic safety standards for protection against the dangers arising from exposure to ionising radiation, SWD (2012) 138 final.
91. The Commission has established that the exclusive nature of the Euratom Community's legislative powers under Articles 30 and 31 of the Euratom Treaty does not in principle require the application of the principle of subsidiarity. *See* Commission Staff Working Document, Executive Summary of the Impact Assessment Accompanying the document Council Directive laying down basic safety standards for protection against the dangers arising from exposure to ionising radiation, SWD(2012)138 final, p. 3.
92. F.-X. Millet, 'The Respect for National Constitutional Identity in the European Legal Space: An Approach to Federalism as Constitutionalism', in L. Azoulai (ed.), *The Question of Competence in the European Union*, Oxford: Oxford University Press, 2014, p. 262.

instruments of exercise. These two elements may have different names,[93] but they constitute a legal two-piece constellation of any given competence. This implies, first, that a competence has certain limits (scope of action), and, second, that it is exercised or 'activated' through instruments of action.[94] Analysis of the relationship between the limits of the competence and the instruments of exercise of that competence plays a significant role when evaluating whether the competence has been exercised to its limits or whether the competence has been exercised within the limits, but not in its full capacity.

It is necessary to identify where a certain competence is defined in order to assess its scope. Any given competence derives from the primary legal act. However, while some are explicitly established in the primary legal act, others are further defined in secondary legal acts or clarified by the Court. The question of where a competence is regulated can be revelatory in terms of its having certain distinguishing features under the Euratom Treaty. As established in defining the parameters of this study, not all Euratom Community competences derive from the Euratom Treaty, since some of them derive from the EU Treaties. Article 106a of the Euratom Treaty refers to the list of articles in the TEU and TFEU as being applicable to the Euratom Treaty. Those articles of the EU Treaties that are listed in Article 106a of the Euratom Treaty primarily regulate horizontal competences and the latter change under the Lisbon Treaty incorporated the application of the TEU and TFEU into Euratom Community's *acquis*. When a competence is established directly in the Euratom Treaty, the general scope of that competence is defined in this primary legal act.

There may also be cases in which a competence derives from the Treaty but is not explicitly set out in the primary legal act. In these circumstances, it may be defined by the CJEU in its case-law or in secondary legislation. However, because in this situation the primary legal act contains no substantive provisions that specify the limits of the competence, identifying those limits would be more difficult. It should also be mentioned that when the secondary legislation provides for the exercise of a competence, attention should be paid to the type of secondary legal act in question, keeping in mind, in particular, the different features of regulations and directives.[95]

In order to identify the content of a competence and instruments of its exercise, the analysis should continue by questioning whether the competence is exercised through any secondary legal act, i.e., whether the primary legal act transfers the exercise of a competence to the provisions of secondary legislation. In this study, reference to exercise of competences implies that an article of the Euratom Treaty has been used as a legal basis for a secondary legal act. Analysis of those legal instruments provides the basis for evaluation of the content and limits of any specific competence. In some cases, provisions in the primary legal act transfer a competence to be exercised

93. Scope or content of a competence; instruments of exercise or 'limits and use', existence and exercise'.
94. Article 106a(1) of the Euratom Treaty, in conjunction with Article 288 TFEU, indicates that the EU's and the Euratom Community's competences are exercised through secondary legal acts – regulations, directives, decisions, recommendations and opinions – adopted by the institutions.
95. Article 288 TFEU is applicable to the Euratom Treaty under Article 106a of the Euratom Treaty.

under secondary legislation, but in practice no secondary legal acts have been adopted. In this situation, the legitimacy of the non-exercise of the competence should be assessed.

In general, the limits of the competences under the primary legal act may be based on at least two different approaches: from the Euratom Community's or EU's point of view, this means a focus on competences delegated by the Member States to the Euratom Community or the EU; and from the point of view of each Member State, it means a focus on competences that remain in the national domain. In other words, in any given field of regulation the focus can be either on identification of the Euratom Community's powers and competences, or on identification of the Member States' powers. Regarding the focus on Member States' powers, the CJEU has stated[96] that the 'transfer' is in itself enough for a Member State to lose the right to take unilateral measures in the area.

In respect of competences in specific regulatory areas that are laid down in the EU Treaties and exercised through secondary legal acts, the CJEU has developed three different approaches to the overall consequences for the regulatory area in question and, more specifically, how they impact upon each Member State's competence to act.[97]

A strict approach in this regard implies that Member States must refrain from taking any unilateral measure, even if that measure is likely to support common EU policy. It is for the EU, not the Member States, to seek a solution to the problems at hand and to exercise its competences to that effect. This approach emerged early in the history of the CJEU's case-law and reflects its dogmatic stance in relation to this issue. In one early case, the Court stated that to the extent to which Member States have transferred legislative powers with the objective of ensuring the satisfactory operation of a common market in agriculture, they no longer have powers to adopt legislative provisions in this field.[98] Examples of this approach can also be found in a more recent case-law.[99] A variation of this strict approach - which seems to me less of an encroachment upon Member States' competences but also closely resembles a situation of exclusive EU competence - is the test of completeness or exhaustiveness: if it can be considered that in respect of a given subject matter there exists a complete regime or an exhaustive body of rules, Member States have no competence to take unilateral measures. Consequently, unilateral national measures concerning an issue covered by EU competence are impermissible, irrespective of content.[100]

---

96. For more on this, *see* Chapter II Section A on the origin of competences.
97. These approaches are discussed in C. Timmermans, 'ECJ Doctrines on Competences', in L. Azoulai (ed.), *The Question of Competence in the European Union*, Oxford: Oxford University Press, 2014.
98. Judgment of 18 February 1970, *Hauptzollamt Hamburg Oberelbe v Bollmann*, C-40/69, ECLI:EU:C:1970:12, paragraph 4. *See also* judgment of 18 June 1970, *Hauptzollamt Bremen-Freihafen v Waren-Import-Gesellschaft Krohn & Co.*, C-74/69, ECLI:EU:C:1970:58, paragraph 4.
99. Judgment of 19 September 2002, *Spain v Commission*, C-113/00, ECLI:EU:C:2002:507, paragraph 74; judgment of 26 May 2005, *Kuipers*, C-283/03, ECLI:EU:C:2005:314, paragraph 49.
100. C. Timmermans, 'ECJ Doctrines on Competences', in L. Azoulai (ed.), *The Question of Competence in the European Union*, Oxford: Oxford University Press, 2014, p. 157.

Another approach that the Court has developed concerns the application of 'conflict of law' rule. In this case, Member States are allowed some margin to take unilateral measures, which extends to the regulatory area covered by the EU, but the CJEU exercises close scrutiny to assess whether these measures conflict with the EU's internal market legislation. This approach was developed when new cases made it apparent that it would be unwise to block entirely the possibility of Member States making autonomous interventions. The decentralised system represented by the EU and its predecessors involved, *inter alia*, the implementation and management of agricultural market organisations, which were the first to encounter daily problems, unexpected events and lacunae in the EC rules. Completely freezing the possibility of autonomous intervention by Member States could in the end be counterproductive and hamper, more than foster, the smooth functioning of the market. Timmermans' analysis of the relevant case-law concludes that the scope of this rule of conflict is very widely drawn. A national measure is regarded as being in conflict with the market regime whenever it jeopardises its aims or interferes with or hinders its functioning.[101]

The third approach is close to the second, but the focus is on compatibility of law rather than conflict. The CJEU has held that whether the national measure is to be deemed legitimate or not is to be decided by applying the classic test of assessing the compatibility of the national measure with existing EU rules.[102] The complexity of the field is reflected in the fact that these different approaches have sometimes been utilised in one and the same case.[103]

These approaches on the part of the CJEU are most relevant in the context of analysing the limits of competences from the national point of view - i.e., when evaluating the Member State's possibility to act - but they may also be useful when analysing and evaluating specific, substantive competences of the Euratom Community.

Consequently, the methodical framework for the analysis and evaluation of each of the Euratom Community's fields of competence consists of three main elements. First, the scope and content of each competence must be addressed, which also entails consideration of the level of detail to which it is regulated in the Euratom Treaty and whether that level of regulatory detail is appropriate in view of the Euratom Community's tasks and objectives. Second, the way in which the competence is exercised should also be assessed, which entails consideration of the instruments utilised for that purpose and whether its exercise is in accordance with the specific wording of the Euratom Treaty or whether it is either narrower or wider in scope than that. Third, it is necessary to search for and review any case-law that interprets or elaborates on the competence at hand and evaluate the way in which the CJEU has defined and delimited the Euratom Community's competences and whether it has done so in the light of the tasks of the Euratom Community.

101. C. Timmermans, 'ECJ Doctrines on Competences', in L. Azoulai (ed.), *The Question of Competence in the European Union*, Oxford: Oxford University Press, 2014, p. 157.
102. Judgment of 25 November 1986, *Cerafel v Le Campion*, C-218/85, ECLI:EU:C:1986:440, paragraph 13.
103. C. Timmermans, 'ECJ Doctrines on Competences', in L. Azoulai (ed.), *The Question of Competence in the European Union*, Oxford: Oxford University Press, 2014, p. 158.

Analysis of the Euratom Community's competences using this methodological framework permits the identification of specific features of competences under the Euratom Treaty. These features in turn allow for the carrying out of a structural systematisation/grouping of competences. In order to provide a basis for comparative analysis, the following three aspects are analysed as features of each of the Euratom Community's fields of competence under Title II of the Euratom Treaty: the level of detail of the provisions of the primary legal act establishing the content and scope of a competence in comparison with the Euratom Community's tasks; the scope of the exercise of the competence as compared with the wording of the Euratom Treaty; the existence of case-law and the effect of the Court's interpretation of the relevant provisions of primary and secondary legislations. These features will allow for evaluation of the effects of stagnation of the Euratom Treaty on the overall legal system of the Euratom Community.

CHAPTER III

General Aspects of the Euratom Community's Competences

Chapter II Section C of this study establishes the method for the analysis and evaluation of each of the Euratom Community's vertical competences and includes three main elements: the scope and content of each competence; its exercise; and relevant case-law. Before analysing the Euratom Community's specific competences, this Chapter III addresses four general aspects of the Euratom Community's competences. These comprise the objectives and tasks of the Community; certain institutional aspects under the Euratom Treaty; the Euratom Community's competences in respect of the military application of nuclear energy; and the specificity of Euratom Treaty's 'flexibility clause' under Article 203 of the Euratom Treaty. Analysis of the third and fourth of these matters is carried out in accordance with the analysis method identified above.

Before proceeding with this analysis, the Euratom Community's competences in respect of the physical protection of nuclear materials should be mentioned. There are no provisions regulating this area under the Euratom Treaty and no secondary legislation, but the CJEU has established that the concept of 'safeguards' within the meaning of the Euratom Treaty is sufficiently comprehensive to include measures of physical protection. The Court takes the view that the Euratom Community's competences in relation to physical protection of nuclear materials extends to measures implemented as part of the safeguards provisions under Chapter 7 of the Euratom Treaty.[104]

104. Ruling of 14 November 1978, Ruling of the Court delivered pursuant to the third paragraph of Article 103 of the Euratom Treaty – Draft Convention of the International Atomic Energy Agency on the Physical Protection of Nuclear Materials, Facilities and Transports, Ruling 1/78, ECLI:EU:C:1978:202, paragraphs 19–21.

A OBJECTIVES AND TASKS OF THE EURATOM COMMUNITY

Article 1 of the Euratom Treaty establishes the main task of the Euratom Community: to contribute to the raising of the standard of living in the Member States and to the development of relations with other countries by creating the conditions necessary for the speedy establishment and growth of nuclear industries. Article 2 provides that, in order to perform its tasks, the Euratom Community shall, as provided in the Euratom Treaty, promote research, establish uniform safety standards, facilitate investments, ensure supply of ores and nuclear fuels, establish nuclear safeguards, exercise the right of ownership to special fissile materials, create a nuclear common market and establish external relations with other countries and international organisations.

The description of the 'tasks' in Article 1 of the Euratom Treaty is indicative of the fact that the substantive law laid down in the Euratom Treaty has never been amended. It is reasonable to infer that these 'tasks' are the Euratom Community's main objectives and the main reason for its existence. The first objective – to raise standards of living – is broad and quite unspecific. One might ask oneself whether nuclear energy stops contributing to rising standards of living if a Member States decides to shift to another source of energy supply, since in formal terms this might imply that the tasks of the Euratom Community are no longer being fully implemented.[105] This objective is also excessively broad, since many different endeavours could potentially fall within the scope of 'raising standards of living'. The second objective – i.e., to develop relations with other countries – is more concrete and is further elaborated under Article 2(h) of the Euratom Treaty, which requires the Euratom Community to establish relations with other countries and international organisations, as well as being regulated under Chapter 10 of the Euratom Treaty.

Article 2 of the Euratom Treaty comprises a list of the Euratom Community's competences. Although it is sometimes interpreted as establishing the objectives of the Community,[106] comparative analysis of the wording of these two articles leads one to conclude that Article 1 establishes the Euratom Community's objectives and Article 2 specifies what it is obliged to do in order to fulfil its objectives, i.e., it sets out the Euratom Community's main tasks. In this context, the Member States are also obliged to take measures to facilitate the achievement of the Euratom Community's tasks and to abstain from taking any measures that may endanger the realisation of its objectives,[107] which resembles the 'conflict of law' rule identified above. Article 2 is

105. Despite the features of the Euratom Treaty that promote the choice of nuclear power by Member States, Article 194 TFEU establishes that no energy policy measures can affect a Member State's right to determine the conditions for exploiting its energy resources, its choice between different energy sources and the general structure of its energy supply. Consequently, Member States are free to choose energy sources, but if they choose nuclear energy, they must comply with the provisions of the Euratom Treaty that regulate the nuclear energy sector.

106. J. Handrlica, 'Harmonisation of Nuclear Liability in the European Union: Challenges, Options and Limits', (2009) 84 *Nuclear Law Bulletin*, p. 45.

107. Article 192 of the Euratom Treaty. *See also* H. J. Hahn, 'Euratom: The Conception of an International Personality', (1958) 71/6 *Harvard Law Review*, p. 1040.

sometimes described as establishing the scope of the Euratom Treaty.[108] Even though the Euratom Community's competences and the scope of the Euratom Treaty may be viewed as similar concepts, the Euratom Community's competences are a framework for regulation that determine the scope of the Treaty. This implies that the Community's competences could be broadened beyond the scope of the Treaty if the Euratom Community regarded this as being necessary and acted under its mandate, for example under Article 203 of the Euratom Treaty.[109]

B GENERAL ASPECTS OF THE EURATOM COMMUNITY'S HORIZONTAL/INSTITUTIONAL COMPETENCES

The CJEU has stated that the provisions of the Euratom Treaty relating to the normative powers of the institutions of the Euratom Community must be interpreted in the light of the overall scheme of the Treaty.[110] Consequently, when analysing and evaluating general aspects of the Euratom Community's competences, i.e., the overall scheme of its competences, certain aspects of the institutional/horizontal powers should be mentioned.

The Euratom Community shares the institutions with the EU. From the establishment of the Euratom Community to the adoption of Lisbon Treaty, the institutions of each Community were separate and during that time Title III of the Euratom Treaty regulated the institutional provisions of the Euratom Community. Protocol no. 2 of the Treaty of Lisbon,[111] which serves to adapt the Euratom Treaty to the new rules laid down by the TEU and the TFEU, in particular in the institutional and financial fields, repealed the articles of the Euratom Treaty regulating the institutional provisions of the Euratom Community. Here it should be mentioned that Article 50 of the TEU is also on the list of Article 106a of the Euratom Treaty. This leads to the implication that with the United Kingdom's withdrawal from the EU under Article 50 TEU, it will also need to leave the Euratom Community.[112]

108. J. G. Polach, *Euratom: Its Background, Issues and Economic Implications*, Dobbs Ferry, NY: Oceana Publications Inc., 1964, pp. 71-72.
109. Article 203 of the Euratom Treaty will be analysed according to the method for analysing and evaluating competences under the Euratom Treaty established in Chapter II Section C of this study.
110. Judgment of 17 September 2007, *France v Commission*, T-240/04, ECLI:EU:T:2007:290, paragraph 36.
111. Protocol No 2 Amending the Treaty Establishing the European Atomic Energy Community, OJ C 306 17.12.2007, pp. 199-201.
112. United Kingdom's withdrawal from the Euratom Community is an important issue. However, it does not per se have an effect on the Euratom Community's competences, which are the objective of this study. For Brexit from the Euratom Community *see, inter alia*, A. Södersten, 'Brexit, Euratom and Nuclear Proliferation', (2016) 98 *Nuclear Law Bulletin*, pp. 47-56; 'Energy Files. Brexit Implications for the Energy Sector - State of Play', (2017) 7/2 *European Energy Journal*, pp. 5-9; A. Circolo and O. Hamulak, 'Euratom and Brexit: Could the United Kingdom Maintain One Foot in the European Union? Current Scenarios and Future Prospects of British Withdrawal from the EAEC, (2018) 18/2 *International and Comparative Law Review*, pp. 134-151; J. Handrlica, 'From the Front Lines of International Nuclear Law: Looking Back at the 'Nuclear Inter Jura' Congress, Held in Abu Dhabi, United Arab Emirates', (2019) 12 *Journal of World Energy Law and Business*, p. 272.

Article 106a of the Euratom Treaty refers to the following articles of the TFEU as being applicable to the Euratom Treaty: Articles 223 to 270, Articles 272 to 274, Articles 277 to 281 and Articles 285 to 304. This means that the institutional provisions concerning the EP, the European Council, the Council (of Ministers), the Commission and the CJEU are common to the EU Treaties and the Euratom Treaty. However, the competences of the institutions under the Euratom Treaty are based on the substantive law contained in the Euratom Treaty and not on the institutional-functional provisions of the EU Treaties. It is therefore reasonable to infer that it is the substantive law of the Euratom Treaty that defines the competences of the institutions, while the provisions of the TFEU, which Article 106a of the Euratom Treaty refers to, allow those institutions to actualise the competences delegated to them.[113] For this reason, the Euratom Community's horizontal competences are not analysed and evaluated separately in this study, but are, where relevant, incorporated in the analysis of vertical competences instead.

Analytical comparative research on how the competences of the same institutions differ under the EU Treaties and the Euratom Treaty has led to the repeated conclusion that the EP does not have the same powers under the Euratom Treaty as it generally does under the EU Treaties.[114] The Euratom Treaty has become an object of criticism on the grounds that it is outdated and undemocratic.[115] This criticism has led to the conclusion that the lack of the ordinary legislative procedure under the Euratom Treaty should be 'made up for' by strengthening the significance of secondary legislation adopted under the EU Treaties that regulates certain specific aspects of the nuclear sector.[116] Keeping in mind that the Euratom Treaty is *lex specialis*, regulating a specific, clearly defined sector, the inference might be drawn that just as the TFEU still entails the use of the special legislative procedure in some areas of regulation, the Euratom Community, as a special sectoral legislative field, also uses the special legislative procedure[117] in exercising its competences. Consequently, the balance

113. For further discussion of the implications of Article 106a of the Euratom Treaty for the relationship between the Euratom Treaty and the EU Treaties, *see* R. Ptasekaite, *The Euratom Treaty v. Treaties of the European Union: Limits of Competence and Interaction*, Swedish Radiation Safety Authority Report, SSM2011:32, Solna: SSM, 2011, pp. 28–35; and I. Cenevska, *The European Atomic Energy Community in the European Union Context: The 'Outsider' Within*, Leiden: Brill Nijhoff, 2016, p. 80.
114. There is no co-decision procedure under the Euratom Treaty. The role of the EP is discussed further in the section below. *See also* I. Cenevska, 'The European Parliament and the European Atomic Energy Community: A Legitimacy Crisis?', (2010) 35/3 *European Law Review*, pp. 415–424; Report on Assessing Euratom: 50 years of European nuclear energy policy, European Parliament, Committee on Industry, Research and Energy, Rapporteur: E. Maldeikis, A6-0129/2007.
115. J. Handrlica, 'The Splendid Durability of the Provisional: A Tribute to Euratom', (2018) 14/14 *Croatian Yearbook of European Law & Policy*, p. 172; P. M. Barnes, 'The Resurrection of the Euratom Treaty: Contributing to the Legal and Constitutional Framework for Secure, Competitive and Sustainable Energy in the European Union', in T. Etty and H. Somsen (eds), *The Yearbook of European Environmental Law*, Volume 8, Oxford: Oxford University Press, 2008, pp. 193–194.
116. I. Cenevska, *The European Atomic Energy Community in the European Union Context: The 'Outsider' Within*, Leiden: Brill Nijhoff, 2016, p. 46.
117. For example, Articles 23, 64 and 113, 182(4) and 192(2)(c) TFEU.

between the horizontal competences of the institutions under the Euratom Treaty differs from the 'classical' balance of institutional competences under the EU Treaties. The EP has made two attempts to obtain greater powers under the Euratom Treaty.[118] Apart from legal challenges, the EP has also attempted to politically challenge the imbalance of institutional competences under the Euratom Treaty, mainly by issuing reports or adopting various legislative and non-legislative resolutions,[119] such as the Maldeikis Report,[120] the Hökmark Report[121] and the Resolution on risk and safety assessments ('stress tests') of nuclear power plants in the EU.[122] Such political pressure does not seem to be an effective tool to change existing legal competences established by and deriving from the Euratom Treaty.

As the EP has limited powers under the Euratom Treaty, it seems to be commonly agreed that the Euratom Community is governed by the Council and the Commission.[123] One of the Commission's most distinctive roles lies in its exclusive right to initiate legislation.[124] The Commission also monitors the implementation of Euratom law in the Member States, and brings legal action before the CJEU against Member States that it considers to have implemented the law in an inadequate manner.[125] This represents the Commission's executive role. Some consider the Commission to be the main instrument under the Euratom 'compact'.[126] As it is the institution that holds the bulk of the regulatory, supervisory and executive powers under the Euratom Treaty, the Commission exercises functional control over national and subnational actors as well as actors at the Euratom Community level, i.e., the Euratom Supply Agency. Some authors conclude that despite the legislative power held by the Council, the 'real' power and authority within the Euratom Community rests with the Commission given its extensive decision-making powers.[127]

It should be noted that the Euratom Treaty establishes some overarching Euratom Community competences, which are not bound to any specific field of vertical competence, but are applicable throughout the Euratom Community's competences and jurisdiction. For example, the Euratom Community has competence to acquire or dispose of movable and immovable property in each of the Member States and be a

118. Judgment of 4 October 1991, *Parliament v Council*, C-70/88, ECLI:EU:C:1991:373; and judgment of 12 February 2015, *Parliament v Council*, C-48/14, ECLI:EU:C:2015:91. *See* Chapter 3 of this study for further information.
119. I. Cenevska, *The European Atomic Energy Community in the European Union Context: The 'Outsider' Within*, Leiden: Brill Nijhoff, 2016, p. 42.
120. European Parliament, Committee on Industry, Research and Energy, Rapporteur: E. Maldeikis, Report on Assessing Euratom: 50 years of European nuclear energy policy, A6-0129/2007.
121. European Parliament, Report on the proposal for a Council Directive (Euratom) setting up a Community framework for nuclear safety of nuclear installations, A6-0236/2009.
122. European Parliament Resolution of 14 March 2013 on risk and safety assessments ('stress tests') of nuclear power plants in the European Union and related activities, 2012/2830 (RSP).
123. S. Wolf, 'Euratom, the European Court of Justice, and the Limits of Nuclear Integration in Europe', (2011) 12/8 *German Law Journal*, p. 1638.
124. *See* Article 17(2) TEU, Article 289 TFEU and Article 106a(1) of the Euratom Treaty.
125. Article 258 TFEU and Article 106a(1) of the Euratom Treaty.
126. H. J. Hahn, 'Control under the Euratom Compact', (1958) 7 *American Journal of Comparative Law*, p. 28.
127. I. Cenevska, *The European Atomic Energy Community in the European Union Context: The 'Outsider' Within*, Leiden: Brill Nijhoff, 2016, p. 31.

party to legal proceedings. To this end, the Euratom Community is represented by the Commission.[128] The Euratom Community via the Commission also has a competence, within the limits and under the conditions laid down by the Council in accordance with the provisions of the Euratom Treaty, to collect any information and carry out any checks required for the performance of the tasks entrusted to it.[129] Furthermore, the Euratom Community has competence to enjoy in the territories of the Member States such privileges and immunities as are necessary for the performance of its tasks, under the conditions laid down in the Protocol on the privileges and immunities of the European Union.[130]

The role of the Council gives rise to less discussion in the context of analysis of institutional competences under the Euratom Treaty. The Council is always the main legislator that establishes the provisions that elaborate the powers transferred to the Euratom Community. The Council can amend the list of research fields under Annex I of the Euratom Treaty.[131] It also determines the research programmes,[132] adopts security regulations for the protection of information,[133] establishes basic safety standards[134] and Joint Undertakings,[135] lays down the statutes of the Supply Agency[136] and even fixes the prices of nuclear supplies.[137] These are only examples, but they all seem to show the same trend: the Council is the institution that has the main competence in decision-making. The Council also supervises the work of the Commission, as the Commission has an obligation to report on its work to the Council.[138]

As was predicted in the early years of the Euratom Community, the CJEU played the strongest role in integrating the three Communities.[139] This arose from its undisputed prerogative to review the work of the institutions and ensure the correct and effective interpretation and application of Euratom and EU law both by the institutions and by the Member States.[140] Almost all the articles in Section 4 of the Euratom Treaty, which established the functioning of the CJEU, have been repealed by the Lisbon Treaty[141] and the Protocol on the Statute of the CJEU[142] has been annexed both to the EU Treaties and the Euratom Treaty on the same terms. The CJEU accordingly has the

128. Article 185 of the Euratom Treaty.
129. Article 187 of the Euratom Treaty.
130. Article 191 of the Euratom Treaty.
131. Article 4 of the Euratom Treaty.
132. Article 7 of the Euratom Treaty.
133. Article 24 of the Euratom Treaty.
134. Article 31 of the Euratom Treaty.
135. Article 49 of the Euratom Treaty.
136. Article 54 of the Euratom Treaty.
137. Article 69 of the Euratom Treaty.
138. For example, Articles 7, 11, 46, 47, 68 and 70 of the Euratom Treaty.
139. H. J. Hahn, 'Control under the Euratom Compact', (1958) 7 *American Journal of Comparative Law*, p. 31.
140. I. Cenevska, *The European Atomic Energy Community in the European Union Context: The 'Outsider' Within*, Leiden: Brill Nijhoff, 2016, p. 51.
141. Articles 144, 145 and 157 of the Euratom Treaty remain valid due to the specific role of the CJEU in disputes concerning dissemination of information under Article 12 and concerning the Commission's decisions on issues concerning safeguards under Article 83.
142. Protocol on the Statute of the Court of Justice of the European Union, annexed to the Euratom Treaty, OJ C 327, 26.10.2012, p. 73.

same competences under the Euratom Treaty as under the EU Treaties, taking account of the specificities in Articles 12 and 83 of the Euratom Treaty.[143] In practice, the CJEU's influence on the Euratom Community's competences arises from its interpretation of the provisions of the Euratom Treaty. Some scholars argue that the Court's judgments have served to reinforce the Euratom Community's legal and political regime in two main ways: by confirming or clarifying an extant Euratom competences; and by adopting a broad approach to the interpretation of the Euratom Treaty that has in practice led to enlargement of its scope of application.[144] Others have referred to this interpretative approach as causing a 'spill over' of Euratom provisions to fields that are not covered by the Euratom Treaty.[145] However, the CJEU has not dealt with all that many cases concerning competences under the Euratom Treaty.[146] The low number of preliminary rulings indicates that Euratom law is rarely used to reinforce positions before national courts. Some scholars identify that the CJEU has extended Euratom law to another policy field in only one preliminary ruling,[147] but most of the cases that have been heard concern poor implementation of certain Euratom Community directives and that does not usually imply an expansion of Euratom competences.[148]

C EURATOM COMMUNITY COMPETENCES IN RESPECT OF THE MILITARY APPLICATION OF NUCLEAR ENERGY

- The provisions of the Euratom Treaty do not provide a clear answer as to whether the Euratom Community has competences in relation to the military application of nuclear energy.
- Although the Commission has interpreted the provisions of the Euratom Treaty as creating Euratom Community competences in the military application of nuclear energy, the Court has concluded that activities falling within

143. Article 12 establishes that failing agreement on the terms referred to in the third paragraph, the licensees may bring the matter before the CJEU so that appropriate terms may be fixed. Article 83 establishes that by way of derogation from Article 157, appeals brought before the CJEU against decisions of the Commission which impose any of the sanctions provided for in paragraph 1 shall have suspensory effect. The CJEU may, however, on application by the Commission or by any Member State concerned, order that the decision be enforced forthwith.
144. I. Cenevska, *The European Atomic Energy Community in the European Union Context: The 'Outsider' Within*, Leiden: Brill Nijhoff, 2016, p. 51.
145. *See* S. Wolf, 'Euratom Before the Court: A Political Theory of Legal Non-Integration', (2011) 15/10 *European Integration Online Papers*. It should be kept in mind that in this context 'spill over' is associated with expanding the Euratom provisions into other sectors. Extensive interpretation of Euratom provisions does not, however, mean that they apply per se to other sectors – it can also imply broadening the meaning of existing provisions in relation to the nuclear sector.
146. There have been approximately fifty cases where the question of competence has been raised. For a case-law selection analysis *see*: S. Wolf, 'Euratom Before the Court: A Political Theory of Legal Non-Integration', (2011) 15/10 *European Integration Online Papers*, pp. 9–10. *See also* S. Wolf, 'Euratom, the European Court of Justice, and the Limits of Nuclear Integration in Europe', (2011) 12/8 *German Law Journal*, p. 1639.
147. Judgment of 27 October 2009, *ČEZ*, C-115/08, ECLI:EU:C:2009:660.
148. S. Wolf, 'Euratom Before the Court: A Political Theory of Legal Non-Integration', (2011) 15/10 *European Integration Online Papers*, p. 13.

> the military sphere are outside the scope of the Euratom Treaty, thus establishing that the Euratom Community does not have a general competence concerning military nuclear activities.

The close link between the regulation of the peaceful use of nuclear energy and the prevention of its destructive use arises out of nuclear energy's dual nature, since peaceful use of nuclear energy can be diverted for military purposes.[149] The issue of whether the Euratom Community's competences extend to cover military activities is therefore often discussed[150] and relevant. The Euratom Community's competences in relation to military nuclear activities is analysed below in accordance with the legal competence analysis and evaluation method established in Chapter II Section C of this study.

The Scope and Content of the Competences

This section considers whether any provisions of the Euratom Treaty may be interpreted as conferring competence in nuclear military activities on the Euratom Community.

Article 2 of the Euratom Treaty establishes that the Euratom Community has a competence to "make certain, by appropriate supervision, that nuclear materials are not diverted to purposes other than those for which they are intended".[151] The wording of this article neither eliminates military activities from the Community's competences, nor confirms that they fall under the scope of those competences. It establishes the Euratom Community's competence to create a safeguards system that is regulated in detail in Chapter 7 of the Euratom Treaty. Article 84, in Chapter 7 of the Euratom Treaty, provides that the safeguards system established under the Euratom Treaty may not be extended to materials intended to meet defence requirements and which are placed or stored in military establishments. Consequently, the scope and content of the Euratom Community's competence in relation to nuclear safeguards does not include military activities and nuclear materials used for military activities. In addition to this, the Euratom Treaty does not prohibit the military use of materials by Member States.[152]

Chapter 2 of the Euratom Treaty on dissemination of information includes a separate section[153] on security provisions that must be applied in respect, for example, of information, a patent or utility model when defence interests of a Member State are

149. V. Lamm, 'Reflections on the Development of International Nuclear Law', (2017) 99 *Nuclear law Bulletin*, p. 32.
150. I. Cenevska, *The European Atomic Energy Community in the European Union Context: The 'Outsider' Within*, Leiden: Brill Nijhoff, 2016, pp. 320–324; G. Mallard, 'Can the Euratom Treaty Inspire the Middle East? The Political Promises of Regional Nuclear Communities', (2018) 15/3 *Non-proliferation Review*, pp. 459–477; S. Wolf, 'Euratom Before the Court: A Political Theory of Legal Non-Integration', (2011) 15/10 *European Integration Online Papers*, pp. 13–14; S. Ferro, *European Nuclear Law (July 10, 2012)*, p. 361, available at SSRN: https://ssrn.com/abstract=2103202 or http://dx.doi.org/10.2139/ssrn.2103202.
151. Article 2(e) of the Euratom Treaty.
152. B. Patel and P. Chare, 'Fifty Years of Safeguards under the Euratom Treaty – A Regulatory Review', in G. Janssens-Maenhout (ed.), *Nuclear Safeguards and Non-Proliferation*, Luxembourg: Office for Official Publications of the European Communities, 2009, p. 97.
153. Chapter 2, Section 3, Articles 24 to 27 of the Euratom Treaty.

at stake. Article 24 of this section provides that information which the Community acquires as a result of carrying out its research programme, and the disclosure of which is liable to harm the defence interests of one or more Member States, shall be subject to a security system. This means that the Community has an obligation to secure information that could harm defence interests of one or several Member States. Article 28 of the Euratom Treaty establishes the Euratom Community's responsibility to compensate for the damage suffered by the party concerned, should patents or utility models classified for defence reasons be improperly used or come to the knowledge of an unauthorised person, as a result of the Commission's communication.[154] In this case, the scope of the Euratom Community's competence in relation to dissemination of information is focused on safe handling of different kinds of sensitive information, information connected to defence interest being one of them. Nevertheless, the provisions of the Euratom Treaty do not provide a clear answer as to whether the Community's right to act in order to protect a Member State's defence interest could constitute a Euratom Community competence in the field. In other words, the Euratom Treaty is ambiguous regarding security and defence policy.[155] This has resulted in conflicting interpretations of the text of the Euratom Treaty and may indicate the existence of a loophole peculiar to the Euratom system in this regard.[156]

The Exercise of the Competences

This section assesses the Euratom Community's competence in respect of the military application of nuclear energy and the instruments through which this competence is exercised.

As the provisions of the Euratom Treaty are ambiguous regarding the applicability of the Euratom Treaty to military activities, the articles of the Euratom Treaty that may serve as legal bases for the secondary legislation cannot be identified either.

The CJEU's Interpretation of the Competences

To provide more clarity in respect of legal argumentation concerning the application of the Euratom Treaty to military activities, the Commission's reasoning is provided first. The Commission had assumed that the Euratom Community has competences concerning military nuclear activities and had exercised its assumed competence by sending the United Kingdom (UK) a letter of formal notice arguing that, by failing to provide to the Commission general data relating to a plan for disposal of radioactive waste resulting from the decommissioning of the military Jason reactor, the UK had

154. The scope of such communications is established, *inter alia*, in Article 25 of the Euratom Treaty.
155. *See* S. Wolf, 'Euratom Before the Court: A Political Theory of Legal Non-Integration', (2011) 15/10 *European Integration Online Papers*, pp. 13–14.
156. *See* I. Cenevska, *The European Atomic Energy Community in the European Union Context: The 'Outsider' Within*, Leiden: Brill Nijhoff, 2016, p. 322.

failed to fulfil its obligations under Article 37 of the Euratom Treaty.[157] The Commission stated that Article 37 of the Euratom Treaty applies to disposal of radioactive waste from both civil and military installations. It argued that provision aims to prevent any risk of radioactive contamination of another Member State and that, since the protection of the general public against the dangers arising from ionising radiations is an indivisible objective, it must extend to all sources of danger including those resulting from the decommissioning of military installations, such as the Jason reactor.[158]

In another case the Commission had exercised its assumed competence in connection with military nuclear activities by stating that the provision of information about health protection measures to the public in the event of a radiological emergency is a civil defence matter, and not a military matter, even when the source of radiation is a military nuclear-powered submarine.[159]

On the specific provisions of the Euratom Treaty concerning defence, the CJEU has stated that the existence of provisions that take account of the defence interests of the Member States, namely Articles 24 to 28 and the third paragraph of Article 84 of the Euratom Treaty, does not necessarily lead to the conclusion that its rules are applicable, save as to express exceptions, to the military uses of nuclear energy. The existence of those provisions may also be explained by the fact that the application of certain rules introduced by the Euratom Treaty, even if they relate only to civil activities, is nevertheless liable to have an impact on activities and interests in the context of Member States' national defence. That is certainly the case for the rules laid down in Title II, Chapter 2 of the Euratom Treaty, which concern dissemination of information; and for those laid down in Chapter 7 of Title II, which relate to safeguards. Furthermore, the Court stated that the provisions in question are limited in scope. Apart from the two chapters in which those provisions are found, the Treaty does not contain any other provisions that take account of interests and specific requirements connected with military activities.[160] The Court concluded that activities falling within the military sphere are outside the scope of the Euratom Treaty,[161] thus establishing that the Euratom Community does not have a general competence concerning military nuclear activities. Consequently, the CJEU rejected the Commission's assumed competences concerning military activities in both cases mentioned above.

The CJEU highlighted that the signatories of the Euratom Treaty intended to emphasise the non-military character of that Treaty and the supremacy of the aim of

157. Judgment of 12 April 2005, *Commission v United Kingdom*, C-61/03, ECLI:EU:C:2005:210, paragraph 15.
158. Judgment of 12 April 2005, *Commission v United Kingdom*, C-61/03, ECLI:EU:C:2005:210, paragraph 22.
159. Judgment of 9 March 2006, *Commission v United Kingdom*, C-65/04, ECLI:EU:C:2006:161, paragraphs 15 and 21.
160. Judgment of 12 April 2005, *Commission v United Kingdom*, C-61/03, ECLI:EU:C:2005:210, paragraphs 32 and 33.
161. Judgment of 12 April 2005, *Commission v United Kingdom*, C-61/03, ECLI:EU:C:2005:210, paragraph 36.

promoting the use of nuclear energy for peaceful purposes.[162] The CJEU further noted that it is clear from background and certain declarations mentioned in the *travaux préparatoires* of the Euratom Treaty that the Treaty's possible application to the military uses of nuclear energy was envisaged and discussed but that the Member States held differing opinions on that issue, as a result of which they decided to leave it unresolved.[163]

D ARTICLE 203 OF THE EURATOM TREATY

- The creation of new competences under Article 203 of the Euratom Treaty requires three conditions to be fulfilled: the new competences must be needed to fulfil the Euratom Community's objectives; the Euratom Treaty lacks the competences required by the Euratom Community to take the envisaged action; and the new competences must be created under a specific legislative procedure, i.e., on a proposal from the Commission, by unanimity of the Council after consulting the EP.
- The exercise of the Euratom Community's competences under Article 203 of the Euratom Treaty allows the Euratom Community to act both when the Euratom Treaty lacks the provisions needed for action to be taken under the existing fields of regulation, and when the Euratom Community needs to act outside the Euratom Treaty's fields of explicit regulation in order to fulfil its objectives.
- The CJEU has not interpreted the Euratom Community's competences under Article 203 of the Euratom Treaty purely as means of filling gaps in the Treaty.[164] Instead, through interpretation of the Euratom Community's objectives, it has established the Community's competence to combat fraud and other illegal activities that affect the financial interests of the Community.

The Scope and Content of the Competences under Article 203

Article 203 of the Euratom Treaty establishes that if action by the Community should prove necessary to attain one of the objectives of the Community and the Euratom Treaty has not provided the necessary powers, the Council shall, acting unanimously on a proposal from the Commission and after consulting the EP, take the appropriate

162. Judgment of 12 April 2005, *Commission v United Kingdom*, C-61/03, ECLI:EU:C:2005:210, paragraph 26.
163. Judgment of 12 April 2005, *Commission v United Kingdom*, C-61/03, ECLI:EU:C:2005:210, paragraph 29. *See also* J. G. Polach, *Euratom: Its Background, Issues and Economic Implications*, Dobbs Ferry, NY: Oceana Publications Inc., 1964, pp. 63–65.
164. I. Cenevska, *The European Atomic Energy Community in the European Union Context: The 'Outsider' Within*, Leiden: Brill Nijhoff, 2016, p. 70.

measures. This competence to act under the Euratom Treaty is referred to as an 'extension clause'[165] or a 'flexibility clause'.[166]

Article 203 of the Euratom Treaty establishes the Euratom Community's right to act if the Community sees a need of an action in order to execute its competences, but the Euratom Treaty does not provide legal means for it. The content of this competence requires three conditions to be fulfilled: first, an action to fulfil a specific objective of the Euratom Community is deemed to be needed; second, the Euratom Treaty lacks the provisions needed for that action; third, the action must be taken under a specific legislative procedure, i.e., on a proposal from the Commission, by unanimity of the Council after consulting the European Parliament.

It is noted above that the Euratom Community's objectives are unspecific and broad. For this reason, the first condition for the creation of new competences under Article 203 (i.e., that they are needed to fulfil the Euratom Community's objectives) can be fulfilled in almost every situation, provided that it raises standards of living and/or creates international relations with other countries.[167] The first condition also indicates that the Euratom Community's objectives are the essential element in defining its competences, and are not strictly bound to the regulatory content of the Euratom Treaty.

The second condition (i.e., that the Euratom Treaty should lack the provisions needed for the action) is complex as it is not clear from the wording of provision whether it requires the Euratom Community to act only under existing fields of regulations when additional action is needed, or whether the wording in Article 203 of the Euratom Treaty empowers the Euratom Community to act outside the Euratom Treaty's fields of explicit regulation, for example by establishing a nuclear liability regime,[168] if that is required to fulfil the Euratom Community's objectives. Some authors argue that this condition should not be restricted to situations where no express provisions exist, but should also apply to situations where the existing powers do not provide for an effective and satisfactory solution.[169]

165. H. J. Hahn, 'Euratom: The Conception of an International Personality', (1958) 71/6 *Harvard Law Review*, p. 1040.
166. I. Cenevska, *The European Atomic Energy Community in the European Union Context: The 'Outsider' Within*, Leiden: Brill Nijhoff, 2016, p. 70; and N. P. Serrano, 'Wakening the Serpent: Reflections on the Possible Modification of the Euratom Treaty', (2006) 1/1 *International Journal of Nuclear Law*, p. 14.
167. For example, in J. Handrlica, 'Harmonisation of Nuclear Liability in the European Union: Challenges, Options and Limits', (2009) 84 *Nuclear Law Bulletin*, the author reasons that Article 203 of the Euratom Treaty could be used as a legal base to establish the European nuclear liability regime.
168. The nuclear liability regime is a legal regime for civil liability in the event of nuclear damage. *See* C. Stoiber, A. Baer, N. Pelzer and W. Tonhauser, *Handbook of Nuclear Law*, Vienna: International Atomic Energy Agency, 2003, pp. 107–108. Analysis of the Euratom Community's competences in the field of nuclear liability is provided in Chapter 9 Sections 01 and 02 of this study.
169. J. Handrlica, 'Harmonisation of Nuclear Liability in the European Union: Challenges, Options and Limits', (2009) 84 *Nuclear Law Bulletin*, p. 45. Handrlica comes to this conclusion by means of a parallel analysis of Article 203 and Article 308 of the EC Treaty (now Article 352 TFEU).

The third condition (i.e., that new competences must be created under a specific legislative procedure) establishes certain horizontal competences of the institutions as a condition for establishing the required vertical competences of the Euratom Community under Article 203.

The Exercise of the Competences under Article 203

This section assesses the instruments used to exercise the Euratom Community's competences under Article 203 of the Euratom Treaty.

The competence to act beyond the regulatory scope of the Euratom Treaty has been exercised through several secondary legal acts. These can be divided into three categories: secondary legal acts that are based on a double legal basis[170] (i.e., Article 203 of the Euratom Treaty and a relevant article of the TFEU);[171] secondary legal acts that have several articles of the Euratom Treaty as a legal basis where Article 203 is one of them;[172] and secondary legal acts that have Article 203 as their only legal basis.[173]

170. Council Regulation (EC, Euratom) No 480/2009 of 25 May 2009 establishing a Guarantee Fund for external actions, OJ L 145, 10.6.2009, pp. 10–14; Council Decision (EC, Euratom) No 2006/908 of 4 December 2006 on the first instalment of the third Community contribution to the European Bank for Reconstruction and Development for the Chernobyl Shelter Fund, OJ L 346, 9.12.2006, pp. 28–29; Council Regulation (EC, Euratom) No 1700/2003 of 22 September 2003 amending Regulation (EEC, Euratom) No 354/83 concerning the opening to the public of the historical archives of the European Economic Community and the European Atomic Energy Community, OJ L 243, 27.9.2003, pp. 1–4; Council Decision (EC/Euratom) No 2001/792 of 23 October 2001 establishing a Community mechanism to facilitate reinforced cooperation in civil protection assistance interventions, OJ L 297, 15.11.2001, pp. 7–11; Council Regulation (Euratom, EC) No 2185/96 of 11 November 1996 concerning on-the-spot checks and inspections carried out by the Commission in order to protect the European Communities' financial interests against fraud and other irregularities, OJ L 292, 15.11.1996, pp. 2–5; Council Regulation (EC, Euratom) No 2988/95 of 18 December 1995 on the protection of the European Communities financial interests, OJ L 312, 23.12.1995, pp. 1–4;Council Decision (EC, Euratom) No 94/557 of 17 June 1994 authorising the European Community and the European Atomic Energy Community to sign and conclude the Convention defining the Statute of the European Schools, OJ L 212, 17.8.1994, pp. 1–2; Council Regulation (EEC, Euratom) No 354/83 of 1 February 1983 concerning the opening to the public of the historical archives of the European Economic Community and the European Atomic Energy Community, OJ L 43, 15.2.1983, pp. 1–3; Council Regulation (EEC, Euratom) No 3308/80 of 16 December 1980 on the replacement of the European unit of account by the ECU in Community legal instruments, OJ L 345, 20.12.1980, p. 1; Regulation (EEC, Euratom) No 1182/71 of the Council of 3 June 1971 determining the rules applicable to periods, dates and time limits, OJ L 124, 8.6.1971, pp. 1–2.
171. For example, Article 308 of the EC Treaty (now Article 352 TFEU).
172. Council Decision 94/179/Euratom of 21 March 1994 amending Decision 77/270/Euratom, to authorise the Commission to contract Euratom borrowings in order to contribute to the financing required for improving the degree of safety and efficiency of nuclear power stations in certain non-member countries, OJ L 84, 29.3.1994, pp. 41–43; Council Decision 77/270/Euratom of 29 March 1977 empowering the Commission to issue Euratom loans for the purpose of contributing to the financing of nuclear power stations, OJ L 88, 6.4.1977, pp. 9–10.
173. Council Regulation (Euratom) No 237/2014 of 13 December 2013 establishing an Instrument for Nuclear Safety Cooperation, OJ L 77, 15.3.2014, pp. 109–116; Council Regulation (Euratom) No 1074/1999 of 25 May 1999 concerning investigations conducted by the European Anti-Fraud Office (OCAF), OJ L 136, 31.5.1999, pp. 8–14 (no longer in force).

The majority of the secondary legislation adopted to exercise the Euratom Community's competences under Article 203 have a dual legal basis, which indicates that the EU and the Euratom Community share competences in that regulatory field. The rarest exercise of competences under Article 203 of the Euratom Treaty arises when it is the only legal basis for the secondary legal act. It is the case in respect of Regulation (Euratom) No 237/2014,[174] which establishes an Instrument for Nuclear Safety Cooperation to finance measures supporting the promotion of a high level of nuclear safety, radiation protection, safe management of spent fuel and radioactive waste and the application of efficient and effective safeguards of nuclear material in third countries. In this situation the Euratom Community's external activities are considered to fall on the technological side of nuclear safety.[175]

Systematic analysis of the instruments used to exercise competences under Article 203 has clarified the second condition as to the content of this article, namely that the Euratom Community has competence to act both when the Euratom Treaty lacks the provision needed for the action under the existing fields of regulations and when the Euratom Community needs to act outside the Euratom Treaty's fields of explicit regulation in order to fulfil its objectives.

The CJEU's Interpretation of the Competences

This section assesses whether any of the CJEU's case-law has elaborated on the competence at hand and, if so, whether the CJEU interpreted the content of the competence by reference to the objectives of the Euratom Community.

In one case the CJEU established that Article 203 of the Euratom Treaty could also be used to regulate notification of investment projects under Articles 41 and 44 of the Euratom Treaty, establishing that the Community's competence under Article 203 of the Euratom Treaty could also be exercised in respect of additional measures within extant fields of regulation under Articles 41 and 44.[176] In another case, the European Investment Bank (EIB) disputed Article 203 as the legal base for Regulation (Euratom)

174. Article 1 of Council Regulation (Euratom) No 237/2014 of 13 December 2013 establishing an Instrument for Nuclear Safety Cooperation, OJ L 77, 15.3.2014, pp. 109–116. It is important to note that the term 'the Union' is used in this regulation and not 'the Community', even though it was adopted under the Euratom Treaty, implying that it falls within the scope of the Euratom Community's competences and not those of the EU. In June 2018 the Commission presented a new Proposal for a Council Regulation establishing a European Instrument for Nuclear Safety complementing the Neighbourhood, Development and International Cooperation Instrument on the basis of the Euratom Treaty in the context of the Multiannual Financial Framework (MFF) 2021–2027, COM(2018) 462, 14.6.2018.

175. Opinion of Advocate General Jacobs, 13 December 2001, *Commission v Council*, C-29/99, ECLI:EU:C:2001:680, paragraph 138.

176. Judgment of 17 September 2007, *France v Commission*, T-240/04, ECLI:EU:T:2007:290, paragraph 41. The CJEU annulled Commission Regulation (Euratom) No 1352/2003 determining procedures for effecting the communications prescribed under Article 41 of the Treaty establishing the European Atomic Energy Community, stating that the Commission had no implicit competence to adopt the contested regulation under Articles 41 and 44 of the Euratom Treaty.

No 1074/1999,[177] arguing that measures adopted under the Euratom Treaty cannot apply to the EIB, since the EIB is not mentioned in that the Euratom Treaty and has no organic relationship with the Euratom Community. The EIB also argued that Article 203 of the Euratom Treaty was not the correct legal basis for Regulation (Euratom) No 1074/1999 as measures can be adopted on the basis of Article 203 only if they are necessary to attain one of the objectives of the Community and Title I of the Euratom Treaty makes no reference to fraud prevention. Therefore, the EIB contended, it cannot be inferred that fraud prevention is one of the Euratom Community's objectives.[178] Advocate General Jacobs dismissed the EIB's submissions and stated that adopting Regulation (Euratom) No 1074/1999 falls under the scope of the Community competence to adopt measures under Article 203 of the Euratom Treaty aimed at combating fraud and other illegal activities affecting the financial interests of the Community, and that the protection of the financial interests of the Community must be regarded as one of the objectives of the Euratom Community within the meaning of Article 203 of the Euratom Treaty.[179] The CJEU followed the reasoning of Advocate General Jacobs and ruled that it cannot be accepted that Regulation (Euratom) No 1074/1999, which has the aim of combating fraud affecting financial interests, was not adopted for the purpose of attaining one of the objectives of that Community and, consequently, could not be adopted on the basis of Article 203 of the Euratom Treaty.[180] The CJEU furthermore noted that it is not disputed that the EIB manages, as an agent, certain loans contracted by the Commission in relation to the Euratom Treaty and therefore concluded that such an activity indisputably concerns the financial interest of the Euratom Community.[181]

Consequently, the CJEU has interpreted the Euratom Community's competences under Article 203 of the Euratom Treaty not as an article for merely enforcing simple adjustments to the Treaty,[182] but through the objectives of the Community. The Court established Community's competence to combat fraud and other illegal activities affecting the financial interests of the Community under Article 203 of the Euratom

177. Council Regulation (Euratom) No 1074/1999 of 25 May 1999 concerning investigations conducted by the European Anti-Fraud Office (OCAF), OJ L 136, 31.5.1999, pp. 8–14.
178. Opinion of Advocate General Jacobs of 3 October 2002, *Commission v EIB*, C-15/00, ECLI: EU:C:2002:557, paragraphs 134–136.
179. Opinion of Advocate General Jacobs of 3 October 2002, *Commission v EIB*, C-15/00, ECLI: EU:C:2002:557, paragraphs 2 and 142.
180. Judgment of 10 July 2003, *Commission v EIB*, C-15/00 ECLI:EU:C:2003:396, paragraphs 140, 143 and 144.
181. Judgment of 10 July 2003, *Commission v EIB*, C-15/00, ECLI:EU:C:2003:396, paragraph 148.
182. I. Cenevska, *The European Atomic Energy Community in the European Union Context: The 'Outsider' Within*, Leiden: Brill Nijhoff, 2016, p. 70.

Treaty. Regulation (Euratom) No 1074/1999 was, however, later repealed by Regulation (EU, Euratom) No 883/2013[183] and the legal base was changed from Article 203 to Article 106a[184] of the Euratom Treaty, which allows direct applicability of the Article 325 TFEU on combatting fraud to the Euratom Treaty.

183. Regulation (EU, Euratom) No 883/2013 of the European Parliament and of the Council concerning investigations conducted by the European Anti-Fraud Office (OLAF) and repealing Regulation (EC) No 1073/1999 of the European Parliament and of the Council and Council Regulation (Euratom) No 1074/1999, OJ L 248, 18.9.2013, pp. 1–22.

184. Article 106a of the Euratom Treaty refers to Article 325 TFEU, which is the EU's legal basis for the adoption of Regulation (EU, Euratom) No 883/2013.

Specific Euratom Community Competences

CHAPTER 1
Promotion of Research

- *The main scope of the Euratom Community's competences is promotion of research that develops the nuclear energy sector. The Euratom Community also possesses research competences in a broader field of radiation protection, such as medical use of radioisotopes.*
- *The exercise of research competences is divided into direct and indirect actions of the Euratom Community. The focus in relation to the exercise of research competences has shifted from the fuel production and operation, which was the main research area under the provisions of the Euratom Treaty, to the safety of nuclear systems, and cover not only fission, but also fusion research. The exercise of competences under Article 7 of the Euratom Treaty also establishes a link to the EU's research activities by referring to the EU's Framework Programme for Research and Innovation – Horizon 2020. The Commission's competence to create the Joint Research Centre (JRC) has been exercised broadly in secondary legislation, establishing the JRC's functions both in research fields that fall under the scope of the Euratom Treaty and in other research areas which are not covered by the Euratom Treaty.*
- *Systematic analysis of the CJEU's case-law concerning Euratom research and training indicates that the Commission's competence to implement the programme under Article 7 is separate from its budgetary competences. The limitation of research and training programmes to five years under the Euratom Treaty is viewed as having a negative impact on officials enrolled in these programmes.*
- *The features of the Euratom Community's competences in relation to research are as follows: there is an appropriate level of detail in the Euratom Treaty to fulfil the Treaty's objective of promoting research; this competence is in some cases exercised in a broader way than the wording of the Euratom Treaty would indicate; and the few cases heard by the CJEU have not affected the relevant competences of the Euratom Community in primary and secondary legislations.*

Promotion of research was and is one of the main tasks assigned to the Euratom Community with a view to acquiring the scientific and technical expertise needed for the development of nuclear energy and other civil applications of nuclear technology. The Euratom Community was regarded as having the potential to become the cornerstone of a new technological revolution[185] and, therefore, the development of nuclear research was at the heart of the Euratom Treaty.[186] This competence was an inspiration to the authors of the Single European Act, which introduced a title on research and technological development into the EC Treaty, in 1992.[187]

The Euratom Community's competences in relation to nuclear research are analysed below, using the competence analysis and evaluation method presented in Chapter II Section C of this study. First, the scope and content of each competence is identified by analysing how it is established in the Euratom Treaty. Second, the question of whether the competence has been exercised and through what legal instruments is discussed. Third, the CJEU's case-law that elaborates on the Euratom Community's competence in relation to research is assessed.

1.01 THE SCOPE AND CONTENT OF THE COMPETENCES

This section assesses the scope and the content of the Euratom Community's competences in relation to research under the Euratom Treaty.

The founders of the Euratom Treaty considered promotion of nuclear research as one of the conditions necessary for the speedy establishment and growth of nuclear industries.[188] Research was singled out as being one of the main areas by which integration could be achieved under the Euratom Treaty, and was seen as being the principal field of activity for the Euratom Community for years to come.[189] The Euratom Treaty specifies that the task of the Euratom Community's competences in this field is to promote nuclear research.[190] The scope and main content of the Euratom Community's competences in relation to research is defined in Chapter 1 of the Euratom Treaty.

The Euratom Community's competences regarding the research and training programme can be divided into two parts: competences to decide on the Community's research and training programmes; and competences to affect research and training programmes in the Member States.

185. A. Södersten, *Euratom at the Crossroads*, Cheltenham, Northampton: Edward Elgar Publishing Limited, 2018, p. 107; L. Guzzetti, *A Brief History of European Union Research Policy*, Brussels: OOPEC, 1995, p. 8.
186. L. Guzzetti, *A Brief History of European Union Research Policy*, Brussels: OOPEC, 1995, p. 11.
187. European Commission, '50 Years of the Euratom Treaty', Memo/07/118, 26 March 2007 Brussels, p. 2.
188. Article 1 of the Euratom Treaty.
189. J. G. Polach, *Euratom: Its Background, Issues and Economic Implications*, Dobbs Ferry, NY: Oceana Publications Inc., 1964, p. 139.
190. Article 2(a) of the Euratom Treaty.

The Council has the competence to decide upon the Euratom Community's research and training programme[191] and to determine the manner in which an institution of university status, established under the Euratom Treaty, functions.[192] The wording of this provision does not clearly specify which institution has the obligation to establish the university, but it states that the way in which it will function shall be determined by the Council. This provision was inserted in the Euratom Treaty following discussions on a European University, but the Commission's latter proposal for a European Institute was not limited to the nuclear field. This resulted in Article 235 of the EEC Treaty (now Article 352 TFEU) being used as a legal basis, removing the Euratom Treaty from the framework of negotiations.[193]

The Council also has a right to amend the list of research fields set out in Annex I of the Euratom Treaty.[194] The established legislative procedure in this chapter of the Euratom Treaty requires either a qualified majority[195] or unanimity[196] of the Council. The EP is not mentioned here, implying that it does not have any established competences in relation to research under the Euratom Treaty.

The Commission is responsible for promoting and facilitating nuclear research of the Member States and carries out Euratom Community's research and training programme.[197] The content of the Commission's competence is specified by limiting the Commission's activities within the fields listed in Annex I to the Treaty.[198] It should be noted that Annex I defines only the Commission's areas of work in the field of research and does not limit the research programmes of the individual Member States. Annex I states that the following fields of research fall under the Euratom Community's

191. Acting unanimously on a proposal from the Commission, which shall consult the Scientific and Technical Committee, Article 7(1) of the Euratom Treaty.
192. Acting by a qualified majority on a proposal from the Commission, Article 9(2) of the Euratom Treaty.
193. A. Södersten, *Euratom at the Crossroads*, Cheltenham, Northampton: Edward Elgar Publishing Limited, 2018, pp. 108–109.
194. *See* Article 4(2) of the Euratom Treaty, which states that the list may be amended by the Council 'acting by a qualified majority on a proposal from the Commission which shall consult the Scientific and Technical Committee established under Article 134'. Some authors take the view that the possibility to amend Annex I of the Euratom Treaty indicates that the scope of the research to be carried out by the Euratom Community was not considered to have been finally decided when the Euratom Treaty was adopted. *See, inter alia*, J. Handrlica, 'The Splendid Durability of the Provisional: A Tribute to Euratom', (2018) 14/14 *Croatian Yearbook of European Law & Policy*, p. 166.
195. Articles 4 and 9 of the Euratom Treaty.
196. Article 7 of the Euratom Treaty.
197. Article 4(1) of the Euratom Treaty.
198. Article 4(2) of the Euratom Treaty.

competences: raw materials;[199] physics applied to nuclear energy;[200] physical chemistry of reactors;[201] processing of radioactive material;[202] applications of radioisotopes;[203] the study of the harmful effects of radiation on living organisms;[204] equipment;[205] and economic aspects of energy production.[206] The specification of research fields contained in Annex I of the Euratom Treaty limits the scope of the Euratom Community's competences to actions that fulfil the Euratom Treaty's objectives.[207] This overview of Annex I allows one to draw the general conclusion that the Euratom Community's nuclear research fields primarily focus on fuel production and reactor operation. A specific mention of concentration and storage of radioactive waste under the processing of radioactive material in Annex I is, however, worth addressing separately. The establishment of research on concentration and storage of radioactive waste as a Commission's competence could allow for a broad interpretation, implying that the Euratom Community has competence over the whole field of radioactive waste management. However, the Commission's competence here could also be interpreted narrowly, as being limited only to research of specific aspects of radioactive waste management, i.e., concentration and storage. Furthermore, mentioning research on other uses of radioisotopes, such as medical uses, in the List of Annex I indicates that this has been one of the Euratom Community's competences from the outset, thus showing that the Euratom Treaty was intended to achieve more than just the establishment and development of the nuclear energy sector. The overview of Annex I of the Euratom Treaty set out above also shows that research on economic aspects of

199. Methods for prospecting and mining of base materials; methods of concentrating and converting materials into pure compounds; methods of converting technically pure compounds into nuclear grade compounds and metals; methods for converting and processing into fuel elements by the chemical, ceramic and metallurgical industries; methods of protecting fuels elements against corrosion or erosion; producing, refining, processing and preserving other special materials used in the field of nuclear energy; and methods of isotope separation.
200. Applied theoretical physics, applied experimental physics and reactor calculations.
201. Study of changes in the physical and chemical structure and of alterations in the technical properties of various materials in reactors brought by different factors; study of degradation and other phenomena produced by irradiation in: fuel elements, structural materials and coolants, moderators; application of analytical chemistry and analytical physical chemistry to reactor components; physical chemistry of homogeneous reactors: radiochemistry, corrosion.
202. Methods of extracting plutonium and uranium 233 from irradiated fuels, and possible recovery of uranium or thorium; chemistry and metallurgy of plutonium; methods of extracting and chemistry of other transuranic elements; methods of extracting and chemistry of useful radioisotopes; concentration and storage of useless radioactive waste.
203. Application of radioisotopes as active elements or tracers in industry and science; medicine and biology; agriculture.
204. Study of the detection and measurement of harmful radiations; study of adequate preventive and protective measures and the appropriate safety standards; and study of the treatment of radiation effects.
205. Studies relating to the construction and improvement of equipment specially intended not only for reactors but also for any of the industrial and research installations required for the research activities listed in Annex I of the Euratom Treaty.
206. Comparative studies, both theoretical and experimental, of the various reactor types; technical and economic study of fuel cycles.
207. A. Södersten, *Euratom at the Crossroads*, Cheltenham, Northampton: Edward Elgar Publishing Limited, 2018, p. 107. There is no equivalent list in the EU Treaties – the EU can carry out research in any area.

nuclear energy production forms part of the Euratom Community's competence (e.g., research into technical issues and economic studies of fuel cycles).

The Commission's other competences entail submitting an annual report on the implementation of the Community's research and training programmes to the Council,[208] publishing research programmes and regular progress reports on their implementation,[209] and keeping the Economic and Social Committee informed of the broad outlines of Community research and training programmes.[210] The Commission is also obliged to call upon the Member States, persons or undertakings to communicate their research programmes.[211] The Commission must also discourage unnecessary duplication of research and direct research towards sectors which are insufficiently explored, and publish a list of those sectors at regular intervals.[212] Finally, the Commission has had an obligation to create a Joint Nuclear Research Centre, after consulting the Scientific and Technical Committee established under Article 134 of the Euratom Treaty,[213] and this responsibility did not involve the Commission being required to enter into consultation with the Council. The Commission also has a competence to deliver a reasoned opinion on each of the programmes communicated to it, if the Member State, person or undertaking which has communicated the programme to the Commission so requests.[214] The Commission may bring together representatives of public and private research centres as well as any experts engaged in research in the same or related fields for mutual consultation and exchanges of information;[215] may encourage the carrying out of national research programmes by different means;[216] may set up schools for training of specialists within the framework of the JRC;[217] and may entrust the carrying out of certain parts of the Community's research programme to Member States, persons or undertakings, or to third countries, international organisations or nationals of third countries.[218]

In addition to the competences of the Council and the Commission, the Euratom Treaty also establishes certain competences of the JRC.[219] The Centre shall ensure that the research programmes and other tasks assigned to it by the Commission are carried out, and a uniform nuclear terminology and a standard system of measurements are

208. Article 7(4) of the Euratom Treaty.
209. Article 11 of the Euratom Treaty.
210. Article 7(5) of the Euratom Treaty.
211. Article 5(1) of the Euratom Treaty.
212. Article 5(3) and (4) of the Euratom Treaty.
213. Article 8(1) of the Euratom Treaty.
214. Article 5(2) of the Euratom Treaty.
215. Article 5(5) of the Euratom Treaty.
216. Article 6 of the Euratom Treaty.
217. Article 9(1) of the Euratom Treaty.
218. Article 10 of the Euratom Treaty.
219. The main competences of the JRC are established in Chapter 1 of the Euratom Treaty, but some competences are also established in other parts of the Euratom Treaty. For example, under Article 39 the JRC assists the Commission in collecting the documentation referred to in Articles 33, 36 and 37.

established.[220] The wording of the Euratom Treaty does not indicate clearly which institution (the JRC or the Commission) has competence to decide whether the Centre's activities could be carried out in separate establishments due to geographical or functional reasons.[221] The provisions of the Euratom Treaty also establish Euratom-specific priority research fields for the Community: prospecting for minerals, the production of high purity nuclear materials, the processing of irradiated fuels, nuclear engineering, health and safety and the production and use of radioisotopes.[222]

The Community's competence to influence research in the Member States is established in Articles 4 to 6 of the Euratom Treaty and is delegated exclusively to the Commission. The fundamental issue of the appropriate relationship between Euratom and national nuclear research programmes should be addressed here. Formally, these programmes should be conducted in mutual harmony, but in practice they cannot avoid competing with each other for available manpower and other resources.[223] The Commission has a competence to promote and facilitate research in the Member States within the research fields identified in Annex I of the Euratom Treaty.[224] The Commission also coordinates research in the Member States[225] and can discourage certain research with a view to avoiding duplication, as well as direct research to certain sectors which are considered to be insufficiently explored.[226] In order to encourage certain research programmes in the Member States, the Commission has a competence to provide financial support; supply available source materials or special fissile materials for the research; place installations, equipment or expert assistance in the disposal of Member States, persons or undertakings; and promote joint financing by the Member States, persons or undertakings concerned.[227] This indicates that the Commission, acting on behalf of the Euratom Community, has a competence to sufficiently steer policy decision-making in respect of research carried out in the Member States. For example, it may have an input into decisions on which research fields should be a priority in order to make the research as effective as possible. Consequently, the Commission has wide-ranging ability to influence research carried out in the Member States, implying that the Community has competences not only to determine the nuclear research carried out by the Euratom Community, but also steer and coordinate research carried out in the Member States.

The analysis of scope and content of the Euratom Community's competences in the research field shows that these competences focus on research that promotes the development of the nuclear energy sector (fuel production, reactor operation and the

220. Article 8(1) of the Euratom Treaty. In order to achieve this, the Euratom Community has set up the Central Nuclear Measurements Bureau (BCMN) in Belgium, which was one of the JRC establishments (source: Euratom, Bulletin of the European Atomic Energy Community, June 1966 vol. V no 2).
221. Article 8(2) of the Euratom Treaty.
222. Article 9(1) of the Euratom Treaty.
223. J. G. Polach, *Euratom: Its Background, Issues and Economic Implications*, Dobbs Ferry, NY: Oceana Publications Inc., 1964, p. 139.
224. Article 4(1) and (2) of the Euratom Treaty.
225. Article 5(1) of the Euratom Treaty.
226. Article 5(3) of the Euratom Treaty.
227. Article 6 of the Euratom Treaty.

economic aspects of nuclear energy production) and that they extend to research in a broader field of radiation protection, such as the medical use of radioisotopes. It is also clear that the Commission has more competences in this field than the Council.[228] Nevertheless, the Council's competences are of key importance for the functioning of the Euratom Community's research programmes, since it establishes the Euratom Community's research and training programme and can determine and prioritise the fields of research that the Community focuses on.

1.02 THE EXERCISE OF THE COMPETENCES

This section assesses whether the Euratom Community's competences in the field of research have been exercised and the instruments through which these competences have been exercised.

Systematic analysis of all secondary legal acts that are based on Articles 4 to 11 of the Euratom Treaty allows one to conclude that Articles 7 and 8[229] of the Euratom Treaty have been used as the legal basis for the most important secondary legislation exercising the Euratom Community's competences in this field. Therefore, this part of the study focuses on the exercise of the competences established in these articles.

A Exercise of Article 7 of the Euratom Treaty

The specificity of the fact that the Euratom Community's research and training programme is adopted for no longer than a five-year period explains why numerous secondary legal acts exercising the Community's competences under Article 7 and establishing the Euratom Community's research and training programme have been in force at various times over the years.[230] The historical aspects of development of the

228. Some researchers consider that the Commission has a key role in promoting research in the Euratom Community. *See* I. Cenevska, *The European Atomic Energy Community in the European Union Context: The 'Outsider' Within*, Leiden: Brill Nijhoff, 2016, p. 32.
229. Under Article 11 of the Euratom Treaty the Commission has an obligation to publish the research programmes referred to in Articles 7, 8 and 10, as well as regular progress reports on their implementation. This competence has been exercised by the Commission by publishing research programmes and reports referred to later in this study when analysing Articles 7 and 8 of the Euratom Treaty. Therefore, Article 11 is not analysed separately.
230. The Council decisions adopted in the three decades before the current programme are as follows: Council Decision 2012/93/Euratom of 19 December 2011 concerning the Framework Programme of the European Atomic Energy Community for nuclear research and training activities (2012 to 2013), OJ L 47, 18.2.2012, pp. 25–32; Council Decision 2006/970/Euratom of 18 December 2006 Concerning the Seventh Framework Programme of the European Atomic Energy Community (Euratom) for nuclear research and training activities (2007 to 2011), OJ L 400, 30.12.2006, pp. 60–85; Council Decision 2002/668/Euratom of 3 June 2002 concerning the sixth framework programme of the European Atomic Energy Community (Euratom) for nuclear research and training activities, also contributing to the creation of the European Research Area (2002 to 2006), OJ L 232, 29.8.2002, pp. 34–42; Council Decision 1999/64/Euratom of 22 December 1998 concerning the Fifth Framework Programme of the European Atomic Energy Community (Euratom) for research and training activities (1998 to 2002), OJ L 26, 1.2.1999, pp. 34–45; Council Decision 94/268/Euratom of 26 April 1994 concerning a framework programme of Community activities in the field of research and training for the European Atomic Energy

nuclear research programmes and their symbiosis with EU research and development programmes may be of some interest,[231] but since this is beyond the scope of this study, analysis of the exercise of Euratom Community's competences under Article 7[232] of the Euratom Treaty is limited to the secondary legislation in force.

Article 7 of the Euratom Treaty is a legal basis for two secondary legal acts that exercise the Euratom Community's competences in the fields of research and training. Council Regulation (Euratom) No 2018/1563 establishes Euratom Community's research and training programme for the period 2019–2020[233] and Council Decision (Euratom) 2017/956 regulates a high flux reactor (HFR) supplementary research programme for the period 2016–2019.[234]

The operation of the HFR has been supported by a series of supplementary research programmes, the last of which[235] expired on 31 December 2015.[236] As was the case with its predecessors, Council Decision (Euratom) 2017/956 is based on a long-term commitment between the Euratom Community and the Netherlands.[237] The main objectives of the supplementary research programme in relation to the HFR is to provide a steady and reliable neutron flux for experimental purposes and to allow the

---

Community (1994 to 1998), OJ L 115, 6.5.1994, pp. 31–37; Council Decision 90/221/Euratom, EEC of 23 April 1990 concerning the framework Programme of Community activities in the field of research and technological development (1990 to 1994), OJ L 117, 8.5.1990, pp. 28–43 and Council Decision 91/626/Euratom of 28 November 1991 adopting a research and education programme in the field of nuclear fission safety (1990 to 1994), OJ L 336, 7.12.1991, pp. 42–47.

231. Research and training programmes under the Euratom Treaty existed from the establishment of the Euratom Community (for further information, *see* J. G. Polach, *Euratom: Its Background, Issues and Economic Implications*, Dobbs Ferry, NY: Oceana Publications Inc., 1964), long before the first European Framework Programme. Council Resolution of 25 July 1983 on framework programmes for Community research, development and demonstration activities and a first framework programme 1984–1987 was established with both Article 235 of the EEC Treaty and Article 7 of the Euratom Treaty as legal bases, covering both nuclear research and other EU research areas. The Euratom Community's research and training programme has now been separated from the EU's framework programme, but the former continues to complement the latter.
232. This also applies to the exercise of competences under Article 8.
233. Council Regulation (Euratom) 2018/1563 of 15 October 2018 on the Research and Training Programme of the European Atomic Energy Community (2019–2020) complementing the Horizon 2020 Framework Programme for Research and Innovation, and repealing Regulation (Euratom) No 1314/2013, OJ L 262, 19.10.2018, pp. 1–19.
234. Council Decision (Euratom) 2017/956 of 29 May 2017 on the adoption of the 2016–2019 high flux reactor supplementary research programme to be implemented by the Joint Research Centre for the European Atomic Energy Community, OJ L 144, 7.6.2017, pp. 23–26.
235. Council Decision 2012/709/Euratom of 13 November 2012 on the adoption of the 2012-2015 High Flux Reactor supplementary research programme to be implemented by the Joint Research Centre for the European Atomic Energy Community, OJ L 321, 20.11.2012, pp. 59–60.
236. To ensure continuity between supplementary research programmes, Article 1 of Council Decision (Euratom) 2017/956 provides for the adoption of the supplementary research programme on the operation of the HFR for a period of four years, starting on 1 January 2016. Under Article 2 and Annex II of the Decision, part of the contributions under the 2016–2019 HFR supplementary research programme may also cover expenditure made during 2016.
237. The HFR is used by the Commission in accordance with the agreement between Euratom and the Netherlands of 25 July 1961. This agreement was signed for a period of ninety-nine years. In order to execute it, the two parties concluded a long lease of ninety-nine years conferring a right in rem ('bail emphytéotique') on 31 October 1962.

efficient use of the HFR by research institutes in various research fields, for example improvement of the safety of nuclear reactors, health, nuclear fusion and waste management.[238] The reactor is also used for the commercial production of radioisotopes for more than 60% of the 10 million medical diagnoses executed each year in Europe.[239] The execution of the programme is financed entirely from contributions from France and the Netherlands,[240] but the Commission has an obligation to exercise its competences to manage the supplementary programme with the help of the JRC[241] and to submit a final report on the implementation of the supplementary programme to the EP and to the Council after the end of the 2016–2019 period.

While the EU's Framework Programme for Research and Innovation (Horizon 2020)[242] is established for the seven-year period (2014–2020), the Euratom Programme is bound by a five-year time frame under Article 7 of the Euratom Treaty. As both programmes fall under the same Multi-annual Financial Framework for 20142020[243], after five years[244] the Council needed to adopt a Regulation (Euratom) No 2018/1563 for a complementary Euratom Community's Research and Training Programme for two more years, i.e., the period 2019–2020. Few changes have been made in comparison with the Euratom Programme under the previous Regulation 1314/2013: the budget for direct and indirect actions was updated for 2019–2020,[245] openness of the 2019–2020 Euratom Programme to countries and territories associated with the 2014–2018 Euratom Programme has been introduced,[246] obsolete provisions concerning the evaluation of the programme have been deleted[247] and Annex I on the activities to be supported by the 2019–2020 Euratom Programme has been updated.[248] In other words, exercise of the competences under Article 7 of the Euratom Treaty has not changed

238. Article 1 and Annex I of Council Decision (Euratom) 2017/956.
239. Commission Proposal for a Council Decision on the adoption of the 2016–2019 High Flux Reactor supplementary research programme to be implemented by the Joint Research Centre for the European Atomic Energy Community, COM (2017) 83 final, Brussels 23.2.2017.
240. Article 2 and Annex II of Council Decision (Euratom) 2017/956.
241. Article 3 of Council Decision (Euratom) 2017/956.
242. Regulation (EU) No 1291/2013 of the European Parliament and of the Council of 17 December 2013 establishing Horizon 2020 – the Framework Programme for Research and Innovation (2014–2020) and repealing Decision No 1982/2006/EC, OJ L 347, 20.12.2013, pp. 104–173. Horizon 2020 is implemented through the consolidated and specific programme established by Council Decision 2013/743/EU of 3 December 2013 establishing the specific programme implementing Horizon 2020 – the Framework Programme for Research and Innovation (2014–2020) and repealing Decisions 2006/971/EC, 2006/972/EC, 2006/973/EC, 2006/974/EC and 2006/975/EC, OJ L 347, 20.12.2013, p. 965.
243. Council Regulation (EU, Euratom) No 1311/2013 of 2 December 2013 laying down the multiannual financial framework for the period 2014–2020, OJ L 347, 20.12.2013, pp. 884–891.
244. The last five-year Euratom Programme was adopted under Council Regulation (Euratom) No 1314/2013 of 16 December 2013 on the Research and Training Programme of the European Atomic Energy Community (2014–2018) complementing the Horizon 2020 Framework Programme for Research and Innovation, OJ L 347, 20.12.2013, pp. 948–964; it was repealed by Council Regulation (Euratom) No 2018/1563.
245. Article 4 of Council Regulation (Euratom) 2018/1563.
246. Article 5 of Council Regulation (Euratom) 2018/1563.
247. Article 22 of Council Regulation (Euratom) 2018/1563.
248. The European Fusion Development Agreement (EFDA) is now replaced by EUROfusion. The wording concerning the Joint European Torus (JET) in Annex 1 was revised in order not to prejudge the funding possibilities under the 2019–2020 Euratom programme.

significantly in the extended Euratom Research and Training Programme for 2019–2020.

Systematic analysis of the provisions of Regulation (Euratom) No 2018/1563[249] leads to the conclusion that the competence to establish the Euratom Community's research and training programme is exercised by dividing implementing actions into direct actions (i.e., actions relating to research and innovation activities undertaken by the Commission through its JRC)[250] and indirect actions (i.e., research and innovation activities for which the Community provides financial support and which are undertaken by participants in the research and training programme).[251] The provisions of Regulation (Euratom) No 2018/1563 regulate objectives of the Euratom research and training programme,[252] the financial envelope for the implementation of the Euratom Programme,[253] the establishment of implementing work programmes[254] and separate evaluations of the implemented programmes[255] for direct and indirect actions.

The objectives of direct and indirect actions under Article 3 of Regulation (Euratom) No 2018/1563 entail the competences to implement research in the fields set out in Annex I of the Euratom Treaty.[256] Comparative analysis of the research field set out in Annex I to the Euratom Treaty and the objectives of direct and indirect actions under the Euratom research and training programme established in Regulation (Euratom) No 2018/1563 indicates that when exercising competences in relation to research the Euratom Community's focus has shifted from being primarily concerned with fuel production and reactor operation towards the safety aspects of nuclear energy, both in direct and indirect actions. This includes the safety of nuclear systems;[257] radiation protection;[258] safe solutions for the management of ultimate nuclear waste,[259] including final geological disposal as well as partitioning and transmutation; decommissioning; and emergency preparedness.[260] This is also indicated in the recitals of Regulation (Euratom) No 2018/1563 by stating that nuclear safety aspects should be given the greatest possible attention in the Euratom Programme.[261] Furthermore, comparative analysis shows that certain research fields are exercised more comprehensively under Regulation (Euratom) No 2018/1563 than established under Annex I of the Euratom Treaty. Radioactive waste management is an example of this phenomenon. The

249. Article 3(2) and (3), Article 4(1)(a) to (c), Article 6(1), Articles 11 and 22 of Council Regulation (Euratom) No 2018/1563.
250. Article 2(b) of Council Regulation (Euratom) No 2018/1563.
251. Article 2(c) of Council Regulation (Euratom) No 2018/1563.
252. Article 3 of Council Regulation (Euratom) No 2018/1563.
253. Article 4 of Council Regulation (Euratom) No 2018/1563. The financial envelope for the implementation of the Euratom research and training programme for the period 2019-2020 is approximately EUR 770 million.
254. Article 11 of Council Regulation (Euratom) No 2018/1563.
255. Article 22(2) of Council Regulation (Euratom) No 2018/1563.
256. Research fields under Annex I of the Euratom Treaty have identified under the scope and the content of the competence in the field of research.
257. Article 3(2)(a) of Council Regulation (Euratom) No 2018/1563.
258. Article 3(2)(d) of Council Regulation (Euratom) No 2018/1563.
259. Article 3(2)(b) of Council Regulation (Euratom) No 2018/1563.
260. Article 3(3)(a) of Council Regulation (Euratom) No 2018/1563.
261. Recital 6 of Council Decision (Euratom) No 2018/1563.

Euratom Treaty only mentions concentration and storage of radioactive waste under the research field of processing of radioactive material in Annex I. By contrast, Regulation (Euratom) No 2018/1563 establishes contribution to the development of safe, long-term solutions for the management of ultimate nuclear waste as one of the objectives of indirect actions,[262] and improving the safety of nuclear waste management, final geological disposal and decommissioning as an objective of direct actions[263] under the Euratom Programme.

Regulation of nuclear fusion research should be analysed in terms of exercise of the competences under Article 7 of the Euratom Treaty. Fusion research is neither mentioned in the list of research fields in Annex I of the Euratom Treaty nor in any other provisions of the Euratom Treaty. Thus, it was not established as forming part of the scope and content of a competence under a primary legal act. Regulation (Euratom) No 2018/1563 states that moving towards demonstration of the feasibility of fusion as a power source[264] is one of the objectives of indirect actions to implement the Euratom research and training programme. This regulation also establishes that the committee relating to the exercise of the Commission's implementing powers sits in two different configurations: one for fission-related aspects and another for fusion-related aspects of the 2019–2020 Euratom Programme.[265] Furthermore, the same regulation refers to the Agreement on the Establishment of the ITER International Fusion Energy Organisation for the Joint Implementation of the ITER Project[266] and Council Decision 2007/198/Euratom,[267] which establishes the European Joint Undertaking for ITER. This indicates that the Euratom Community has the competence and responsibility to promote fusion by participating in the construction of the ITER Project and its future exploitation. The importance attached to the ITER Project follows from the research carried out by the Euratom Community in this field since the First Community Research Programme, which enabled the setting up of the Joint European Torus (JET, Culham) in 1978, the results of which have been an essential step forward in fusion energy research.[268] Council Decision 2007/198/Euratom was, however, established under another legal basis – Articles 47 and 48 of the Euratom Treaty, which regulate the Euratom Community's competence to establish Joint Undertakings. Consequently, the

262. Article 3(2)(b) of Council Regulation (Euratom) No 2018/1563.
263. Article 3(3)(a) of Council Regulation (Euratom) No 2018/1563.
264. Article 3(2)(e) of Council Regulation (Euratom) No 2018/1563.
265. Article 12 of Council Regulation (Euratom) No 2018/1563. The committee is a committee within the meaning of Regulation (EU) No 182/2011 of the European Parliament and of the Council of 16 February 2011 laying down the rules and general principles concerning mechanisms for control by Member States of the Commission's exercise of implementing powers, OJ L 55, 28.2.2011, pp. 13–18.
266. ITER stands for International Thermonuclear Experimental Reactor. Recital 10 of Council Regulation (Euratom) No 2018/1563. Agreement on the Establishment of the ITER International Fusion Energy Organization for the Joint Implementation of the ITER Project, OJ L 358, 16.12.2006, p. 62.
267. Council Decision 2007/198/Euratom of 27 March 2007 establishing the European Joint Undertaking for ITER and the Development of Fusion Energy and conferring advantages upon it, OJ L 90, 30.3.2007, pp. 58–72.
268. R. Ptasekaite, *The Euratom Treaty v. Treaties of the European Union: Limits of Competence and Interaction*, Swedish Radiation Safety Authority Report, SSM2011:32, Solna: SSM, 2011, p. 5.

details of the Community's competences related to the ITER Project are analysed in Chapter 5 of this study regarding Joint Undertakings. The Euratom Community's engagement in fusion is also reflected in the allocations in respect of the financial envelope for the implementation of the Euratom research and training programme. Fusion research remains the single largest element of the current Euratom Programme: in the Euratom Programmes for both the 2014–2018 and the 2019–2020 periods, it accounts for approximately 45 % of the total cost of the implementation of the Programme.[269] Regulation (Euratom) No 2018/1563 establishes the general objectives and the financial envelope for fusion research, but refers to Council Decision 2007/198/Euratom for the specific aspects of the ITER Project. Consequently, the Euratom research and training programme covers the Euratom Community's competences in relation to research and training more comprehensively than the wording of Article 7 of the Euratom Treaty.

The interaction between the Euratom research and training programme and the Horizon 2020 should be analysed in relation to exercise of the competences under Article 7 of the Euratom Treaty. In respect of the Euratom Programme, Article 1 of Regulation (Euratom) No 2018/1563 is a legal basis for participation in activities conducted jointly under that regulation and Regulation (EU) 1291/2013. Regulation (Euratom) No 2018/1563 also states that the Euratom Programme contributes to achieving the objectives of the Horizon 2020 Framework Programme for Research[270] and that achieving the objectives of the Euratom Programme in relevant areas requires support for cross-cutting activities, both within the Euratom Programme and jointly with the activities of the Horizon 2020 Framework Programme.[271] It also indicates that participation in the Euratom Programme and dissemination of research results should be subject to the rules applicable to the Horizon 2020 Framework Programme.[272] Article 6(2) of Regulation (Euratom) No 2018/1563 provides that the Commission may entrust the implementation of indirect action under the Euratom Programme to bodies created under, or referred to in, the Horizon 2020 Framework Programme. Furthermore, Article 8(1) of the same Regulation notes that there may be activities that cut across the indirect actions set out in both Euratom Programme and Horizon 2020, and Article 11(4) requires the Commission to identify these cross-cutting activities in the work programme for the implementation of the indirect actions and the multi-annual work programme for direct actions of the JRC.

These provisions show that the Euratom research and training programme establishes a link to Horizon 2020 when exercising competences under Article 7 of the Euratom Treaty. Regulation (EU) 1291/2013, which establishes Horizon 2020, mentions the Euratom by indicating that the priorities of Horizon 2020 should also be

269. In the 2014–2018 Programme, the total amount for implementation is EUR 1,603,329,000, of which fusion research accounts for EUR 728,232,000; while in the 2019–2020 Programme the total amount for implementation is EUR 770.220,000, of which fusion research accounts for EUR 349,834,000.
270. Recital 5 of Council Regulation (Euratom) No 2018/1563.
271. Recital 32 of Council Regulation (Euratom) No 2018/1563.
272. Recital 27 of Council Regulation (Euratom) No 2018/1563.

supported through the Euratom Programme on nuclear research and training[273] and, where appropriate, possible synergies between Horizon 2020 and the Euratom Programme should be envisaged.[274] Comparative analysis of these cross-references between the two research programmes allows one to conclude that the Euratom Programme has a stronger connection with the Horizon 2020 Framework than does Horizon 2020 with the Euratom. Furthermore, the impact assessment in respect of the Euratom research and training programme was done for the whole seven-year period (2014–2020) as part of the Horizon 2020 impact assessment.[275] This accordingly confirms that the Euratom Programme complements the broader EU framework programme of Horizon 2020.[276] The fact that the provisions of the Euratom Programme refer to the cross-cutting activities of both programmes implies that the activities under Regulation (EU) 1291/2013, which does not have the Euratom Treaty as a legal basis, can indirectly exercise the Euratom Community's competences established in Article 7, via a reference in Regulation (Euratom) No 2018/1563. By achieving the objectives set out for the indirect and direct actions to implement the Euratom research and training programme the Euratom Programme will also reinforce outcomes under three priorities of the Horizon 2020 Framework Programme, namely excellent science, industrial leadership and societal challenges.[277]

Concerning exercise of horizontal/institutional competences under Article 7 of the Euratom Treaty, two issues should be mentioned: the EP's role in the adoption of the Euratom research and training programme and the Commission's exercise of implementing powers in the field.

Under the Euratom Treaty, the research and training programme is adopted by the Council acting unanimously on a proposal from the Commission, after the Commission has consulted the Scientific and Technical Committee.[278] The adoption of the Euratom Programme does not require the opinion of other institutions or bodies and, therefore, the EP has no formal legislative or consultative role in the matter. The Council has, however, decided to consult the EP on the proposal for the Euratom

273. Recital 11 of Regulation (EU) No 1291/2013.
274. Annex I, Part I, Point 3 ('Secure, clean and efficient energy') of Regulation (EU) No 1291/2013.
275. Commission Staff Working Paper, Impact Assessment Accompanying the Communication from the Commission 'Horizon 2020 – The Framework Programme for Research and Innovation'; Proposal for a Regulation of the European Parliament and of the Council establishing Horizon 2020 – the Framework Programme for Research and Innovation (2014–2020); Proposal for a Council Decision establishing the Specific Programme implementing Horizon 2020 – The Framework Programme for Research and Innovation (2014–2020); Proposal for a Council Regulation on the Research and Training Programme of the European Atomic Energy Community (2014–2018) contributing to the Horizon 2020 – The Framework Programme for Research and Innovation, SEC (2011) 1427 final, Brussels, 30.11.2011, Annex 6.
276. Södersten also expresses the view that EU research and Euratom research has become increasingly intertwined, in A. Södersten, *Euratom at the Crossroads*, Cheltenham, Northampton: Edward Elgar Publishing Limited, 2018, p. 111.
277. Annexe I to the proposal for a Council Regulation on the Research and Training Programme of the European Atomic Energy Community (2019–2020) complementing the Horizon 2020 Framework Programme for Research and Innovation, COM (2017) 698 final, p. 2.
278. Article 7 of the Euratom Treaty.

Research and Training Programme.[279] The EP issued a European Parliament Legislative Resolution with its opinion on the Euratom Research and Training Programme for 2019–2020[280] in which it proposed changes to the Euratom Programme. The use of this informal consultation procedure involving the EP indicates that the horizontal/institutional competences under Article 7 are de facto exercised on a broader basis than the wording of the Euratom Treaty would appear to require. However, the EP's broad role in relation to Euratom research cannot be compared with its competences in relation to EU research, as the Horizon 2020 Framework Programme was adopted under the ordinary legislative procedure.[281]

Articles 290 and 291 TFEU, which establish the Commission's delegated and implementing powers, apply to the Euratom Treaty under Article 106a of the Euratom Treaty. Consequently, Regulation (EU) No 182/2011 establishing the rules of exercise of implementing powers is also applicable under the Euratom Treaty.

The recitals of Regulation (Euratom) No 2018/1563 indicate a need to confer implementing powers on the Commission in order to ensure uniform conditions for the implementation of the indirect actions under the Euratom Programme.[282] Article 11 of Regulation (Euratom) No 2018/1563 establishes implementing powers of the Commission in relation to Euratom research and training, requiring the Commission to adopt work programmes for the implementation of the indirect actions[283] in accordance with Regulation (EU) No 182/2011.[284] The Commission has exercised its implementing power by adopting the Work Programmes annually, the latest being for 2019 and 2020.[285] In addition to supporting research on nuclear safety, decommissioning, waste management and radiation protection, the Euratom Work Programme 2019–2020 places emphasis on research in respect of the education and training and research infrastructure. It is divided into fifteen topics and supports the implementation of Directive 2009/71/Euratom[286] and other related legislation.[287] Consequently, despite

279. Under Article 19(7)(h) of the Council's Rules of Procedure, Coreper may adopt a procedural decision to consult an institution or body wherever such consultation is not required by the Treaties.
280. Draft European Parliament Legislative Resolution on the proposal for a Council Regulation on the Research and Training Programme of the European Atomic Energy Community (2019–2020) complementing the Horizon 2020 Framework Programme for Research and Innovation, Committee on Industry, Research and Energy, 2017/0312(NLE).
281. Article 182 TFEU. Under Article 289 TFEU the ordinary legislative procedure comprises the joint adoption by the EP and the Council of a legislative act.
282. Recital 31 of Council Regulation (Euratom) No 2018/1563.
283. The Commission's implementing powers under Regulation (EU) No 182/2011 cover only indirect actions. The Commission's obligations concerning direct actions require the Commission to draw up a multi-annual work programme in accordance with Commission Decision 96/282/Euratom of 10 April 1996 on the reorganization of the Joint Research Centre, OJ L 107, 30.4.1996, pp. 12–15; *see* Article 11(2) of Regulation No 2018/1563.
284. Article 12 of Council Regulation (Euratom) No 2018/1563.
285. Commission Implementing Decision C(2018) 8412 of 14 December 2018 on the financing of indirect actions within the framework of Council Regulation (Euratom) No 2018/1563 and on the adoption of the work programme for 2019–2020.
286. Council Directive 2009/71/Euratom of 25 June 2009 establishing a Community framework for the nuclear safety of nuclear installations, OJ L 172, 2.7.2009, pp. 18–22.
287. Euratom Work programme 2019–2020, Commission Implementing Decision C(2018) 8412 of 14 December 2018, p. 5.

the fact that Article 7 of the Euratom Treaty does not mention the Commission's implementing powers, Article 106a of the Euratom Treaty in tandem with Article 291 TFEU establish a legal basis for the Commission to exercise its implementing powers in relation to Euratom research and training. Consequently, the Euratom Treaty provides the horizontal competences to establish delegated or implementing powers of the Commission not only in relation to research and training, but also in any field of substantive law in the Euratom Community realm.

In conclusion, competences under Article 7 of the Euratom Treaty are exercised more broadly than the strict wording of the article - both in terms of vertical and horizontal competences - would tend to indicate. The Euratom research and training programme covers both fusion and fission research, the EP is consulted in relation to the adoption of the Euratom research and training programme, and implementing powers have been conferred on the Commission to establish work programme for indirect research actions of the Euratom Community.

B Exercise of Article 8 of the Euratom Treaty

Article 8 of the Euratom Treaty establishes the Commission's competence to create a JRC. As resources in this field were limited, it was decided not to establish an entirely new venture, but to incorporate a number of existing establishments into one JRC, without impeding the work being done on a national basis.[288] The process of securing signature of the different site agreements has been done gradually[289] and the JRC now comprises seven institutes: the Institute for Reference Materials and Measurements located in Geel, Belgium; the Institute for Transuranium Elements located in Karlsruhe, Germany; the Institute for Prospective Technological Studies located in Seville, Spain; the Institute for Energy, which is located in Petten in the Netherlands; the Institute for the Protection and Security of the Citizen located in Ispra, Italy; the Institute for Environment and Sustainability located in Ispra, Italy; and the Institute for Health and Consumer Protection located in Ispra, Italy. The JRC has seen three periods of significant change. In the 1970s, its mandate was extended to cover non-nuclear work. In the 1980s its activities became part of the European Framework Programme for Research and late in the 1990s, the Council endorsed the JRC's broad policy support mission.[290] Now the functions of the JRC are much broader than was originally intended under Article 8 of the Euratom Treaty. Due to the scope of this study, the analysis will focus on the JRC's functions under the Euratom Treaty. In a similar manner to the analysis in Chapter 1 Section 02.A on the exercise of competences under Article 7 of the Euratom Treaty, exercise of the Euratom Community's competences

288. Euratom Commission's Third General Report on the Activities of the Community (March 1959–April 1960), April 1960, pp. 18–19.
289. JRC, The European Commission's science and knowledge service: 60 stories for the 60th anniversary, Brussels 2017, p. 78.
290. JRC Implementation Review 2017: In the context of the interim evaluation of the Horizon 2020 Programme, July 2017, European Commission Joint Research Centre (JRC), Adviser for Evaluation and Scientific Integrity Brussels, Belgium, p. 9.

under Article 8 of the Euratom Treaty is limited to the secondary legislation currently in force.

The main secondary legal act through which the Commission's competence to establish and organise the JRC is exercised is Commission Decision 96/282/Euratom, which deals with the reorganisation of the JRC and sets out its structure and functions.[291] The JRC has three main organs – the Director-General, the Board of Governors and the Scientific Committee.[292] The Director-General is appointed by the Commission and is responsible for, *inter alia*, preparation of the draft programmes and establishing a strategy for the JRC, negotiation and conclusion of research contracts with third parties, implementation of programmes and the financial administration of the JRC.[293] Even though the JRC is under the authority of the Director-General, who has the right to determine its internal organisation,[294] the Commission appoints officers responsible for control of commitments, authorisation of expenditures and control of receipt of revenues, as well as officers responsible for the payment of expenditure and receipt of revenue and for the handling of funds and securities (who are also responsible for its safe custody).[295] The Board of Governors comprises high-level representatives from the Member States, appointed by the Commission on the basis of nominations by the authorities of the Member States. The Board of Governors assists the Director-General and delivers opinions for submission to the Commission on questions relating to: the role of the JRC within the Community research and technological development strategy; the scientific/technical and financial management of the JRC; and the performance of the tasks entrusted to it. The Board of Governors may also, through the Commission, submit opinions to the Council and EP on all matters relating to the JRC.[296] The Scientific Committee of the JRC assists the Director-General. The Scientific Committee is to be regularly consulted by the Director-General on all questions of a scientific or technical nature relating to the activities of the JRC. In this connection, it must, in particular, take part in the preparation of draft Euratom Programmes.[297]

As noted in the analysis of the scope and content of the competences in Chapter 1 Section 01 of this study, Article 7 and Article 8 of the Euratom Treaty also establish a division of horizontal competences between the Council and the Commission. The Council adopts the Euratom research and training programme and the Commission establishes the JRC, implying that the Commission also ensures the functioning of the JRC. It may even be assumed that the Commission has exclusive competence over the

291. Commission Decision 96/282/Euratom of 10 April 1996 on the reorganization of the Joint Research Centre, ELI: OJ L 107, 30.4.1996, pp. 12–15. There is also Commission Decision 71/57/Euratom of 13 January 1971 on the reorganization of the Joint Nuclear Research Centre (JRC), OJ L 016, 20.1.1971, p. 14. Although Commission Decision 71/57/Euratom has not been formally repealed, it is structurally almost identical to Commission Decision 96/282/Euratom. Therefore, *lex posterior derogat priori* is applied here.
292. Article 2 of Commission Decision 96/282/Euratom.
293. Article 3 of Commission Decision 96/282/Euratom.
294. Article 3 of Commission Decision 96/282/Euratom.
295. Article 8(4) and (5) of Commission Decision 96/282/Euratom.
296. Articles 4 and 6 of Commission Decision 96/282/Euratom.
297. Article 5 of Commission Decision 96/282/Euratom.

JRC's mandate and work framework. However, the JRC's functioning has, on various occasions, been an important issue for the Council and it has felt the need to express its views on JRC's role via the adoption of resolutions[298] and conclusions.[299] The Council has stressed the need for the JRC to be better integrated in networks with partners belonging to all the Member States, both in its institutional and competitive activities, which would result in JRC playing a significant role in European scientific integration.[300] The Council also encouraged the Commission to include the JRC's activities in the Commission's annual report on the implementation of the Euratom research and training programme,[301] which indicates that the Council wanted to be involved in, or at least informed about, the JRC's activities. In the Council's conclusions of 26 April 1994 the Council also specified that the proportion of JRC activities in the framework programmes to be transferred to the competitive system should average 10% for the Euratom framework programme for the period from 1995 to 1998.[302] This indicates that the Council, being responsible for the overall research and training programme of the Euratom Community, has exercised its general competences in the field by indicating to the Commission the measures that should be taken concerning the function and role of the JRC to ensure European scientific integration.

The wording of Article 8 of the Euratom Treaty implies that the Commission has competence to establish the JRC. The competences of the JRC are therefore not established under Article 8, but derive from the secondary legislation establishing the Euratom research and training programme. Regulation (Euratom) No 2018/1563 has established that the Euratom research and training programme would, in addition to indirect actions, also consist of direct actions in the form of research and innovation activities undertaken by the JRC.[303] The regulation also specified that in the context of the Euratom research and training programme, the JRC had the following functions:

- improving nuclear safety, including: nuclear reactor and fuel safety; waste management including final geological disposal as well as partitioning and transmutation; decommissioning; and emergency preparedness;
- improving nuclear security, including: nuclear safeguards, non-proliferation, combating illicit trafficking and nuclear forensics;
- increasing excellence in the nuclear science base for standardisation;
- fostering knowledge management, education and training; and
- supporting the policy of the Union on nuclear safety and security.[304]

298. Council Resolution of 29 April 1992 concerning the activities to be undertaken by the Joint Research Centre, OJ C 118, 9.5.1992, pp. 8–10, CELEX 31992Y0509(01).
299. Council conclusions of 26 April 1994 on the role of the Joint Research Centre (JRC), 94/C 126/01, OJ C 126, 7.5.1994, pp. 1–4, CELEX 31994Y0507(01).
300. Paragraph 3 of the Council Resolution of 29 April 1992 and paragraph 13 of the Council conclusions of 26 April 1994.
301. Paragraphs 6 and 8 of the Council Resolution of 29 April 1992 concerning the activities to be undertaken by the Joint Research Centre.
302. Paragraph 6 of the Council conclusions of 26 April 1994 on the role of the Joint Research Centre (JRC).
303. Article 6(1) of Council Regulation (Euratom) No 2018/1563.
304. Annex I of Council Regulation (Euratom) No 2018/1563.

Furthermore, the nuclear activities of the JRC under the Euratom research and training programme must aim to support the implementation of Directives 2009/71/Euratom[305] and 2011/70/Euratom,[306] as well as Council conclusions giving priority to the highest standards for nuclear safety in the EU and internationally. The JRC must, in particular, contribute to the nuclear safety research needed to ensure the safe, secure and peaceful use of nuclear energy and non-fission applications. The Centre should provide a scientific basis for the relevant EU policies and, where necessary, react within the limits of its mission and competences to nuclear events, incidents and accidents. To that end, the JRC carries out research and assessments, provides references and standards and delivers dedicated training and education.[307] A JRC strategy was adopted in order to support and improve the visibility of the JRC's nuclear and technical expertise[308] and a new unit dealing with knowledge relating to nuclear safety, security and safeguards was established under the Directorate for Nuclear Safety and Security. Its mission is to manage and disseminate knowledge generated by the scientific units of the Nuclear Safety and Security Directorate by mapping, collating, analysing, quality checking and communicating, in a systematic and digestible way, relevant scientific data, methods and tools. It also monitors the knowledge available worldwide and facilitates open access to JRC nuclear facilities including training and education.[309] To ensure that direct actions are in line with and complement the research and training needs of Member States, the JRC continuously interacts with the main research and scientific institutions in the Member States.[310] The JRC's nuclear research activities in respect of improving nuclear safety, security and safeguards in Europe and globally are designed to complement the activities developed either by Member States or under indirect actions of the Euratom Community and provide an independent scientific basis for EU policies.[311] The JRC also ensures that the Commission can fulfil its obligations and commitments in the fields of nuclear safety, radioactive waste management, radiation protection and nuclear security. The JRC has provided scientific and technical support to the Commission in the implementation of the directives on nuclear safety,[312] radioactive waste management,[313] and basic safety standards.[314] The fulfilment of this task is also exemplified in the JRC's provision of

305. Council Directive 2009/71/Euratom.
306. Council Directive 2011/70/Euratom.
307. Annex I of Council Regulation (Euratom) No 2018/1563.
308. The European Commission's science and knowledge service: JRC Strategy 2030, adopted in the spring of 2016.
309. Report from the Commission to the European Parliament, the Council and the European Economic and Social Committee, Interim evaluation of the Euratom Research and Training Programme 2014–2018, COM (2017) 697 final, pp. 12–13.
310. Report from the Commission to the European Parliament, the Council and the European Economic and Social Committee, Interim evaluation of the Euratom Research and Training Programme 2014–2018, COM (2017) 697 final, p. 3.
311. Report from the Commission to the European Parliament, the Council and the European Economic and Social Committee, Interim evaluation of the Euratom Research and Training Programme 2014–2018, COM (2017) 697 final, p. 4.
312. Council Directive 2009/71/Euratom.
313. Council Directive 2011/70/Euratom.
314. Council Directive 2013/59/Euratom of 5 December 2013 laying down basic safety standards for protection against the dangers arising from exposure to ionising radiation, and repealing

scientific and technical support for EU outreach activities through the implementation of the Instrument for Nuclear Safety Cooperation[315] and the Instrument Contributing to Stability and Peace.[316] Regarding nuclear safeguards, the JRC is a member of the European Safeguards Research and Development Association (ESARDA). The JRC also provides support to the Commission for the implementation of the Euratom nuclear safeguards system in Europe. It helps to improve nuclear security in Europe by supporting EU Member States with nuclear detection technologies and nuclear forensics.[317]

As noted at the beginning of the Chapter 1 Section 02.B on the analysis of the exercise of competences under Article 8 of the Euratom Treaty, the JRC now has a broad policy mission, meaning that its research activities are not limited to the nuclear field. Under Regulation (EU) 1291/2013, which specifies the non-nuclear direct actions to be carried out by the JRC, the JRC's competence areas are also extended to energy, transport, environment and climate change, agriculture and food security, health and consumer protection, information and communication technologies, reference materials and safety and security.[318] The JRC's activities in these areas are conducted taking into account relevant initiatives at the level of regions, Members States or the Union, within the perspective of shaping the European Research Area.[319] Consequently, the Commission's competence to establish the JRC under the Euratom Treaty has been exercised broadly in secondary legislation, establishing the JRC's functions both in the nuclear research field and in other research areas that do not fall under the scope of the Euratom Treaty.

In conclusion, the exercise of the Euratom Community's competences in relation to research covers both fission and fusion research. The exercise of competences under Chapter 1 of the Euratom Treaty establishes a link to the EU's research activities both by referring to Horizon 2020 and by defining the JRC's functions broader than the scope of the Euratom Treaty.

1.03 THE CJEU'S INTERPRETATION OF THE COMPETENCES

This section assesses the CJEU's case-law concerning the Euratom Community's competences in relation to research and considers whether the CJEU has interpreted these competences by reference to the objectives of the Euratom Treaty.

Directives 89/618/Euratom, 90/641/Euratom, 96/29/Euratom, 97/43/Euratom and 2003/122/Euratom, OJ L 13, 17.1.2014, pp. 1-73.

315. For the Instrument for Nuclear Safety Cooperation, *see also* Chapter III Section D of this study.
316. Report from the Commission to the European Parliament, the Council and the European Economic and Social Committee, Interim evaluation of the Euratom Research and Training Programme 2014-2018, COM (2017) 697 final, p. 15.
317. Report from the Commission to the European Parliament, the Council and the European Economic and Social Committee, Interim evaluation of the Euratom Research and Training Programme 2014-2018, COM (2017) 697 final, pp. 3-4.
318. *See* Annex I, Part VI of Regulation (EU) 1291/2013.
319. Annex I, Part IV of Regulation (EU) 1291/2013.

There is limited case-law on the competences at hand and the cases that have been heard have focused on horizontal competences as opposed to substantive law under the Euratom Treaty. The CJEU has interpreted the delimitation of competencies between the Council and the Commission in relation to research in the fisheries sector by finding a parallel between Article 145 of the Treaty, as amended by the Single European Act, and Article 7 of the Euratom Treaty.[320] The CJEU concluded that the power to carry out the programmes under Article 7 of the Euratom Treaty – including the decision to conclude research contracts – is separate from the power to implement the budget that the Commission possesses in any event.[321] Consequently, the Court has interpreted the Commission's competences in relation to research in the fisheries sector by reference to Article 7 of the Euratom Treaty. The Court has also interpreted the length of the Euratom research and training programme by reference to Article 7 in light of the equality between the officials who are assigned to that programme.[322] On this point, the Court stated that the fact that the programme under Article 7 of the Euratom Treaty has a fixed duration of not more than five years causes a certain degree of insecurity for officials assigned to the Euratom Programme.[323] The Court stated that in order to encourage officials to take part in these programmes, certain advantages could be provided to them, such as salary and promotion from one category to another without competition, and that those advantages would not be in breach of the principle of equality between officials.[324]

Systematic analysis of the case-law in relation to Euratom research and training leads one to conclude that that the Commission's competence to implement research and training programmes under Article 7 of the Euratom Treaty is separate from its competence to implement its budget, which indicates that the competences under the substantive law are separate from the Commission's budgetary competences. It may also be noted that the Court interprets the fact that the Euratom research and training programmes are limited to five years as having a negative impact on officials engaged in these programmes.

1.04 FEATURES OF THE COMPETENCES

As noted in Chapter II Section C of this study, this section assesses the following features with a view to ensuring a basis for a comparative analysis: the level of detail of the provisions of the Euratom Treaty; the exercise of the competences in comparison with the wording of the Euratom Treaty; the existence of case-law and the effect of the Court's interpretation of the relevant provisions of primary and secondary legislations to the competences of the Euratom Community.

320. Judgment of 24 October 1989, *Commission v Council*, C-16/88, ECLI:EU:C:1989:397.
321. Judgment of 24 October 1989, *Commission v Council*, C-16/88, ECLI:EU:C:1989:397, paragraph 20.
322. Judgment of 20 October 1977, *Jänsch v Commission*, C-5/76, ECLI:EU:C:1977:163.
323. Judgment of 20 October 1977, *Jänsch v Commission*, C-5/76, ECLI:EU:C:1977:163, paragraphs 15 and 16.
324. Judgment of 20 October 1977, *Jänsch v Commission*, C-5/76, ECLI:EU:C:1977:163, paragraphs 17–19.

The level of detail of the provisions of the Euratom Treaty that establish the Euratom Community's competences in relation to research is appropriate to the objective of promoting nuclear research. These provisions establish the division of competences between the institutions and the key substantive provisions in the field, for example the purpose and length of the research programme, the budgetary provisions to finance it, and requirements concerning implementation and reporting.

The exercise of the competences in relation to research has in some respects been wider than the strict wording of the Euratom Treaty would indicate: the Euratom Community's competences cover not only fission but also fusion research, and the exercise of competences under Article 7 of the Euratom Treaty establishes a link to the EU's research activities. This is done by referring to Horizon 2020 and by defining the JRC's functions both in research fields that fall under the scope of the Euratom Treaty and in other research areas that fall under the competences of the EU.

The CJEU has interpreted the provisions of the Euratom Treaty in relation to research on two occasions, referring to Article 7 in both cases. The case-law relevant to defining the Euratom Community's competences has established a separation between the Commission's implementation and budgetary competences. However, as the Court has interpreted the Commission's competences in relation to research in the fisheries sector by reference to the provisions of Article 7 of the Euratom Treaty, it may be concluded that the extant case-law has not had a significant effect on the provisions of the Euratom Treaty.

Chapter 2
Dissemination of Information

- *The main scope of the Euratom Community's competences in this field is dissemination of information and knowledge in the Community and protecting sensitive information from unauthorised access. The Euratom Community's competences in relation to dissemination of information are broad and the level of detail of the provisions of the Euratom Treaty is high. The Euratom Community not only has a competence to disseminate the information that the Euratom Community owns or has at its disposal, but also has wide powers to access information by using amicable agreements, compulsory notifications, arbitration or compulsory powers. Regarding division of horizontal competences, the Commission dominates the field, with the exception of the competences of the Arbitration Committee.*
- *The exercise of these competences in secondary legislation is relatively limited. Of the eighteen articles establishing the Community's competences in the Euratom Treaty, only Articles 18, 24 and 25 have been used as legal bases for secondary legislation. The Euratom Treaty contains articles that are worded as obligations of the Community, but which are not exercised by secondary legislation.*
- *The CJEU has mentioned Articles 24 to 28 of the Euratom Treaty, without going into the content of those provisions. Hence, the Court has not specifically defined or delimited the Euratom Community's competences in relation to the dissemination of information.*
- *The features of the Euratom Community's competences in relation to the dissemination of information are as follows: a high level of detail in the Euratom Treaty; some obligations that are not given further definition in secondary legal acts, and in those cases, the exercise of competences may be narrower than the wording of the Euratom Treaty; the CJEU has not analysed the content of the relevant competences of the Euratom Community concerning the dissemination of information.*

2.01 THE SCOPE AND CONTENT OF THE COMPETENCES

This section assesses the scope and content of the Euratom Community's competences in relation to the dissemination of information under the Euratom Treaty.

To prevent national restrictive practices from impeding the free flow of nuclear information, there was strong emphasis from the outset on the idea that integration must ensure the free exchange of atomic knowledge throughout the Euratom Community.[325] Consequently, the Euratom Treaty obliges the Euratom Community to ensure the dissemination of information[326] in order to satisfy the clear need for the free flow of technical information.[327] The Euratom Community's competences in this area are established in eighteen articles of the Euratom Treaty.[328] These provide a detailed level of regulation and, in some cases, establish procedures and time frames,[329] which are usually attributes of secondary legislation as opposed to those of a primary legal act.

The Euratom Community promoted the conduct of research both by the Community and in the Member States. This inevitably would have resulted in production and significant increase of nuclear knowledge, including information that should be shared in the Community to promote continuous development and research, by way of dissemination, but also information that could be sensitive in terms of the defence interest of one or several Member States. Therefore, at the point at which the Euratom Community was established, the correct handling of that information (dissemination and security) may have been one of its main priorities. Consequently, the level of detail of the Euratom Treaty's provisions may have been a way of ensuring appropriate handling of that information from the outset, with no immediate need to enact secondary legislation.

Chapter 2 of the Euratom Treaty contains provisions on dissemination of information regarding the Euratom Community's competences as well as provisions on the rights and obligations of the Euratom Member States, persons and undertakings in the Member States, Joint Undertakings, licence applicants, licensees, licence owners, etc. Given the ambit of this study, analysis in this area focuses exclusively on identifying the scope and content of the Euratom Community's competences in this field.

The provisions contained in Chapter 2 have been described as ambitious,[330] extensive[331] and complex.[332] The complexity of these provisions also proves that

325. J. G. Polach, *Euratom: Its Background, Issues and Economic Implications*, Dobbs Ferry, NY: Oceana Publications Inc., 1964, pp. 74–75.
326. Article 2(a) of the Euratom Treaty.
327. A. Södersten, *Euratom at the Crossroads*, Cheltenham, Northampton: Edward Elgar Publishing Limited, 2018, p. 107; L. Guzzetti, *A Brief History of European Union Research Policy*, Brussels: OOPEC 1995, p. 113.
328. Articles 12–29 of the Euratom Treaty.
329. For example, Articles 16, 20 and 21 of the Euratom Treaty.
330. M. Gaudet, *Euratom*, London: Pergamon Press, 1959, p. 164.
331. P. Mathijsen, 'Problems Connected with the Creation of Euratom', (1961) 26/3 *Law and Contemporary Problems*, p. 441.
332. A. Södersten, *Euratom at the Crossroads*, Cheltenham, Northampton: Edward Elgar Publishing Limited, 2018, p.107; L. Guzzetti, *A Brief History of European Union Research Policy*, Brussels: OOPEC 1995, p. 113.

dissemination of information was considered by the drafters of the Treaty as essential to the public interest.[333] The structure of Chapter 2 of the Euratom Treaty leads one to the conclusion that the applicable rules on the dissemination of information depend on whether such information is the property of or is at the disposal of the Euratom Community.

The Euratom Treaty confers on the Commission the competence to grant non-exclusive licences under patents, provisionally protected patent rights, utility models or patent applications, owned by the Community and sublicences under patents, provisionally protected patent rights, utility models or patent applications, where the Community holds contractual licences conferring power to grant sublicences.[334] The Commission also has a competence to communicate other information acquired by the Euratom Community from its own research programme or communicated to it with authority to make free use of it, to Member States, persons and undertakings.[335] In other words, if the information is at the disposal of the Euratom Community, the main rule is that information and knowledge shall be accessible to anybody in the Community, provided that the applicant is in a position to exploit such information effectively.[336] If the Euratom Community, as a result of its research, acquires information, disclosure of which is liable to harm the defence interest of one or more Member States, that information will be subject to a security system established by the Euratom Community.[337] The Council has a competence and an obligation to adopt security regulations, laying down various security gradings to be applied and the security measures that are appropriate to each grading.[338] The Commission provisionally applies the appropriate security grading to the information if one is needed. The Member States concerned may then decide whether to keep the same grading, change it or declassify the information, but the Council can, acting unanimously, change the grading or declassify information at any time.[339]

The Euratom Treaty confers broad competences on the Euratom Community to acquire information or knowledge that is not owned by or at the disposal of the Euratom Community. The array of competences available to the Euratom Community to secure information that will be of use in achieving its objectives[340] ranges from amicable agreements to compulsory powers. The Commission has a competence to establish a confidential procedure by which the provisional and final results of research can be exchanged between the Euratom Community and Member States, persons and undertakings.[341] The Commission has a competence to require a Member State to

333. P. Mathijsen, 'Problems Connected with the Creation of Euratom', (1961) 26/3 *Law and Contemporary Problems*, p. 442.
334. Article 12 of the Euratom Treaty.
335. Article 13 of the Euratom Treaty.
336. J. G. Polach, *Euratom: Its Background, Issues and Economic Implications*, Dobbs Ferry, NY: Oceana Publications Inc., 1964, pp. 75–76; M. Gaudet, *Euratom*, London: Pergamon Press, 1959, p. 165.
337. Article 24 of the Euratom Treaty.
338. Article 24(1) of the Euratom Treaty.
339. Article 24(2) of the Euratom Treaty.
340. Article 14 of the Euratom Treaty.
341. Article 15 of the Euratom Treaty.

communicate the content of an application for a patent or a utility model relating to a specifically nuclear subject after it has been filed in that Member State.[342] Communication of the contents of patents or patent applications under these rules does not entitle the Euratom Community to make use of them, but is for the purpose of documentation.[343] To this end, the Commission is entitled to be notified of all information for which some form of protection is applied for in a Member State, whether it relates to a nuclear matter or to a matter which, without being nuclear, is directly linked to the development of nuclear energy within the Community.[344] The security grading system also applies to the information communicated to the Commission, meaning that the Member State has to notify the Commission as to whether any security grading should be applied to the information communicated to the Commission under the provisions on compulsory communication. In some cases, such information may be disseminated to other Member States. Consequently, the Commission and the Member States, which have access to that information, must apply the security grading required by the Member State from which the information originated.[345] This Euratom Community competence to require communication from the Member States is accompanied by certain responsibilities. In return for communication as to the availability of classified patents, the Community assumes liability for any damage arising out of improper use or communication to unauthorised third persons.[346] If information communicated to the Commission is improperly used or becomes accessible to unauthorised persons, the Community is responsible for making good the damage suffered by the party concerned.[347] The Euratom Community then has a right to take action against the person responsible for the damage.[348] In addition to this, provisions outside Chapter 2 of the Euratom Treaty establish the responsibility of the members of the institutions, officials and servants of the Euratom Community or any other person, who by reason of their duties acquire or obtain any facts, information, knowledge, documents or objects which are subject to a security system, to keep the information secret from any unauthorised person and from the general public even after their duties have ceased.[349]

Where granting a certain licence is necessary for the continuance of the Euratom Community's own research or is indispensable to the operation of Community's installations, the Euratom Community has a right to be granted a non-exclusive licence in respect of patents, provisionally protected patent rights or utility models relating to inventions directly connected with nuclear research. The granting of a non-exclusive licence to the Euratom Community is done either by arbitration procedure or under the

342. Article 16(1) and (2) of the Euratom Treaty.
343. P. H. Hay, 'Patent Aspects of Domestic Law, Euratom, and the International Atomic Energy Agency', (1958) 56/5 *Michigan Law Review*, p. 778.
344. M. Gaudet, *Euratom*, London: Pergamon Press, 1959, p. 165.
345. Article 25(1) of the Euratom Treaty.
346. P. H. Hay, 'Patent Aspects of Domestic Law, EURATOM, and the International Atomic Energy Agency', (1958) 56/5 *Michigan Law Review*, p. 782.
347. Article 28(1) of the Euratom Treaty.
348. Article 28(2) of the Euratom Treaty.
349. Article 194 of the Euratom Treaty.

Community's compulsory powers.[350] In order for the arbitration procedure to take place, the Euratom Community has a competence and an obligation to establish an Arbitration Committee. The Council appoints the members of the Arbitration Committee and lays down the rules of procedure of this committee, acting on a proposal from the CJEU.[351] Consequently, the Euratom Treaty confers on the CJEU the specific competence to propose the rules of procedure and members of the Arbitration Committee. Therefore, the Commission does not have right of legislative initiative when it comes to the exercise of competences concerning the Arbitration Committee, as that right belongs to the CJEU. That is the only exception to the Commission's competence to initiate legislation in relation to the Euratom Treaty. The final decision of the Arbitration Committee has the force of res judicata between the parties concerned.[352] The Arbitration Committee has a competence to determine whether the conditions prescribed in Article 17 of the Euratom Treaty have been met and to lay down the terms of the licence and the appropriate remuneration. In this regard, it is, in effect, interpreting the law for the parties.[353] If the arbitration procedure is not chosen by the licence proprietor, the Commission has the right to call upon the Member State concerned or its appropriate authorities to grant the licence or cause it to be granted, i.e., to invoke the compulsory powers of the Euratom Community. If the Member State refuses to comply with this request, or if, within four months of the date of the request the Commission does not receive any information with regard to the granting of the licence, the Commission has a right to bring the matter before the CJEU within two months.[354]

The Commission also has the competence - where such agreements or contracts require the signature of a State acting in its sovereign capacity - to conclude agreements or contracts for the exchange of scientific or industrial information in the nuclear field, between any Member State, person or undertaking and any third state, international organisation or national organisation of a third state. In other words, no agreement that entails the participation of a fully sovereign third state can be concluded without the Commission's authorisation or participation if its purpose is to exchange scientific or industrial information on nuclear matters.[355] The Commission may, however, delegate the authorisation to a Member State, person or undertaking to conclude the agreement.[356] These provisions are similar to those set out in Chapter 10 of the Euratom Treaty on external relations. The main difference between them lies in the role of the Council. The provisions on external relations laid down in the Euratom Treaty[357] stipulate that agreements or contracts must be negotiated by the Commission in accordance with the directives of the Council and the agreements must be concluded

350. Article 17(1) of the Euratom Treaty.
351. Article 18(1) of the Euratom Treaty.
352. Article 18(3) of the Euratom Treaty.
353. E. Lauterpacht, 'Aspects of the Administration of International Justice', (1991) 9 *Hersch Lauterpacht Memorial Lecture Series*, p. 144.
354. Article 21(1) and (3) of the Euratom Treaty.
355. M. Gaudet, *Euratom*, London: Pergamon Press, 1959, p. 165.
356. Article 29 of the Euratom Treaty.
357. Article 101 of the Euratom Treaty.

by the Commission with the approval of the Council. Under the provisions on agreements on dissemination of information there is, however, no need for the Council's approval. Consequently, the Commission's powers in relation to external relation under Chapter 2 of the Euratom Treaty are broader than those established in Chapter 10 of the Euratom Treaty.

Analysis of division of competences between the institutions indicates that the Commission dominates the field with its broad executive competences in, *inter alia*, granting licences, communicating information, disseminating knowledge, establishing amicable agreements, requesting compulsory communication of information, applying security gradings, etc. The Council has two main competences. Acting on a proposal from the CJEU it can appoint members of the Arbitration Committee; and acting on a proposal from the Commission it can adopt security regulations for the handling of information.

In conclusion, analysis of the scope and content of the Euratom Community's competences concerning the dissemination of information under the Euratom Treaty shows that the scope of the Community's competences in this field extends not only to the dissemination of information that it owns or has at its disposal, but also to the acquisition of such information by means of amicable agreements, compulsory notifications, arbitration or compulsory powers. The content of the Euratom Community's competences in this regard are laid down in the Euratom Treaty to a level of detail that is more characteristic of a secondary than a primary legal act.

2.02 EXERCISE OF THE COMPETENCES

This section assesses the Euratom Community's competences in relation to the dissemination of information and the instruments through which these competences have been exercised.

Systematic analysis of all secondary legal acts based on Articles 12 to 29 of the Euratom Treaty leads one to conclude that Article 18 and Articles 24 to 25 have been used as legal bases for secondary legislation. Therefore, this part of the study focuses on the exercise of the competences established in these articles. Due to the ambit of this study, the scope of this analysis is limited to the secondary legislation in force.

Two points should be noted at the outset. First, in a 1963 communication[358] the Commission specified that the Euratom Community's obligation under Article 13 of the Euratom Treaty to disseminate information and knowledge to persons and undertakings in the Community is to be carried out by distributing confidential documents through national correspondents and by organising technical meetings, conferences, symposia, exchanges of personnel, contacts between researchers and industrialists. Second, the wording of Article 15 of the Euratom Treaty indicates that the Commission has a responsibility to establish a procedure for the exchange of provisional or final results of research conducted by Member States, persons and undertakings, insofar as

358. Commission communication of information to persons and undertakings in the Community 63/56/Euratom, OJ 154, 26.10.1963, p. 2569.

these results have not been acquired by the Community. Analysis of current secondary legislation based on Chapter 2 of the Euratom Treaty leads one to conclude that this procedure for exchange of research and knowledge in the Euratom Community has not been formally established by the Commission as no secondary legislation based on Article 15 of the Euratom Treaty has been enacted.

Article 18 of the Euratom Treaty establishes the Euratom Community's competences to establish an Arbitration Committee. Regulation 7/63/Euratom[359] adopted by the Council, acting on a proposal from the CJEU, exercises this competence by laying down the rules of procedure of the Arbitration Committee and specifying the way in which the Arbitration Committee should be organised and operate, and the procedure to be followed in the Committee.[360] Regulation 7/63/Euratom establishes that the Arbitration Committee is to consist of nationals of Member States who have the legal or technical training or experience necessary for the proper functioning of the Committee in various fields. It also requires the Council to ensure a proper balance in the Arbitration Committee between members that have legal training or experience and members that have technical training or experience. The Arbitration Committee is to consist of a Chairman, two Vice-Chairmen and twelve other members who are nationals of the Member States of the Euratom Community, and who are appointed for six years by the Council.[361] Regulation 7/63/Euratom also contains provisions on the independence and immunity of members of the Arbitration Committee as well as the consequences if the members do not meet the obligations arising from their office.[362] The Commission's competences with respect to the exercise of competences under Article 18 of the Euratom Treaty are limited. For example, even the remuneration to be paid to members of the Arbitration Committee, which is an executive function, is decided by the Council, on a proposal from the Court.[363] In accordance with the Euratom Treaty and with general principles common to the laws of the Member States, the arbitration board (i.e., the configuration in which the Committee sits) is to make awards on an *ex aequo et bono* basis.[364] The Chairman of the Committee may propose suggestions for amending or supplementing the rules of procedure contained in Regulation 7/63/Euratom to the Court,[365] which in its turn proposes the amendments to the Council. Systematic analysis of secondary legislation in this field leads one to conclude that up to now no amendments to Regulation 7/63/Euratom have been made. Finally, it should be mentioned that Articles 20 and 22 of the Euratom Treaty are indirectly exercised by Regulation 7/63/Euratom, as they are referred to in Article 10(1) of Regulation 7/63/Euratom, implying that the provisions governing arbitration

359. Regulation No 7/63/Euratom of the Council of 3 December 1963 on rules of procedure of the Arbitration Committee provided for in Article 18 of the Treaty establishing the European Atomic Energy Community, OJ 180, 10.12.1963, pp. 2849–2853.
360. *See* the recitals of Regulation 7/63/Euratom.
361. Article 1(1) of Regulation 7/63/Euratom.
362. Articles 2 to 5 of Regulation 7/63/Euratom.
363. Article 7 of Regulation 7/63/Euratom.
364. Article 23 of Regulation 7/63/Euratom.
365. Article 28 of Regulation 7/63/Euratom.

procedures laid down in the Euratom Treaty are linked to the functioning of the Arbitration Committee under Regulation 7/63/Euratom.

As identified under the scope and content of the Euratom Community's competences concerning the dissemination of information in Chapter 2 Section 01 of this study, Articles 24 and 25 of the Euratom Treaty indicate that the Euratom Community has the competence to stipulate provisions governing the security of information available to the Euratom Community, disclosure of which is liable to harm the defence interests of one or more Member States. Competences established in Articles 24 and 25 of the Euratom Treaty are exercised in Regulation (Euratom) No 3 implementing Article 24 of the Treaty establishing the European Atomic Energy Community,[366] which was adopted in 1958 and is based on Articles 24 and 25 of the Euratom Treaty.

The main focus of Regulation (Euratom) No 3 is to establish security gradings and measures for each of the security gradings to be applied to information acquired by the Community or communicated by Member States and covered by Articles 24 and 25 of the Euratom Treaty, namely Euratom Classified Information, and to specify how the Commission should supervise the exercise of these measures.[367] The unclear part of the definition of the scope of Regulation (Euratom) No 3 lies in its Article 1, which states that when a Member State communicates information covered by Article 25 of the Euratom Treaty the regulation shall apply only if the use to which the information is put falls within the scope of the Euratom Treaty. Articles 16 and 25 of the Treaty provide that Member States must communicate information on a potential patent or a utility model relating to a specifically nuclear subject and that when they do this, they must also draw attention to the need to apply a given security grading for defence reasons while also stating the probable duration of such grading. Article 25 of the Euratom Treaty also states that further communications and, where appropriate, the use of that information should correspond to the security grading required by the Member State of origin. The meaning of the reference in Article 1 of the Regulation (Euratom) No 3 to the scope of the Euratom Treaty is hence debatable, as it is unclear how the use of the information according to the scope of the Euratom Treaty could affect the security grading proposed by the Member State of origin.

To assist the Commission, the Council established the Security Bureau, which is under the authority and responsibility of the Commission.[368] The Council defines the functions of the Security Bureau in Regulation (Euratom) No 3, but delegates to the Commission to set it. The Security Bureau has a competence to coordinate and ensure the general application of security measures; supervise the application of those measures in the Euratom Community; require the national authorities of a Member State to verify the security measures required by Regulation (Euratom) No 3 and even carry out such verification itself in collaboration with those national authorities; and propose any amendments it considers necessary for the application of Regulation (Euratom) No 3. Keeping in mind that this institution is not even mentioned in the

366. Regulation (Euratom) No 3 implementing Article 24 of the Treaty establishing the European Atomic Energy Community, OJ 17, 6.10.1958, pp. 406–416.
367. Recital and Article (1)(1) of Regulation (Euratom) No 3.
368. Article 6 of Regulation (Euratom) No 3.

Euratom Treaty, the competences of the Security Bureau are considerably wide.[369] The Euratom Community's competence to establish security grading finds expression in Regulation (Euratom) No 3, which requires Euratom Classified Information to be classified under one of four security gradings: Eura-Top Secret, Eura-Secret, Eura-Confidential, Eura-Restricted.[370] These security gradings are applied only to the extent strictly necessary[371] and security gradings of documents relating to Euratom Classified Information is determined solely on the basis of the content.[372] Regulation (Euratom) No 3 also specifies that the Commission has an obligation to classify information first provisionally, when it considers that the information is liable to harm the defence of interest of the Member States, and then permanently in accordance with the security grading requested by the Member State.[373] Article 11 of Regulation (Euratom) No 3, which governs provisional classification, contains similar wording to Article 24(2) of the Euratom Treaty, without actually referring to it. However, the wording contained in Article 11 as to definite classification is not mirroring the provisions in the Euratom Treaty, with the implication that this results from the Council's exercise of its competence to establish the security system.

Regulation (Euratom) No 3 exercises the competence to establish security system in the Euratom Community by establishing specific procedures governing who is entitled to access Euratom Classified Information. Such access is granted only to persons who are duly authorised following a screening procedure, and strictly on a need-to-know basis, on account of their duties.[374] Regulation (Euratom) No 3, which provides for the Euratom Community's security system, also sets out detailed provisions on the physical protection of Euratom Classified Information[375] and measures to be taken in the event of infringement of the security regulations.[376]

Consequently, the Euratom Community had a clear priority to put in place, as soon as possible after the adoption of the Euratom Treaty, a detailed security system concerning information disclosure which is liable to harm the defence interests of the Member States. The instrument that gave effect to the competences established in Articles 24 and 25 of the Euratom Treaty was adopted one year after the adoption of the Euratom Treaty and has not been amended since then. This implies that some of the provisions of the Euratom Treaty were repeated in Regulation (Euratom) No 3 without reference to the primary legal act, which diminishes their legal weight. In giving effect to the Euratom Community's competences concerning the dissemination of information, the regulation contains a high level of detail and, while the Commission had a limited role in exercising competences concerning arbitration issues in respect of the

369. There is no publicly accessible information confirming that the Security Bureau under Regulation No 3 was ever established by the Commission.
370. Article 10 of Regulation (Euratom) No 3.
371. Article 9 of Regulation (Euratom) No 3.
372. Article 12 of Regulation (Euratom) No 3.
373. Article 11 of Regulation (Euratom) No 3.
374. Articles 14 to 16 of Regulation (Euratom) No 3.
375. Articles 19 to 31 of Regulation (Euratom) No 3.
376. Article 32 and 33 of Regulation (Euratom) No 3.

dissemination of information, the Commission dominates the exercise of competences regarding the Euratom Community's security system.

In conclusion, keeping in mind that the scope and content of the Euratom Community's competences concerning the dissemination of information is established in eighteen articles of the Euratom Treaty, the exercise of this competence by secondary legislation is relatively limited. Certain articles of the relevant chapter[377] are worded as obligations (i.e., using 'shall'), but are not given effect in any secondary legislation. This may mean either that these provisions have direct effect without the need to adopt secondary legislation or that the Commission is not exercising some of its obligations under the Euratom Treaty. In the latter case, the exercise of competences of the Euratom Community may be considered to be narrower, in practice, than the wording of Chapter 2 of the Euratom Treaty indicates.

2.03 THE CJEU'S INTERPRETATION OF THE COMPETENCES

This section assesses whether and how the case-law defines or elaborates on the Euratom Community's competence in relation to the dissemination of information.

In one case the Court referred to arguments raised by the Commission and the UK respectively and analysed whether the existence of Articles 24 to 28 of the Euratom Treaty imply that the Treaty is applicable to military activities.[378] The Commission's position in that case was that Articles 24 to 28 of the Euratom Treaty show that Member States' defence interests were taken into consideration in the establishment of the Euratom Community and that these interests were the subject of appropriate provisions of the Euratom Treaty.[379] The CJEU supported the UK's response to that argument, stating that the existence of Articles 24 to 28 of the Euratom Treaty does not necessarily lead to the conclusion that its rules are applicable to the military uses of nuclear energy. The reason for this, the Court went on to say, was the existence of these provisions may also be explained by the fact that the application of certain rules laid down in the Euratom Treaty, even if they relate only to civil activities, is nevertheless liable to have an impact on activities and interests concerning Member States' national defence.[380] Consequently, the CJEU used the existence of Articles 24 to 28 of the Euratom Treaty, which refer to Member States' defence interests, as an argument by which to establish that the Euratom Treaty is not applicable to military activities. The Court did not, however, analyse the content of those provisions and did not, therefore, interpret the Euratom Community's competences as to the dissemination of information.

377. For example, Articles 14 and 15 of the Euratom Treaty.
378. Judgment of 12 April 2005, *Commission v United Kingdom*, C-61/03, ECLI:EU:C:2005:210. *See also* Chapter III Section C on the Euratom Community's competences in relation to the military application of nuclear energy.
379. Judgment of 12 April 2005, *Commission v United Kingdom*, C-61/03, ECLI:EU:C:2005:210, paragraph 31.
380. Judgment of 12 April 2005, *Commission v United Kingdom*, C-61/03, ECLI:EU:C:2005:210, paragraph 32.

In conclusion, the CJEU has only analysed Chapter 2 of the Euratom Treaty in one case in which it mentioned Articles 24 to 28 of the Euratom Treaty without discussing their content. Therefore, the Court has not had the opportunity to specifically define the Euratom Community's competences in relation to the dissemination of information.

2.04 FEATURES OF THE COMPETENCES

As noted in Chapter II Section C of this study, to ensure a basis for a comparative analysis the following features are identified in this section: the level of detail of the provisions of the Euratom Treaty; the exercise of the competences in comparison with the wording of the Euratom Treaty; the existence of case-law and the effect of the Court's interpretation of the relevant provisions of primary and secondary legislation to the competences of the Euratom Community.

The level of detail of the provisions in Chapter 2 of the Euratom Treaty that establish the Euratom Community's competences in relation to the dissemination of information is in some cases very high. In particular, the nature of the wording of the provisions contained in this Chapter 2 is more suited to secondary legislation.

The competences laid down in the Euratom Treaty have been exercised to a relatively limited extent in terms of secondary legal acts concerning the dissemination of information and certain articles that specify Euratom Community obligations have not been exercised in secondary legislation. The reason for this may be that these articles have direct effect – i.e., they are applicable without the need for secondary legislation – or that the Commission is not exercising some of its obligations under the Euratom Treaty. In the latter situation, the exercise of the Euratom Community's competences may be considered narrower in scope than the wording of the Euratom Treaty indicates.

The CJEU made one reference to the existence of Articles 24 to 28 of the Euratom Treaty when determining the Euratom Treaty's application to military activities. However, it has not interpreted the provisions of Chapter 2 of the Euratom Treaty concerning the dissemination of information in its case-law and, therefore, has had no influence on the relevant competences of the Euratom Community in this field.

CHAPTER 3
Health and Safety

- *The main scope of the Euratom Community's competences in relation to health and safety is the establishment and updating of basic safety standards in accordance with the scientific knowledge available and ensuring adherence to those standards, inter alia, within the legislative and regulatory system.*
- *The Euratom Community's competences in respect of health and safety are exercised to the broadest extent under Articles 31, 32 and 37 of the Euratom Treaty. Exercise of the Euratom Community's competences under Articles 31 and 32 covers four different areas of regulation: radiation protection; nuclear safety; safe radioactive waste management; and emergency preparedness and response. Exercise of the Euratom Community's competences under Article 37 has resulted in the Commission issuing 180 opinions, and the adoption of practices that show the Commission's broad competences concerning the content of notifications to be submitted by Member States.*
- *The CJEU has interpreted the provisions of the Euratom Treaty in respect of health and safety in nine cases. This has produced the following: the establishment of the Euratom Community's broad competences under the objectives of Chapter 3 of the Euratom Treaty; flexibility to regulate the level of harmonisation in its secondary legislation; confirmation of the Euratom Community's competences in respect of emergency preparedness and response; and establishment of the Euratom Community's competences in respect of nuclear safety.*
- *The features of the Euratom Community's competences in respect of health and safety are as follows: the Euratom Treaty contains a low level of detail, which nonetheless suffices to fulfil the Treaty's objective of protecting workers and the general public from the harmful effects of ionising radiation; these competences are exercised in a broader manner than the wording of the Euratom Treaty would indicate, and they cover four different fields of regulation, some of which are not mentioned in the Euratom Treaty; the CJEU has had an important role in terms of expanding and defining the Euratom Community's broad competences in respect of health and safety.*

3.01 THE SCOPE AND CONTENT OF THE COMPETENCES

This section assesses the scope and content of the Euratom Community's competences in the field of health and safety under the Euratom Treaty.

Under Article 2 of the Euratom Treaty the Euratom Community has a general obligation to establish uniform safety standards for the protection of the health of workers and of the general public, and to ensure that they are applied.[381] The founding States were keen to create the conditions of safety necessary to eliminate hazards to the life and health of the public. They conferred extensive powers on the Euratom Community to protect the public and workers against the risks of ionising radiation.[382] The Euratom Community's competences in relation to health and safety under the Euratom Treaty are sometimes regarded as being one area in which its competences are predominant to those of the Member States, given that health and safety is one of the most prominent fields covered by the Euratom Treaty and constitutes a substantial part of the subject matter covered by it.[383]

The Euratom Community's competences in respect of health and safety are established in ten articles of Chapter 3 of the Euratom Treaty, the core objective of which is to lay down basic standards within the Community for the protection of the health of workers and the general public against dangers arising from ionising radiation.[384] Article 2 of the Euratom Treaty, however, clearly indicates that the Euratom Community's tasks in this area under the Euratom Treaty are not only to establish a level of protection from ionising radiation, but also to ensure that the relevant safety standards are applied in the Member States and to underline the need for uniformity of those basic standards. Some authors argue that the founders of the Euratom Treaty were aware of the potential hazards posed by nuclear energy and established requirements as to basic safety standards solely for this reason.[385] Others take the view that the original reasons for imposing harmonisation in relation to health and safety did not arise purely from concern for increasing the level of protection, but were also prompted by economic reasons motivated by internal market incentives. While health and safety measures are expensive to put in place, harmonising them

381. Article 2(b) of the Euratom Treaty.
382. European Commission, '50 Years of the Euratom Treaty', Memo/07/118, 26 March 2007 Brussels, p. 2.
383. I. Cenevska, *The European Atomic Energy Community in the European Union Context: The 'Outsider' Within*, Leiden: Brill Nijhoff, 2016, pp. 3-4 and 111; and I. Cenevska, 'Protection of the Health of Workers and the General Public under the Euratom Treaty and the EU Environmental Policy - The Ratio between Human Health Protection and Environmental Protection', (2012) 21 *European Energy and Environmental Law Review*, p. 180.
384. I. Cenevska, *The European Atomic Energy Community in the European Union Context: The 'Outsider' Within*, Leiden: Brill Nijhoff, 2016, p. 112.
385. A. Södersten, *Euratom at the Crossroads*, Cheltenham, Northampton: Edward Elgar Publishing Limited, 2018, p. 107; L. Guzzetti, *A Brief History of European Union Research Policy*, Brussels: OOPEC, 1995, p. 141.

across the Euratom Community may have been thought likely to equalise production costs between Member States thus increasing competition.[386]

The Euratom Treaty confers on the Euratom Community the competence to establish and update[387] basic safety standards. Basic safety standards are defined as maximum permissible doses to ensure safety; maximum permissible levels of exposure and levels of contamination with ionising radiation; and fundamental principles on health surveillance of workers.[388] Radiation protection is generally defined as protection of people from the harmful effects of exposure to ionising radiation, including the means of achieving this, and the means of preventing accidents and mitigating their consequences if they do occur.[389] Setting the fundamental principles of surveillance, maximum permissible doses, levels of exposure and levels of contamination are the means of achieving radiation protection. Consequently, the Euratom Treaty establishes the Euratom Community's competences in respect of radiation protection. The general principles of radiation protection are broadly applicable to all nuclear-related activities and to all facilities at which ionising radiation is produced, from dental X-ray equipment to power reactors. The competence to establish basic standards cover all situations which might lead to the general public and workers being exposed to ionising radiation. This competence does not relate solely to the field of nuclear power production but also to other applications concerning the ionisation of radiation in respect of industry and medicine.[390]

Radiation protection is perceived as a 'chapeau' of all nuclear legislation.[391] Two disciplines originally developed from nuclear science in the context of protection from nuclear hazards: radiation protection and nuclear safety.[392] The terminology implies that nuclear safety primarily entails the maintenance of control over sources, while radiation protection primarily entails the control of exposure to radiation and its effects.[393] The safe management of radioactive waste and spent nuclear fuel[394] is

386. J. G. Polach, *Euratom: Its Background, Issues and Economic Implications*, Dobbs Ferry, NY: Oceana Publications Inc., 1964, p. 39; A. Moravcsik, *The Choice for Europe: Social Purpose and State Power from Messina to Maastricht*, Ithaca, NY: Cornell University Press, 1998, p. 94.
387. Under Article 32 of the Euratom Treaty, Member States have a right to require revision of the basic safety standards established under Article 31 of the Euratom Treaty.
388. Articles 30 and 32 of the Euratom Treaty.
389. International Atomic Energy Agency, *IAEA Safety Glossary. Terminology Used in Nuclear Safety and Radiation Protection*, Vienna: IAEA, 2016, pp. 131–132.
390. Communication from the Commission to the Council and the European Parliament, '50 Years of the Euratom Treaty', Brussels, 20.3.2007, pp. 3–4.
391. C. Stoiber, A. Baer, N. Pelzer and W. Tonhauser, *Handbook of Nuclear Law*, Vienna: International Atomic Energy Agency, 2003, p. 47.
392. E. Molodstova, 'Nuclear Energy and Environmental Protection: Responses of International Law', (1994) 12/1 *Pace Environmental Law Review*, p. 190; N. L. Char and B. J. Csik, 'Nuclear Power Development: History and Outlook', (1987) 29/3 *IAEA Bulletin*, pp. 19–25.
393. International Atomic Energy Agency, *IAEA Safety Glossary. Terminology Used in Nuclear Safety and Radiation Protection*, Vienna: IAEA, 2016, p. 131.
394. For legal and regulatory purposes, radioactive waste is defined as waste that contains, or is contaminated with, radionuclides at activity concentrations greater than clearance levels as established by the regulatory body. Spent nuclear fuel is defined as nuclear fuel removed from a reactor following irradiation that is no longer usable in its present form because of depletion of fissile material, poison build-up or radiation damage, *see*: International Atomic Energy Agency, *IAEA Safety Glossary. Terminology Used in Nuclear Safety and Radiation Protection*,

another area that has developed over time in connection with radiation protection and nuclear safety.

The Euratom Treaty provides a horizontal division of competences between the Euratom Community's institutions by establishing a legislative procedure for the adoption of basic safety standards in the Community. These basic standards are established by the Council, on a proposal from the Commission and after consulting the EP. Before submitting a proposal to the Council, the Commission is obliged to obtain the opinion of the expert group appointed by the Scientific and Technical Committee[395] and the opinion of the Economic and Social Committee.[396]

Articles 33 to 38 of the Euratom Treaty establish the Commission's competences concerning the implementation of the basic safety standards referred to in Article 2(b). All of these articles have a similar structure: they require a communication of certain information to the Commission and establish the Commission's competence to act on that information in a certain manner, i.e., by issuing a recommendation,[397] an opinion,[398] or assent;[399] by obtaining access to facilities;[400] or by issuing a mandatory directive that ultimately allows it to bring the matter before the Court.[401] These provisions are analysed in detail below.

The Euratom Treaty requires Member States' legislative and regulatory systems[402] to comply with basic safety standards. Member States are obliged to communicate national implementation and compliance with the basic standards to the Commission before they are adopted, and the Commission has competence to issue recommendations on those notified provisions within three months.[403]

Article 34 of the Euratom Treaty stipulates that the Commission's opinion or assent is required when particularly dangerous experiments are conducted in the territory of a Member State. However, it is clear that in order for the Commission to be able to give its opinion on or assent to such experiments, it requires prior notice of the intention to carry them out. Consequently, Article 34 also specifies the Commission's right to be informed about any particularly dangerous experiments that are planned to take place in the territory of any Member State. The article also provides that the Commission's assent is required when the experiments are liable to affect the territories

---

Vienna: IAEA, 2016, pp.169 and 188. Scientifically and legally the term of radioactive waste is separated from the term spent nuclear fuel, due to the fact that spent fuel can be reprocessed to recover fissile material and close the nuclear fuel cycle.

395. This is known as the 'Article 31 Group of Experts' and comprises scientific experts, particularly public health experts, appointed by the Member States. It is consulted by the Commission under Article 37 of the Euratom Treaty. Article 134 of the Euratom Treaty lays down the provisions for the establishment of a Scientific and Technical Committee.
396. Article 31 of the Euratom Treaty.
397. Article 33 of the Euratom Treaty.
398. Articles 34 and 37 of the Euratom Treaty.
399. Article 34 of the Euratom Treaty.
400. Article 35 of the Euratom Treaty.
401. Article 38 of the Euratom Treaty.
402. Legislation, regulation and administrative actions, under Article 33 of the Euratom Treaty.
403. Under Article 33 of the Euratom Treaty, Member States are required to communicate to the Commission draft provisions implementing basic safety standards.

of other Member States, although the assent of those Member States is not required by the Euratom Treaty.

Article 37 of the Euratom Treaty is constructed in a similar manner to Article 33 and requires Member States to provide the Commission with general data relating to their plans for the disposal of radioactive waste in such a way as to make it possible to determine whether the implementation of that plan is liable to result in the radioactive contamination of the water, soil or airspace of another Member State. The objective of this provision is to avoid transboundary contamination, not contamination within a Member State.[404] The article also establishes the Commission's obligation to deliver its opinion within six months.

The Euratom Treaty contains a few references to the management of radioactive waste,[405] but the wording of Article 37, which mentions radioactive waste, is problematic for several reasons. First, it is not clear from the primary legal act whether disposal of radioactive waste under Article 37 covers plans for disposal of spent nuclear fuel. Second, the wording of the provisions does not make it clear as to whether the obligation to notify the Commission concerns only the disposal of radioactive waste or whether it also covers the storage and interim storage of radioactive waste. Third, the concept of general data is problematic. The wording of Article 37 implies that the Commission needs to receive sufficient data to be able to determine whether a disposal plan is liable to result in contamination, but whether it is enough to submit general data appears to be unclear. These issues are addressed in detail in the context of the analysis of the exercise of competences under the Euratom Community under Chapter 3 Section 02.B of this study.

To ensure compliance with basic standards, the Euratom Treaty requires Member States to establish facilities for continuous monitoring of radioactivity levels in air, water and soil.[406] The Commission has a competence to access those national facilities, to verify their operation and efficiency and to be informed about the levels of radioactivity to which the public is exposed, as measured in those facilities.[407] Furthermore, the Commission is obliged to propose recommendations as to radioactivity levels in air, water and soil.[408]

Despite the fact that the term 'environment' is not used in the Euratom Treaty, interpretation of the provisions on monitoring air, water and soil has led to legal discussion on whether the Euratom Community has any competences in respect of environmental protection. Some authors argue that measures based on the Euratom Treaty do not target the impact of nuclear energy on the environment in any significant way since they mainly consider nuclear energy's impact on human health and not on

404. A. Södersten, *Euratom at the Crossroads*, Cheltenham, Northampton: Edward Elgar Publishing Limited, 2018, p. 107; L. Guzzetti, *A Brief History of European Union Research Policy*, Brussels: OOPEC, 1995, p. 144.
405. P. D. Cameron, 'The Revival of Nuclear Power: An Analysis of the Legal Implications', (2007) 19/1 *Journal of Environmental Law*, p. 3.
406. Article 35 of the Euratom Treaty.
407. Article 36 of the Euratom Treaty.
408. Article 38(1) of the Euratom Treaty.

fauna, flora and other environmental assets,[409] and that the provisions of Chapter 3 of the Euratom Treaty focus on health protection.[410] It is also understood in international nuclear law circles that the term 'radiation protection' denotes the protection of people only.[411] Other authors have argued that the concepts of the protection of human health and of air, water and soil are inextricably linked because human health depends directly on the quality of their living environment, i.e., the surrounding air, water and soil.[412]

In the context of this study's objectives, the question of whether the Euratom Community possesses competences in respect of environmental protection may be addressed by establishing whether the articles under Chapter 3 of the Euratom Treaty – specifically those that require the monitoring of radioactivity in air, water and soil – might offer a legal basis for secondary legislation on environmental protection. The wording of Articles 35 and 36 of the Euratom Treaty implies that the facilities for continuous monitoring of air, water and soil are to be established not to protect these elements of the environment, but to monitor the level of radioactivity to which the public is exposed,[413] i.e., to protect public health and to maintain preparedness to act in the event of radioactive contamination that could affect the general public. The EP has also reasoned that protection of the environment is not covered by Article 31 of the Euratom Treaty. Air, water and soil are referred to in Articles 37 and 38 of the Euratom Treaty and those provisions do not offer a legal basis for the adoption of legislative measures, but only for the carrying out of data collection and the issuance of recommendations.[414] Therefore, the articles of the Euratom Treaty that establish requirements to monitor radioactivity in air, soil and water do not seem to constitute a legal basis for secondary legislation on environmental protection. However, analysis of the provisions in the primary legal act does not allow one to reach a final conclusion, as it is also necessary to analyse secondary legislation and the available case-law. These are discussed further in Chapter 3 Sections 02 and 03 of this study.

Since the Commission has the right to be kept informed about radiation levels to which the public is exposed, it can also determine when the levels are too high and when urgent cases arise. In this situation, the Commission may issue a directive requiring the Member State concerned to take all necessary measures to prevent infringement of basic safety standards and, if the Member State does not comply,

409. L. Krämer, *EU Environmental Law*, London: Sweet & Maxwell, 2011, p. 419.
410. European Commission, '50 Years of the Euratom Treaty', Memo/07/118, 26 March 2007 Brussels, p. 2.
411. International Atomic Energy Agency, *IAEA Safety Glossary. Terminology Used in Nuclear Safety and Radiation Protection*, Vienna: IAEA, 2016, p. 132.
412. I. Cenevska, *The European Atomic Energy Community in the European Union Context: The 'Outsider' Within*, Leiden: Brill Nijhoff, 2016, p. 114. For academic discussion on the distinctions between nuclear law and environmental law, *see also*: J. Handrlica, 'Nuclear Law Revisited as an Academic Discipline', (2019) 12 *Journal of World Energy Law and Business*, p. 58.
413. Article 36 of the Euratom Treaty.
414. European Parliament Report on the proposal for a Council Directive (Euratom) setting up a Community framework for nuclear safety of nuclear installations (Hökmark Report) A6-0236/2009, pp. 47–48.

directly[415] bring the matter before the CJEU.[416] Consequently, it may be concluded that provisions under Article 38, in combination with Articles 31 and 32, of the Euratom Treaty indicate that the Euratom Treaty establishes Euratom Community competences concerning radiation protection, and emergency preparedness and response.

In conclusion, analysis of the provisions of Chapter 3 of the Euratom Treaty shows that the scope and content of the Euratom Community's competences in the field of health and safety include two main areas: establishing and updating basic safety standards based on the available scientific knowledge; and ensuring compliance with those standards, *inter alia*, in legislative and regulatory systems, when conducting experiments, by requiring establishment of monitoring facilities, when making plans for radioactive waste disposal, and in cases of radiological urgency.

3.02 THE EXERCISE OF THE COMPETENCES

This section assesses the exercise of the Euratom Community's competence in respect of health and safety and the instruments through which this occurs.

The competences established in Chapter 3 of the Euratom Treaty - which covers health and safety - have enabled the Euratom Community to develop a large body of Community law.[417] The Euratom Community has exercised its competences under majority of the articles contained in Chapter 3 of the Euratom Treaty using them as legal bases for secondary legislation,[418] and covering a wide range of secondary legal acts, including regulations, directives, decisions, recommendations and opinions.[419] Articles 31, 32 and 37 have been used most often as legal bases for such secondary legislation.

Articles 35 and 36 of the Euratom Treaty have not been utilised to the same extent as the articles mentioned above. Nevertheless, concerning the issue of the Euratom

415. *Id est*, without prior formal notification under Articles 258 and 259 TFEU.
416. Article 38(2) and (3) of the Euratom Treaty.
417. European Commission, '50 Years of the Euratom Treaty', Memo/07/118, 26 March 2007 Brussels, p. 2.
418. The exercise of competences under Articles 31, 32, 35, 36 and 37 of the Euratom Treaty is analysed below. The remaining articles of Chapter 3 of the Euratom Treaty are exercised by secondary legal acts in force, as follows: Article 30 by Commission Recommendation of 20 December 2001 on the protection of the public against exposure to radon in drinking water supplies (notified under document number C(2001) 4580), OJ L 344, 28.12.2001, pp. 85-88; Article 33 by Commission Recommendation of 7 July 2009 for a secure and effective system of transmission of documents and information relating to the provisions of Council Directive 2006/117/Euratom, OJ L 177, 8.7.2009, pp. 5-6; Commission Recommendation of 20 December 2001 on the protection of the public against exposure to radon in drinking water supplies (notified under document number C(2001) 4580), OJ L 344, 28.12.2001, pp. 85-88; Commission Recommendation 90/143/Euratom of 21 February 1990 on the protection of the public against indoor exposure to radon, OJ L 80, 27.3.1990, pp. 26-28; Article 34 is not exercised by any secondary legal acts; Article 38 by Commission Recommendation of 20 December 2001 on the protection of the public against exposure to radon in drinking water supplies (notified under document number C(2001) 4580), OJ L 344, 28.12.2001, pp. 85-88; Article 39 is not exercised by any secondary legal acts.
419. Under Article 106a(1) of the Euratom Treaty and Article 288 TFEU, in order to exercise the Union's and the Euratom Community's competences, the institutions can adopt regulations, directives, decisions, recommendations and opinions.

Treaty covering environmental protection, there is a need to revisit the concept of 'air, water and soil' as constituting the environment under Article 35 of the Euratom Treaty,[420] analyse whether any secondary legislation has been based on Article 35 and 36 of the Euratom Treaty, and assess whether that legislation provides any clarity on this issue. Systematic analysis of Commission recommendations and other guidance documents issued by the Commission[421] reveals that the Commission's position on the concept of air, water and soil is inconsistent. In some recommendations and guidance documents the Commission refers to the monitoring of radioactivity in air, water and soil as the monitoring of environmental radioactivity and interprets the concept of air, water and soil under Article 35 of the Euratom Treaty as the environment as a whole, implying that environmental monitoring per se is an objective of the Euratom Treaty.[422] Other Commission recommendations and reports indicate that the main purpose of the monitoring of levels of environmental radioactivity is to control radioactivity and to assess the general population's overall exposure to it in order to protect the health of members of the public.[423] Consequently, it seems that the question of whether the monitoring of air, water and soil covers environmental protection cannot be answered by analysing the exercise of competences under Article 35 of the Euratom Treaty.

The continuation of the analysis of the exercise of the Euratom Community's competences in relation to health and safety focuses on the competences established in Articles 31, 32 and 37 of the Euratom Treaty. In view of the scope and objectives of this study, analysis of the exercise of the Euratom Community's competences under these articles is limited to the secondary legislation in force.

420. *See* Chapter 3 Section 01 on scope and content of the Euratom Community's competences in relation to health and safety above.
421. Commission Recommendation 2004/2/Euratom of 18 December 2003 on standardised information on radioactive airborne and liquid discharges into the environment from nuclear power reactors and reprocessing plants in normal operation, OJ L 2, 6.1.2004, pp. 36–46; Commission Recommendation 2000/473/Euratom of 8 June 2000 on the application of Article 36 of the Euratom Treaty concerning the monitoring of the levels of radioactivity in the environment for the purpose of assessing the exposure of the population as a whole (notified under document number C(2000) 1299), OJ L 191, 27.7.2000, p. 37; Verification of environmental radioactivity monitoring facilities under the terms of Article 35 of the Euratom Treaty – Practical arrangements for the conduct of verification visits in Member States, 2006/C 155/02, OJ C 155, 4.7.2006, pp. 2–5; Communication from the Commission – Application of Article 35 of the Euratom Treaty – Verification of the operation and efficiency of facilities for continuous monitoring of the level of radioactivity in the air, water and soil – Report, 1990–2007, COM (2007) 847 final.
422. Recitals 1 and 3 of Commission Recommendation 2004/2/Euratom; recitals 1, 8 and 10 and clarification of 'environmental monitoring' in Verification of environmental radioactivity monitoring facilities under the terms of Article 35 of the Euratom Treaty – Practical arrangements for the conduct of verification visits in Member States, 2006/C 155/02, OJ C 155, 4.7.2006, pp. 2–5.
423. Title and recital 4 of Commission Recommendation 2000/473/Euratom; Communication from the Commission – Application of Article 35 of the Euratom Treaty – Verification of the operation and efficiency of facilities for continuous monitoring of the level of radioactivity in the air, water and soil – Report, 1990–2007. COM (2007) 847 final, p. 2.

A Exercise of Articles 31 and 32 of the Euratom Treaty

Articles 31 and 32 of the Euratom Treaty lay down the legislative procedure for establishing and revising basic safety standards. Eight secondary legal acts currently in force were adopted on the basis of these articles. Analysis of the content of these secondary legal acts indicates the way in which the Euratom Community's competences have been exercised in relation to health and safety. Even though the Euratom Treaty does not explicitly mention the operational safety of nuclear power plants, radioactive waste storage or the development of disposal facilities,[424] comprehensive analysis of these eight secondary legal acts reveals that they may be divided into the following four regulatory fields: radiation protection;[425] nuclear safety of nuclear installations;[426] safe management of radioactive waste and spent nuclear fuel;[427] and emergency preparedness and response.[428]

It should be noted from the outset that Directive 2013/59/Euratom not only exercises competences established in Articles 31 and 32 of the Euratom Treaty, but also addresses the issue of environmental protection under the Euratom Treaty.[429] While acknowledging the need for a policy that protects the environment against the harmful effects of ionising radiation, the directive states that the Euratom Community's secondary legislation so far has regarded the contamination of the environment only as a pathway of exposure to members of the public directly affected by radioactive discharges to the environment.[430] It also states that its provisions apply in relation to the environment only in the context of the long-term protection of human health.[431] In other words, the provisions of Directive 2013/59/Euratom that mention the environment[432] take the environment into account for the purpose of protecting human

424. P. M. Barnes, 'Nuclear Safety for Nuclear Electricity – The Search for a Solid Legal Basis for Nuclear Safety in an Enlarged European Union', (2003) 45 *Managerial Law*, p. 129.
425. Council Directive 2013/59/Euratom; Council Directive 2013/51/Euratom of 22 October 2013 laying down requirements for the protection of the health of the general public with regard to radioactive substances in water intended for human consumption, OJ L 296, 7.11.2013, pp. 12–21; Council Regulation (Euratom) No 1493/93 of 8 June 1993 on shipments of radioactive substances between Member States, OJ L 148, 19.6.1993, pp. 1–7.
426. Council Directive 2009/71/Euratom.
427. Council Directive 2011/70/Euratom; Council Directive 2006/117/Euratom of 20 November 2006 on the supervision and control of shipments of radioactive waste and spent fuel, OJ L 337, 5.12.2006, pp. 21–32.
428. Council Regulation (Euratom) 2016/52 of 15 January 2016 laying down maximum permitted levels of radioactive contamination of food and feed following a nuclear accident or any other case of radiological emergency, and repealing Regulation (Euratom) No 3954/87 and Commission Regulations (Euratom) No 944/89 and (Euratom) No 770/90, OJ L 13, 20.1.2016, pp. 2–11; Council Decision 87/600/Euratom of 14 December 1987 on Community arrangements for the early exchange of information in the event of a radiological emergency, OJ L 371, 30.12.1987, pp. 76–78.
429. Council Directive 2013/59/Euratom is not mentioned in the context of the analysis of the exercise of competences under Articles 35 and 36 of the Euratom Treaty, as it does not have Articles 35 and 36 as legal bases.
430. Recital 27 of Council Directive 2013/59/Euratom.
431. Article 2(1) of Council Directive 2013/59/Euratom.
432. Articles 28(f), 29(4), 67(1) and 72 of Council Directive 2013/59/Euratom.

health.[433] Consequently, the objective of protecting the environment from the harmful effects of ionising radiation is explicitly excluded from the scope of the directive, which lays down the basic safety standards of radiation protection.[434]

1 *Radiation Protection*

The Euratom Community's competences under Articles 31 and 32 of the Euratom Treaty in respect of radiation protection are exercised through three secondary legal acts: Directive 2013/59/Euratom, which covers basic safety standards for protection against the dangers arising from exposure to ionising radiation; Directive 2013/51/Euratom, which covers requirements for the protection of health of the general public with regard to radioactive substances in water intended for human consumption; and Regulation (Euratom) No 1493/93 to ensure radiation protection control during shipments of radioactive substances.

The provisions of Directive 2013/59/Euratom, which impose obligations on the Member States, are applicable to planned, existing or emergency exposure situations that involve risk of exposure to ionising radiation that cannot be disregarded from a radiation protection perspective.[435] This wording indicates that the Euratom Community's competences under the directive cover any situation that might call for radiation protection measures.[436] A general feature of Directive 2013/59/Euratom is that it almost exclusively focuses on imposing clear requirements on the Member States, without involvement from the institutions of the Euratom Community, implying that the Euratom Community's horizontal competences are scarcely exercised under this directive.[437]

Analysis of the Euratom Community's vertical competences under Directive 2013/59/Euratom leads one to conclude that the Euratom Community exercises its competences in respect of radiation protection by ensuring: first, the establishment of fundamental principles concerning radiation protection in Member States' national legal frameworks; second, the establishment of radiation protection provisions for ionising radiation occurring in specific situations (occupational exposure, medical

433. In the Commission's proposal for a Council Directive laying down basic safety standards for protection against the dangers arising from exposure to ionising radiation COM(2012) 242 final, there was a separate chapter on protection of the environment. However, reference to the protection of the environment was removed from the final version of the directive.
434. For further discussion of the interaction between nuclear and environmental law at international level, *see* S. Emmerechts, 'Environmental Law and Nuclear Law: A Growing Symbiosis', (2008) 82 *Nuclear Law Bulletin*, pp. 91–110.
435. Article 2 of Council Directive 2013/59/Euratom.
436. Article 3 of Council Directive 2013/59/Euratom provides that the directive does not apply to exposure to a natural level of radiation, such as radionuclides contained in the human body and cosmic radiation prevailing at ground level; exposure of members of the public or workers other than air or space crew to cosmic radiation in flight or in space; and above-ground exposure to radionuclides present in the undisturbed earth's crust.
437. Articles 76(5) and 79(2) of Council Directive 2013/59/Euratom are the only provisions that establish the Commission's competences, which are limited to receiving certain information from each Member State and making it available to all Member States of the Euratom Community.

exposure, existing exposure, emergency exposure); and third, the establishment of regulatory provisions.

First, Directive 2013/59/Euratom lays down the three fundamental principles of radiation protection: justification, optimisation and dose limitation. The justification principle requires that in relation to exposure to ionising radiation it must be ensured that the individual or societal benefit resulting from the practice that led to such exposure outweighs the health detriment that it may cause, i.e., that it does more good than harm.[438] The Euratom Community also imposes requirements on the Member States concerning the justification of practices resulting in exposure to ionising radiation[439] and the prohibition of certain practices, including the deliberate addition of radioactive substances to consumer products,[440] as well as the identification of practices that involve human exposure to ionising radiation for non-medical purposes.[441] The optimisation principle requires that in the event of public or occupational exposure the magnitude of individual doses, the likelihood of exposure and the number of individuals exposed are as low as reasonably achievable.[442] The optimisation principle is referred to by the acronym ALARA ('as low as reasonably achievable').[443] The Euratom Community establishes tools for optimisation in the form of dose constraints and reference levels.[444] The dose limitation principle requires that in planned exposure situations, the total amount of doses for an individual shall not exceed the dose limits laid down for occupational exposure or public exposure. This principle is not applicable in medical exposure situations.[445] The Euratom Community also exercises its competences under Articles 30 and 31 of the Euratom Treaty by establishing the principle of dose limitation for exposed workers, pregnant and breastfeeding workers, apprentices and students, and dose limits for public exposure.[446] Directive 2013/59/Euratom also indicates that its provisions lay down minimum rules, and that Member States are free to adopt or maintain more stringent measures in the subject matter covered by this directive.[447] The latter wording implies the right for the Member States to adopt more stringent basic standards than those established by the Euratom Community.[448]

438. Article 5(a) of Council Directive 2013/59/Euratom.
439. Article 19 of Council Directive 2013/59/Euratom.
440. Article 21 of Council Directive 2013/59/Euratom.
441. Article 22 of Council Directive 2013/59/Euratom.
442. Article 5(b) of Council Directive 2013/59/Euratom.
443. *See* International Atomic Energy Agency, *IAEA Safety Glossary. Terminology Used in Nuclear Safety and Radiation Protection*, Vienna: IAEA, 2016, pp. 7 and 121. For further discussion of the optimisation principle, *see* S. Lierman and L. Veuchelen, 'The Optimisation Approach of ALARA in Nuclear Practice: An Early Application of the Precautionary Principle? Scientific Uncertainty Versus Legal Uncertainty and Its Role in Tort Law', (2006) 15/4 *European Environmental Law Review*.
444. Articles 6 and 7 of Council Directive 2013/59/Euratom.
445. Article 5(c) of Council Directive 2013/59/Euratom.
446. Articles 8 to 12 of Council Directive 2013/59/Euratom.
447. Recital 5 of Council Directive 2013/59/Euratom.
448. For further discussion of the level of harmonisation, *see* analysis of the CJEU's case-law below.

Second, the Euratom Community exercises its competences by establishing requirements, the organisation of work and responsibilities of parties involved in the field of occupational exposure, in planned and emergency exposure situations.[449] Directive 2013/59/Euratom also lays down a framework for medical exposure situations,[450] provisions concerning the protection of members of the public,[451] and imposes requirements on the Member States concerning the management of existing exposure situations[452] and emergency exposure situations.[453]

Third, as the Euratom Community's competences under Chapter 3 of the Euratom Treaty include both the establishment of basic safety standards and ensuring that these basic standards are adhered to by the Member States, Directive 2013/59/Euratom exercises these competences by establishing requirements concerning the following: a graded approach to regulatory control;[454] institutional infrastructure;[455] a system of control governing radioactive sources and orphan sources;[456] and the establishment of an enforcement system.[457]

Directive 2013/51/Euratom regulates certain specific aspect of radiation protection, i.e., radioactivity in drinking water. It establishes parametric values and methods for monitoring radioactive substances in water intended for human consumption.[458]

To ensure radiation protection control during transports of radioactive substances, the Euratom Community took the view that it was necessary to establish a Community system governing the declaration and provision of information for shipments of radioactive sources.[459] The Euratom Community exercises its competences in relation to radiation protection through the procedure for shipments of radioactive sources between the Member States laid down in Regulation (Euratom) No 1493/93.[460] The Euratom Community also requires controls of shipments to be performed as part of the control procedures applied in a non-discriminatory manner throughout the territory of the Member States.[461]

449. Articles 31 to 54 of Council Directive 2013/59/Euratom.
450. Articles 55 to 64 of Council Directive 2013/59/Euratom.
451. Articles 65 to 68 of Council Directive 2013/59/Euratom. The term 'general public' used in Chapter 2 of the Euratom Treaty is replaced in Council Directive 2013/59/Euratom with 'members of the public'.
452. Articles 72 to 75 and 100 to 103 of Council Directive 2013/59/Euratom. Existing exposure situations include contaminated areas, indoor radon concentrations or gamma radiation from building materials.
453. Articles 69 to 71 and 97 to 99 of Council Directive 2013/59/Euratom. For further discussion of the exercise of the Euratom Community's competences in relation to emergency preparedness and response, *see* Chapter 3 Section 02.A.4 below.
454. Articles 23 to 30 of Council Directive 2013/59/Euratom. A graded approach implies that regulatory control should be commensurate with the magnitude and likelihood of exposures resulting from the practice. Under Council Directive 2013/59/Euratom, regulatory control can be done by notification, registration or licensing.
455. Articles 76 to 84 of Council Directive 2013/59/Euratom.
456. Articles 85 to 95 of Council Directive 2013/59/Euratom.
457. Articles 104 to 105 of Council Directive 2013/59/Euratom.
458. Articles 1, 5, 6 and Annexes I and II of Council Directive 2013/51/Euratom.
459. Recitals of Council Regulation (Euratom) No 1493/93.
460. Articles 1, 4 to 8 of Council Regulation (Euratom) No 1493/93.
461. Article 3 of Council Regulation (Euratom) No 1493/93.

Consequently, Directive 2013/59/Euratom is an overarching directive, exercising the Euratom Community's competences in relation to radiation protection by establishing fundamental principles of radiation protection and uniform basic safety standards for the protection of individuals subject to occupational, medical and public exposures against the dangers arising from ionising radiation, in planned and emergency exposure situations. Directive 2013/51/Euratom and Regulation (Euratom) No 1493/93 exercises the Euratom Community's competences in specific situations, where risk of radiological exposure may occur, i.e., radioactivity in drinking water and during shipments of radioactive sources.

2 Nuclear Safety

The nuclear safety regime is built on the legal framework for the protection of workers and the general public laid down in the Euratom Treaty.[462] The Euratom Community's competences under Articles 31 and 32 of the Euratom Treaty in relation to nuclear safety are exercised through Directive 2009/71/Euratom. The primary reason for the revision of Directive 2009/71/Euratom was the Fukushima Daiichi nuclear accident,[463] but the added value of Directive 2009/71/Euratom for nuclear safety is sometimes questioned.[464]

The aim here is to analyse the exercise of the Euratom Community's competences under Directive 2009/71/Euratom by identifying its key aspects that may be regarded as bringing added value. These comprise a nuclear safety framework; nuclear safety objective; the imposition of obligations on regulatory authority and licence holders; periodic safety reviews; the continuous improvement of nuclear safety; and the fostering of a safety culture.

As is the case for radiation protection, limited exercise of horizontal competences has taken place in relation to nuclear safety under Directive 2009/71/Euratom. The focus here is on vertical competences, i.e., the obligations imposed by the Euratom Community on the Member States.[465]

462. P. M. Barnes, 'Nuclear Safety for Nuclear Electricity - The Search for a Solid Legal Basis for Nuclear Safety in an Enlarged European Union', (2003) 45 *Managerial Law*, p. 117.
463. Although it was triggered by an earthquake and tsunami of immense magnitude, investigation of the nuclear accident at the Fukushima Daiichi nuclear power plant has revealed a range of foreseeable technical issues as well as persistent institutional failures, which, taken together, produced a catastrophic outcome. The EU's response to the events was immediate and resulted in the comprehensive risk and safety review and assessment of all the nuclear power plants EU-wide, known as the Stress Tests (for the Final Stress Tests Report, *see* COM (2012) 571 final). In March 2011 the Commission also received a clear legislative mandate from the European Council to review the existing legal and regulatory framework for the safety of nuclear installations and propose any improvements that may be necessary. The EU called for a stronger legal framework in the nuclear safety area through binding standards, and the appointment of a strong, transparent and independent regulator while at the same time increasing monitoring and transparency.
464. L. Krämer, *EU Environmental Law*, London: Sweet & Maxwell, 2011, p. 169.
465. The Commission's powers under Council Directive 2009/71/Euratom essentially involve participation in the peer review as an observer under Article 8e and obligations under transposition provisions in Article 10.

Nuclear safety is defined as the achievement of proper operating conditions, the prevention of accidents and mitigation of their consequences, resulting in protection of workers and the general public from dangers arising from ionising radiations from nuclear installations.[466] The Euratom Community requires the Member States to establish and maintain a national legislative, regulatory and organisational framework for the nuclear safety of nuclear installations. This framework should consist of allocation of responsibilities between relevant bodies, establishment of national nuclear safety requirements that cover the whole lifecycle of nuclear installations, a system of licensing of nuclear installations, a system of regulatory control and effective and proportionate enforcement actions.[467] The national nuclear safety framework must also include nuclear safety objective for nuclear installations.[468]

The nuclear safety objective is to prevent accidents and, should they occur, mitigate their consequences, and avoid early radioactive release that would require immediate off-site emergency measures. The nuclear safety objective applies to nuclear installations in all stages – design, siting, construction, commissioning, operation and decommissioning.[469]

The Euratom Community further exercises its competences by requiring the Member States to establish and maintain an independent competent regulatory authority in the field of nuclear safety of nuclear installations. Independence means that the national competent authority is protected from undue influence in its regulatory decision-making, by functional separation from any bodies or organisation concerned with the promotion or utilisation of nuclear energy.[470] The Euratom Community's requirement concerning a responsible licence holder implies, *inter alia*, that the Member States need to ensure that the prime responsibility for the nuclear safety of a nuclear installation rests with the licence holder and that responsibility cannot be delegated to contractors and subcontractors.[471] The requirement concerning a system of initial assessments and periodic safety review consists of two parts: the grant of a licence has to be based on an appropriate and installation-specific assessment that comprises a nuclear safety demonstration; and systematic and regular reassessment of the safety of nuclear installation has to be done at least every ten years.[472]

466. Article 3(2) of Council Directive 2009/71/Euratom.
467. Article 4(a) to (e) of Council Directive 2009/71/Euratom.
468. Article 8a of Council Directive 2009/71/Euratom.
469. Under Article 8a(2) of Council Directive 2009/71/Euratom, the nuclear safety objective applies in its full extent only to those nuclear installation that have a granted construction licence after 14 August 2014. To the existing nuclear installations licenced before 14 August 2014, the nuclear safety objective is used as a reference for timely implementation of reasonably practicable nuclear safety improvements. Consequently, the nuclear safety objective fully applies only to the newly built nuclear installations.
470. Article 5(1) and (2) of Council Directive 2009/71/Euratom. On the international principle of independence of regulatory authority in nuclear law, *see inter alia*: C. Stoiber, A. Baer, N. Pelzer and W. Tonhauser, *Handbook of Nuclear Law*, Vienna: International Atomic Energy Agency, 2003, p. 9; L. G. Williams, 'Nuclear Safety and Nuclear Security Regulatory Challenges Facing a Country Embarking on a Nuclear Power Programme', (2019) 12 *Journal of World Energy Law and Business*, pp. 73 and 83.
471. Article 6 of Council Directive 2009/71/Euratom.
472. Articles 8c and 8e of Council Directive 2009/71/Euratom.

It should be mentioned at this point that although the Euratom Community has a competence to ensure that the basic standards established under Articles 31 and 32 of the Euratom Treaty are implemented and adhered to by the Member States,[473] the peer review mechanism under Directive 2009/71/Euratom is based on self-assessment between the Member States, where the Commission is only an observer.[474]

The Euratom Community's requirement with respect to continuous improvement[475] of nuclear safety recurs throughout Directive 2009/71/Euratom: the Member States are obliged to continuously improve their national frameworks for nuclear safety;[476] licence holders are obliged to continuously improve the nuclear safety of their nuclear installations;[477] and a periodic safety review should be established in the national frameworks as a tool to identify further safety improvements.[478]

The Euratom Community regards the establishment of a strong safety culture within nuclear installations as one of the fundamental safety management principles necessary to achieve their safe operation.[479] Under Directive 2009/71/Euratom, the Member States are obliged to ensure that their competent regulatory authorities and licence holders promote and enhance an effective nuclear safety culture. The main elements involved in achieving a strong nuclear safety culture include effective management systems; the registration, evaluation and documentation of licence holders' internal and external operating experience; licence holder's effective resolution of issues that have been raised; the imposition of an obligation on a licence holder to report events that have the potential to impact nuclear safety to the competent regulatory authority; and appropriate education and training.[480]

Consequently, analysis of Directive 2009/71/Euratom shows that the Euratom Community exercises its competences under Articles 31 and 32 of the Euratom Treaty in the field of nuclear safety by imposing on Member States the obligation to establish and maintain a nuclear safety framework, an independent competent regulatory authority and a responsible licence holder; as well as further obligations, which include a system of periodic safety review, requirements concerning the continuous improvement of nuclear safety and good nuclear safety culture.

473. *See* scope and content of the Euratom Community competences regarding health and safety under Chapter 3 Section 01 of this study.
474. Article 8e(2)(b) of Council Directive 2009/71/Euratom.
475. For further discussion of continuous improvement, *see* R. Ptasekaite, 'Continuous Improvement of Nuclear Safety', in C. Raetzke (ed.), *Nuclear Law and Beyond*, Baden-Baden: Nomos, 2014, pp. 71–97.
476. Article 4(2) of Council Directive 2009/71/Euratom.
477. Article 6(c) of Council Directive 2009/71/Euratom.
478. Article 8c(b) of Council Directive 2009/71/Euratom.
479. Recital 19 of Council Directive 2009/71/Euratom.
480. Article 8b(2) of Council Directive 2009/71/Euratom. Nuclear safety culture can be defined as an assembly of characteristics and attitudes in organisations and individuals that establish nuclear safety as an overriding priority, and is a much-discussed issue in the international nuclear regulation arena. For further information on this topic, *see* R. Ptasekaite, 'The Role of the Regulator: Nuclear Safety and Nuclear Safety Culture', (2013) 1 *Nuclear Law and Policy*.

3 *Safe Management of Spent Fuel and Radioactive Waste*

The Euratom Community's competences under Articles 31 and 32 of the Euratom Treaty in relation to the safe management of radioactive waste and spent nuclear fuel (often referred to as the back end of the nuclear fuel cycle),[481] are exercised through Council Directive 2011/70/Euratom, which concerns responsible and safe management of spent fuel and radioactive waste; and Council Directive 2006/117/Euratom, which concerns the shipment of radioactive waste and spent fuel.

In Directive 2006/117/Euratom, the Euratom Community exercises its competences in relation to safe management of spent fuel and radioactive waste by establishing a Euratom Community system of supervision and control of transboundary shipments of radioactive waste and spent fuel, to guarantee adequate protection of the population.[482] Directive 2006/117/Euratom establishes a specific system of requirements for both intra-community shipments[483] and extra-community shipments.[484] This directive contains provisions concerning prohibited exports,[485] indicating that some shipments are prohibited even if they fulfil all the technical requirements.[486]

The Euratom Community's competences in respect of spent fuel and radioactive waste management are exercised through Directive 2011/70/Euratom, which imposes obligations on Member States to ensure the responsible and safe management of spent fuel and radioactive waste and to avoid imposing undue burdens on future generations.[487] This directive represents an important step towards building and strengthening the most advanced legal framework that could be envisaged for nuclear energy in Europe.[488]

The Euratom Community requires the Member States to ensure safe management of radioactive waste and spent fuel in their national policies,[489] national frameworks[490] and national programmes.[491] National policy is required to be based on the following principles: keeping generation of waste to the minimum; taking into account the interdependencies between all steps in waste generation and management; managing

481. For the definition of the nuclear fuel cycle, *see* International Atomic Energy Agency, *IAEA Safety Glossary. Terminology Used in Nuclear Safety and Radiation Protection*, Vienna: IAEA, 2016, p. 114.
482. Article 1(1) of Council Directive 2006/117/Euratom.
483. Articles 6 to 12 of Council Directive 2006/117/Euratom.
484. Articles 13 to 16 of Council Directive 2006/117/Euratom.
485. Article 16 of Council Directive 2006/117/Euratom. For further discussion of this issue, *see* U. Blohm-Hieber, 'The Radioactive Waste Directive: A Necessary Step in the Management of Spent Fuel and Radioactive Waste in the European Union', (2011) 88 *Nuclear Law Bulletin*, p. 26.
486. *See* L. Krämer, *EU Environmental Law*, London: Sweet & Maxwell, 2011, pp. 354–355.
487. Article 1(1) of Council Directive 2011/70/Euratom.
488. U. Blohm-Hieber, 'The Radioactive Waste Directive: A Necessary Step in the Management of Spent Fuel and Radioactive Waste in the European Union', (2011) 88 *Nuclear Law Bulletin*, p. 21.
489. Article 4(1) of Council Directive 2011/70/Euratom.
490. Article 5 of Council Directive 2011/70/Euratom.
491. Articles 11 and 12 of Council Directive 2011/70/Euratom.

radioactive waste and spent fuel safely; following a graded approach[492] in the implementation of measures; applying an evidence-based and documented decision-making process; and the polluter pays principle.[493] The obligation to define national policies and to transpose them into national programmes that cover all types of spent fuel and radioactive waste under their jurisdictions and all stages of spent fuel and radioactive waste management from generation to disposal is key to address the ethical obligation not to impose undue burdens on future generations.[494] Furthermore, the Member States are required to establish and maintain a national legislative, regulatory and organisational framework. This national framework must comprise national programme and national arrangements for management; a system of licensing; a system of control and enforcement actions; allocation of responsibilities between different bodies; provisions concerning public information and participation; and a financing scheme to cover the waste management costs.[495] Systematic analysis of these components leads one to the conclusion that a national framework comprises a legal and regulatory 'backbone' that ensures the safe management of radioactive waste and spent fuel. A specific and continuously updated[496] national programme for the management of spent fuel and radioactive waste is required to cover all types of spent fuel and radioactive waste under a Member State's jurisdiction and at all stages from generation to disposal.[497]

Exercise of the Euratom Community's competences under Articles 31 and 32 of the Euratom Treaty in the field of the safe management of spent fuel and radioactive waste also requires national frameworks and national programmes to be regularly reviewed and updated;[498] and to undergo periodical self-assessments and international peer review at least every ten years.[499] The Euratom Community framework also allocates responsibilities in the field such that each Member State has ultimate responsibility for the management of spent nuclear fuel and radioactive waste generated in it.[500] This means that radioactive waste must be disposed of in the Member State in which it was generated, unless there is a specific shipment agreement in place.[501] The fact that each Member State bears ultimate responsibility in this regard also means

492. A graded approach means that implemented measures are commensurate with the magnitude and likelihood of exposures resulting from the practice and commensurate with the impact that the implemented measure may have in reducing such exposures or improving safety.
493. Article 4(3) of Council Directive 2011/70/Euratom.
494. U. Blohm-Hieber, 'The Radioactive Waste Directive: A Necessary Step in the Management of Spent Fuel and Radioactive Waste in the European Union', (2011) 88 *Nuclear Law Bulletin*, p. 28.
495. Article 5 of Council Directive 2011/70/Euratom.
496. Article 11(2) of Council Directive 2011/70/Euratom.
497. Article 11(1) of Council Directive 2011/70/Euratom.
498. Article 11(2) of Council Directive 2011/70/Euratom.
499. Article 14(3) of Council Directive 2011/70/Euratom. Self-assessment and peer review under Council Directive 2011/70/Euratom and under Article 8e of the Council Directive 2009/71/Euratom are similar. *See also* Chapter 3 Section 02.A.2 of this study.
500. Article 4(1) of Council Directive 2011/70/Euratom.
501. Article 4(4) of Council Directive 2011/70/Euratom. This article requires a shipment agreement between two Member States, which means that both a general authorisation mechanism under Articles 6 to 12 of Council Directive 2006/117/Euratom and an intergovernmental agreement between Member States are required for the shipment of radioactive waste.

that if radioactive waste or spent nuclear fuel is shipped for processing or reprocessing to another Member State or third country, responsibility for disposal of that waste or spent fuel remains with the state of origin.[502] In this case, control and authorisation provisions under Directive 2006/117/Euratom do not affect the right of the Member State to which radioactive waste is to be shipped for processing to return that waste after treatment to its country of origin.[503] The primary responsibility for the spent fuel and radioactive waste lies with those who have generated it or, under specific circumstances, with a licence holder to whom this responsibility has been entrusted by competent bodies.[504] This prime responsibility for the safety of spent fuel and radioactive waste management facilities and/or activities rests with the licence holder and that responsibility cannot be delegated.[505] Comparative analysis as between the ultimate responsibility of a Member State and the prime responsibility of the waste-generator is required on this point.[506]

The ultimate responsibility borne by each Member State ensures that there is always a party that has responsibility for the management of radioactive waste and spent fuel. If the licence holder or generator ceases to exist, the Member State itself bears that responsibility. Consequently, the Member State concerned must ensure the existence of an undertaking that holds the required licence and has the obligation to manage the waste. The Member State's ultimate responsibility is not triggered as long as such an undertaking (licence holder or generator) responsible for the safe management of radioactive waste and spent fuel exists. The prime responsibility of a generator or licence holder requires that this entity establishes and maintains a plan as to how the waste should be managed and finally disposed of, and also has financing for its implementation.[507] Similar to the regulatory fields discussed above,[508] Member States are also required to ensure that there is a responsible licence holder that regularly assesses, verifies and continuously improves, as far as is reasonably achievable, the safety of the radioactive waste and spent fuel management.[509] The licence holder must also establish and implement integrated management systems, including quality assurance, which give due priority to safety and are regularly verified by the competent regulatory authority.[510]

Finally, the Euratom Community's competences in respect of spent fuel and radioactive waste management are exercised by requiring a restrictive approach

502. Article 4(2) of Council Directive 2011/70/Euratom.
503. Article 2 of Council Directive 2006/117/Euratom.
504. Article 5(1)(f) of Council Directive 2011/70/Euratom.
505. Article 7(1) of Council Directive 2011/70/Euratom. Under Article 3(6) of Council Directive 2011/70/Euratom, a licence holder is defined as a legal or natural person having overall responsibility for any activity or facility related to the management of spent fuel or radioactive waste as specified in a licence.
506. *See also* J. Handrlica, 'Between the Public and Private Responsibility for the Management of Spent Nuclear Fuel and Radioactive Waste in EU', in B. Delvaux, M. Hunt and K. Talus (eds), *EU Energy Law and Policy Issues*, Volume 4, Cambridge – Antwerp – Portland: Intersentia, 2014, pp. 5992.
507. Article 4(3)(e) of Council Directive 2011/70/Euratom.
508. *See* Chapter 3 Section 02.A.1 on radiation protection and Section 02.A.2 on nuclear safety.
509. Article 7(2) of Council Directive 2011/70/Euratom.
510. Article 7(4) of Council Directive 2011/70/Euratom.

towards the export of radioactive waste to countries outside the EU.[511] Export to a third country is permitted only if that country has concluded an agreement with the Euratom Community or is a party to the Joint Convention.[512] A country of destination is also required to maintain radioactive waste management and disposal programme that reflects the objective of achieving a high level of safety, and must also maintain a disposal facility that operates in accordance with the safety requirements set down in the radioactive waste management and disposal programme of that country of destination.[513]

In conclusion, the Euratom Community exercises its competences under Articles 31 and 32 of the Euratom Treaty in relation to the safe management of spent fuel and radioactive waste by establishing requirements for the safe management of radioactive waste and spent fuel in every Member State, as well as requirements for the safe shipment of radioactive waste and spent fuel within the Euratom Community and for its import and export.

4 Emergency Preparedness and Response

The Euratom Community's competences under Articles 31 and 32 of the Euratom Treaty in relation to emergency preparedness and response are exercised through Council Regulation (Euratom) 2016/52, which concerns the maximum permitted levels of radioactive contamination of food and feed in the event of a nuclear accident or radiological emergency; and Council Decision 87/600/Euratom, which concerns the early exchange of information in the event of radiological emergency. In addition, Directive 2013/59/Euratom establishes basic safety standards in respect of radiation protection; and Directive 2009/71/Euratom, which concerns nuclear safety, and is analysed above, requires Member States to ensure that specific measures concerning emergency preparedness and response are in place in nuclear installations.

Study of the relevant secondary legislation indicates that the Euratom Community exercises its competences under Articles 31 and 32 of the Euratom Treaty in respect of emergency preparedness and response by laying down maximum permitted levels of radioactive contamination of food,[514] minor food[515] and feed,[516] which may be placed in the market following a nuclear accident or any other case of radiological emergency which is likely to lead to or has led to significant radioactive contamination of food and feed, in order to protect the population.[517]

511. Article 4(4) of Council Directive 2011/70/Euratom.
512. Joint Convention on the Safety of Spent Fuel Management and on the Safety of Radioactive Waste Management, IAEA document INFCIRC/546, 24 December 1997.
513. The wording of Article 4(4) of Council Directive 2011/70/Euratom appears to indicate that a restrictive approach to export only applies to radioactive waste and not spent nuclear fuel. Nevertheless, spent fuel that has no further purpose of use falls under the concept of radioactive waste. Therefore, the provisions of Article 4(4) of Council Directive 2011/70/Euratom are also applicable to spent fuel.
514. Annex I of Council Regulation (Euratom) 2016/52.
515. Annex II of Council Regulation (Euratom) 2016/52.
516. Annex III of Council Regulation (Euratom) 2016/52.
517. Recital 5 and Article 1 of Council Regulation (Euratom) 2016/52.

As Regulation (Euratom) 2016/52 establishes maximum permissible levels of radioactivity in food and feed, and Directive 2013/51/Euratom establishes maximum permissible radioactivity levels in water for human consumption,[518] the relationship between these two secondary legal acts should be explored.

Regulation (Euratom) 2016/52 does not apply to water intended for human consumption to which Directive 2013/51/Euratom applies. However, in the event of a radiological emergency, the Euratom Community grants Member States flexibility to refer to the maximum levels for liquid food laid down in Regulation (Euratom) 2016/52 in order to manage the use of water intended for human consumption.[519] As noted above,[520] Regulation (EU) No 182/2011, which establishes the rules governing the exercise of implementing powers,[521] is applicable under the Euratom Treaty. The applicability of implementing powers is also confirmed in Regulation (Euratom) 2016/52, which states that in order to ensure uniform conditions for the implementation of this regulation as regards establishing applicable maximum permitted levels, implementing powers should be conferred on the Commission. Those powers should be exercised in accordance with Regulation (EU) No 182/2011 notwithstanding the fact that it does not refer explicitly to Article 106a of the Euratom Treaty.[522] Regulation (Euratom) 2016/52 confers implementing powers on the Commission in relation to emergency preparedness and response by requiring it to adopt an implementing regulation that lays down maximum permitted levels for potentially contaminated food or feed that may be placed on the market.[523] This means that the provisions of Regulation (Euratom) 2016/52 that establish maximum radioactivity levels do not apply under normal circumstances, but are activated by the Commission's implementing act when there is a risk of contamination of feed and food placed on the internal market.

The Euratom Community also exercises its competences under Articles 31 and 32 of the Euratom Treaty in the field of emergency preparedness and response by establishing, in Council Decision 87/600/Euratom, arrangements for the early exchange of information in the event of a radiological emergency, ensuring that all Member States are promptly informed in order to provide the uniform standards for the protection of the population.[524] Decision 87/600/Euratom contains provisions governing when the exchange of information is to be carried out (i.e., what is considered to be a radiological emergency, how the notification of other Member States and the Commission should be carried out, and what kind of information is to be provided in the context of such notification) and specifies the measures to be taken by Member

518. *See* Chapter 3 Section 02.A.1 regarding exercise of the Euratom Community competences under Articles 31 and 32 of the Euratom Treaty in the field of radiation protection.
519. Recital 6 of Council Regulation (Euratom) 2016/52.
520. *See* Chapter 1 Section 02.A regarding exercise of the Euratom Community's competences in the field of promotion of research.
521. Regulation (EU) No 182/2011 of the European Parliament and of the Council.
522. Recital 12, Article 5 of Council Regulation (Euratom) 2016/52.
523. Articles 3 and 5 of Council Regulation (Euratom) 2016/52.
524. Recitals of Council Decision 87/600/Euratom.

States when they receive such information, and establishes the Commission's competences and obligations to distribute it within the Euratom Community.[525] In this decision the Euratom Community also established the European Community Urgent Radiological Information Exchange (ECURIE) system.[526]

Although Council Decision 87/600/Euratom provides for urgent information exchange between the Member States and the Commission in the event of an emergency, the Euratom Community took the view that there was a need to put in place arrangements for information exchange beyond the scope of that decision to allow for cooperation with all other Member States and with third countries that might be involved or likely to be affected.[527] As noted in this study, Directive 2013/59/Euratom establishes a system of requirements applicable, *inter alia,* in emergency exposure situations that involve a risk of exposure to ionising radiation that cannot be disregarded from a radiation protection perspective.[528] The Euratom Community's competences in the field are exercised under Directive 2013/59/Euratom through the establishment of a comprehensive emergency preparedness and response system comprising an assessment of potential emergency exposure situations, an overall emergency management system, emergency response plans and pre-planned strategies for the management of each postulated event.[529] In addition to provisions on prior information and training for emergency workers[530] and on emergency occupational exposure,[531] two sections of Directive 2013/59/Euratom are dedicated to emergency exposure situations.[532] The Euratom Community exercises its competences by requiring the Member States impose obligations on undertakings to notify emergency situations to the competent authorities, make an initial provisional assessment of the situation, take protective measures and ensure that members of the public that are likely to be affected and that actually are affected by the radiological emergency are informed.[533] The Euratom Community also obliges the Member States to establish national emergency management systems as well as emergency response plans for the various types of emergencies, and to cooperate with other Member States and with third countries in addressing possible emergencies on their territory that may affect other Member States or third countries.[534]

The Euratom Community exercises its competences in respect of emergency preparedness and response under Directive 2009/71/Euratom on nuclear safety by imposing requirements on the Member States to ensure that their national frameworks

525. Articles 1 to 5 of Council Decision 87/600/Euratom.
526. For further information on this issue, *see* A. Södersten, *Euratom at the Crossroads*, Cheltenham, Northampton: Edward Elgar Publishing Limited, 2018, p. 107; and L. Guzzetti, *A Brief History of European Union Research Policy*, Brussels: OOPEC 1995, pp.181–182.
527. Recital 44 of Council Directive 2013/59/Euratom.
528. Article 2 of Council Directive 2013/59/Euratom. *See* Chapter 3 Section 02.A.1 regarding exercise of the Euratom Community's competences in the field of radiation protection.
529. Recital 41 of Council Directive 2013/59/Euratom.
530. Article 17 of Council Directive 2013/59/Euratom.
531. Article 52 of Council Directive 2013/59/Euratom.
532. Sections 2 and 5.
533. Articles 69 to 71 of Council Directive 2013/59/Euratom.
534. Articles 97 to 99 of Council Directive 2013/59/Euratom.

require licence holders to provide for appropriate on-site emergency procedures and arrangements, including severe accident management guidelines, in the nuclear installations.[535] The Member States must also ensure that their national frameworks require an organisational structure for on-site emergency preparedness and response that clearly allocates responsibilities between the licence holder, the competent authority and other organisations, establishes coordination rules between the latter, and in so doing takes into account all phases of an emergency.[536] However, this provision is without prejudice to the provisions of Directive 2013/59/Euratom[537] and the Member States have to ensure consistency and continuity between the various on-site emergency preparedness and response arrangements required by each of these directives.[538]

In conclusion, the content of Article 38 of the Euratom Treaty concerns emergency preparedness and response, but the Euratom Community's competences in this area are exercised through the secondary legal acts established under Articles 31 and 32 of the Euratom Treaty. The Euratom Community's competences encompass requirements concerning all aspects of activities that deal with ionising radiation. These range from the protection of workers in emergency situations and the obligation imposed on the licence holders to maintain emergency management systems to the obligation imposed on Member States to establish national emergency management systems and emergency response plans and the obligation to communicate with other Member States and/or third countries that might be affected.

By way of consolidation of the analysis of the exercise of the Euratom Community's competences under Articles 31 and 32 of the Euratom Treaty, it may be concluded that Articles 31 and 32 of the Euratom Treaty are the legal bases for the Euratom Community's broad competences regarding health and safety. The exercise of these competences stretches to four different regulatory areas: radiation protection; nuclear safety; safe radioactive waste management; and emergency preparedness and response. Obligations are imposed on all parties involved in these regulatory areas in order to ensure the protection of the health of workers and the general public against the dangers arising from ionising radiations, under Article 30 of the Euratom Treaty.

B Exercise of Article 37 of the Euratom Treaty

This section assesses the Euratom Community's exercise of competences established under Article 37 of the Euratom Treaty. Article 37 imposes an obligation on the Member States to provide the Commission with such general data relating to plans for the disposal of radioactive waste which will make it possible for the Commission to determine whether the implementation of such plan is liable to result in the radioactive contamination of the water, soil or airspace of another Member State. Some authors consider that Article 37 has no real regulatory 'bite' as it does not lend itself as a

535. Article 6(e) of Council Directive 2009/71/Euratom.
536. Article 8d(1) of Council Directive 2009/71/Euratom.
537. Article 2(3) of Council Directive 2009/71/Euratom.
538. Article 8d(2) of Council Directive 2009/71/Euratom.

potential legal basis for the adoption of legislative measures and can only be relied upon as a ground for conducting data collection and the adoption of recommendations.[539] Article 37 of the Euratom Treaty provides the legal basis for Commission Recommendation 2010/635/Euratom[540] and a number of Commission opinions relating to specific plans for the disposal of radioactive waste in the Member States. The Commission has issued a total of 180 opinions on disposal plans of radioactive waste under Article 37 of the Euratom Treaty. Consequently, there is a need for detailed analysis of the exercise of the Euratom Community's competences under Article 37.

This analysis focuses on the questions posed in relation to the scope and content of the Euratom Community's competences concerning Article 37 of the Euratom Treaty.[541] These comprise whether the obligation to notify the Commission extends to the disposal of spent nuclear fuel, whether plans for storage and interim storage of radioactive waste should be notified under Article 37 of the Euratom Treaty, and how the concept of general data is defined.

First, the concepts of radioactive waste and spent fuel should be defined.[542] Radioactive waste is generally defined as radioactive material in gaseous, liquid or solid form for which no further use is foreseen or considered by the Member State.[543] Spent fuel is defined as nuclear fuel that has been irradiated in and permanently removed from a reactor core, and may either be considered as a usable resource that can be reprocessed or be destined for disposal if regarded as radioactive waste.[544] The specificity of the regulation of safe management of spent fuel lies in the fact that it can be reprocessed[545] and reused in a fuel cycle or disposed of with no further use, and each Member State remains free to define its fuel cycle policy.[546] Consequently, spent fuel with no further purpose of use is included in the concept of radioactive waste. As there are other types of radioactive waste that are not spent fuel, it follows that radioactive waste is a broader concept than spent nuclear fuel with no further use. The Commission exercises the competences in this field by using an overarching term (plan for the disposal of radioactive substances) that covers both radioactive waste and spent

539. I. Cenevska, *The European Atomic Energy Community in the European Union Context: The 'Outsider' Within*, Leiden: Brill Nijhoff, 2016, p. 113.
540. Commission Recommendation 2010/635/Euratom of 11 October 2010 on the application of Article 37 of the Euratom Treaty, OJ L 279, 23.10.2010, pp. 36–67.
541. *See* Chapter 3 Section 01 regarding the scope and content of the Euratom Community's competences in the field of health and safety.
542. The definitions laid down in Article 3 of Council Directive 2011/70/Euratom are consistent with other secondary Euratom law and particularly with the definitions laid down in Council Directive 2009/71/Euratom, Council Directive 2006/117/Euratom and in the 2007 IAEA Safety Glossary. *See also* U. Blohm-Hieber, 'The Radioactive Waste Directive: A Necessary Step in the Management of Spent Fuel and Radioactive Waste in the European Union', (2011) 88 *Nuclear Law Bulletin*, p. 24.
543. Article 2(7) of Council Directive 2011/70/Euratom.
544. Article 2(11) of Council Directive 2011/70/Euratom.
545. Reprocessing is defined as a process or operation, the purpose of which is to extract radioactive isotopes from spent fuel for further use. *See* International Atomic Energy Agency, *IAEA Safety Glossary. Terminology Used in Nuclear Safety and Radiation Protection*, Vienna: IAEA, 2016, p. 150.
546. Recital 20 of Council Directive 2011/70/Euratom.

fuel.[547] Consequently, the obligation to notify the Commission under Article 37 of the Euratom Treaty is exercised as being applicable to any planned disposal or accidental release of radioactive substances.

Second, Article 37 of the Euratom Treaty requires Member States to notify disposal plans to the Commission. Disposal is defined as one of the aspects of radioactive waste management, in addition to handling, pretreatment, treatment, conditioning and storage.[548] The question of whether the obligation to notify is exercised as applicable only to disposal or whether it requires notification of broader waste management plans, specifically storage plans, should be discussed. Disposal is defined as the emplacement of spent fuel or radioactive waste in a facility without the intention of retrieval.[549] Storage is defined as the holding of spent fuel or of radioactive waste in a facility with the intention of retrieval.[550] The intention of retrieval is, therefore, the key point of differentiation between storage and disposal.[551] It is sometimes considered that the concepts of interim storage and disposal should not be considered as mutually exclusive, but as being consecutive steps in a chain of management steps towards the final stage, i.e., final disposal.[552] The Euratom Community is clear, however, that storage cannot become de facto disposal: storage of radioactive waste, including long-term storage, is an interim solution as opposed to an alternative to disposal.[553] Consequently, disposal and storage are defined in binding secondary legislation as separate concepts, reflecting different stages in the radioactive waste management cycle. Analysis of the Commission's recommendations shows that the Commission exercises its competences under Article 37 of the Euratom Treaty by specifying the types of operations that may result in the disposal of radioactive waste within the meaning of Article 37 and the information that is to be supplied as the general data for these different types of operations.[554] The Commission stipulates that the disposal of radioactive waste within the meaning of Article 37 covers any planned or accidental release of radioactive substances associated with, *inter alia*, the operation of nuclear reactors, the reprocessing of irradiated nuclear fuel, the mining and enrichment of uranium, the fabrication of nuclear fuel, the storage of irradiated nuclear fuel, the handling and processing of artificial radioactive substances on an industrial scale, the dismantling of nuclear reactors, mixed-oxide fuel fabrication plants and

547. Paragraph 1 of Commission Recommendation 2010/635/Euratom.
548. Under Article 3(8) of Council Directive 2011/70/Euratom, radioactive waste management means all activities that relate to handling, pretreatment, treatment, conditioning, storage, or disposal of radioactive waste, excluding off-site transportation.
549. Article 2(3) of Council Directive 2011/70/Euratom.
550. Article 2(14) of Council Directive 2011/70/Euratom.
551. Article 5(1)(c) of Council Directive 2011/70/Euratom does not, however, differentiate between storage and disposal in terms of licence requirements, since a licence is needed for all radioactive waste management activities.
552. U. Blohm-Hieber, 'The Radioactive Waste Directive: A Necessary Step in the Management of Spent Fuel and Radioactive Waste in the European Union', (2011) 88 *Nuclear Law Bulletin*, p. 34.
553. Recital 21 of Council Directive 2011/70/Euratom.
554. Recital 6 of Commission Recommendation 2010/635/Euratom.

reprocessing plants and the predisposal management, i.e. including storage, of radioactive waste arising from these operations.[555] Consequently, the Euratom Community exercises its competences under Article 37 of the Euratom Treaty by broadening the concept of disposal plan to covering all the main activities in the nuclear fuel cycle, including storage of radioactive waste and spent nuclear fuel.[556]

Third, under Article 37 of the Euratom Treaty, general data must be submitted to the Commission. The Commission exercises its competences in this field by defining the content of the concept of general data.[557] The Member States are required, *inter alia*, to submit information on the technical aspects of installations, such as annual discharges foreseen; origins of the radioactive effluents, their composition and physicochemical forms; and management of these effluents, methods and paths of release.[558] The level of specificity and technicality of these requirements indicates that the Euratom Community exercises its competences in the field in a manner that makes it clear that the specific and technical aspects of disposal plans qualify as general data under Article 37 of Euratom Treaty.

In conclusion, the Euratom Community exercises its competences under Article 37 of the Euratom Treaty broadly: the Commission's competence to receive notifications covers any planned or accidental release of radioactive substances, throughout the nuclear fuel cycle, and includes both general data and information on specific technical aspects.

3.03 THE CJEU'S INTERPRETATION OF THE COMPETENCES

This section assesses the extent to which the CJEU's case-law defines and elaborates on the Euratom Community's competence in the field of health and safety.

Quantitative analysis of the CJEU's case-law in relation to health and safety shows that it has been active in defining and delimiting the Euratom Community's competences under Chapter 3 of the Euratom Treaty.[559]

555. Paragraph 1 of Commission Recommendation 2010/635/Euratom.
556. A survey of the Commission's opinions shows that different types of nuclear facilities have been notified under Article 37 of the Euratom Treaty. Examples include: New build: DE – Brunsbüttel LasmA radioactive waste storage facility, OJ C 199, 04.06.2016, p. 1; SE – European Spallation Source, OJ C 72, 28.02.2015, p. 1; FR – Marcoule DIADEM interim storage facility, OJ C 381, 28.10.2014, p. 1; UK – Sellafield LSTP sludge treatment plant, OJ C 209, 25.6.2015, p. 1; Dismantling: DE – Brunsbüttel KKB nuclear power plant, OJ C 199, 04.06.2016, p. 3; FR – La Hague UP2-400 reprocessing plant (dismantling), OJ C 405, 05.12.2015, p. 1; Decommissioning: SK – Bohunice A-1 nuclear power plant (decommissioning stages III & IV), OJ C 362, 31.10.2015, p. 1; UK – Sellafield MOX fabrication plant (modification/decommissioning), OJ C 420, 22.11.2014, p. 1; SE – Studsvik R2 and R02 research reactors (decommissioning), OJ C 54, 23.02.2013, p. 1.
557. Paragraph 2 of Commission Recommendation 2010/635/Euratom.
558. Points 3.2 and 4.2 in Annexes I to IV of Commission Recommendation 2010/635/Euratom.
559. The CJEU had defined and delimited the Euratom Community's competences in respect of health and safety under Chapter 3 of the Euratom Treaty in nine cases. Some authors are of the opinion that over the past few decades, the CJEU has not had to deal much with substantive Euratom law, and that most of the cases that have been heard have been similar and rather unspectacular actions initiated by the Commission for a declaration to the effect that a Member State has failed to fulfil its obligations under certain Euratom directives. *See* S. Wolf, 'Euratom,

In defining the Euratom Community's competences, the Court has repeatedly interpreted the scope and purpose of Chapter 3 of the Euratom Treaty and has established in several cases that the provisions of Chapter 3 of the Euratom Treaty are to be interpreted broadly in order to give them practical effect.[560] These provisions form a coherent whole that confers on the Commission powers of considerable scope.[561] The CJEU has confirmed that the legal structure of Chapter 3 of the Euratom Treaty on Health and Safety is not limited to setting out basic standards, but also comprises an important section as regards compliance with those standards and monitoring of radioactivity,[562] and that basic standards must be governed, *inter alia*, by the principle of optimisation of protection.[563]

The Court has defined the scope of Articles 30 and 31 of the Euratom Treaty as being intended to ensure the consistent and effective protection of the health of the general public against the dangers arising from ionising radiation, whatever their source and whatever the categories of persons exposed to such radiation,[564] and has accordingly expanded the Euratom Community's competences in respect of health and safety to cover all types of ionising radiation. Consequently, the Court has interpreted the scope and purpose of Chapter 3 of the Euratom Treaty systematically to ensure that the Euratom Community has the broad competences it needs to establish all the necessary basic safety standards and to ensure that they are applied in order to protect the health of workers and of the general public.[565]

The CJEU has also addressed the issue of whether the basic standards established under the Euratom Treaty have harmonising power in the Euratom Community, i.e., whether Member States are entitled to adopt more stringent requirements in respect of radiation protection than those established by the Euratom Community. In one case the CJEU ruled that the uniformity of safety rules in the field of health and safety does not

---

the European Court of Justice and the Limits of Nuclear Integration in Europe', (2011) 12/8 *German Law Journal*, p. 1639. Other authors consider that the consequences of, e.g., the case of *ČEZ*, are far-reaching because the Court has strengthened the position of the European Atomic Energy Community (EAEC) in respect of nuclear safety. *See* W.-G. Schärf, 'The Temelín-Judgement of the European Court of Justice', (2010) 85 *Nuclear Law Bulletin*, p. 79.

560. Judgment of 12 February 2015, *Parliament v Council*, C-48/14, ECLI:EU:C:2015:91, paragraph 35; judgment of 10 December 2002, *Commission v Council*, C-29/99, ECLI:EU:C:2002:734, paragraph 78; judgment of 27 October 2009, *ČEZ*, C-115/08, ECLI:EU:C:2009:660, paragraph 100.
561. Judgment of 10 December 2002, *Commission v Council*, C-29/99, ECLI:EU:C:2002:734, paragraph 79; judgment of 22 September 1988, *Land de Sarre v Ministre de l'Industrie*, C-187/87, ECLI:EU:C:1988:439, paragraph 11; judgment of 27 October 2009, *ČEZ*, C-115/08, ECLI:EU:C:2009:660, paragraphs 119 and 124.
562. Judgment of 27 October 2009, *ČEZ*, C-115/08, ECLI:EU:C:2009:660, paragraph 117. The interesting aspect of this case was that neither the Land Oberosterreich and the Landesgericht Linz nor Advocate General Maduro realised that Euratom Community law was decisive. For further discussion of this issue, *see* S. Wolf, 'Euratom, the European Court of Justice and the Limits of Nuclear Integration in Europe', (2011) 12/8 *German Law Journal*, p. 1644.
563. Judgment of 27 October 2009, *ČEZ*, C-115/08, ECLI:EU:C:2009:660, paragraph 115; judgment of 25 November 1992, *Commission v Belgium*, C-376/90, ECLI:EU:C:1992:457, paragraph 27.
564. Judgment of 4 October 1991, *Parliament v Council*, C-70/88, ECLI:EU:C:1991:373, paragraphs 13 and 14; judgment of 27 October 2009, *ČEZ*, C-115/08, ECLI:EU:C:2009:660, paragraph 112.
565. Article 2(b) of the Euratom Treaty.

mean that more stringent protection is not permissible.[566] In this case the Court interpreted the harmonisation of basic standards in the Euratom Community in the light of the principle of optimisation of radiation protection[567] by stating that if the Euratom Community legislature had intended to prohibit the introduction by the Member States of a higher level of protection than that provided for in the Euratom Community's secondary legal act (in this case Directive 80/836/Euratom), it would have included an express provision to that effect in this directive.[568] This implies that the Euratom Community has a competence to regulate the level of harmonisation in secondary legislation. In another judgment the CJEU dismissed the possibility of more stringent measures being imposed in relation to a nuclear installation that had already been authorised and which was located in another Member State.[569] It may appear that in the second of these cases the CJEU reached completely the opposite conclusion to the conclusion it reached in the first. However, the Court's reasoning in the second case was based on the fact that the nuclear installation was already licensed in the other Member State and fulfilled the legislative requirements applicable to it. It seems reasonable to conclude that uniformity of safety standards is assured through the imposition of minimum basic standards rather than through harmonised (i.e., same level) basic standards. Concerning the issue of harmonisation, the Court also ruled that the regulation of radioactivity in feed and food within the Community is harmonised to avoid the need for unilateral national measures relating to contaminated feed and food.[570] However, in another case that concerned radioactivity levels in feed and food imported into the Community from third countries, the Court ruled that Article 30 of the Euratom Treaty regulates health and safety in the nuclear sector, not the trade between the EU and third countries. Here the Court prioritised the EU's common commercial policy above the health and safety objectives under the Euratom Treaty.[571]

The Court has confirmed the Euratom Community's competences in relation to emergency preparedness and response by ruling that Articles 30 and 32 of the Euratom Treaty confer on the Euratom Community competence to lay down basic standards for emergency measures.[572] This may be regarded as an example of the Court's willingness to define the Euratom Community's competences in specific fields of regulation.

The safety of nuclear installations was for many years considered to be an inherent national competence of the Member States.[573] The CJEU case that brought the

566. Judgment of 25 November 1992, *Commission v Belgium*, C-376/90, ECLI:EU:C:1992:457, paragraph 19.
567. For further information on the optimisation principle in relation to radiation protection *see* Chapter 3 Section 02.A.1 of this study.
568. Judgment of 25 November 1992, *Commission v Belgium*, C-376/90, ECLI:EU:C:1992:457, paragraph 27.
569. Judgment of 27 October 2009, *ČEZ*, C-115/08, ECLI:EU:C:2009:660, paragraphs 135 and 141.
570. Judgment of 4 October 1991, *Parliament v Council*, C-70/88, ECLI:EU:C:1991:373, paragraph 17.
571. Judgment of 29 March 1990, *Greece v Council*, C-62/88, ECLI:EU:C:1990:153, paragraphs 17 and 18.
572. Judgment of 10 December 2002, *Commission v Council*, C-29/99, ECLI:EU:C:2002:734, paragraph 97.
573. I. Cenevska, *The European Atomic Energy Community in the European Union Context: The 'Outsider' Within*, Leiden: Brill Nijhoff, 2016, p. 54.

biggest breakthrough in terms of the Euratom Community's competences in the field of health and safety was one in which the Court identified the Euratom Community's competences in the field of nuclear safety.[574] The Court took the view that whether the Euratom Treaty contains competences in relation to nuclear safety or not depends on the interpretation of the provisions of Chapter 3 of the Euratom Treaty. It went on to say that such interpretation must be carried out in the light of the objective set out in the preamble to the Euratom Treaty of creating safety conditions necessary to eliminate hazards to the life and health of the public.[575] The CJEU stated that the protection of the health of workers and of the general public from dangers arising from ionising radiation cannot be achieved without controlling the sources of harmful radiation.[576] The Court concluded, therefore, that it is not appropriate, in order to define the Community's competences, to draw an artificial distinction between the protection of the health of the general public and the safety of sources of ionising radiation.[577] The Court also ruled that the Euratom Community's competences under Articles 30 and 32 of the Euratom Treaty include legislative competence to establish, for the purpose of health protection, an authorisation system for nuclear installations which must be applied by the Member States. The CJEU has, however, clearly specified that a competence to establish an authorisation system does not grant the Euratom Community competence to authorise the construction or operation of nuclear installations.[578]

The Court engaged in a detailed examination of all the provisions of the Convention mentioned in the Commission's submissions,[579] and interpreted Article 33 of the Euratom Treaty as providing that the Euratom Community possesses certain competences as to the siting, design, construction and operation of nuclear installations.[580] Consequently, the Court broadened the Euratom Community's regulatory competences so that they extended to the technological aspects of nuclear safety, and justified this approach by reference to the lack of a clear dividing line between nuclear safety in purely technological terms and general nuclear safety.[581] The CJEU's judgment did not, however, alter the role of the national safety authorities as the pre-eminent authorities in the oversight of safety regimes at the nuclear installations. The Court recognised that the technical competence of the national safety authorities

574. Judgment of 10 December 2002, *Commission v Council*, C-29/99, ECLI:EU:C:2002:734.
575. Judgment of 10 December 2002, *Commission v Council*, C-29/99, ECLI:EU:C:2002:734, paragraphs 74 and 75.
576. Judgment of 10 December 2002, *Commission v Council*, C-29/99, ECLI:EU:C:2002:734, paragraph 76.
577. Judgment of 10 December 2002, *Commission v Council*, C-29/99, ECLI:EU:C:2002:734, paragraph 82; judgment of 27 October 2009, *ČEZ*, C-115/08, ECLI:EU:C:2009:660, paragraph 102.
578. Judgment of 10 December 2002, *Commission v Council*, C-29/99, ECLI:EU:C:2002:734, paragraph 89; judgment of 27 October 2009, *ČEZ*, C-115/08, ECLI:EU:C:2009:660, paragraph 103.
579. *See* P. Koutrakos, 'Case C-29/99 Commission v Council (re: Nuclear Safety Convention)', (2004) 41 *Common Market Law Review*, p. 197.
580. Judgment of 10 December 2002, *Commission v Council*, C-29/99, ECLI:EU:C:2002:734, paragraphs 103 and 105.
581. P. Koutrakos, 'Case C-29/99 Commission v Council (re: Nuclear Safety Convention)', (2004) 41 *Common Market Law Review*, p. 205.

did not prevent the Euratom Community from introducing legislation concerning the safety of nuclear installations.[582]

The Euratom Community's competences under Article 34 of the Euratom Treaty have not been substantially analysed by the Court, but the Order of the President concerning a request for provisional measures ruled on certain issues relevant to the Euratom Community's competences. The President of the Court stated that the Commission has the right to take a decision on whether Article 34 should be applied or not,[583] and that the Commission's competence and obligation under this article is to assess the effects that nuclear tests can cause on all members of the general public and workers, within the context of the general objective of protecting the health of workers and the general public as a whole. The Commission, therefore, cannot be required to take into consideration the particular situation of each individual resident and worker within the geographical area affected by a particular experiment unless there are specific grounds for taking such considerations into account in the light of the objectives envisaged.[584]

Concerning the obligation imposed on Member States under Article 37 of the Euratom Treaty to notify the Commission on disposal plans, the Court has assessed whether the notification to the Commission should be submitted before authorisation of the disposal plan or before the disposal is effected.[585] The CJEU emphasised the importance of the Commission's guidance under Article 37 of the Euratom Treaty[586] and took the view that it must be possible for the Commission's opinion concerning the disposal plan to be examined and taken into account. The Court concluded that the Commission's opinion must, therefore, be sought before the authorisation.[587] Furthermore, the Court elaborated that Member States' partial or late communication with the Commission contradicts the purpose of the provisions of Article 37.[588] In another case the CJEU took the view that the wording of Article 37 implies that the Euratom Community has competences in relation to the siting of nuclear installations.[589]

582. P. M. Barnes, 'Nuclear Safety for Nuclear Electricity – The Search for a Solid Legal Basis for Nuclear Safety in an Enlarged European Union', (2003) 45 *Managerial Law*, p. 131.
583. Order of the President of the Court of First Instance of 22 December 1995, *Marie-Thérèse Danielsson, Pierre Largenteau and Edwin Haoa v Commission of the European Communities*, T-219/95, ECLI:EU:T:1995:219, paragraph 64.
584. Order of the President of the Court of First Instance of 22 December 1995, *Marie-Thérèse Danielsson, Pierre Largenteau and Edwin Haoa v Commission of the European Communities*, T-219/95, ECLI:EU:T:1995:219, paragraph 74.
585. Judgment of 22 September 1988, *Land de Sarre v Ministrie de l'Industrie*, C-187/87, ECLI:EU:C:1988:439, paragraph 6.
586. Judgment of 22 September 1988, *Land de Sarre v Ministre de l'Industrie*, C-187/87, ECLI:EU:C:1988:439, paragraph 13.
587. Judgment of 22 September 1988, *Land de Sarre v Ministre de l'Industrie*, C-187/77, ECLI:EU:C:1988:439, paragraphs 14 and 18–20; judgment of 27 October 2009, *ČEZ*, C-115/08, ECLI:EU:C:2009:660, paragraph 104.
588. Judgment of 12 April 2005, *Commission v United Kingdom*, C-61/03, ECLI:EU:C:2005:210, paragraphs 39 and 40; judgment of 27 October 2009, *ČEZ*, C-115/08, ECLI:EU:C:2009:660, paragraph 104.
589. Judgment of 10 December 2002, *Commission v Council*, C-29/99, ECLI:EU:C:2002:734, paragraph 103.

This chapter has analysed the Euratom Community's competences in relation to environmental protection.[590] Systematic analysis of the relevant case-law shows that the CJEU has not analysed the explicit question of whether protection of the environment falls under the competence of the Euratom Treaty. In the majority of its judgments concerning health and safety, especially radiation protection, the Court has used the term environmental protection in the context of the protection of workers and the general public.[591] Some researchers have concluded that references to the protection of the environment in the Court's case-law indicates that it has endorsed an environmental approach to radiation protection, treating the concepts of 'radiation protection' and 'environmental protection' as inextricably linked and giving a green light to the practice of extrapolating the Euratom health and safety provisions to the field of environmental protection.[592] However, defining the Euratom Community's competences should be based on the Court's legal reasoning on the issue, which in this case is scarce. Furthermore, it has already been established that existing secondary legislation in the field of health and safety excludes the protection of the environment from its scope. Consequently, while the fact that the CJEU mentioned the protection of the environment could be interpreted as indicating an overarching environmental approach,[593] the ultimate conclusion on the basis of the analysis set out above must be that it remains unclear whether the Euratom Community has competences in the field of environmental protection under the Euratom Treaty.

In conclusion, systematic analysis of the available case-law leads one to conclude that the CJEU has been active in defining and delimiting the Euratom Community's competences in the field of health and safety under Chapter 3 of the Euratom Treaty. Through its interpretative approach to the purpose and objectives of the health and safety chapter of the Euratom Treaty, the Court has concluded that the Euratom Community has broad competences to establish the necessary basic safety standards and to ensure that they are applied. It has also clarified that the Euratom Community has the competence to regulate the level of harmonisation in its secondary legislation. The CJEU has confirmed the Euratom Community's competences in the field of emergency preparedness and response and established the Euratom Community's competences in the field of nuclear safety. The latter have resulted in secondary legal acts exercising the Euratom Community's competences in respect of nuclear safety and the safe management of radioactive waste and spent fuel, as well as broader and more

590. For further information regarding environmental protection, *see* Chapter 3 Section 01 and Section 02.A of this study.
591. Judgment of 27 October 2009, *ČEZ*, C-115/08, ECLI:EU:C:2009:660, paragraph 83; judgment of 12 February 2015, *Parliament v Council*, C-48/14, ECLI:EU:C:2015:91, paragraph 37; judgment of 22 September 1988, *Land de Sarre v Ministre de l'Industrie*, C-187/87, ECLI:EU:C:1988:439, paragraph 11; judgment of 12 April 2005, *Commission v United Kingdom*, C-61/03, ECLI: EU:C:2005:210, paragraph 44; judgment of 10 December 2002, *Commission v Council*, C-29/99, ECLI:EU:C:2002:734, paragraph 79; judgment of 12 April 2005, *Commission v United Kingdom*, C-65/04, ECLI:EU:C:2006:161, paragraph 28.
592. I. Cenevska, *The European Atomic Energy Community in the European Union Context: The 'Outsider' Within*, Leiden: Brill Nijhoff, 2016, p. 125.
593. I. Cenevska, 'Protection of the Health of Workers and the General Public under the Euratom Treaty and the EU Environmental Policy – The Ratio Between Human Health Protection and Environmental Protection', (2012) 21 *European Energy and Environmental Law Review*, p. 185.

detailed regulation of measures for emergency preparedness and response at Euratom Community level.[594] Concerning Article 37 of the Euratom Treaty, the Court has clarified that Member States need to seek the Commission's opinion before authorising disposal plans, and has also specified that partial or late communication to the Commission by Member States constitutes a breach of Article 37. The Euratom Community's competences to protect the environment are, however, still unclear: protection of the environment is excluded from the existing secondary legislation, but has been repeatedly mentioned by the Court, which has not, however, analysed the issue in substance.

3.04 FEATURES OF THE COMPETENCES

This section assesses the following features with a view to ensuring a basis for comparative analysis: the level of detail of the provisions of the Euratom Treaty; the exercise of the competences as compared with the bare wording of the Euratom Treaty; and the existence of case-law and the effect of the Court's interpretation of the relevant provisions of primary and secondary legislations to the competences of the Euratom Community.

The level of detail of the provisions of the Euratom Treaty, that lay down the Euratom Community's competences in the field of health and safety, is relatively low in relation to the task of protecting the health of workers and the general public against the dangers arising from ionising radiation. The Euratom Community's competences under the health and safety chapter of the Euratom Treaty structurally cover two main issues: establishing and updating basic safety standards by reference to the available scientific knowledge; and ensuring compliance with those standards. Radiation protection is an overarching field of regulation that covers nuclear safety, the safe management of radioactive waste and spent nuclear fuel and emergency preparedness and response. Consequently, it may be concluded that the objectives that the Euratom Community's competences are designed to achieve in relation to health and safety would be better met if the Euratom Treaty included provisions on basic safety standards in respect of nuclear safety, safe management of radioactive waste and spent nuclear fuel and emergency preparedness and response.

The exercise of the Euratom Community's competences in relation to health and safety is significantly wider than the wording of the Euratom Treaty would tend to indicate. Articles 31 and 32 of the Euratom Treaty are the legal bases of the Euratom Community's broad competences. Exercise of these competences extends to four different regulatory areas: radiation protection; nuclear safety; safe radioactive waste management; and emergency preparedness and response. The exercise of the Euratom Community's competences under Article 37 of the Euratom Treaty has resulted in the

594. For further discussion of this issue, *see* P. Koutrakos, 'Case C-29/99 Commission v Council (re: Nuclear Safety Convention)', (2004) 41 *Common Market Law Review*, pp. 207-208.

Commission issuing 180 opinions and in practices that are indicative of the Commission's broad discretion concerning the content of notifications to be submitted by the Member States.

The CJEU has interpreted the provisions of the Euratom Treaty in relation to health and safety in nine cases and its rulings show that the Euratom Community has broad competences to fulfil the objectives of Chapter 3 of the Euratom Treaty and flexibility to regulate the level of harmonisation in its secondary legislation. The CJEU has also confirmed the Euratom Community's competences in relation to emergency preparedness and response and defined the Euratom Community's competences regarding nuclear safety. The latter had a great effect on the secondary legislation as it led to the adoption of directives on nuclear safety, the safe management of radioactive waste and spent fuel and more detailed regulation of emergency preparedness and response.

CHAPTER 4
Investments

- *The scope of the Euratom Community's competences in the field of investments is stimulating investment actions by persons and undertakings and facilitating coordinated development of their investments in the nuclear field. The Euratom Community's competences in this area cover both the front end and back end of the nuclear fuel cycle.*
- *The Euratom Community's competences in relation to investments are exercised in accordance with the wording of provisions of Chapter 4 of the Euratom Treaty. However, the Commission does not fully exercise its competences under Article 40 of the Euratom Treaty as it does not provide nuclear energy production targets in its Nuclear Illustrative Programme.*
- *The CJEU's case-law in relation to investments under the Euratom Treaty is limited. In one case the Court analysed the Euratom Community's competences and established that the Commission's competences under Article 41 of the Euratom Treaty do not extend to adopting legislation that establishes procedures for assessing investment projects.*
- *The features of the Euratom Community's competences in relation to investments are as follows: the Euratom Treaty contains an appropriate level of detail to allow for the fulfilment of its task of facilitating and coordinating investment in the nuclear field; competences are exercised more narrowly under Article 40 of the Euratom Treaty than the wording of the Treaty would imply; the case-law is limited and the CJEU has concluded that the Commission does not have a competence to adopt regulations establishing procedures for the examination of investment projects.*

4.01 THE SCOPE AND CONTENT OF THE COMPETENCES

This part of the study analyses the scope and content of the Euratom Community's competences in relation to investments under the Euratom Treaty.

Investments are essential in order to achieve development in the nuclear field.[595] The Euratom Treaty confers competences on the Euratom Community as an incentive to encourage and coordinate national stakeholders' investments in the nuclear field from a Community perspective.[596] One of the Euratom Community's main tasks in respect of investments is to stimulate actions by persons and undertakings and to facilitate coordinated development of their investments in the nuclear field. In other words, the Euratom Community has a competence to facilitate nuclear investment.[597]

To ensure that this occurs, the Euratom Treaty bestows a competence upon the Commission to periodically publish nuclear illustrative programmes that show the nuclear energy production targets and the types of investments required to meet them.[598] Furthermore, the Commission has a competence to require persons and undertakings engaged in certain nuclear activities to communicate to the Commission their investment projects.[599] Systematic analysis of the activities that must be communicated to the Commission[600] indicates that most of them relate to the front end of the nuclear fuel cycle,[601] except for the facilities for the industrial processing of radioactive waste.[602] The fact that persons and undertakings have an obligation to communicate information concerning investments in the processing of radioactive waste under the investments chapter of the Euratom Treaty implies that the Euratom Community's competences in the field of investments are not limited to investment in the expanding nuclear sector, but also extend to investment projects that entail taking care of the back end of the nuclear fuel cycle. The wording of Chapter 4 of the Euratom Treaty also implies that not all investment projects are to be communicated, but only those of a certain type and size. The criteria governing this issue are to be determined by the Council on a proposal from the Commission in the secondary legislation.[603] The

595. The rationale behind Chapter 4 of the Euratom Treaty has been explained as follows: 'it would, in effect, have made poor economic sense for each of the original Member States to try to establish, nationally, a complete fuel cycle. The thrust of Chapter 4 is to encourage each Member State to look at what its neighbours are doing or planning to do before deciding on investment, for example, in its own isotope/separation or fuel-fabrication project'. *See* T. F. Cusack, 'A Tale of Two Treaties', (2003) 40 *Common Market Law Review*, p. 120.
596. Communication from the Commission to the Council and the European Parliament, '50 Years of the Euratom Treaty', Brussels, 20.3.2007, pp. 3–4.
597. Article 2(c) of the Euratom Treaty.
598. Article 40 of the Euratom Treaty.
599. Article 41 of the Euratom Treaty.
600. For example, mining of uranium and thorium ore, preparation of nuclear fuels, fabrication of nuclear fuel elements, production of enriched uranium, nuclear reactors of all types and for all purposes. Complete list is in Annex II of the Euratom Treaty.
601. For the definition of the nuclear fuel cycle, *see* International Atomic Energy Agency, *IAEA Safety Glossary. Terminology Used in Nuclear Safety and Radiation Protection*, Vienna: IAEA, 2016, p. 114.
602. Annex II point 13 of the Euratom Treaty.
603. Analysis of this legislation is carried out in Chapter 4 Section 02 of this study, which deals with the exercise of the Euratom Community's competences in relation to investment.

wording of Chapter 4 of the Euratom Treaty also implies that the Commission has an obligation to discuss with individuals or undertakings all aspects of investment projects that relate to the objectives of the Euratom Treaty.[604] Consequently, the Commission has broad competences in this area as they refer to the objectives of the Euratom Treaty.

Analysis of the provisions of Chapter 4 reveals that the Euratom Community's competences in respect of investments under the Euratom Treaty focus on the interaction and communication between the Commission and persons and undertakings in the Member States. It is sometimes thought that the Commission may require both private firms and governments to file notice of investment programmes in the field of nuclear energy.[605] However, the provisions of Chapter 4 of the Euratom Treaty clearly state that persons and undertakings (i.e., not Member States) communicate their investment projects directly to the Commission and the Commission discusses these investment projects with those individuals or undertakings directly. The Member States concerned receive the notifications sent to the Commission and the Commission's views on those projects for information purposes.[606] The Commission needs, however, the consent of the Member State concerned, in addition to person and undertaking concerned, when it wants to publish information on the investment project communicated to it.[607] Systematic analysis of the provisions in Article 2 and Chapter 4 of the Euratom Treaty leads one to the conclusion that the competences under the Euratom Treaty that relate to investments do not merely concern the communication of investment information,[608] but have the broader objective of encouraging, coordinating and facilitating national stakeholders' investments in the nuclear field.

A State Aid Aspects

This section assesses whether the Euratom Community's competences in relation to investments have features that promote state aid in respect of nuclear investment projects.[609]

As noted above, the Euratom Community's competences include facilitating investment to ensure the establishment of the installations needed to develop nuclear

604. Article 43 of the Euratom Treaty. Some authors regard Chapter 4 of the Euratom Treaty as constituting the Euratom Community's advice on investments. *See* M. Gaudet, *Euratom*, London: Pergamon Press 1959, p. 166.
605. A. Nanes, 'The Evolution of Euratom', (1957/58) 13/1 *International Journal*, p. 15.
606. Articles 41(1), 42(1) and 43 of the Euratom Treaty.
607. Article 44 of the Euratom Treaty.
608. *See* A. Södersten *Euratom at the Crossroads*, Cheltenham, Northampton: Edward Elgar Publishing Limited, 2018, p. 102; J. G. Polach, *Euratom: Its Background, Issues and Economic Implications*, Dobbs Ferry, NY: Oceana Publications Inc., 1964, p. 132.
609. For broader analysis of competition law and the Euratom Treaty, *see* R. Ptasekaite, 'Competition Law and Nuclear Regulation: European Perspective', in B. Delvaux, M. Hunt and K. Talus (eds), *EU Energy Law and Policy Issues*, Volume 4, Cambridge - Antwerp - Portland: Intersentia, 2014, pp. 93–108.

energy.[610] Although the extent to which competition law applies to the nuclear sector is sometimes disputed,[611] it is generally agreed that the provisions of the Euratom Treaty, especially Chapter 4 of the Euratom Treaty, do not include a prohibition on subsidies or any other provisions dealing with the prevention or regulation of state aid.[612] The above analysis of the scope and content of the Euratom Community's competences in relation to investment could also imply that, in some circumstances, subsidies from the Member States may be encouraged, especially when they contribute to the Euratom Community's tasks under Article 2(c) of the Euratom Treaty.

The Commission's position is, however, that the fact that nuclear investments fall within the scope of the Euratom Treaty does not exclude them from the ambit of state aid regulation. In fact, whilst Article 2(c) of the Euratom Treaty obliges the Euratom Community to facilitate investments in the field of nuclear energy and Article 40 of the Euratom Treaty obliges it to publish illustrative programmes in order to facilitate the development of nuclear investments, the Euratom Treaty does not provide for any specific rules to govern the financing, by a Member State, of such investments. No state aid control rules are provided for in the Euratom Treaty and the state aid control carried out by the Commission does not impede fulfilment of the objective of promotion of new nuclear investments enshrined in the Euratom Treaty.[613]

However, the Commission takes the view that the provisions of the Euratom Treaty were expressly confirmed by the Treaty of Lisbon. The preamble of the Euratom Treaty recognises that the conditions necessary for the development of a powerful nuclear industry should be created. The Commission accordingly considers that the promotion of nuclear energy is a key objective of the Euratom Treaty and therefore of the EU at large. The Commission highlights that as set out in the preamble of the Euratom Treaty, the Commission is an institution of the Euratom Community and is obliged to 'create the conditions necessary for the development of a powerful nuclear industry which will provide extensive energy resources'. This obligation should be

---

610. Article 2(c) of the Euratom Treaty.
611. M. Sousa Ferro, 'Competition Law and the Nuclear Sector: An EU Outlook', (2010) 86 *Nuclear Law Bulletin*, p. 14. However, Södersten argues that there can hardly be any incompatibility between state aid control and the investment regulation under the Euratom Treaty, as the investment provisions are 'merely about communication of investment information'. *See* A. Södersten, *Euratom at the Crossroads*, Cheltenham, Northampton: Edward Elgar Publishing Limited, 2018, p. 132.
612. L. Garzaniti, 'Competition Law in the Nuclear Sector', in INLA/AIDN (ed.), *Nuclear Inter Jura 2007: Proceedings – Actes du Congrès, 1–4 Octobre 2007*, Bruxelles: Emilie Bruylant, 2008, p. 1251; A. Bouquet, 'Which Competition Rules for Nuclear Energy in a (Progressively) Liberalised European Market Environment?', in INLA/AIDN (ed.), *Nuclear Inter Jura 2007: Proceedings – Actes du Congrès, 1–4 Octobre 2007*, Bruxelles: Emilie Bruylant, 2008, p. 1201; Report by Working Group III on Legal Certainty in International Nuclear Trade, in Lamm V. (ed.), *Nuclear Inter Jura 2001: Proceedings of the 15th Nuclear Inter Jura Congress 'Nuclear Law under the Sign of Safety and Confidence'*, Budapest: Archaeolingua, 2002, p. 298; R. J. Heffron, *Deconstructing Energy Law and Policy: The Case of Nuclear Energy*, Edinburgh: Edinburgh University Press, 2015, p. 48.
613. Commission Decision (EU) 2017/2112 of 6 March 2017 on the measure/aid scheme/State aid SA.38454 – 2015/C (ex 2015/N) which Hungary is planning to implement for supporting the development of two new nuclear reactors at Paks II nuclear power station, C 2017/1486, OJ L 317, 1.12.2017, pp. 45–118, paragraphs 276–278.

taken into account when the Commission is exercising its discretion to authorise state aid in accordance with the TFEU.[614] This essentially means that the Commission's competences under Chapter 4 of the Euratom Treaty in relation to investments cannot be undermined by its competences in relation to state aid control under the TFEU.[615] In practice the Commission did not decline to approve any of the state subsidies that were needed in the nuclear sector: some were authorised as state aid subject to certain conditions,[616] while others were either not considered to be state aid[617] or no objections to them were raised by the Commission.[618]

In conclusion, even though it is sometimes considered that the Euratom Community's competences in relation to investments are limited to the collection and analysis of information,[619] the analysis of the scope and content of its competences in this area under the Euratom Treaty shows that the scope of the Euratom Community's competences extend to stimulating actions by persons and undertakings and facilitating coordinated development of their investments in the nuclear field, covering both the front end and back end of the nuclear fuel cycle. The Commission's competences dominate the field: among other things, it publishes nuclear illustrative programmes and communicates with persons and undertakings concerning their investment projects in the nuclear field. The Commission's competences in the field of investments

614. *See* Commission Decision 2005/407/EC of 22 September 2004 on the State aid which the United Kingdom is planning to implement for British Energy plc, OJ L 142, 6.6.2005, pp. 26–80; Commission Decision (EU) 2015/658 of 8 October 2014 on the aid measure SA.34947 (2013/C) (ex 2013/N) which the United Kingdom is planning to implement for support to the Hinkley Point C nuclear power station, OJ L 109, 28.4.2015, pp. 44–116; and Commission Decision (EU) 2017/2112 of 6 March 2017 on the measure/aid scheme/State aid SA.38454 - 2015/C (ex 2015/N) which Hungary is planning to implement for supporting the development of two new nuclear reactors at Paks II nuclear power station, C/2017/1486, OJ L 317, 1.12.2017, pp. 45–118.
615. This point has been formulated as follows: 'when a certain subsidy is necessary for the objective of the Euratom Treaty, it will not be prohibited under the EC treaty'. *See* A. Bouquet, 'Which Competition Rules for Nuclear Energy in a (Progressively) Liberalised European Market Environment?', in INLA/AIDN (ed.), *Nuclear Inter Jura 2007: Proceedings – Actes du Congrès, 1–4 Octobre 2007*, Bruxelles: Emilie Bruylant, 2008, p. 1203.
616. State aid was authorised for UK reorganisation of electricity generation and distribution. *See* EU Press Release, Commission authorises aid for nuclear electricity sector, IP/90/267, 3 March 1990; aid in favour of British Energy II was authorised with certain conditions, *see* Case C52/2003; aid for UK Nuclear Decommissioning Authority was authorised with certain conditions, *see* Case C 39/2004. These are only example cases.
617. Not considered to be state aid: German reserves for nuclear power plant, *see* Commission Press Release, Commission decides on reserves for nuclear power plant decommissioning, IP/01/1799, 11 December 2001; Coface guarantee for the building of a Framatome nuclear power plant, *see* State aid C 45/2006 (ex NN 62/A/2006) – Coface guarantee – construction by Framatome AN P of a nuclear power station for Teollisuuden Voima Oy, OJ C 23, of 1 February 2007. These are only example cases.
618. The Commission had no objections: Aid in favour of British Energy I, *see* Case NN 101/2002; Tax exemptions for Ignalina nuclear power plant, *see* Case N 337/2005. These are only example cases.
619. A. Södersten, *Euratom at the Crossroads*, Cheltenham, Northampton: Edward Elgar Publishing Limited, 2018, p. 102; J. G. Polach, *Euratom: Its Background, Issues and Economic Implications*, Dobbs Ferry, NY: Oceana Publications Inc., 1964, p. 85; P. Mathijsen, 'Problems Connected with the Creation of Euratom', (1961) 26/3 *Law and Contemporary Problems*, p. 444.

under Chapter 4 of the Euratom Treaty are not to be undermined by its competences in the field of state aid control under the TFEU[620].

4.02 THE EXERCISE OF THE COMPETENCES

This section assesses the Euratom Community's competences in relation to investments and analyses the instruments through which these competences have been exercised.

Systematic analysis of secondary legal acts based on articles in Chapter 4 of the Euratom Treaty shows that only Articles 40 and 41 of the Euratom Treaty have been used as legal bases for secondary legislation through which the Euratom Community's competences have been exercised. Therefore, the focus in this part of the study is on the competences established in these two articles. Given the scope and objectives of this study, analysis of the exercise of the Euratom Community's competences is limited to the secondary legislation in force.

Article 40 of the Euratom Treaty states that the Commission has a competence and an obligation to periodically publish a nuclear illustrative programme, especially indicating nuclear energy production targets and all the types of investments required for their attainment. The most recent exercise of this competence is the Commission's latest Communication on a Nuclear Illustrative Programme (PINC).[621] The latest PINC provides a basis for discussion of how nuclear energy can help achieve the EU's energy objectives, as the Commission estimates that nuclear energy is expected to remain an important component of the EU's energy mix in the 2050 horizon.[622] The Commission has predicted a decline in nuclear generation capacity at EU level up to 2025 due to certain Member States (such as Germany and France) having decided to phase out nuclear energy or to reduce its share in the national energy mix. The trend is expected to be reversed by 2030 as it is predicted that new reactors will be connected to the grid and that the lifetime of others will be extended. The Commission has also established that significant investments will be needed to support the transformation of the energy systems in line with the Energy Union Strategy.[623] The Commission has noted though that investments in the nuclear sector are a small part of the overall effort to be made in relation to this transformation and must be made within the framework established

620. For political, economic and geo-strategic aspects regarding state aid support in nuclear sector, *see inter alia*: S. Tromans Q.C., 'State Support for Nuclear New Build', (2019) 12 *Journal of World Energy Law and Business*, pp. 36–51.
621. Communication from the Commission on Nuclear Illustrative Programme presented under Article 40 of the Euratom Treaty – Final (after opinion of EESC) COM (2017) 237 final. This is the first Communication from the Commission on Nuclear Illustrative Programme after the Fukushima Daiichi accident in March 2011. The one before this was presented in 2008.
622. Communication from the Commission on Nuclear Illustrative Programme presented under Article 40 of the Euratom Treaty, COM (2017) 237 final, p. 11.
623. Communication from the Commission to the European Parliament, the Council, the European Economic and Social Committee, the Committee of the Regions and the European Investment Bank, A Framework Strategy for a Resilient Energy Union with a Forward-Looking Climate Change Policy, COM (2015) 80 final.

in EU legislation.[624] Significant cost-overruns in plant construction have been common in recent nuclear projects[625] and the Commission has noted that the expected construction time and project discount rate play a significant role in cost components, when discussing investments and business environment for new nuclear plants. The Commission has also indicated that greater attention should be paid to the possibility of cooperation between regulators when licensing new reactors and to encouraging the industry to standardise nuclear reactor designs.[626] In the latest PINC the Commission focused not only on nuclear energy production, but also on nuclear safety and the back end of the nuclear fuel cycle – the PINC includes investments related to post-Fukushima safety upgrades, investments related to the long-term operation of existing nuclear power plants and discusses the need for investments in relation to the management of radioactive waste and spent fuel.[627] The Commission has indicated that it is estimated that more than 50 of the 129 reactors currently operating in the EU will be shut down by 2025, which offers both challenges and opportunities in relation to the spent fuel and nuclear waste management, decommissioning and funding requirements for spent fuel, radioactive waste management and decommissioning.[628] The Commission has also considered the non-power applications of nuclear and radiation technology in the medical sector, industry, agriculture and research, and concluded that there is a need for a more coordinated European approach in these areas.[629]

Consequently, while Article 40 of the Euratom Treaty states that the purpose of the PINC is to stimulate actions by persons and undertakings and facilitate coordinated development of their investment in the nuclear field, the Commission's latest PINC simply surveys the current state of the nuclear sector. The fact that the PINC's content seems to be shifting from nuclear energy market to nuclear safety and the back end of the nuclear fuel cycle indicates that the Commission exercises its competences under Article 40 by taking into account the changing situation of the nuclear energy sector in Europe, which is characterised, *inter alia*, by a high level of decommissioning. However, it should be noted that the content of the latest PINC indicates that the Commission is no longer fulfilling its obligation under Article 40 to include nuclear

624. Communication from the Commission on Nuclear Illustrative Programme presented under Article 40 of the Euratom Treaty, COM (2017) 237 final, pp. 4–5.
625. *See* P. D. Cameron, 'The Revival of Nuclear Power: An Analysis of the Legal Implications', (2007) 19/1 *Journal of Environmental Law*, pp. 1 and 4.
626. Communication from the Commission on Nuclear Illustrative Programme presented under Article 40 of the Euratom Treaty, COM (2017) 237 final, p. 7.
627. Communication from the Commission on Nuclear Illustrative Programme presented under Article 40 of the Euratom Treaty, COM (2017) 237 final, p. 2. For more on the from-end and back end of nuclear fuel cycle in the nuclear illustrative programme, *see*: Commission Staff Working Document Accompanying the Communication from the Commission Nuclear Illustrative Programme Presented under Article 40 of the Euratom Treaty – Final COM (2017) 237 final, SWD (2017) 158 final, pp. 6–11 and 24–40.
628. Communication from the Commission on Nuclear Illustrative Programme presented under Article 40 of the Euratom Treaty, COM (2017) 237 final, pp. 8–10.
629. Communication from the Commission on Nuclear Illustrative Programme presented under Article 40 of the Euratom Treaty, COM (2017) 237 final, p. 10. *See also* the Council Conclusions of 6 June 2019 on non-power nuclear and radiological technologies and applications.

energy production targets in the PINC. It is accordingly clear that the Euratom Community exercises its competences under Article 40 of the Euratom Treaty in a narrower way than the wording in the primary legal act indicates.

As noted in relation to the scope and content of the Euratom Community's competences in respect of investments in Chapter 4 Section 01 of this study, Article 41 establishes a competence of the Euratom Community to require persons and undertakings to notify their investment projects to the Commission and to define the type and size of those investment projects in secondary legislation. Regulation (Euratom) No 2587/1999 exercises the Euratom Community's competences under Article 41 of the Euratom Treaty by defining the investment projects to be communicated to the Commission.[630] It provides that investment projects creating a production capacity, maintaining quantitative and qualitative production capacity, directly increasing production capacity, directly increasing productivity, improving the quality of production and creating facilities for the management of spent fuel or radioactive waste, including treatment, interim or final storage and/or disposal are to be communicated to the Commission.[631] In Regulation (Euratom) No 2587/1999 the size criteria of the investment projects is defined not by reference to the planned capacity of the investment project, but by reference to costs. All expenditures arising directly from carrying out the investment project is to be taken into account, irrespective of the time that they occurred.[632] Investment projects that are smaller than the established cost-threshold criteria can be notified to the Commission on a voluntary basis.[633] In general terms, Regulation (Euratom) No 2587/1999 requires that the notification should include and be limited to the details needed for the discussion under Article 43 of the Euratom Treaty, and should include, in particular, types of products or activities, production or storage capacity, total amount of expenditure, time required to carry out the project and prospects as regards supplies for and operation of the installation.[634]

The Commission has a responsibility to determine the procedure for notification under Article 41 of the Euratom Treaty and Commission Regulation (EC) No 1209/2000 specifies a detailed form and procedure for that.[635] In addition to the annexed form of notification, Regulation (EC) No 1209/2000 reiterates that the obligation to communicate the investment projects devolves on persons and undertakings engaged in nuclear activities that ought to be notified under the Euratom Treaty and establishes that any changes made to the investment project during the course of its implementation is

630. Council Regulation (Euratom) No 2587/1999 of 2 December 1999 defining the investment projects to be communicated to the Commission in accordance with Article 41 of the Treaty establishing the European Atomic Energy Community, OJ L 315, 9.12.1999, pp. 1-3. Council Regulation (Euratom) No 2587/1999 has replaced Regulation No 4 from 1958, which defined the investment projects to be communicated to the Commission in accordance with Article 41 of the Treaty establishing the European Atomic Energy Community (OJ 17, 6.10.1958, p. 417).
631. Article 1 of Council Regulation (Euratom) No 2587/1999.
632. Article 2 of Council Regulation (Euratom) No 2587/1999.
633. Articles 1(1), (3) and 4, and Annex of Council Regulation (Euratom) No 2587/1999.
634. Article 3 of Council Regulation (Euratom) No 2587/1999.
635. Commission Regulation (EC) No 1209/2000 of 8 June 2000 determining procedures for effecting the communications prescribed under Article 41 of the Treaty establishing the European Atomic Energy Community, OJ L 138, 9.6.2000, p. 12.

subject to further notification.[636] Furthermore, it clarifies the interaction between notification of disposal plans in respect of radioactive waste and spent fuel under Article 37 and notification under Article 41 of the Euratom Treaty to avoid unnecessary duplication of information.[637] One difference not clarified by the Commission is that while the obligation to notify the Commission under Article 37 lies with the Member State concerned, notification under Article 41 – as established in the scope of the competences discussed in Chapter 4 Section 01 of this study and reiterated in Regulation (EC) No 1209/2000 – devolves only on persons and undertakings.

During the period between 2008 and 2016, a total of forty-eight projects were notified: nine were for facilities dedicated to front-end activities, twenty for major modifications or upgrades in nuclear power plants related to long-term operations or to post-Fukushima improvements, seven for new commercial or research reactors, and twelve for back-end installations. All of these projects were the subject of non-binding Commission opinions in which comments and/or suggestions for improvements to be taken into account when authorising the projects were made.[638] Consequently, it is hard to agree with those authors who take the view that the investment provisions under the Euratom Treaty are only marginally used.[639] Furthermore, the Commission has been planning a legislative update of the modalities of the implementing framework for Articles 41 to 44 of the Euratom Treaty to provide clarity and legal certainty for investors in the nuclear field as well as transparency and equality of treatment,[640] but on this issue a proposal has not been presented yet.[641]

The above analysis of the secondary legislation leads one to the conclusion that the Euratom Community's competences in relation to investments are generally exercised in accordance with the wording of the provisions of Chapter 4 of the Euratom Treaty. The secondary legal acts that have Article 41 of the Euratom Treaty as a legal basis do not broaden the scope of these provisions. The Commission's exercise of its obligations and competences concerning the PINC under Article 40 does not, however, fully reflect the provisions of the Euratom Treaty, especially concerning the Commission's obligation to indicate nuclear energy production targets. On this issue, it may be considered that the Euratom Community exercises its competences under Article 40 of the Euratom Treaty more narrowly than the wording of Article 40 would tend to indicate.

636. Articles 2 and 4 of Commission Regulation (EC) No 1209/2000.
637. Article 3 of Commission Regulation (EC) No 1209/2000.
638. Communication from the Commission on Nuclear Illustrative Programme presented under Article 40 of the Euratom Treaty, COM (2017) 237 final, p. 5.
639. Södersten argues that the Euratom Community's competences in respect of nuclear investments are 'very limited' and 'marginally used'. *See* A. Södersten *Euratom at the Crossroads*, Cheltenham, Northampton: Edward Elgar Publishing Limited, 2018, p. 106.
640. Commission Staff Working Document Regulatory Fitness and Performance Programme (REFIT): State of Play and Outlook Accompanying the document Better Regulation for Better Results – An EU Agenda, SWD (2015) 110 final, p. 57.
641. By the end of 2019.

4.03 THE CJEU'S INTERPRETATION OF THE COMPETENCES

This section assesses the CJEU's case-law in respect of the Euratom Community's competences in relation to investment and considers how the CJEU has interpreted these competences.

The CJEU has heard two cases that are relevant to analysis of the Euratom Community's competences in the field of investments. In the first of these the Court analysed whether the Commission had implied powers to adopt the regulation establishing the procedures for the examination of investment projects under Chapter 4 of the Euratom Treaty.[642] The CJEU ruled that when an article of the Euratom Treaty gives the Commission a specific and precise task, it must be accepted that it implicitly confers on the Commission necessary powers which are indispensable in order to carry out that task.[643] The CJEU interpreted the provisions contained in Articles 41 to 44 of the Euratom Treaty and established that the Euratom Treaty does not confer on the Commission regulatory powers to establish procedures for the examination of investment projects.[644] The Court also ruled that Regulation (Euratom) No 2587/1999 is limited to specifying which investment projects are to be communicated to the Commission in accordance with Article 41 of the Euratom Treaty and does not, in any way, concern the process of discussing these projects with the Commission. The CJEU accordingly concluded that the Commission does not have the implicit competence to adopt a regulation establishing procedures for the examination of the investment projects under Chapter 4 of the Euratom Treaty.[645]

In the second case, the Court interpreted the provisions of Chapter 4 of the Euratom Treaty as having the purpose of promoting or coordinating investments in the nuclear field. This means that all individual investment projects relating to new installations and all replacements or conversions of a certain size must be communicated to the Commission.[646]

In conclusion, there is limited CJEU case-law in relation to investments under the Euratom Treaty. The Court has analysed the Euratom Community's competences on one occasion, which involved delimiting the Commission's competences under Article 41 of the Euratom Treaty and concluding that they do not include a competence to

642. Judgment of 17 September 2007, *France v Commission*, T-240/04, ECLI:EU:T:2007:290, paragraph 36.
643. Judgment of 17 September 2007, *France v Commission*, T-240/04, ECLI:EU:T:2007:290, paragraph 35.
644. Judgment of 17 September 2007, *France v Commission*, T-240/04, ECLI:EU:T:2007:290, paragraph 33.
645. Judgment of 17 September 2007, *France v Commission*, T-240/04, ECLI:EU:T:2007:290, paragraph 41. The CJEU annulled Commission Regulation (Euratom) No 1352/2003, which concerned the determination of procedures for effecting the communications prescribed under Article 41 of the Euratom Treaty. The Court also indicated that Article 203 of the Euratom Treaty could be used as a legal basis if the Euratom Community sees a need for legal measures to be adopted in addition to already existing regulation field in Articles 41 and 44 of the Euratom Treaty. *See* Chapter III Section D of this study.
646. Judgment of 6 September 2012, *Parliament v Council*, C-490/10, ECLI:EU:C:2012:525, paragraph 84.

adopt secondary legislation establishing procedures for the examination of the investment projects. In the other case the CJEU merely reiterated the content of Chapter 4 of the Euratom Treaty.

4.04 FEATURES OF THE COMPETENCES

This section assesses the following features with a view to ensuring a basis for a comparative analysis: the level of detail of the provisions of the Euratom Treaty; the exercise of the competences as compared with the bare wording of the Euratom Treaty; and the existence of case-law and the effect of the Court's interpretation of the relevant provisions of primary and secondary legislation to the competences of the Euratom Community.

The level of detail of the provisions of the Euratom Treaty that establish the Euratom Community's competences in the field of investments is appropriate to the Community's tasks of stimulating investment actions by persons and undertakings and facilitating coordinated development of their investments in the nuclear field.

The Euratom Community's competences in the field of investments are generally exercised in accordance with the wording of the provisions of Chapter 4 of the Euratom Treaty. The secondary legal acts established under Article 41 of the Euratom Treaty do not broaden the scope of the Euratom Treaty's provisions, but implement them. The Commission does not, however, indicate nuclear energy production targets in the latest PINC, as required in Article 40 of the Euratom Treaty. It may therefore be concluded that the Euratom Community exercises its competences under Article 40 more narrowly than the wording of Article 40 would tend to indicate.

The Court has delimited the Euratom Community's competences in relation to investments on one occasion and ruled that the Commission does not have a competence under Article 41 of the Euratom Treaty to adopt secondary legislation that establishes procedures for the examination of investment projects.

CHAPTER 5

Joint Undertakings

- *The scope and content of the Euratom Community's competences in relation to establishing Joint Undertakings comprises two aspects: establishing Joint Undertakings under the legislative procedure set out in Chapter 5 of the Euratom Treaty; and giving certain privileges to Joint Undertakings due to their fundamental importance to the development of the nuclear industry in the Euratom Community.*
- *The Euratom Community exercises its competences in relation to Joint Undertakings in accordance with the wording of the provisions of Chapter 5 of the Euratom Treaty, and this is currently carried out solely through Council Decision 2007/198/Euratom, which established the ITER Joint Undertaking. One of the distinctive attributes of exercise of the Euratom Community's competences under Chapter 5 of the Euratom Treaty is that it is time-limited.*
- *There is limited CJEU case-law in relation to Joint Undertakings, but the Court has clarified the legal status of a Joint Undertaking by clarifying that a Joint Undertaking established by the Euratom Community under Article 48 of the Euratom Treaty is not an institution of the Euratom Community and does not form a part of the Euratom Community. The Court has also concluded that a host organisation of a Joint Undertaking might have a significantly different status from other members of that Joint Undertaking, including the status of the staff.*
- *The features of the Euratom Community's competences in relation to Joint Undertakings is as follows: the relevant provisions of the Euratom Treaty are drafted in sufficient detail to fulfil the Community's task of encouraging ventures in a form of Joint Undertakings for the development of nuclear energy in the Euratom Community; these competences are exercised in accordance with the wording of the provisions of Chapter 5 of the Euratom Treaty; and the case-law is limited, but establishes that a Joint Undertaking does not form part of the Euratom Community.*

5.01 THE SCOPE AND CONTENT OF THE COMPETENCES

The scope and the content of the Euratom Community's competences in respect of Joint Undertakings under the Euratom Treaty is analysed here.

From the date of its establishment, the Euratom Community took the view that it was necessary to encourage ventures in the form of Joint Undertakings in order to establish the installations necessary for the development of nuclear energy in the Euratom Community.[647] This is particularly needed in those cases where private initiative is not able to meet, in sufficient quantity and at the required speed, the need for industrial equipment within the Euratom Community.[648] The Euratom Treaty establishes that the Euratom Community has the competence to award the status of a Joint Undertaking to projects of fundamental importance to the development of the nuclear industry in the Euratom Community.[649] 'Joint Undertaking' means an enterprise established by a decision of the Council.[650] In other words, the Euratom Community is enabled to set up Joint Undertakings, i.e., entities with their own legal personality, to carry out specific projects which are of prime importance for the nuclear industry.[651] This broad wording concerning projects of fundamental importance to the development of the nuclear industry allows the Euratom Community to prioritise the most diversified undertakings.[652] The Euratom Community's competence to bestow the status of Joint Undertaking on a project brings significant advantages. It means that the project can be at least partially financed by the Euratom Community;[653] the Euratom Community can grant certain privileges to the project under the Euratom Treaty, such as exemption from all duties and charges when Joint Undertaking is established, exemption from all direct taxes, exemption from all customs duties and charges having equivalent effect, which also means that Member States are required to confer these advantages under their national legislative systems;[654] and in each Member State a Joint Undertaking is given the most extensive legal capacity accorded to legal persons under its national law – it can, *inter alia*, acquire or dispose of movable and immovable property and may be a party to legal proceedings.[655] The Euratom Treaty also requires that each Joint Undertaking has its own statutes and is to be governed by the rules applicable to industrial or commercial undertakings in the

647. Article 2(c) of the Euratom Treaty.
648. M. Gaudet, *Euratom*, London: Pergamon Press 1959, pp. 166–167.
649. Article 45 of the Euratom Treaty.
650. P. Mathijsen, 'Problems Connected with the Creation of Euratom', (1961) 26/3 *Law and Contemporary Problems*, p. 444.
651. European Commission, '50 Years of the Euratom Treaty', Memo/07/118, 26 March 2007 Brussels, p. 3.
652. J. G. Polach, *Euratom: Its Background, Issues and Economic Implications*, Dobbs Ferry, NY: Oceana Publications Inc., 1964, p. 89.
653. Articles 46(2) and 47(4) of the Euratom Treaty.
654. Article 48(1) and Annex III of the Euratom Treaty, which contains a list of possible advantages. Some authors consider these advantages to be State aids if scrutinised under Treaty rules. *See* T. F. Cusack, 'A Tale of Two Treaties', (2003) 40 *Common Market Law Review*, p. 132; and A. Södersten, *Euratom at the Crossroads*, Cheltenham, Northampton: Edward Elgar Publishing Limited, 2018, p. 132.
655. Article 49(3) of the Euratom Treaty.

Member States. The statutes of Joint Undertakings can be amended but these amendments must be approved by the Council.[656]

The Commission has a competence and an obligation to carry out an enquiry into any project that is a candidate for Joint Undertaking status and deliver its opinion to the Council.[657] The Council is, however, not bound by the Commission's opinion and can decide to give a project the status of a Joint Undertaking despite the Commission's unfavourable opinion.[658] The Council establishes a Joint Undertaking by a Council decision,[659] acting in most cases by qualified majority, except in relation to participation by the Euratom Community in the financing of the Joint Undertaking; participation by a third state, an international organisation or a national of a third state in the financing or management of the Joint Undertaking; and granting any or all of the advantages listed in Annex III to the Euratom Treaty to the Joint Undertaking – in these cases the Council's unanimous decision is required.[660] After the Council adopts its decision on the establishment of a Joint Undertaking, the Commission has a competence and a responsibility to implement this decision until the bodies responsible for the operation of such undertaking have been set up.[661]

Consequently, in accordance with the Euratom Community's task of encouraging ventures in the form of Joint Undertakings for the development of the nuclear energy in the Euratom Community, the scope and content of its competences in this area comprise two aspects: establishing Joint Undertakings under the legislative procedure set out in Chapter 5 of the Euratom Treaty; and giving certain privileges to Joint Undertakings due to their fundamental importance for the development of the nuclear industry in the Euratom Community.

5.02 THE EXERCISE OF THE COMPETENCES

This section assesses the exercise of the Euratom Community's competences in relation to Joint Undertakings and the instruments through which this occurs.

Analysis of secondary legal acts based on Chapter 5 of the Euratom Treaty leads one to conclude that Articles 47 and 48 are the legal bases for the secondary legislation that exercises the Euratom Community's competences in relation to Joint Undertakings.[662] Therefore, this part of the study focuses on the exercise of the competences

656. Article 50 of the Euratom Treaty.
657. Article 46 of the Euratom Treaty.
658. Article 47(2) of the Euratom Treaty.
659. Article 49(1) of the Euratom Treaty.
660. Articles 47(4) and 48(1) of the Euratom Treaty.
661. Article 51 of the Euratom Treaty.
662. Article 49 of the Euratom Treaty was a legal basis for Council Decision 2011/362/Euratom of 17 June 2011 on extension of the joint-undertaking status of Hochtemperatur-Kernkraftwerk GmbH (HKG), OJ L 163, 23.6.2011, pp. 24–25, but the status awarded under this decision ended on 31 December 2017. Article 50 of the Euratom Treaty was one of the legal bases of Council Decision (Euratom) 2015/224 of 10 February 2015 amending Decision 2007/198/Euratom establishing the European Joint Undertaking for ITER and the Development of Fusion Energy and conferring advantages upon it, OJ L 37, 13.2.2015, pp. 8–14. As Council Decision 2007/198/Euratom is based on Articles 47 and 48 of the Euratom Treaty, Council

established in these articles. Given the scope and objectives of this study, this analysis is limited to the secondary legislation in force.

Under Articles 47 and 48 of the Euratom Treaty, the Council, based on a Commission proposal to establish a Joint Undertaking, acts by a qualified majority, except in specific cases where unanimity is required. This implies that the Euratom Community primarily exercises its competences in this area through Council decisions on establishing Joint Undertakings. In this regard, it may be noted that the Euratom Community has previously established seven Joint Undertakings[663] that no longer exist, and one Joint Undertaking currently in existence – the European Joint Undertaking for ITER[664] and the Development of Fusion Energy.[665] The exercise of competences under Articles 47 and 48 of the Euratom Treaty has a distinctive time attribute: all Joint Undertakings are established for a limited period of time. The ITER Joint Undertaking was established for a period of thirty-five years, starting from April 2007.[666] The Euratom Community's competences in relation to the ITER Project were first exercised in the form of an international agreement under Article 101 of the Euratom Treaty, between the Euratom Community, the Government of Japan, the Government of the Russian Federation[667] and the Government of the United States of America on the development of a next step international fusion project – from conceptual design to

Decision (Euratom) 2015/224 is not analysed separately, but in the context of the exercise of competences under Articles 47 and 48 of the Euratom Treaty below.

663. Previously established Joint Undertakings: EAEC Council Decision on the establishment of the 'Société d'energie nucléaire franco-belge des Ardennes' Joint Undertaking, OJ 65, 9.10.1961, pp. 1173–1189; Council Decision 63/27/Euratom of 18 June 1963 on the establishment of the 'Kernkraftwerk RWE-Bayernwerk GmbH' Joint Undertaking, OJ 93, 22.6.1963, pp. 1745–1748; Council Decision 64/64/Euratom of 12 December 1964 on the establishment of the 'Kernkraftwerk Lingen GmbH' Joint Undertaking, OJ 214, 24.12.1964, pp. 3642–3645; Council Decision 66/30/Euratom of 28 July 1966 on the establishment of the 'Kernkraftwerk Obrigheim GmbH' Joint Undertaking, OJ 147, 9.8.1966, pp. 2681–2686; Council Decision 74/295/Euratom of 4 June 1974 on the establishment of the Joint Undertaking Hochtemperatur-Kernkraftwerk GmbH (HKG), OJ L 165, 20.6.1974, pp. 7–13; Council Decision 75/328/Euratom of 20 May 1975 on the establishment of the Joint Undertaking 'Schnell-Brüter-Kernkraftwerksgesellschaft mbH' (SBK), OJ L 152, 12.6.1975, pp. 8–10; Council Decision 78/471/Euratom of 30 May 1978 on the establishment of the 'Joint European Torus (JET), Joint Undertaking', OJ L 151, 7.6.1978, p. 10.
664. ITER is a large-scale scientific experiment that aims to demonstrate the technological and scientific feasibility of fusion energy being built in France. It is an international collaborative effort between the Parties to the ITER Agreement: EU, China, India, Japan, South Korea, Russia and the USA.
665. Council Decision 2007/198/Euratom of 27 March 2007 establishing the European Joint Undertaking for ITER and the Development of Fusion Energy and conferring advantages upon it, OJ L 90, 30.3.2007, pp. 58–72.
666. Article 1(1) of Council Decision 2007/198/Euratom.
667. It was the Union of Soviet Socialist Republics, not the Russian Federation, that participated in the first ITER international agreement. *See* Commission Decision 88/229/Euratom of 26 February 1988 concerning the conclusion of an Agreement of participation in the International Thermonuclear Experimental Reactor (ITER) Conceptual Design Activities, by the European Atomic Energy Community, with Japan, the Union of Soviet Socialist Republics, and the United States of America, by the Commission for and on behalf of the Community, ELI: http://data.europa.eu/eli/dec/1988/229(2)/oj.

engineering design activities.[668] In the latter stages of the development of the ITER Project, the Euratom Community argued that due to the project's fundamental importance in harnessing fusion as a potentially limitless, safe, sustainable, environmentally responsible and economically competitive source of energy, it was necessary to establish a Joint Undertaking as provided for in Chapter 5 of the Euratom Treaty.[669] The ITER Joint Undertaking was not designed to fulfil an economic purpose, but is responsible for managing the Euratom Community's participation in an international research project of public interest – one of its main tasks is to provide the Euratom Community's contribution to the ITER International Fusion Energy Organisation.[670]

Article 2 of Decision 2007/198/Euratom establishes that the Euratom Community is one of the members of the ITER Joint Undertaking and implies that the Commission has a competence to represent the Euratom Community in the ITER Joint Undertaking. ITER represents a unique first-of-its-kind project developed through international scientific collaboration, which allows for synergies and mobilisation of financial resources that would not be possible for a single state.[671] The financing structure of the ITER Joint Undertaking comprises, *inter alia*, a contribution from the Euratom Community, contributions from the ITER host State, the annual membership contributions and voluntary contribution from other members of the ITER Joint Undertaking. The Euratom Community's financial contribution for the period 2014–2020 is EUR 2,915,015,000.[672] It is noted in Chapter 5 Section 01 of this study that the Euratom Community has a competence to decide to make applicable to Joint Undertakings any or all of the advantages listed in Annex III of the Euratom Treaty and to require the Member States to ensure that these advantages are conferred. Decision

668. Commission Decision 88/229/Euratom of 26 February 1988 concerning the conclusion of an Agreement of participation in the International Thermonuclear Experimental Reactor (ITER) Conceptual Design Activities, by the European Atomic Energy Community, with Japan, the Union of Soviet Socialist Republics, and the United States of America, by the Commission for and on behalf of the Community, OJ L 102, 21.4.1988, pp. 31–44; Commission Decision 92/439/Euratom of 22 April 1992 concerning the conclusion of an Agreement between the European Atomic Energy Community, the Government of Japan, the Government of the Russian Federation, and the Government of the United States of America on cooperation in the engineering design activities for the International Thermonuclear Experimental Reactor (ITER) and of its Protocol 1, by the Commission for and on behalf of the Community, OJ L 244, 26.8.1992, pp. 13–31; Commission Decision 94/267/Euratom of 21 March 1994 concerning the conclusion of Protocol 2 to the Agreement among the European Atomic Energy Community, the Government of Japan, the Government of the Russian Federation, and the Government of the United States of America on cooperation in the engineering design activities for the International Thermonuclear Experimental Reactor (ITER), by the Commission for and on behalf of the Community, OJ L 114, 5.5.1994, p. 25; Council Decision 98/704/Euratom of 22 June 1998 concerning the extension of the duration of the Agreement among the European Atomic Energy Community, the Government of Japan, the Government of the Russian Federation and the Government of the United States of America on cooperation in the engineering design activities (EDA) for the international thermonuclear experimental reactor (ITER), OJ L 335, 10.12.1998, pp. 61–65.
669. Recital 9 of Council Decision 2007/198/Euratom.
670. Recital 16 and Article 1(2)(a) of Council Decision 2007/198/Euratom.
671. Proposal for a Council Decision amending Decision 2007/198/Euratom establishing the European Joint Undertaking for ITER and the Development of Fusion Energy and conferring advantages upon it, COM (2018) 445 final, p. 1.
672. In current values. Article 4(2) and (3) of Council Decision 2007/198/Euratom.

2007/198/Euratom exercises this competence by specifying that Member States must confer all the advantages provided for in Annex III to the Euratom Treaty on the ITER Joint Undertaking within the scope of its official activities for as long as this Joint Undertaking exists.[673]

The Euratom Community has amended Decision 2007/198/Euratom to strengthen the competences of the Euratom Community and the EU concerning the protection of the financial interests of the Euratom Community and the EU.[674] These amendments imply that the Commission has a competence and an obligation to ensure the application of preventive measures against fraud, corruption and illegal activities, that effective checks are carried out and, where irregularities are detected, amounts wrongly paid are recovered and proportionate and dissuasive penalties are applied. The Commission and the Court of Auditors have the power of audit over all grant beneficiaries, contractors, subcontractors and other third parties in the ITER Joint Undertaking that have received Euratom funds under Council Decision 2013/791/Euratom. The European Anti-Fraud Office (OLAF) has a right to carry out investigations, including on-the-spot checks and inspections[675] and the Commission, the Court of Auditors and OLAF are empowered to conduct audits, on-the-spot checks and inspections, concerning cooperation agreements with third countries and international organisations, contracts, agreements and decisions resulting from the application of Council Decision 2007/198/Euratom.[676]

In 2015 the ITER Parties launched a major overhaul of the project, which included the appointment of new senior management personnel in the ITER Organization and the preparation of a new baseline. The changes in the management of the ITER Joint Undertaking took place in parallel with those in the ITER Organization and entailed changing the director (in early 2016) and the majority of the members in the top level of management and its organisation (in 2016 and 2017). The critical mass of funding now needed to make the ITER-related EU-actions work effectively corresponds to the new baseline for the construction of ITER.[677]

In the middle of 2018 the Commission presented a new proposal for a Council Decision amending Decision 2007/198/Euratom, which provides a new basis for the financing of the ITER Joint Undertaking's activities for the period 2021–2027 under the Euratom Treaty and is connected with the proposal for the next Multi-annual Financial

673. Article 8 of Council Decision 2007/198/Euratom.
674. Council Decision 2013/791/Euratom of 13 December 2013 amending Decision 2007/198/Euratom establishing the European Joint Undertaking for ITER and the Development of Fusion Energy and conferring advantages upon it, OJ L 349, 21.12.2013, pp. 100–102.
675. In accordance with the provisions and procedures laid down in Regulation (EU, Euratom) No 883/2013 and Regulation (Euratom, EC) No 2185/96 with a view to establishing whether there has been fraud, corruption or any other illegal activity affecting the financial interests of the EU in connection with an agreement or decision or a contract funded under this Decision.
676. Article 5a of Council Decision 2007/198/Euratom. Article 5a was adopted by Council Decision 2013/791/Euratom.
677. Commission Staff Working Document Executive Summary of the Ex-ante Evaluation, accompanying the document Proposal for a Council Decision amending Decision 2007/198/Euratom establishing the European Joint Undertaking for ITER and the Development of Fusion Energy and conferring advantages upon it, SWD (2018) 326 final, p. 1.

Framework (MFF) 2021–2027.[678] The proposed changes focus on financing issues, proper evaluation of Decision 2007/198/Euratom, increased communication, visibility and publicity of the ITER Joint Undertaking. The proposal estimates the required Euratom budget, including the Commission's administrative expenditure related to the ITER Joint Undertaking's tasks and any other relevant activities, at about EUR 6.1 billion.[679] The comparison of the budget for 2014–2020 and that proposed for 2021–2027 shows that the Commission sees the need to double the available financial resources for the next MFF period. The Commission also proposed to remove the existing mid-term review and include a more detailed evaluation of the ITER Joint Undertaking.[680] The Commission also takes the view that Council Decision 2007/198/Euratom should ensure the visibility of the funding through coherent, effective and proportionate targeted information. To ensure that this occurs, the Commission has proposed that it should be subject to an obligation to implement information and communication actions relating to the ITER Joint Undertaking and that the recipients of the funding should be required to ensure its visibility (particularly when promoting the actions taken and their results) by providing coherent, effective and proportionate targeted information to multiple audiences, including the media and the public.[681]

Before the Commission presented its proposal, the Council underlined the fundamental importance of the ITER Project in the European fusion roadmap and reaffirmed the Euratom Community's ongoing commitment to its successful completion.[682] The Council also stated that it would endeavour to make available resources within the limits of the next MFF. The Council regretted, however, past significant cost increases and delays in the ITER Project and stressed the importance of staying strictly within the new approved baseline.[683]

Systematic analysis of the exercise of the Euratom Community's competences under Chapter 5 of the Euratom Treaty shows that the ITER Joint Undertaking has a connection with competences established in Chapter 1 of the Euratom Treaty, on the establishment of the Euratom Community's research and training programme, and Chapter 2 on the dissemination of information.

Council Decision 2007/198/Euratom provides that resources required for the ITER Joint Undertaking to carry out its tasks concerning preparation and coordination of activities in preparation for the construction of a demonstration fusion reactor and related facilities are to be determined in accordance with research and training

678. Proposal for a Council Decision amending Decision 2007/198/Euratom establishing the European Joint Undertaking for ITER and the Development of Fusion Energy and conferring advantages upon it, COM (2018) 445 final, p. 1.
679. Article 1(1) and (2) of the Commission's proposal COM(2018) 445 final, amending Article 4(3) and adding Article 4(4) to Council Decision 2007/198/Euratom.
680. Article 1(3) and (4) of the Commission's proposal COM(2018) 445 final, deleting Article 5b and adding Article 5c to Council Decision 2007/198/Euratom.
681. Article 1(5) of the Commission's proposal COM(2018) 445 final, adding Article 5d to Council Decision 2007/198/Euratom.
682. Commission proposal COM (2018) 445 final, p. 2.
683. Paragraphs 2, 3 and 12 of the Council's conclusions on the reformed ITER Project, Brussels, 12 April 2018.

programmes adopted pursuant to Article 7 of the Euratom Treaty.[684] Chapter 1 Section 02.A of this study notes that Regulation (Euratom) No 2018/1563, which concerns the Euratom Community's research and training programme for the period 2019–2020, refers to the ITER Agreement.[685] This regulation also provides that in order to secure the achievements of ongoing fusion research activities, as well as the long-term commitment of, and collaboration between, the fusion stakeholders, the continuity of the Euratom Community's support should be ensured. One of the activities necessary to achieve the objectives of the Euratom Research and Training Programme is to move towards demonstration of the feasibility of fusion as a power source and supporting common research activities to ensure the swift start of high performance operation of ITER.[686] The reference to Article 7 of the Euratom Treaty in the Council Decision 2007/198/Euratom on ITER and references to ITER in Regulation (Euratom) No 2018/1563 shows that the research carried out by the Euratom Community in the field of fusion energy has led it to having a competence to participate in the construction of the ITER Project and its future exploitation.[687]

Chapter 2 of the Euratom Treaty establishes that, as one of the advantages afforded to Joint Undertakings under Article 48 of the Euratom Treaty, a Joint Undertaking can be granted a non-exclusive licence in respect of patents, provisionally protected patent rights or utility models relating to inventions directly connected with nuclear research, where the granting of such licences is necessary for the continuance of their own research or indispensable to the operation of their installations.[688] Provisions in Council Decision 2007/198/Euratom require the ITER Joint Undertaking to apply the Commission's appropriate provisions which allow the Community to exercise its competences under Chapter 2 of the Euratom Treaty.[689] Consequently, the ITER Joint Undertaking receives all the advantages provided in Annex III of the Euratom Treaty and privileges in terms of receiving non-exclusive licences under Chapter 2 of the Euratom Treaty, but has to fulfil the Commission's provisions that allow the Euratom Community to exercise its competences in the field of dissemination of information.

In conclusion, a distinctive attribute of the exercise of the Euratom Community's competences in the field of Joint Undertakings is that it is limited in time. The Euratom Community's competences under Chapter 5 of the Euratom Treaty are currently exercised through one secondary legal act: Council Decision 2007/198/Euratom. The

684. Article 1(2) and Article 4(1)(c) of Council Decision 2007/198/Euratom.
685. Agreement on the Establishment of the ITER International Fusion Energy Organization for the Joint Implementation of the ITER Project, OJ L 358, 16.12.2006, p. 62.
686. Recital 10 and Annex I(1)(e), together with Article 3(2)(e) of Council Regulation (Euratom) No 2018/1563.
687. Recital 10 of Council Regulation (Euratom) No 2018/1563.
688. Article 17(1) of the Euratom Treaty. Under Chapter 2, Article 25(2) of the Euratom Treaty, Joint Undertakings may also receive communications from the Commission on the possible application of the information security grading due to defence reasons for information which the Community acquires as a result of carrying out its research programme from the Member State of origin. This connection between Joint Undertakings and dissemination of information is however less relevant for this study in terms of analysis of competences.
689. Recital 19 and Article 10 of Council Decision 2007/198/Euratom.

Euratom Community exercises its competences in accordance with the wording of the primary legal act, *inter alia*, by establishing the Euratom Community as one of the members of the ITER Joint Undertaking and by providing significant financial contributions to the ITER Project. The exercise of the Euratom Community's competences under Chapter 5 of the Euratom Treaty focuses on research, the promotion of fusion energy and its future exploitation.

5.03 THE CJEU'S INTERPRETATION OF THE COMPETENCES

This section assesses whether the CJEU's case-law defines or elaborates on the Euratom Community's competence in relation to Joint Undertakings.

Analysis of the case-law in relation to Joint Undertakings reveals that there are three cases - one 1978 ruling,[690] one 1987 judgment[691] and one 1994 order[692] of the Court - which have a connection with the Euratom Community's competences under Chapter 5 of the Euratom Treaty.

In its 1978 ruling, the Court only mentioned the provisions of the Treaty in relation to Joint Undertakings in the context of an analysis of the systemic coherence of the Euratom Community's competences and the effect the conclusion of the Convention on Physical Protection of Nuclear Materials, Facilities and Transports (CPPNM) would have on those competences.

In its 1987 judgment, the Court analysed the position of the staff of the host organisation of the JET Joint Undertaking as compared with the position of staff of other members of the JET Joint Undertaking. The facts of the case were that the staff made available to the JET Joint Undertaking by the host organisation - the United Kingdom Atomic Energy Authority (UKAEA)[693] - remained in the employment of that organisation on its terms and conditions of service, while staff made available to JET Joint Undertaking by other members of JET were recruited to posts as temporary servants of the Euratom Community.[694] The question for the Court was whether this situation was discriminatory towards the staff of the UKAEA.[695] The Court analysed the special nature of the UKAE and found that the JET Joint Undertaking was in the very unusual position of having to manage staff who had the same qualifications and were employed on the same site and doing the same kind of work but were assigned to two

690. Ruling of 14 November 1978 delivered pursuant to the third paragraph of Article 103 of the EAEC Treaty - Draft Convention of the International Atomic Energy Agency on the Physical Protection of Nuclear Materials, Facilities and Transports, Ruling 1/78, ECLI:EU:C:1978:202, paragraph 30.
691. Judgment of 15 January 1987, *Ainsworth v Commission and Council*, Joined Cases 271/83, 15, 36, 113, 158, 203/84 and 13/85, ECLI:EU:C:1987:7.
692. Order of 16 December 1994, *Altmann and Others v Commission*, Case T-177/94, ECLI: EU:T:1994:314.
693. The Joint European Torus (JET) Joint Undertaking's host organisation is the United Kingdom Atomic Energy Authority (the UKAEA). Besides the host organisation, the members of JET Joint Undertaking were twelve other research organisations of European States.
694. The Court noted that recruitment to a post as a temporary servant of the Euratom Community involves the payment of appreciably higher salary than paid to employees of the UKAEA.
695. Judgment of 15 January 1987, *Ainsworth v Commission and Council*, Joined Cases 271/83, 15, 36, 113, 158, 203/84 and 13/85, ECLI:EU:C:1987:7, paragraph 31.

legally distinct organisations. In the negotiations for the establishment of the JET Joint Undertaking, the UK government had requested that the staff which it would make available to the JET Joint Undertaking would remain subject to its own conditions of service.[696] The Court accordingly concluded that the very particular position of the host organisation, in relation to the Joint Undertaking, which is not comparable with the position of any other member organisation, constitutes an objective justification for the difference in treatment.[697]

In its 1994 order, the Court analysed the legal status of the JET Joint Undertaking, which was established under Chapter 5 of the Euratom Treaty, with a view to ascertaining whether it was an institution of the Euratom Community. The Court took the view, *inter alia*, that the JET Joint Undertaking was not set up under the Euratom Treaty itself but under a Council Decision[698] based on Articles 46, 47 and 49 of the Euratom Treaty. The Court also stated that the members of the JET Joint Undertaking are the Euratom Community itself, certain Member States and certain national organisations – including one from a non-member country – with responsibility in the field of atomic energy.[699] The Court therefore concluded that the JET Joint Undertaking is not an institution of the Community and does not form part of the Euratom Community.[700] This could be regarded as an indication that a Joint Undertaking is an outcome of the exercise of the Euratom Community's competences by its institutions – the Commission, which provides its reasoned opinion; and the Council, which adopts a decision establishing a Joint Undertaking.

In conclusion, although there is limited case-law in this area, the CJEU has established two significant aspects of the Euratom Community's competences. First, the Court established that a Joint Undertaking established under Article 48 of the Euratom Treaty does not form part of the Euratom Community. Second, when the Community exercises its competences under Articles 46 and 48 of the Euratom Treaty and establishes a Joint Undertaking with a specific location and a host organisation, it should be taken into account that the host organisation of a Joint Undertaking may have a significantly different status from other members of that Joint Undertaking, which implies that the staff of the host organisation has a different status as well.

5.04 FEATURES OF THE COMPETENCES

This section assesses the following features with a view to ensuring a basis for a comparative analysis: the level of detail of the provisions of the Euratom Treaty; the

696. Judgment of 15 January 1987, *Ainsworth v Commission and Council*, Joined Cases 271/83, 15, 36, 113, 158, 203/84 and 13/85, ECLI:EU:C:1987:7, paragraphs 34 and 37.
697. Judgment of 15 January 1987, *Ainsworth v Commission and Council*, Joined Cases 271/83, 15, 36, 113, 158, 203/84 and 13/85, ECLI:EU:C:1987:7, paragraph 38.
698. Council Decision 78/471/Euratom of 30 May 1978 on the establishment of the 'Joint European Torus (JET), Joint Undertaking', OJ L 151, 7.6.1978, p. 10.
699. Order of 16 December 1994, *Altmann and Others v Commission*, Case T-177/94, ECLI:EU:T:1994:314, paragraph 41.
700. Order of 16 December 1994, *Altmann and Others v Commission*, Case T-177/94, ECLI:EU:T:1994:314, paragraphs 38 and 44.

exercise of the competences as compared with the bare wording of the Euratom Treaty; and the existence of case-law and the effect of the Court's interpretation of the relevant provisions of primary and secondary legislations to the competences of the Euratom Community.

The level of detail of the provisions of the Euratom Treaty that establish the Euratom Community's competences in relation to Joint Undertakings is appropriate to the Community's task of encouraging ventures in the form of Joint Undertakings for the development of nuclear energy in the Euratom Community.

The Euratom Community's competences in relation to Joint Undertakings are exercised in accordance with the wording of the provisions in Chapter 5 of the Euratom Treaty. These competences focus on research and promotion of fusion energy and its future exploitation and amount to one secondary legal act - Council Decision 2007/198/Euratom - which establishes the European Joint Undertaking for ITER and the Development of Fusion Energy.

The Court has delimited the Euratom Community's competences in the field of Joint Undertakings by establishing that a Joint Undertaking established by the Council under Chapter 5 of the Euratom Treaty is not an institution of the Euratom Community and does not form part of the Community.

Chapter 6
Supplies

- *The main scope of the Euratom Community's competences in relation to nuclear supply is to ensure a regular and equitable supply of nuclear fuels. The content of Euratom Community's competences constitutes establishing the common supply policy and competences in respect of specific elements of the nuclear supply chain.*
- *The exercise of the Euratom Community's competences in this area is somewhat limited and most of the competences are exercised in accordance with the wording of the Euratom Treaty, except for Article 53 of the Euratom Treaty, which is exercised broader than the wording of the primary legal act. Exercise of the Euratom Community's competences inter alia implies that there is no 'Community preference' for nuclear supplies and that the Euratom Community has competence to protect and promote the diversification of supplies under the common supply policy.*
- *The CJEU has been active in defining and delimiting the Euratom Community's competences under Chapter 6 of the Euratom Treaty. The Court has established the valid, binding and exclusive nature of the Euratom Community's competences in the field of nuclear supply; delimited the Euratom Community's competences by ruling that the Euratom Treaty does not establish an obligation to guarantee preferential disposal of production coming from inside the Euratom Community; emphasised the importance of geographical diversification of supplies; and concluded that the provisions of Chapter 6 of the Euratom Treaty are now maintained on a temporary basis.*
- *The features of the Euratom Community's competences in relation to nuclear supply are as follows: a high level of detail in the Euratom Treaty; limited exercise of the competences through secondary legal acts; the CJEU plays an active role in defining and delimiting the Euratom Community's broad competences in this area.*

6.01 THE SCOPE AND CONTENT OF THE COMPETENCES

This section analyses the scope and content of the Euratom Community's competences in the field of nuclear supply under Chapter 6 of the Euratom Treaty.

There is a basic unwillingness on the part of sovereign States to give up control over their fuel supply to regional or international organisations and nuclear fuel supply constitutes a national concern of sufficient sensitivity to prevent most States from turning over production and delivery responsibilities to multilateral organisations. The Euratom Community is the sole exception to this, as no other international arrangement possesses comparable features.[701] The Euratom Treaty lays down the Euratom Community's obligation to ensure that all users in the Euratom Community have regular and equitable access to nuclear supplies.[702] Some authors refer to the regulation of the nuclear supply system under the Euratom Treaty as a compromise between public authority interventionism and a more free market approach,[703] while others view it as a monopoly involving total control over and responsibility for supply.[704] The Euratom Treaty makes clear the scope of the Euratom Community's competences: they do not entail the creation of a common nuclear supply market,[705] but the establishment of a common nuclear supply policy that ensures regular and equitable supply of ores, source materials and special fissile materials.[706]

Supply of the basic raw materials under Chapter 6, the longest chapter in Title II of the Euratom Treaty, is sometimes considered to be one of the six pillars of the Euratom Community and the axis around which all the rest of the Euratom Treaty turns.[707] The Euratom Community's competences in relation to supply are laid down in twenty-five articles,[708] which provide a high level of regulatory detail. This indicates that regular and secure access to nuclear supplies has been a high priority for the Euratom Community from the start. The Euratom Treaty establishes a system for the pooling of available nuclear resources in the Euratom Community and provides for

---

701. L. Weiss, 'Reliable Energy Supply and Nonproliferation', (2009) 16/2 *Nonproliferation Review*, p. 279; and H. J. Hahn, 'Control under the Euratom Compact', (1958) 7 *American Journal of Comparative Law*, p. 38.
702. Article 2(d) of the Euratom Treaty.
703. A. Bouquet, 'How Current Are Euratom Provisions on Nuclear Supply and Ownership in View of the European Union's Enlargement?', (2001) 68 *Nuclear Law Bulletin*, p. 8.
704. D. Allen, 'The Euratom Treaty, Chapter VI: New Hope Or False Dawn?', (1983) 20 *Common Market Law Review*, p. 474; J. Grunwald, 'Peaceful Uses of Nuclear Energy under Euratom Law', in J. L. Black-Branch and D. Fleck (eds), *Nuclear Non-Proliferation in International Law, Volume III: Legal Aspects of the Use of Nuclear Energy for Peaceful Purposes*, The Hague: Asser Press, 2016, p. 186; and H. J. Hahn, 'Control under the Euratom Compact', (1958) 7 *American Journal of Comparative Law*, p. 37.
705. Some authors generalise that the scope of the Euratom Community's competences is such as to create a nuclear common market for trade in nuclear ores and materials within the EU. *See* P. Barnes, 'Nuclear Safety for Nuclear Electricity – The Search for a Solid Legal Basis for Nuclear Safety in an Enlarged EU', (2003) 45 *Managerial Law*, p. 9.
706. Ores, source materials and special fissile materials are defined in Article 197of the Euratom Treaty.
707. T. F. Cusack, 'A Tale of Two Treaties', (2003) 40 *Common Market Law Review*, pp. 121 and 134.
708. Articles 52 to 76 of the Euratom Treaty.

their distribution through a central apparatus.[709] Chapter 6 of the Euratom Treaty is divided into six sections,[710] but three main areas of Euratom Community competences emerge from close reading of its provisions. These are competences in establishing a common supply policy, the allocation of competences between the institutions and competences in specific areas of the nuclear supply chain to ensure a common supply policy.

The Euratom Treaty establishes the Euratom Community's common supply policy, which means equal access to sources of supply, the prohibition of a privileged position for certain users, the prohibition of discrimination between users and the establishment of the Euratom Supply Agency (ESA).[711] A common supply policy was established to ensure security of supply for the whole of the Euratom Community.[712] The concept of a common policy refers to a comprehensive set of rules under which the Community has exclusive powers and conducts its policy in a certain field[713] and the Euratom Treaty established the instruments needed to achieve diversity and security of energy supply.[714] The rules governing the common supply policy in respect of ores, source materials and special fissile materials that come from inside the Euratom Community require potential users to periodically inform the ESA of the supplies they require and producers of supplies to inform the ESA of offers they are able to make. The ESA then informs the users of the offers and calls upon them to place their orders by a specified time limit.[715] In other words, the nuclear supply policy under the Euratom

709. J. G. Polach, *Euratom: Its Background, Issues and Economic Implications*, Dobbs Ferry, NY: Oceana Publications Inc., 1964, p. 78.
710. Section 1 – the Agency; Section 2 – Ores, source materials and special fissile materials coming from inside the Community; Section 3 – Ores, source materials and special fissile materials coming from outside the Community; Section 4 – Prices; Section 5 – Provisions relating to supply policy; Section – 6 Special provisions.
711. Article 52 of the Euratom Treaty.
712. Commission Staff Working Document accompanying the document Communication from the Commission Nuclear Illustrative Programme Presented under Article 40 of the Euratom Treaty – Final, SWD(2017) 158 final, pp. 9–10. Current uranium inventories can fuel EU utilities' nuclear power reactors for approximately three years. Most vulnerable in terms of security of supply are those utilities that depend on Russian fabricated fuel assemblies, which cannot be quickly replaced by fuel assemblies from another manufacturer.
713. A. Bouquet, 'How Current Are Euratom Provisions on Nuclear Supply and Ownership in View of the European Union's Enlargement?', (2001) 68 *Nuclear Law Bulletin*, p. 10. As noted in Chapter II Section B of this study, the Euratom Community's competences are not classified as shared or exclusive, but some authors argue that the common supply policy, as a common policy, is equivalent to policies for which the Union has exclusive competence under Article 3 TFEU. *See, e.g.*, J. Grunwald, 'Peaceful Uses of Nuclear Energy under Euratom Law', in J. L. Black-Branch and D. Fleck (eds), *Nuclear Non-Proliferation in International Law, Volume III: Legal Aspects of the Use of Nuclear Energy for Peaceful Purposes*, The Hague: Asser Press, 2016, p. 186.
714. Paragraph 211 of Commission Decision (EU) 2017/1021 of 10 January 2017 on State aid SA.44727 2016/C (ex 2016/N) which France is planning to implement in favour of the Areva group, C/2016/9029, OJ L 155, 17.6.2017, pp. 23–75. It should be mentioned, however, that Article 195 of the Euratom Treaty establishes an exception when the institutions of the Euratom Community, the ESA and Joint Undertakings are to comply with a Member State's national rules and regulations regarding access to ores, source materials and special fissile materials if these national rules and regulations have been established for reasons of public policy or public health.
715. Article 60(1) to (4) of the Euratom Treaty.

Treaty gives the ESA the power to mediate deliveries between the potential users and the producers of supplies.[716] The ESA has a general obligation to fulfil all orders[717] and the ESA Rules[718] determine the manner in which demand is to be balanced against supply. If the ESA cannot meet the orders received in their entirety, it has a power and an obligation to share out the supplies proportionally among the orders relating to each offer.[719] For ores, source materials and special fissile materials that come from outside the Euratom Community, the same rules apply, but the ESA has an additional competence to decide on the geographical origin of supplies, provided that conditions at least as favourable as those specified in the order are thereby secured for the user.[720]

The Euratom Community's common supply policy also entails that the Euratom Community has right of option on ores, source materials and special fissile materials, and this right of option is exercised by the ESA. [721] It is applicable to the full ownership of ores and source materials and to the right of use and consumption of special fissile materials, because special fissile materials are already under the ownership of the Euratom Community under Chapter 8 of the Euratom Treaty.[722] The Euratom Community implements the right of option by requiring every producer to offer to the ESA the ores, source materials and special fissile materials that it produces, before they are used, transferred or stored. If the producer carries out several stages of production (from the extraction of the ore up to and including production of the metal), the products can be offered to the ESA at whichever stage the producer chooses.[723] The right of option is established under Section 2 of Chapter 6 of the Euratom Treaty, which regulates supplies coming from inside the Euratom Community. There is no reference to it in Section 3 of the same chapter, which regulates supplies coming from outside the Euratom Community. Therefore, taking into account the wording of Article 52(2)(b), the conclusion may be drawn that the ESA cannot exercise a right of option on supplies coming from outside the Euratom Community.

The Euratom Treaty also lays down exemptions from the common supply policy, which mainly concern situations when ores, source materials or special fissile materials are processed, converted or shaped either inside or outside the Euratom Community

716. J. G. Polach, *Euratom: Its Background, Issues and Economic Implications*, Dobbs Ferry, NY: Oceana Publications Inc., 1964, p. 80.
717. Article 61 of the Euratom Treaty.
718. Rules of the Supply Agency of the European Atomic Energy Community of 5 May 1960 determining the manner in which demand is to be balanced against the supply of ores, source materials and special fissile materials, OJ 32, 11.5.1960, pp. 777–779; and Regulation of the Supply Agency of the European Atomic Energy Community amending the rules of the Supply Agency of 5 May 1960 determining the manner in which demand is to be balanced against the supply of ores, source materials and special fissile materials, OJ L 193, 25.7.1975, pp. 37–38.
719. Article 60(4) and (5) of the Euratom Treaty.
720. Article 65 of the Euratom Treaty.
721. Article 52(2)(b) and Article 57(1) of the Euratom Treaty. Ownership of nuclear materials is regulated under Chapter 8 of the Euratom Treaty.
722. A. Bouquet, 'How Current Are Euratom Provisions on Nuclear Supply and Ownership in View of the European Union's Enlargement?', (2001) 68 *Nuclear Law Bulletin*, p. 14. *See also* Chapter 8 of this study on property ownership.
723. Articles 57(2) and 58(1) of the Euratom Treaty. The obligation to offer the supplies to the ESA applies to the processing aspects of the nuclear supplies as well. *See* Article 59(a) of the Euratom Treaty.

and the materials are then to be returned to the original person, undertaking or international organisation concerned.[724]

In conclusion, the Euratom Community's common supply policy is based on two main elements: the ESA's mediation between the potential users and the producers, and the Euratom Community's right of option.

The Euratom Community's horizontal competences are allocated between three main institutions: the ESA, the Commission and the Council. The ESA was designed to be the central and sole supplier of nuclear materials in the Euratom Community and has been in operation since 1960.[725] The ESA has a legal personality and financial autonomy.[726] The ESA focuses on improving security of supply to users located in the Euratom Community, thus also contributing to the viability of the Euratom Community's nuclear industry.[727] To exercise its competences in the implementation of the common supply policy, the ESA has a right to receive all the necessary information from the Member States and to operate freely in the territories of the Member States.[728] The Commission supervises the ESA by, *inter alia*, issuing directives, appointing its Director-General, and having a competence to veto the ESA's decisions and overrule its acts.[729] In addition to the Commission's general supervision power and right of veto, it also has the right to review decisions made by the ESA in exercising its right of option or its exclusive right to conclude supply contracts.[730] One might say that the Commission exercises functional control over the ESA.[731] As the ESA, despite having legal personality and financial autonomy, is under the control of the Commission, it may therefore be inferred that the Commission has an indirect competence to ensure that all users in the Euratom Community receive a regular and equitable supply of nuclear fuels.[732] On a proposal from the Commission, the Council has a competence to adopt the statutes of the ESA, which determines its capital and the rules for the commercial management of its activities.[733] Consequently, the ESA has broad competences in the field, *inter alia*, by operating freely in the Member States and having a right to receive

---

724. Article 75 of the Euratom Treaty.
725. European Commission, '50 Years of the Euratom Treaty', Memo/07/118, 26 March 2007 Brussels, p. 3.
726. Article 54(1) of the Euratom Treaty.
727. Euratom Supply Agency Annual Report 2017, p. 6.
728. Articles 55 and 56 of the Euratom Treaty. The wording of Article 55 of the Euratom Treaty is broad as it seems to require the Member States to determine what information needs to be communicated and whether that information is necessary to the ESA for it to be able to exercise its competences. The provision basically implies that all information connected to nuclear supplies should be communicated to the ESA.
729. Article 53 of the Euratom Treaty.
730. *See* A. Bouquet, 'How Current Are Euratom Provisions on Nuclear Supply and Ownership in View of the European Union's Enlargement?', (2001) 68 *Nuclear Law Bulletin*, p. 11. The author argues that the Commission's right to veto the ESA's decisions under Article 53(1) of the Euratom Treaty should not be confused with its right to take the final decision on cases referred to it as set out in Article 53(2).
731. I. Cenevska, *The European Atomic Energy Community in the European Union Context: The 'Outsider' Within*, Leiden: Brill Nijhoff, 2016, p. 31.
732. P. Mathijsen, 'Some Legal Aspects of Euratom', (1965–1966) 3 *Common Market Law Review*, p. 334.
733. Article 54(2) to (5) of the Euratom Treaty.

all the relevant information from the Member States in the field of nuclear supply. Some authors consider that the ESA's competences are so broad that the ESA is as much a means of assuring equal access to the nuclear supplies as a means of exercising surveillance over nuclear activities in the Euratom Community.[734] The ESA is under the control of the Commission and the Council, as the Commission supervises the ESA's decisions and the Council adopts its statutes.

The Euratom Treaty has also established the Euratom Community's competences throughout the nuclear supply chain – from prospecting for minerals, mining, production and processing of supplies, concluding contracts, setting prices, exporting, importing and transferring supplies; to storage and stocking of supplies, and disposal of the production of supplies outside the Euratom Community. The content of these competences is set out below.

The Euratom Community, via the Commission, has a competence to give financial support for prospecting programmes in the territories of the Member States,[735] make recommendations to the Member States concerning the development of, prospecting for, and exploitation of mineral deposits[736] and make recommendations to the Member States with regard to revenue or mining regulations.[737] Furthermore, the Council may decide that a Member State has waived its right to equal access to supplies within the Euratom Community, if that Member State does not prospect and expand mining operations in its territory when the prospects of extraction appear to be economically justified on a long-term basis.[738] As noted above, producers and processors of ores, source materials and special fissile materials have an obligation to offer the supplies to ESA. This indicates that the Euratom Community has an imbedded competence to implement its right of option throughout the production and processing stages of nuclear supplies.

The various aspects of the Euratom Community's competence to conclude contracts in respect of nuclear supply is divided between seven different provisions in Chapter 6 of the Euratom Treaty. The exclusive competence to conclude contracts is considered to be the ESA's key operating tool.[739] Only the ESA can deal with supply and, as some authors state, it must, on behalf of the Euratom Community, ensure the exclusion of intervention by the Member States, and make the Euratom Community the natural and necessary partner of third countries and international organisations.[740]

The first article of Chapter 6 of the Euratom Treaty specifies that the ESA has an exclusive right to conclude contracts relating to the supply of ores, source materials and special fissile materials coming from inside or outside the Euratom Community.[741]

734. L. Scheinmann, 'Euratom: Nuclear Integration in Europe', (1967) 563 *International Conciliation*, p. 17.
735. Article 70(1) of the Euratom Treaty.
736. Article 70(2) of the Euratom Treaty.
737. Article 71 of the Euratom Treaty.
738. Article 70(4) of the Euratom Treaty.
739. A. Bouquet, 'How Current Are Euratom Provisions on Nuclear Supply and Ownership in View of the European Union's Enlargement?', (2001) 68 *Nuclear Law Bulletin*, p. 14.
740. D. Allen, 'The Euratom Treaty, Chapter VI: New Hope or False Dawn?', (1983) 20 *Common Market Law Review*, p. 482.
741. Article 52(2)(b) of the Euratom Treaty.

Regarding ores, source materials and special fissile materials coming from inside the Euratom Community, the ESA may require users to make appropriate advance payments either as security or to assist in meeting the ESA's own long-term commitments to producers, when the ESA exercises its right to conclude contracts with producers of ores, source materials and special fissile materials.[742] The Euratom Treaty provides that when regulating ores, source materials and special fissile materials coming from outside the Euratom Community, the ESA, acting where appropriate within the framework of agreements concluded between the Community and a third state or an international organisation, has (subject to certain exceptions under the Treaty) an exclusive right to enter into agreements or contracts whose principal aim is the supply of ores, source materials or special fissile materials coming from outside the Community.[743] The ESA's right to conclude contracts for the supply of ores, source materials and special fissile materials coming from outside of the Euratom Community is established in two provisions of the Euratom Treaty: Article 52(2)(b) and Article 64. Comparative analysis of these provisions indicates that the ESA's competence in this respect is established as absolute at the beginning of Chapter 6 of the Euratom Treaty, but phrased in conditional terms – i.e., there is provision for an assessment of appropriateness within the framework of agreements and this right to conclude contracts is subject to exceptions provided under the Euratom Treaty.

These provisions seem to conflict with each other, but as Article 52 of the Euratom Treaty is an overarching article that does not belong to any section of the chapter, the implication may be that it establishes a *lex generalis* rule, while the other provisions are *lex specialis* in relation to it. The difference between these provisions also relates to the fact that, by way of an exemption from *lex generalis*, the Commission has a competence to give users the right to conclude direct contracts for supplies from outside the Community, if the Commission finds that the ESA is not in a position to deliver all or part of the supplies ordered within a reasonable period of time, or that it can only do so at excessively high prices.[744] Here the prior consent of the Commission is required for the conclusion or renewal of an agreement or contract between a Member State, a person or an undertaking on the one hand, and a third state, an international organisation or a national of a third state on the other, which provides, *inter alia*, for delivery of products which come within the province of the ESA.[745]

One might say that these provisions of the Euratom Treaty brought international agreements and cooperation within the ambit of the Commission's competence as a necessary element of the common supply policy.[746] Commitments relating to the processing, conversion or shaping of ores, source materials and special fissile materials that do not fall under the common supply policy also need to be notified to the ESA – both the existence of such commitments and, as soon as contracts are signed, the

742. Articles 57(2) and 61(2) of the Euratom Treaty.
743. Article 64 of the Euratom Treaty.
744. Article 66(1) of the Euratom Treaty.
745. Article 73 of the Euratom Treaty.
746. P. Barnes, 'Nuclear Safety for Nuclear Electricity – The Search for a Solid Legal Basis for Nuclear Safety in an Enlarged EU', (2003) 45 *Managerial Law*, p. 9.

quantities of material involved in the movements.[747] The regulatory system establishing the Euratom Community's competences to conclude supply contracts is detailed, but sometimes considered to be incomplete as it does not specify the contractual consequences of an infringement of Article 52 of the Euratom Treaty and is thus missing a key legal element.[748]

In respect of the pricing of nuclear supplies, the general rule is that prices are to be determined by balancing supply against demand[749] and the ESA's rules, approved by the Commission, determine the manner in which this balance is to be reached.[750] This implies that the ESA has a competence to oversee the pricing of nuclear supply so that it corresponds to an existing demand. The general rule of price balancing implies that Member States' national regulations cannot contravene the requirement that prices are to be determined by balancing supply against demand and all pricing practices designed to secure a privileged position for certain users are prohibited.[751] The Euratom Treaty establishes an exception to the general rule of price balancing by giving the Council the competence to fix prices by a unanimous decision.[752] The Treaty does not require the Council to fulfil any other conditions in order to adopt a decision on fixed prices. Consequently, the Council has an exclusive competence to determine when fixed prices are needed.[753] Fixing supply prices, together with the right of option, implies the Euratom Community's competence to interfere in the nuclear supply chain in order to ensure that all users in the Euratom Community receive a regular and equitable supply of nuclear fuels.

Regarding the Euratom Community's competences in relation to the export, import and transfer of ores, source materials and special fissile materials, the Commission has a competence to authorise producer's export of supplies outside the Euratom Community[754] and the ESA must be notified of every transfer, import or export operation.[755] Special rules apply to the export of special fissile materials, as they are the property of the Euratom Community:[756] special fissile materials may only be exported through the ESA after authorisation by the Commission.[757] Under the provisions of the

747. Article 75(2) of the Euratom Treaty.
748. As distinct from EU competition law, in respect of which Article 101(2) TFEU provides that prohibited agreements are automatically void. For further discussion of this issue, *see* A. Bouquet, 'How Current Are Euratom Provisions on Nuclear Supply and Ownership in View of the European Union's Enlargement?', (2001) 68 *Nuclear Law Bulletin*, p. 14.
749. Article 67 of the Euratom Treaty.
750. Article 60(6) of the Euratom Treaty.
751. Articles 67 and 68(1) of the Euratom Treaty.
752. Article 69(1) of the Euratom Treaty.
753. Some authors consider that by establishing a common supply policy, subject to the principle of equal access, the Euratom Treaty effectively excludes such supplies from the normal scope of competition on the market, with a specific impact at the level of prices. *See* M. Sousa Ferro, 'Competition Law and the Nuclear Sector: An EU Outlook', (2010) 86 *Nuclear Law Bulletin*, p. 15.
754. Article 62(1)(c) of the Euratom Treaty. However, under Article 74(2) of the Euratom Treaty, the transfer, import or export of small quantities of ores, source materials and special fissile materials may be exempted from the need to obtain the Commission's authorisation.
755. Article 74(2) of the Euratom Treaty.
756. *See* Article 86 of the Euratom Treaty and Chapter 8 of this study.
757. Article 59(b) and Article 62 of the Euratom Treaty.

Euratom Treaty, the Commission cannot give its authorisation if the recipients of the supplies fail to satisfy the Commission that the general interests of the Euratom Community will be safeguarded. This 'general interest' test is usually understood to focus on the political aspects of the export.[758] The ESA has a competence to store special fissile materials itself or give an authorisation for storage to a producer.[759]

Furthermore, the Euratom Treaty provides for some additional means of intervention in the nuclear fuel cycle.[760] It gives the Euratom Community the competence to build up necessary commercial or emergency stocks, from materials available inside or outside of the Euratom Community, to facilitate supplies to or normal deliveries by the Euratom Community.[761] The Euratom Treaty also provides that if the ESA does not exercise its right of option, the producer shall be authorised by a decision of the Commission to dispose of its available production of supplies outside the Euratom Community.[762] The term 'to dispose of' or 'disposal' is used in nuclear law to define the process of emplacement of waste in an appropriate facility without an intention of retrieval.[763] If this provision of the Euratom Treaty were to be interpreted by reference to the classical definition of disposal, it would imply that the Commission has a competence to authorise a disposal of supplies outside the Euratom Community. However, as the Euratom Community's competences regarding disposal activities are defined and regulated under Chapter 3 of the Euratom Treaty,[764] the grammatical meaning of this provision should be interpreted as a competence to transfer the supplies to person or undertaking outside the Euratom Community, and not a competence to discard the supplies outside the Euratom Community.

Finally, the Euratom Treaty establishes the Euratom Community's competence to amend the provisions of Chapter 6 of the Euratom Treaty by means of a special amendment procedure, if unforeseen circumstances create a situation of general shortage of supply.[765] The provisions of Chapter 6 can be amended by the Council acting unanimously on a proposal from the Commission and after consulting the EP.[766]

758. A. Bouquet, 'How Current Are Euratom Provisions on Nuclear Supply and Ownership in View of the European Union's Enlargement?', (2001) 68 *Nuclear Law Bulletin*, p. 18.
759. Article 62(1)(b) and (2)(a) of the Euratom Treaty.
760. For the tools of the Supply Agency, *see* A. Bouquet, 'How Current Are Euratom Provisions on Nuclear Supply and Ownership in View of the European Union's Enlargement?', (2001) 68 *Nuclear Law Bulletin*, p. 13.
761. Article 72 of the Euratom Treaty. Competence to build commercial stocks belongs to the ESA and the Commission has a competence to decide to build up emergency stocks, the financing of which is determined by the Council.
762. Article 59(b) of the Euratom Treaty.
763. International Atomic Energy Agency, *IAEA Safety Glossary. Terminology Used in Nuclear Safety and Radiation Protection*, Vienna: IAEA, 2016 – definition of disposal as emplacement of waste in an appropriate facility without the intention of retrieval, p. 41, and definition of radioactive waste management facility, p. 194.
764. *See also* Chapter 3 of this study.
765. Article 76(1) of the Euratom Treaty. The requirement of shortage under Article 76 of the Euratom Treaty is sometimes disregarded by those who approach Chapter 6 of the Euratom Treaty as if it had been designed expressly to cope with a situation of general shortage. *See* D. Allen, 'The Euratom Treaty, Chapter VI: New Hope or False Dawn?', (1983) 20 *Common Market Law Review*, p. 475.
766. The regular amendment procedure of the Euratom Treaty is the ordinary revision procedure under Article 48(2) to (5) TEU, which is applicable to the Euratom Treaty under Article 106a(1)

This is considered to be the Euratom Treaty's acknowledgment of the dynamism of the nuclear industry and the need for the Euratom Community's legislation to keep abreast of it.[767]

This analysis of the scope and content of the Euratom Community's competences in relation to nuclear supplies under the Euratom Treaty may be concluded by stating that the main scope of the Euratom Community's competences is to ensure a regular and equitable supply of nuclear fuels in the Community. The content of the Euratom Community's competences in the field cover three main areas: establishing a common supply policy, defining competences in specific areas of the nuclear supply chain and the allocating of competences between the institutions. The Euratom Treaty contains a high level of detail in regulating this area, which indicates that it was a high priority at the time the Treaty was established.

6.02 THE EXERCISE OF THE COMPETENCES

This section assesses the Euratom Community's competences in relation to nuclear supplies and the instruments through which those competences are exercised.

Systematic analysis of the existing secondary legislation, adopted on the basis of one of the articles in Chapter 6 of the Euratom Treaty, shows that the competences under the majority of the articles in this chapter have not been exercised by the Euratom Community: twenty out of twenty-five articles in this chapter have not been used as legal bases for secondary legislation.[768] The Euratom Community's competences in relation to nuclear supply that are exercised by secondary legislation are to be found in Articles 52 to 54, 60 and 74 of the Euratom Treaty. Due to the scope and objectives of this study, analysis of the exercise of the Euratom Community's competences is limited to the secondary legislation in force.

Article 52 of the Euratom Treaty establishes the Euratom Community's fundamental competences in the field of the common supply policy, but these are exercised through just one secondary legal act: the Commission decision approving the ESA Rules of 5 May 1960 determining the manner in which demand is to be balanced against the supply of ores, source materials and special fissile materials.[769] Article 52 of

---

of the Euratom Treaty. On 8 December 1982 the Commission submitted to the Council its proposal for a Council Decision adopting new provisions relating to Chapter VI (Supplies) of the Treaty establishing the European Atomic Energy Community, OJ C 330, 16.12.1982, pp. 4–8. The EP adopted the Resolution on the Commission's proposal advising the Council to refrain from adopting a final position with regard to the Commission's proposal, OJ C 172, 2.7.1984, p. 152, The Commission withdrew its proposal in 2004, by issuing a Communication from the Commission – Withdrawal of Commission Proposals which are no longer of topical interest, COM (2004) 542 final. Consequently, exercise of the competences under Article 76 of the Euratom Treaty is not analysed in relation to exercise of the Euratom Community's competences in relation to supplies.

767. D. Allen, 'The Euratom Treaty, Chapter VI: New Hope or False Dawn?', (1983) 20 *Common Market Law Review*, p. 475.

768. The Euratom Community's competences established in Articles 56 to 59, 61 to 69, 71 to 73 and 75 to 76 of the Euratom Treaty have not been exercised through secondary legislation.

769. The EAEC Commission Decision fixing the date on which the Euratom Supply Agency shall take up its duties and approving the Agency Rules of 5 May 1960 determining the manner in

the Euratom Treaty is the legal basis for this Commission decision, alongside Articles 53 and 60 of the Euratom Treaty, but analysis of the provisions of this decision reveals that the Article 52 competences are not exercised to any significant degree in this secondary legal act.

As noted in the analysis of the scope and content of the Euratom Community's competences in relation to common nuclear supply,[770] Article 53 of the Euratom Treaty lays down the ESA's institutional competences and the Commission's competence to veto the ESA's decisions. This Commission competence has been exercised twice through the adoption of Commission decisions on a procedure for the application of Article 53(2).[771] In Commission Decision 93/428/Euratom and Commission Decision 94/285/Euratom, the Commission has exercised the Euratom Community's competences by adopting decisions relating to requests submitted to the Commission under Article 53. Even though both Commission decisions are addressed to a specific applicant,[772] they indicate the Commission's position on certain provisions contained in Chapter 6 of the Euratom Treaty, and are accordingly worth noting here.

In Commission Decision 93/428/Euratom, the Commission first specified that the proper functioning of the machinery established by Chapter 6 of the Euratom Treaty is ensured by the ESA Rules, which provide a mechanism for balancing supply and demand, and noted that this machinery - including the ESA's right of option and its exclusive right to conclude supply contracts - has never been repealed.[773] In other words, the Commission confirmed the validity of the provisions establishing the common supply policy under Chapter 6 of the Euratom Treaty.

Second, the Commission indicated that neither the Euratom Treaty nor the secondary legislation provide for a 'Community preference' concerning nuclear supplies. The ESA is, therefore, not required to order Community users to obtain supplies from Community producers before they can conclude supply contracts with non-Community suppliers. The applicable rules authorise Euratom Community users to negotiate with producers of their choice.[774] The Commission also specified that Article 5 bis of the ESA Rules authorises Community users to negotiate with the producers of their choice, under a simplified procedure, both inside and outside the Euratom Community, without the Euratom Treaty or the ESA Rules laying down a 'Community preference'.[775] The Commission concluded its assessment by stating that no action should therefore be taken against Community users who obtain supplies from outside

which demand is to be balanced against the supply of ores, source materials and special fissile materials, OJ 32, 11.5.1960, p. 776.

770. For more information *see* Chapter 6 Section 01 of this study.

771. Commission Decision 93/428/Euratom of 19 July 1993 on a procedure for the application of the second paragraph of Article 53 of the EAEC Treaty, OJ L 197, 6.8.1993, pp. 54–56; and Commission Decision 94/285/Euratom of 21 February 1994 relating to a procedure in application of the second paragraph of Article 53 of the Euratom Treaty, OJ L 122, 17.5.1994, pp. 30–36.

772. The Empresa Nacional de Uranio SA (ENU), company constituted under Portuguese law - *see* Article 2 of Commission Decision 93/428/Euratom; the German company Kernkraftwerke Lippe-Ems GmbH (KLE) - *see* Article 2 of Commission Decision 94/285/Euratom.

773. Recital 7 of Commission Decision 93/428/Euratom.

774. Recital 12 of Commission Decision 93/428/Euratom.

775. Recital 8 of Commission Decision 93/428/Euratom.

the Euratom Community and submit their contracts to the ESA for signature for the purpose of their conclusion.[776] Although the Commission came to a general conclusion on the Community users' prerogative to negotiate contracts on their own, Article 5 bis of the ESA Rules explicitly states that the latter prerogative is applicable only to ores and source materials, which implies that contracts relating to the supply of special fissile materials coming from outside the Euratom Community can only be negotiated by the ESA. Consequently, the Commission separates the ESA's exclusive right to conclude contracts established under Article 52 of the Euratom Treaty from the right to negotiate contracts, but this right to negotiate does not include contracts for supply of special fissile materials. On the one hand, the Commission's exercise of its competences seems to weaken the competences of the ESA laid down, *inter alia*, in Article 52 of the Euratom Treaty, because, through the Commission's interpretation, the ESA is distanced from contract negotiations. On the other hand, under the provisions of the ESA Rules, the ESA has a right to refuse to conclude a contract, and any amendment to a supply contract shall require a new signature of the ESA, in accordance with the procedure for the original contract.[777]

Third, when exercising competences under Article 53 of the Euratom Treaty, the Commission interprets provisions of Article 66 of the Euratom Treaty, by stating that Article 66 does not apply in cases where the tenders offered are too high to be competitive in the Euratom Community and no Community user accepts them. The Commission takes the view that Article 66 only covers crisis situations in which the ESA is not in a position to supply users except at excessively high prices, with the consequence that users may, under certain conditions, be granted the right to obtain supplies from outside the Euratom Community without any intervention whatsoever for the ESA.[778]

In Commission Decision 94/285/Euratom, the Commission exercised its competences under Article 53 of the Euratom Treaty by confirming the importance of diversification of supplies in the Euratom Community's common supply policy and the ESA's role in that, and by elaborating on its position concerning the conclusion of contracts. First, the Commission indicated that, with regard to the general objective of diversifying sources of supply in the energy sector, there has long been agreement on this objective in the communities[779] and referred to the Council Resolution of 16 September 1986.[780] Concerning supplies of nuclear material, the Commission indicated that the Euratom Community's common supply policy under Article 52 of the Euratom

776. Recital 10 of Commission Decision 93/428/Euratom.
777. Article 5 bis(f) and (i) of the Rules of the Supply Agency of the Euratom Community.
778. Recital 9 of Commission Decision 93/428/Euratom.
779. Recital 16 of Commission Decision 94/285/Euratom.
780. Council Resolution of 16 September 1986 concerning new Community energy policy objectives for 1995 and convergence of the policies of the Member States, OJ C 241, 25.9.1986, pp. 1-3. This Council Resolution provides that, concerning new Community energy policy objectives for 1995 and convergence of the policies of the Member States, the Council emphatically took the view that the energy policy of the Community and of the Member States must endeavour to achieve certain horizontal objectives, *inter alia*, more secure conditions of supply and reduced risks of sudden fluctuations in energy prices through, *inter alia*, geographical diversification of the Community's external sources of supply.

Treaty must be directed towards the tasks set out in Article 2(d) of the Euratom Treaty; i.e., to ensure that users in the Euratom Community receive a regular and equitable supply of ores and nuclear fuels.[781] The latter task and the common supply policy furthermore imply that the ESA is not only authorised to decide whether and with which partners agreements or contracts should be concluded for the supply of ores, source materials or special fissile materials coming from outside the Euratom Community but also has a competence to determine the modalities of such supply arrangements that it considers necessary.[782] The Commission also reiterated the provisions of the Euratom Treaty by stating that, under Article 61 of the Euratom Treaty, the ESA is not obliged to meet supply orders of the Euratom Treaty where there are 'legal or material obstacles' to doing so. Such a legal obstacle exists in particular if, by meeting the order, the ESA were to secure a privileged position for certain users.

Second, in the Commission Decision 94/285/Euratom the Commission elaborated on its position concerning the conclusion of contracts, by stating that the fact that the ESA allows producers and users themselves to draw up contracts more easily and directly under a simplified procedure in accordance with the ESA Rules does not mean that the ESA loses the competences conferred on it in this regard under the Euratom Treaty. Under Article 52(2)(b) of the Euratom Treaty, the ESA still has the exclusive right to conclude supply contracts for materials coming from outside the Community and is therefore still authorised to exercise its rights under the Euratom Treaty in respect of the common supply policy. Hence, the validity of these rights does not depend on the ESA Rules.[783] In addition, the Commission has confirmed the implications of Article 5 bis of the ESA Rules, i.e., that it does not require the conclusion of a supply contract, as under paragraphs (f) and (g) of that Article, the ESA also has the right to refuse to conclude a contract if necessary.[784]

In conclusion, by exercising its competences under Article 53 of the Euratom Treaty, the Commission endorsed the validity of the provisions establishing the common supply policy under Chapter 6 of the Euratom Treaty and established its position that neither the Euratom Treaty nor the secondary legislation provide for a 'Community preference' concerning nuclear supplies. Furthermore, the exercise of the Euratom Community's competences under Article 53 of the Euratom Treaty established the importance of diversification of supplies in the Euratom Community's common supply policy. Finally, the Commission exercised its competences under Article 53 by separating the concept of negotiation of contracts, which can be done by the Community users under a simplified procedure, and the conclusion of contracts, which is a competence of the ESA under the Euratom Treaty. The Commission, however, underlined that the fact that the ESA allows producers and users themselves to draw up contracts more easily and directly under a simplified procedure in accordance with the ESA Rules, does not mean that the ESA loses the powers conferred on it in this regard under the Euratom Treaty.

781. Recital 17 of Commission Decision 94/285/Euratom.
782. Recital 20 of Commission Decision 94/285/Euratom.
783. Recital 20 of Commission Decision 94/285/Euratom.
784. Recital 14 of Commission Decision 94/285/Euratom.

It is established under Chapter 6 Section 01 of this study that Article 54 of the Euratom Treaty establishes the legal status of the ESA and gives the Council competence to adopt the ESA's statutes on a proposal from the Commission. Under Article 54 of the Euratom Treaty, the ESA's statutes must determine the ESA's capital and the rules for the commercial management of the activities of the ESA. Analysis of the secondary legislation shows that the Council exercises its competences under Article 54 of the Euratom Treaty by adopting two types of Council decisions: – decisions on establishing statutes for the ESA[785] and decisions on appointing members of the ESA's Advisory Committee.[786] Due to the scope of this study the focus here will be on Council Decision 2008/114/EC, Euratom, on establishing statutes for the ESA.[787]

The statutes specify that ESA's aim is to perform the tasks entrusted to it under Chapter 6 of the Euratom Treaty in accordance with the objectives of the Euratom Treaty. In addition to this general aim, the statutes identify three specific tasks that the ESA is to carry out. These are: the provision of expertise to the Euratom Community on the operation of the nuclear market; monitoring and identification of nuclear market trends that could affect the security of supply; and establishment of the Advisory Committee for advice, support and cooperation.[788] The statutes regulate the ESA's internal structure and functioning,[789] financial provisions[790] and the composition and functioning of the Advisory Committee of the ESA.[791] Regarding the internal structure and functioning of the ESA, the statutes establish that it has a seat in Luxembourg and

785. Three Council decisions were adopted to this effect: the Euratom Community Council Decision on the Statutes of the Euratom Supply Agency, OJ 27, 6.12.1958, pp. 534–540 (repealed by Council Decision 2008/114/EC, Euratom); Council Decision 73/45/Euratom of 8 March 1973 amending the Statutes of the Euratom Supply Agency following the Accession of new Member States to the Community, OJ L 83, 30.3.1973, p. 20; and Council Decision 2008/114/EC, Euratom of 12 February 2008 establishing Statutes for the Euratom Supply Agency, OJ L 41, 15.2.2008, pp. 15–20.
786. Thirty-four Council decisions appointing members of the Advisory Committee of the ESA were adopted.
787. Council Decision 2008/114/EC, Euratom of 12 February 2008 establishing Statutes for the Euratom Supply Agency, OJ L 41, 15.2.2008, pp. 15–20. Council Decision 2008/114/EC was amended by Euratom Regulation (EU) No 517/2013 of 13 May 2013 adapting certain regulations and decisions in the fields of free movement of goods, freedom of movement for persons, company law, competition policy, agriculture, food safety, veterinary and phytosanitary policy, transport policy, energy, taxation, statistics, trans-European networks, judiciary and fundamental rights, justice, freedom and security, environment, customs union, external relations, foreign, security and defence policy and institutions, by reason of the accession of the Republic of Croatia, OJ L 158, 10.6.2013, pp. 1–71, but the latter amendment was repealed by Council Regulation (EU) 2015/1589 of 13 July 2015 laying down detailed rules for the application of Article 108 of the Treaty on the Functioning of the European Union, OJ L 248, 24.9.2015, pp. 9–29.
788. Article 1 in the Statutes of the Euratom Supply Agency, Annex to Council Decision 2008/114/EC, Euratom.
789. Articles 1 to 5 in the Statutes of the Euratom Supply Agency, Annex to Council Decision 2008/114/EC, Euratom.
790. Articles 6 to 10 in the Statutes of the Euratom Supply Agency, Annex to Council Decision 2008/114/EC, Euratom.
791. Articles 11 to 14 in the Statutes of the Euratom Supply Agency, Annex to Council Decision 2008/114/EC, Euratom.

operates on a non-profit-making basis.[792] The Director-General of the ESA is be appointed by the Commission and must submit a yearly report to the EP, the Council and the Commission covering the activities of the ESA in the previous year and a work programme for the coming year, after obtaining the opinion of the Advisory Committee.[793] Both the Director-General and the staff of the ESA have the status of officials of the European Communities: they are appointed by and their salaries are paid by the Commission.[794]

The ESA's statutes repeat the wording of Article 53 of the Euratom Treaty without actually referring to it, by saying that the ESA is under the supervision of the Commission, which may issue directives to it and have a right of veto over its decisions.[795] Article 5 of the ESA's statutes contains provisions that govern the procedure and time frames as to the vetoing of the ESA's decisions. In so doing, Article 5 also exercises the Euratom Community's competences under Article 53 of the Euratom Treaty. Furthermore, in each of the Member States the ESA enjoys the most extensive legal capacity accorded to legal persons under its laws. For example, it may acquire or dispose of movable and immovable property and be a party to legal proceedings.[796]

The requirement laid down in Article 54 of the Euratom Treaty for rules of commercial management to be laid down under the ESA's statutes has been exercised by means of the financial provisions contained therein. The ESA's financial autonomy means that it may carry out financial operations, transfer its assets into another currency in order to carry out financial or commercial operations and contract borrowings for a limited time on behalf of the Euratom Community.[797] Article 54 of the Euratom Treaty also requires the ESA's statutes to determine the ESA's capital, which is EUR 5,824,000. The system under which the capital is subscribed from all Member States is based on seven levels of payments, which range from no payment to EUR 672,000.[798]

Finally, the ESA's statutes regulate the status, composition and functioning of the Advisory Committee by, *inter alia*, establishing that it acts as a link between the ESA

792. Article 2(1) and (3) in the Statutes of the Euratom Supply Agency, Annex to Council Decision 2008/114/EC, Euratom.
793. Article 3(1) and (4) in the Statutes of the Euratom Supply Agency, Annex to Council Decision 2008/114/EC, Euratom.
794. Article 4(1) and (4) in the Statutes of the Euratom Supply Agency, Annex to Council Decision 2008/114/EC, Euratom.
795. Article 5(1) and (4) of the Statutes of the Euratom Supply Agency; Annex to Decision 2008/114/EC, Euratom.
796. Article 2(5) of the Statutes of the Euratom Supply Agency; Annex to Decision 2008/114/EC, Euratom.
797. Article 6(2) and (3) of the Statutes of the Euratom Supply Agency; Annex to Decision 2008/114/EC, Euratom.
798. Article 9 of the Statutes of the Euratom Supply Agency; Annex to Council Decision 2008/114/EC, Euratom; No payment – Luxembourg, Malta; EUR 32,000 – Estonia, Ireland, Cyprus, Latvia, Lithuania and Slovenia; EUR 96,000 – Bulgaria, Denmark, Austria, Slovakia and Finland; EUR 192,000 – Belgium, Czech Republic, Greece, Hungary, Netherlands, Portugal and Sweden; EUR 288,000 – Romania; EUR 416,000 – Spain and Poland; EUR 672,000 – Germany, France, Italy and the UK.

and both producers and users in the nuclear industry.[799] The Advisory Committee provides a forum for discussion and guides the ESA on nuclear supply and trade matters.[800] In the exercise of its competences under Chapter 6 of the Euratom Treaty, the Commission has established that the producers and users of nuclear material in the Euratom Community participate in implementing the common supply policy through the Advisory Committee.[801]

In conclusion, the Euratom Community's competences under Article 54 of the Euratom Treaty are exercised in accordance with the wording of the Treaty. They are exercised through two types of Council decisions: one which adopts the ESA's statutes and another which appoints members of the Advisory Committee. The exercise of competences under the ESA's statutes focus on implementation of competences laid down in Article 54 of the Euratom Treaty. These include provisions concerning the seat, financial autonomy and capital of the ESA.

Article 60 of the Euratom Treaty establishes the functioning of the Euratom Community's common supply policy. The ESA Rules determining the manner in which demand is to be balanced against the supply and the regulation of the Supply Agency, amending the ESA Rules[802] exercise the Euratom Community's competences under Article 60(6) of the Euratom Treaty. The ESA Rules exercise the Euratom Community's competences in the field by establishing two main functions of the ESA. The first of these is the acquisition of complete knowledge of the situation on the nuclear supplies market in the Euratom Community – i.e., information on general data and market trends, supply potential and possible outlets in third countries – and the provision of that information to users and producers in the Community.[803] The second is the balancing of demand against supply by the ESA exercising its right of option on tenders from the producers of the Community, and in that way controlling the supply of ores,

799. Article 13(1) of Council Decision 2008/114/EC, Euratom of 12 February 2008 establishing Statutes for the Euratom Supply Agency, OJ L 41, 15.2.2008, pp. 15–20.
800. A. Bouquet, 'How Current Are Euratom Provisions on Nuclear Supply and Ownership in View of the European Union's Enlargement?', (2001) 68 *Nuclear Law Bulletin*, p. 13.
801. Recital 24 of Commission Decision 94/285/Euratom.
802. Rules of the Supply Agency of the European Atomic Energy Community of 5 May 1960 determining the manner in which demand is to be balanced against the supply of ores, source materials and special fissile materials, OJ 32, 11.5.1960, pp. 777–779; and Regulation of the Supply Agency of the European Atomic Energy Community amending the rules of the Supply Agency of 5 May 1960 determining the manner in which demand is to be balanced against the supply of ores, source materials and special fissile materials, OJ L 193, 25.7.1975, pp. 37–38. The Commission has indicated that as the existing Rules of the Supply Agency have not been modified since 1975, it is therefore necessary to update and clarify them to take into account changes in the functioning of the nuclear fuel market. The main objective of simplifying the existing Rules of the Supply Agency would include extending the application of simplified contract procedures to cover special fissile materials as well as natural uranium. *See* Commission Staff Working Document Regulatory Fitness and Performance Programme (REFIT): State of Play and Outlook accompanying the document Better Regulation for Better Results – An EU Agenda, SWD (2015) 110 final, p. 58.
803. Paragraph 5 in the Preamble and Articles 1, 2 and 4 of the Rules of the Supply Agency determining the manner in which demand is to be balanced against the supply of ores, source materials and special fissile materials. The preamble notes that in order to carry out its duties in accordance with the principles set out in Article 52 of the Euratom Treaty, the ESA must have a complete knowledge of the situation on the market.

source materials and special fissile materials in the Euratom Community and adjusting it to existing demand.[804] It has been noted in the context of an analysis of the exercise of the Euratom Community's competences under Article 53 of the Euratom Treaty that the ESA Rules also establish a simplified procedure for the conclusion of contracts.[805] In order for this procedure to be applied the Commission must carry out an assessment that concludes that the market shows a clear supply surplus in respect of supply over demand of a specific product. The procedure implies that the ESA lays down the general conditions to be fulfilled under supply contracts covering a specific product, the parties concerned are then empowered to negotiate directly to sign the contracts and those contracts are then communicated to the ESA and deemed to be concluded if no objection is raised by the ESA. Any amendment to such a supply contract requires a new signature of the ESA in accordance with the original procedure for signature.[806] However, as established above, this simplified procedure cannot be used in relation to supply contracts for special fissile materials.

Consequently, the Euratom Community's competences under Article 60 of the Euratom Treaty are exercised through the following: defining the ESA's role in monitoring the nuclear market; establishing a procedure to control the supply in order to be able to balance it against demand; and establishing a simplified procedure through which to conclude contracts when supply of ores and source materials is higher than demand in the Euratom Community.

Article 74 of the Euratom Treaty establishes the Commission's competence to exempt transfer, import or export of small quantities of ores, source materials or special fissile materials from the provisions of Chapter 6 of the Euratom Treaty, and is a form of *de minimis* clause.[807] This competence is exercised through Commission Regulation (Euratom) No 66/2006,[808] which defines quantities of ores, uranium and thorium source materials and special fissile materials that are to be considered as small quantities.[809] Commission Regulation (Euratom) No 66/2006 also imposes an obligation on all persons that effect import, export or transfer within the Euratom Community under the exemptions provided for in Articles 1 and 2 of this regulation to submit a quarterly statement of the transactions to the ESA.[810] Consequently, Regulation

804. Article 6 of the Rules of the Supply Agency determining the manner in which demand is to be balanced against the supply of ores, source materials and special fissile materials.
805. Initially the procedure for balancing offers and demands for nuclear materials, as laid down in Article 60 of the Euratom Treaty, was not applied to natural uranium: the industry wanted to make its own bargains, not depend on the Supply Agency to receive all offers and demands and decide the terms on which it could meet the orders. This situation is considered to have led to the establishment of the simplified procedure. *See* D. Allen, 'The Euratom Treaty, Chapter VI: New Hope or False Dawn?', (1983) 20 *Common Market Law Review*, p. 479.
806. Articles 5 and 5 bis of the Rules of the Supply Agency determining the manner in which demand is to be balanced against the supply of ores, source materials and special fissile materials.
807. D. Allen, 'The Euratom Treaty, Chapter VI: New Hope or False Dawn?', (1983) 20 *Common Market Law Review*, p. 476.
808. Commission Regulation (Euratom) No 66/2006 of 16 January 2006 exempting the transfer of small quantities of ores, source materials and special fissile materials from the rules of the chapter on supplies, OJ L 11, 17.1.2006, pp. 6–8.
809. Articles 1 and 2 of Regulation (Euratom) No 66/2006.
810. Article 3 of Regulation (Euratom) No 66/2006.

(Euratom) No 66/2006 exercises the Euratom Community's competences under Article 74 of the Euratom Treaty in accordance with the wording of the Treaty.

In conclusion, keeping in mind that the scope and content of the Euratom Community's competences in the field of nuclear supplies are established in twenty-five articles of the Euratom Treaty under Chapter 6, the Euratom Community's competences in this area are exercised to a relatively limited extent. This fact sometimes raises the question as to whether the common supply policy has been exercised in its full form.[811] The majority of the Euratom Community's competences under Chapter 6 are exercised in accordance with the wording of the Euratom Treaty. The exercise of the Euratom Community's competences under Article 53 of the Euratom Treaty is carried out on a broader basis than the wording of the Treaty would appear to indicate. The secondary legal acts adopted under this article endorse the validity of the provisions establishing the common supply policy under Chapter 6 of the Euratom Treaty, establish that there is no 'Community preference' for nuclear supplies under the Euratom Treaty, and separate the concept of negotiation of contracts from that of the conclusion of contracts. Analysis of the exercise of the Euratom Community's competences under Chapter 6 of the Euratom Treaty shows that the Euratom Community has a competence to protect and promote the diversification of supplies in the context of the common supply policy. Furthermore, the fact that the Euratom Community's secondary legislation establishes a simplified procedure through which producers and users may, in certain situations, negotiate contracts more easily and directly does not mean that the ESA loses the powers to this effect conferred on it by the Euratom Treaty. The exercise of the Euratom Community's competences under Chapter 6 of the Euratom Treaty also elaborates on the role of the ESA, which must not only ensure a balance between supply and demand, but is also responsible for monitoring the nuclear supplies market and providing the relevant knowledge on the supplies market to users and producers within the Euratom Community.

6.03 THE CJEU'S INTERPRETATION OF THE COMPETENCES

This section analyses whether and how the CJEU's case-law defines and delimits the Euratom Community's competence in the field of nuclear supply.

Analysis of the CJEU's case-law in relation to nuclear supply shows that the CJEU has been active in defining and delimiting the Euratom Community's competences under Chapter 6 of the Euratom Treaty.[812]

In defining the Euratom Community's competences in relation to nuclear supply, the Court has confirmed the valid, binding and mandatory nature of the competences

811. *See* A. Bouquet, 'How Current Are Euratom Provisions on Nuclear Supply and Ownership in View of the European Union's Enlargement?', (2001) 68 *Nuclear Law Bulletin*, p. 11.
812. The Court had heard eight cases, in which it defined and delimited the Euratom Community's competences in relation to nuclear supply under Chapter 6 of the Euratom Treaty. Some authors are still of the opinion that the provisions concerning equal access to sources of supply, stockpiles and right of option are obsolete. *See* A. Bouquet, 'How Current Are Euratom Provisions on Nuclear Supply and Ownership in View of the European Union's Enlargement?', (2001) 68 *Nuclear Law Bulletin*, p. 7.

under Chapter 6 of the Euratom Treaty and the exclusivity of these competences in relation to nuclear supply. Referring to the prerogatives conferred on the Euratom Community by the provisions of the Euratom Treaty, the Court has emphasised the care taken to define in a precise and binding manner the exclusive right exercised by the Euratom Community in relation to nuclear supply in the context of both internal and external relations.[813] Furthermore, the Court has stated that the fact that market conditions have rendered less necessary the use of the supply mechanisms stipulated in the Euratom Treaty, this does not suffice to deprive those provisions of their mandatory character.[814] It has also been clear that even where the ESA does not exercise its exclusive right, the Euratom Community's real interest in all things relating to materials falling within the definitions of the Euratom Treaty must be recognised.[815]

In several cases, the Court has defined the ESA's competences and role in relation to nuclear supply. It has ruled that the ESA was established to guarantee, under the conditions laid down in Chapter 6 of the Euratom Treaty, one of the essential aims which the Euratom Treaty assigns to the Euratom Community, namely to ensure that all users in the Euratom Community receive a regular and equitable supply of ores and nuclear fuels.[816] The ESA was established under Article 52(2)(b) of the Euratom Treaty expressly for this purpose and that provision conferred upon the ESA exclusive rights in order to ensure that Community users receive regular and equitable supplies of ores and nuclear fuels coming from both the Euratom Community and non-member countries.[817] According to the CJEU, the ESA plays an essential role in the common supply policy and, where decisions concerning economic and commercial policy and nuclear policy are involved, the ESA has a broad discretion when exercising its powers.[818] The Court confirmed that in order to fulfil its functions relating to supplies, the ESA has the two rights provided for in the Euratom Treaty: a right of option on ores, source materials and special fissile materials produced in the territories of Member States; and an exclusive right to conclude contracts relating to the supply of ores,

813. Ruling of 14 November 1978, Ruling of the Court delivered pursuant to the third paragraph of Article 103 of the Euratom Treaty - Draft Convention of the International Atomic Energy Agency on the Physical Protection of Nuclear Materials, Facilities and Transports, Ruling 1/78, ECLI:EU:C:1978:202, paragraph 14; judgment of 15 September 1995, *ENU v Commission*, Joined Cases T-458/93 and T-523/93, ECLI:EU:T:1995:165, paragraph 56.
814. Judgment of 14 December 1971, *Commission v France*, C-7/71, ECLI:EU:C:1971:121, paragraphs 41 and 43; judgment of 15 September 1995, *ENU v Commission*, Joined Cases T-458/93 and T-523/93, ECLI:EU:T:1995:165, paragraph 56.
815. Ruling of 14 November 1978, Ruling of the Court delivered pursuant to the third paragraph of Article 103 of the Euratom Treaty - Draft Convention of the International Atomic Energy Agency on the Physical Protection of Nuclear Materials, Facilities and Transports, Ruling 1/78, ECLI:EU:C:1978:202, paragraph 17.
816. Judgment of 11 March 1997, *ENU v Commission*, C-357/95 P, ECLI:EU:C:1997:144, paragraph 45.
817. Judgment of 15 September 1995, *ENU v Commission*, Joined Cases T-458/93 and T-523/93, ECLI:EU:T:1995:165, paragraph 57.
818. Judgment of 22 April 1999, *Kernkraftwerke Lippe-Ems v Commission*, C-161/97 P, ECLI:EU:C:1999:193, paragraph 63; judgment of 25 February 1997, *Kernkraftwerke Lippe-Ems v Commission*, Joined Cases T-149/94 and T-181/94, ECLI:EU:T:1997:21, paragraph 90.

source materials and special fissile materials coming from inside the Euratom Community or outside.[819] Furthermore, the case-law has elaborated that under the first paragraph of Article 61 of the Euratom Treaty and Article 5 bis(f) of the ESA Rules, the ESA has not only the right but also the duty to refuse to conclude a contract as a whole, without making any amendments, where it considers that there is a legal obstacle. The ESA does not, however, have the right to amend the substance of the contract by adding conditions. The CJEU also concluded that the bounds the overstepping of which would constitute a legal obstacle within the meaning of Article 61 of the Euratom Treaty undeniably include compliance with the aim of achieving a regular and equitable supply, and that this obliges the ESA to ensure that certain orders do not affect the diversification of supply or breach the principle of non-discrimination, whatever the origin of those supplies, whether from inside or outside the Community.[820] The Court took the view that it is clear that the ESA's tasks are limited to implementing the system for ensuring supplies established under Chapter 6 of the Euratom Treaty.[821]

The CJEU has also addressed the issue of a 'Community preference' concerning nuclear supplies[822] and took the view that the Euratom Treaty does not contain any provision guaranteeing, expressly or implicitly, preferential disposal of production coming from the Euratom Community. On the contrary, under the system by which offers from Community producers and applications from Community users are centralised with the ESA so as to enable it to ensure that all users have regular and equitable supplies, no distinction is made by reference to the origin of products. Therefore, the ESA is not bound to guarantee the disposal of ores and nuclear fuels coming from within the Euratom Community, offers of which are notified to the ESA pursuant to the second paragraph of Article 60 of the Euratom Treaty. The system for regulating supplies only lays down the principle of preference for Community users, in accordance with Article 2(d) of the Euratom Treaty, and does not guarantee the disposal of Community production of ores.[823] The price-fixing mechanism established by the Euratom Treaty under the system governing supplies thus confirms that that system does not allow preferential treatment to be given to ores and other nuclear fuels coming from within the Euratom Community when they are offered at prices higher than those prevailing on the world market, in the absence of specific circumstances which would impede attainment of the aims of the Euratom Treaty pursued by Chapter 6 of the

819. Judgment of 11 March 1997, *ENU v Commission*, C-357/95 P, ECLI:EU:C:1997:144, paragraph 6; judgment of 25 February 1997, *Kernkraftwerke Lippe-Ems v Commission*, Joined Cases T-149/94 and T-181/94, ECLI:EU:T:1997:21, paragraph 85; judgment of 15 September 1995, *ENU v Commission*, Joined Cases T-458/93 and T-523/93, ECLI:EU:T:1995:165, paragraph 57.
820. Judgment of 22 April 1999, *Kernkraftwerke Lippe-Ems v Commission*, C-161/97 P, ECLI:EU:C:1999:193, paragraphs 63 and 89.
821. Judgment of 15 September 1995, *ENU v Commission*, Joined Cases T-458/93 and T-523/93, ECLI:EU:T:1995:165, paragraphs 58 and 59.
822. *See also* analysis of the exercise of the Euratom Community's competences in relation to nuclear supply in Chapter 6 Section 02 of this study.
823. Judgment of 15 September 1995, *ENU v Commission*, Joined Cases T-458/93 and T-523/93, ECLI:EU:T:1995:165, paragraphs 59–63; judgment of 11 March 1997, *ENU v Commission*, C-357/95 P, ECLI:EU:C:1997:144, paragraph 46.

Euratom Treaty, without Council intervention under Article 69 of the Euratom Treaty. Consequently, showing a systematic Community preference for producers of nuclear ores would run counter to the objectives of the Euratom Treaty.[824] Some authors take the view that the supply system provided for in the Euratom Treaty was designed not only to intervene effectively in the event of scarcity of nuclear supplies, but that it can also be applied in the event of an oversupply crisis.[825] It is, however, clear from the exercise of the Euratom Community's competences and the Court's interpretation of the provisions under Chapter 6 of the Euratom Treaty that the Euratom Treaty does not establish a 'Community preference' for supplies produced inside the Euratom Community. This indicates that the Euratom Community does not have competence to intervene in the cases of oversupply.

The CJEU has also emphasised the importance of the geographical diversification of supplies. The Court has established that the requirements of reliability and diversifying sources of supply follow directly from the principle of the regular and equitable supply for all Community users set out in Article 2(d) of the Euratom Treaty.[826] The geographical origin of the materials to be supplied is thus one of the principal elements of a supply contract which must be communicated to the ESA. Consequently, it is essential for the ESA to know the geographical origin of the nuclear supplies in order to ensure reliability of supply, which is the aim of the supply policy pursued.[827] The Court has, furthermore, indicated that regularity of supply is closely linked with diversity of sources. According to the CJEU, Article 60 of the Euratom Treaty, under which users of raw materials must periodically inform the ESA of the place of origin of supplies, confirms the importance of knowledge of the geographical origin of supplies for implementation of the common supply policy by the ESA.[828] In order to ensure, in particular, geographical diversification in outside sources of supply, the ESA has a competence to bar certain imports of uranium which would reduce such diversification, using its exclusive right to conclude contracts for the supply of ores and other nuclear fuels, in accordance with the task conferred upon it by the Euratom Treaty.[829]

The simplified procedure for concluding supply contracts under Article 5 bis of the ESA Rules has been challenged by industry players, who argue that it creates disparity between the strict letter of the law as represented by Chapter 6 of the Euratom Treaty and the practice followed since 1960.[830] The CJEU has ruled that the simplified procedure, which allows users to negotiate supply contracts directly with producers of

824. Judgment of 15 September 1995, *ENU v Commission*, Joined Cases T-458/93 and T-523/93, ECLI:EU:T:1995:165, paragraphs 64 and 65.
825. A. Bouquet, 'How current are Euratom provisions on nuclear supply and ownership in view of the European Union's enlargement?', (2001) 68 *Nuclear Law Bulletin*, p. 8.
826. Judgment of 22 April 1999, *Kernkraftwerke Lippe-Ems v Commission*, C-161/97 P, ECLI:EU:C:1999:193, paragraph 110.
827. Judgment of 25 February 1997, *Kernkraftwerke Lippe-Ems v Commission*, Joined Cases T-149/94 and T-181/94, ECLI:EU:T:1997:21, paragraph 35.
828. Judgment of 22 April 1999, *Kernkraftwerke Lippe-Ems v Commission*, C-161/97 P, ECLI:EU:C:1999:193, paragraphs 62 and 67.
829. Judgment of 15 September 1995, *ENU v Commission*, Joined Cases T-458/93 and T-523/93, ECLI:EU:T:1995:165, paragraph 68; judgment of 25 February 1997, *Kernkraftwerke Lippe-Ems v Commission*, Joined Cases T-149/94 and T-181/94, ECLI:EU:T:1997:21, paragraph 92.
830. T. F. Cusack, 'A Tale of Two Treaties', (2003) 40 *Common Market Law Review*, p. 123.

their choice, does not deprive the ESA of its exclusive competences, and is in conformity with the system governing supplies established by the Euratom Treaty. The Court went on to say that even within the framework of the simplified procedure, the ESA has the right to object to a contract that might prejudice the achievement of the objectives of the Euratom Treaty.[831] The Court has also taken the view that the simplified procedure, as defined in Article 5 bis of the ESA Rules, applies not only to supplies from the Euratom Community but also to those imported from non-member countries in accordance with Article 65 of the Euratom Treaty, which refers to Article 60 as a whole, the sixth paragraph of which is the legal basis of the ESA Rules. Moreover, that procedure is not contrary to Article 66 of the Euratom Treaty, since it does not infringe the ESA's exclusive right to conclude contracts.[832] Some authors are of the opinion that the Court's conclusion that the simplified procedure for the conclusion of contracts is in conformity with the provisions of the Euratom Treaty could be invoked to achieve the application of this procedure to contracts concerning special fissile materials.[833] It has been established that special fissile materials are explicitly exempted from the simplified procedure set out in the ESA Rules and it is hard, therefore, to find arguments supporting this interpretation.[834]

Concerning the Commission's horizontal competences under Article 53 of the Euratom Treaty, the CJEU has ruled that the special feature of Article 53(2) of the Euratom Treaty is to give interested parties seeking to contest an ESA decision the opportunity to bring the matter before the Commission and to oblige that institution to take a decision within a one-month period. The Court interprets the wording of Article 53(2) as requiring the Commission to give a decision if an act, whether implied or expressed, performed by the ESA in the exercise of its right of option or of its exclusive right to conclude supply contracts, is referred to it by a concerned party. Consequently, the Court concluded that the Commission has an obligation to issue a decision under Article 53(2) of the Euratom Treaty.[835]

Finally, the Court has elaborated on the Euratom Community's competences under Articles 75 and 76 of the Euratom Treaty.

The Court ruled that the effect of Article 75 of the Euratom Treaty, which establishes the Euratom Community's competence to exempt certain activities from its common supply policy, is to remove substances that are the subject of the contract

---

831. Judgment of 15 September 1995, *ENU v Commission*, Joined Cases T-458/93 and T-523/93, ECLI:EU:T:1995:165, paragraph 73; judgment of 25 February 1997, *Kernkraftwerke Lippe-Ems v Commission*, Joined Cases T-149/94 and T-181/94, ECLI:EU:T:1997:21, paragraph 86.
832. Judgment of 11 March 1997, *ENU v Commission*, C-357/95 P, ECLI:EU:C:1997:144, paragraph 50.
833. A. Bouquet, 'How Current Are Euratom Provisions on Nuclear Supply and Ownership in View of the European Union's Enlargement?', (2001) 68 *Nuclear Law Bulletin*, p. 15; D. Allen, 'The Euratom Treaty, Chapter VI: New Hope or False Dawn?', (1983) 20 *Common Market Law Review*, p. 480.
834. The fact that a parallel practice was developed by the Agency, where it, by its own representative's signature, concludes special fissile material contracts, in fact, already negotiated and signed by the parties, does not change the legal implications of the provisions.
835. Judgment of 16 February 1993, *ENU v Commission*, C-107/91, ECLI:EU:C:1993:56, paragraphs 11, 26 and 32–34; judgment of 15 September 1995, *ENU v Commission*, Joined Cases T-458/93 and T-523/93, ECLI:EU:T:1995:165, paragraph 13.

work operations referred to in that provision from the ambit of the provisions relating to the supply system.[836] It follows that Article 75 concerns situations that are deemed not to affect, or not sufficiently to affect, the regular and equitable nuclear supply to all users in the Euratom Community, in order to justify the full application of the system laid down under Chapter 6 of the Euratom Treaty. That applies to a process, such as that referred to in Article 75(1)(c) of the Euratom Treaty, which involves the enrichment in the Euratom Community of uranium from a third state and which is to be returned to that third state. Such a process is inherently neutral as regards the supply of uranium to users established in the Euratom Community. Therefore, Article 75(1) of the Euratom Treaty is to be interpreted as meaning that the terms 'processing', 'conversion' and 'shaping' in that provision also encompass the enrichment of uranium. The Court, however, indicated that the fact that uranium enrichment constitutes a process, conversion or shaping within the meaning of Article 75 of the Euratom Treaty does not mean that such a process is free of all forms of control. The CJEU highlighted that the materials that may form the subject matter of the commitments referred to in Article 75 are, in any event, subject within the territories of the Member States to the safeguards set out in Chapter 7 of the Euratom Treaty.[837]

The Court has stated, with regard to Article 76 of the Euratom Treaty and the Euratom Community's competence to amend the provisions of Chapter 6 of the Euratom Treaty under a special procedure, that Article 76 does not contain any express stipulation that the Euratom Community will be relieved of the tasks conferred on it by Article 2 of the Euratom Treaty or that these tasks should be restored to the authority of the Member States. According to the CJEU, the objective of Article 76 of the Euratom Treaty is to enable the supply system to be adapted to changing circumstances. It cannot therefore be interpreted as depriving the Euratom Community of a means of action designed to achieve one of the objectives of the Euratom Treaty. The Court also indicated that until the decision is taken either to make the existing rules permanent, or to replace them by new rules, the provisions of Chapter 6 of the Euratom Treaty are only maintained on a temporary basis, so that they may be replaced at any given point by a set of new provisions constituting a different supply system.[838] As mentioned above, this does not prevent the existence of simplified procedures in the ESA Rules.[839]

In conclusion, the Court ruled in favour of the Euratom Community's competences under Chapter 6 of the Euratom Treaty having a valid, binding and exclusive nature. It has defined the ESA's central role in the Euratom Community's common

836. Ruling of 14 November 1978, Ruling of the Court delivered pursuant to the third paragraph of Article 103 of the Euratom Treaty – Draft Convention of the International Atomic Energy Agency on the Physical Protection of Nuclear Materials, Facilities and Transports, Ruling 1/78, ECLI:EU:C:1978:202, paragraph 16; judgment of 12 September 2006, *Industrias Nucleares do Brasil and Siemens*, Joined Cases C-123/04 and C-124/04, ECLI:EU:C:2006:542, paragraph 39.
837. Judgment of 12 September 2006, *Industrias Nucleares do Brasil and Siemens*, Joined Cases C-123/04 and C-124/04, ECLI:EU:C:2006:542, paragraphs 40, 45 and 46. *See also* Article 75(3) of the Euratom Treaty.
838. Judgment of 14 December 1971, *Commission v France*, C-7/71, ECLI:EU:C:1971:121, paragraphs 22, 26 and 28.
839. A. Bouquet, 'How Current Are Euratom Provisions on Nuclear Supply and Ownership in View of the European Union's Enlargement?', (2001) 68 *Nuclear Law Bulletin*, p. 10.

supply policy, including the duty to refuse to conclude a contract where it considers that there is a legal obstacle under Article 61 of the Euratom Treaty. The Court also delimited the Euratom Community's competences by establishing that the Euratom Treaty does not establish an obligation to guarantee preferential treatment of production coming from inside the Euratom Community, and by emphasising the importance of the geographical diversification of supplies. The CJEU also concluded that the simplified procedure does not deprive the ESA of its exclusive competences and is in conformity with the system governing supplies established by the Euratom Treaty. Finally, the Court interpreted the competences under the provisions of the Euratom Treaty as indicating that the Commission is obliged to issue a decision under Article 53(2) of the Euratom Treaty, that the terms 'processing', 'conversion' and 'shaping' also encompass the enrichment of uranium under Article 75 of the Euratom Treaty, and that Article 76 of the Euratom Treaty contains no express provision to the effect that the Euratom Community will be relieved of its tasks conferred on it by Article 2 of the Euratom Treaty or that these tasks should be restored to the authority of the Member States. Until a decision is taken under Article 76 either to make the existing rules permanent, or to replace them with new rules, the provisions of Chapter 6 of the Euratom Treaty are, therefore, only maintained on a temporary basis. Consequently, the CJEU defined the competences of the Euratom Community under Chapter 6 of the Euratom Treaty in a wider manner than the explicit wording of the Euratom Treaty would tend to indicate.

6.04 FEATURES OF THE COMPETENCES

This section assesses the following features with a view to ensuring a basis for a comparative analysis: the level of detail of the provisions of the Euratom Treaty; the exercise of the competences as compared with the bare wording of the Euratom Treaty; and the existence of case-law and the effect of the Court's interpretation of the relevant provisions of primary and secondary legislation to the competences of the Euratom Community.

The level of detail of the provisions of the Euratom Treaty that establish the Euratom Community's competences in relation to nuclear supply is high both in respect of the regulation of the common supply policy and in respect of the Euratom Community's competences in the specific areas of the nuclear supply chain. This high level of detail shows that this area had high priority at the time the Euratom Community was established and fulfils the Euratom Community's task of ensuring regular and equitable supply of ores and nuclear fuels for Community users.

In relation to nuclear supply, the Euratom Community's competences are exercised to a relatively limited extent through secondary legal acts: these competences are established in twenty-five articles of Chapter 6 of the Euratom Treaty, but only five articles have been used as legal bases for secondary legislation. Most of the Euratom Community's competences are exercised according to the wording of the Euratom Treaty. However, the competences established in Article 53 of the Euratom Treaty are exercised more broadly than the wording of this provision would tend to indicate, as the secondary legal acts adopted under it endorse the validity of the provisions establishing the common supply policy under Chapter 6 of the Euratom Treaty; establish that there is no 'Community preference' for nuclear supplies under the Euratom Treaty; and separate the concept of negotiation of contracts from that of their conclusion. The exercise of the Euratom Community's competences under Chapter 6 of the Euratom Treaty also elaborates on the importance of diversification of supplies in the common supply policy and on the ESA's role - in addition to the competences explicitly established under the Euratom Treaty, the ESA is also responsible for monitoring the nuclear supply market and providing the relevant knowledge about it to users and producers within the Euratom Community.

Despite the low level of exercise of the Euratom Community's competences in relation to nuclear supply, the Court has actively defined and delimited the Euratom Community's competences in this area in eight cases. It has established that the Euratom Community's competences under Chapter 6 of the Euratom Treaty have a valid, binding and exclusive nature, and has also ruled that until a decision is taken under Article 76 of the Euratom Treaty either to make the existing rules permanent, or to replace them with new rules, the provisions of Chapter 6 of the Euratom Treaty are to be maintained on a temporary basis. Furthermore, the Court has confirmed the ESA's central role in the Euratom Community's common supply policy, delimited the Euratom Community's competences by establishing that it has no obligation to guarantee preferential treatment of production coming from inside the Euratom Community, and emphasised the importance of geographical diversification of nuclear supplies.

CHAPTER 7

Safeguards

- *The main scope of the Euratom Community's competences in the field of nuclear safeguards is to ensure that ores, source materials and special fissile materials are not diverted from their originally intended uses. The content of the Community's competences in relation to nuclear safeguards comprises the three main elements: inspections, infringement procedures and sanctions. All the horizontal competences in the field are concentrated in one institution – the Commission.*
- *The exercise of the Euratom Community's competences in relation to nuclear safeguards is carried out to a broader extent than the wording of the Euratom Treaty would tend to imply, as it makes the safeguards provisions of the Euratom Treaty applicable to civil nuclear materials in military nuclear installations and expands the application of safeguards to certain nuclear waste. When exercising its competence to apply sanctions, the Commission carries out its objective and subjective analyses on a case-by-case basis.*
- *The Court has heard relatively few cases concerning safeguards, but the available case-law defines the Commission's competences under Chapter 7 of the Euratom Treaty as being fundamental to the accomplishment of the Euratom Community's tasks and wider in scope than the explicit wording of the Euratom Treaty indicates.*
- *The Euratom Community's competences in relation to nuclear safeguards have the following features: the Euratom Treaty contains an appropriate level of detail to fulfil the Euratom Community's task of ensuring that ores, source materials and special fissile materials are not diverted from their intended uses; the Euratom Community's competences are exercised more broadly than the wording of the Euratom Treaty indicates; case-law is limited, but the cases that have been heard establish that the Commission's competences in relation to nuclear safeguards are fundamental to the accomplishment of the Euratom Community's tasks.*

7.01 THE SCOPE AND CONTENT OF THE COMPETENCES

This chapter assesses the scope and the content of the Euratom Community's competences in relation to safeguards under Chapter 7 of the Euratom Treaty.

In order to mitigate the risks of militarisation of nuclear materials associated with the civil nuclear industry, it was thought essential to put in place a safeguards system capable of accounting for the movement and stocks of nuclear materials.[840] The Euratom Treaty provides that the Euratom Community, through the Commission, has a competence and an obligation ensure that ores, source materials and special fissile materials are not diverted from their intended uses as declared by the users in the Member States of the Euratom Community, and that agreements between the Euratom Community and third States regarding, *inter alia*, safeguarding obligations assumed by the Euratom Community are complied with in the territories of Member States.[841] As a result of the Euratom Community's competences under Chapter 7 of the Euratom Treaty, the Euratom Community is a party to cooperation agreements with a number of third States, including the US, Canada, Japan, Australia, Kazakhstan, Uzbekistan and Ukraine.[842] The rationale behind the Euratom Community's competences regarding agreements with third States is sometimes considered to be that it guarantees its trading parties that the safeguards provisions are complied with on a national level.[843] This conclusion may be confirmed by comparing the Euratom Community's competences under Article 77(1)(b) with those under Article 101 of the Euratom Treaty. While Article 101 establishes the Euratom Community's competence to conclude external agreements with, *inter alia*, a third state or an international organisation, Article 77(1)(b) establishes its competence, via the Commission, to ensure that provisions relating to supply and safeguarding obligations assumed by the Euratom Community under an external agreement are complied with in the territories of the Member States.[844]

The focus of the Euratom Community's competences under Chapter 7 of the Euratom Treaty is to ensure, by means of appropriate supervision, that nuclear materials are not diverted to purposes other than those for which they are intended.[845] Some authors take the view that the safeguards provisions contained in the Euratom Treaty lack precision in failing to specify whether they strictly cover only peaceful uses.[846] Analysis of the provisions of Chapter 7 of the Euratom Treaty shows, however,

840. B. Patel and P. Chare, 'Fifty Years of Safeguards under the Euratom Treaty – A Regulatory Review', in G. Janssens-Maenhout (ed.), *Nuclear Safeguards and Non-Proliferation*, Luxembourg: Office for Official Publications of the European Communities, 2009, p. 95.
841. Article 77 of the Euratom Treaty.
842. European Commission Report on the Implementation of Euratom Safeguards in 2014, p. 1.
843. A. Södersten, *Euratom at the Crossroads*, Cheltenham, Northampton: Edward Elgar Publishing Limited, 2018, p. 203.
844. *See also* W. Kilb, 'The Nuclear Safeguards Regime of Euratom: A Regional Cornerstone of the Verification of Non-Proliferation Obligations in the European Union', in J. L. Black-Branch and D. Fleck (eds), *Nuclear Non-Proliferation in International Law, Volume II: Verification and Compliance*, The Hague: Asser Press, 2016, pp. 157–159.
845. Article 2(e) of the Euratom Treaty.
846. *See* I. Cenevska, *The European Atomic Energy Community in the European Union Context: The 'Outsider' Within*, Leiden: Brill Nijhoff, 2016, pp. 254–255.

a clear limitation of scope of the Euratom Community's competences in relation to nuclear safeguards, since these provisions do not apply in respect of materials intended to meet defence requirements.[847] The provisions of the Euratom Treaty were intended to ensure that internal nuclear material accounting and control systems would be in place at installations concerned with non-military use.[848] This may be regarded as additional confirmation that the Euratom Treaty's provisions do not apply in relation to military activities.[849] Some authors argue that the Euratom Treaty competences were created to ensure peaceful use of the nuclear materials.[850] However, there is nothing in the Treaty that forbids the use of nuclear materials for military purposes or prohibits the manufacturing or possession of nuclear weapons or explosives in terms of non-proliferation.[851]

To ensure that the nuclear materials are not diverted from their original purpose, the Euratom Treaty empowers the Commission by means of a three-tier system of competences comprising inspections, infringement procedures and sanctions.[852] This comprises the Euratom Community's safeguards regime.[853]

First, the Commission has a competence to perform inspections in the Member States to verify the way in which Member States fulfil their obligations under Chapter 7 of the Euratom Treaty. The Commission may send inspectors into the territories of Member States and these inspectors have access to all places, data and people that deal with materials, equipment or installations that are subject to the safeguards provisions under Chapter 7 of the Euratom Treaty.[854] The Euratom Treaty limits the Commission's right to send inspectors to Member States by means of two conditions only: consultation with the Member State concerned, which means neither that the Member State has to approve the nomination of an inspector at the beginning of his or her career in the

847. Article 84 of the Euratom Treaty.

848. P. M. Barnes, 'Nuclear Safety for Nuclear Electricity – The Search for a Solid Legal Basis for Nuclear Safety in an Enlarged European Union', (2003) 45 *Managerial Law*, p. 122.

849. For more information on Euratom Community's competences in respect of military application, *see* Chapter III Section C of this study.

850. *See* W. Kilb, 'The Nuclear Safeguards System of the European Atomic Energy Community (Euratom)', in C. Raetzke (ed.), *Nuclear Law in the EU and Beyond*, Baden-Baden: Nomos, 2014, p. 98. There has also been some suggestion that the Euratom Community's safeguards regime has a role in the non-proliferation regime. *See* R. Kobia, 'The EU and Non-Proliferation: Need for a Quantum Leap', (2008) 81 *Nuclear Law Bulletin*, pp. 39–40.

851. *See also* B. Patel and P. Chare, 'Fifty Years of Safeguards under the Euratom Treaty – A Regulatory Review', in G. Janssens-Maenhout (ed.), *Nuclear Safeguards and Non-Proliferation*, Luxembourg: Office for Official Publications of the European Communities, 2009, p. 97; and A. Lindroos, 'The Role of Euratom in the Non-Proliferation Regime', (1997) 8 *Finnish Yearbook of International Law*, p. 321.

852. Some authors regard the safeguards system as comprising four separate legal dimensions: supranational relations with the Member States; international relations with third States outside the Community; the cooperation relationship with the IAEA; and the direct supervision relationship with nuclear operators. *See* W. Kilb, 'The Nuclear Safeguards System of the European Atomic Energy Community (Euratom)', in C. Raetzke (ed.), *Nuclear Law in the EU and Beyond*, Baden-Baden: Nomos, 2014, pp. 98–111.

853. It is sometimes called a supranational system, with no police force: *see* H. W. Schleicher, 'Nuclear Safeguards in the European Community: A Regional Approach', (1980) 22 *IAEA Bulletin*, p. 46; or a regime of stringent and incisive 'conformity control': *see* H. J. Hahn, 'Control under the Euratom Compact', (1958) 7 *American Journal of Comparative Law*, p. 39.

854. Article 81(1) and (2) of the Euratom Treaty.

Commission, nor that such consultation takes place before every inspection; and presentation of an inspector's authority, i.e., by showing at least his or her inspector's card to the nuclear operator.[855]

The Euratom Community's body of inspectors established under the Euratom Treaty is regarded as being the first of its kind, and it comes with extensive powers.[856]

First, Euratom Community has a competence to force the inspection upon a Member State by the Commission applying to the President of the CJEU for an order to ensure that the inspection is compulsorily carried out, or, if there is a danger of delay, by the Commission issuing a written order which is then submitted to the President of the CJEU for subsequent approval.[857]

Second, if the Commission's inspectors find any infringements in the accounting records required under Article 79 of the Euratom Treaty, the Commission has a competence to issue a directive calling upon the Member State concerned to take all measures necessary to bring the infringement to an end, and has an obligation to inform the Council.[858] If the Member State concerned does not comply, the Commission or any Member State concerned may, in derogation from Articles 258 and 259 TFEU,[859] refer the matter directly to the CJEU.[860] The Euratom Treaty identifies the

855. W. Kilb, 'The Nuclear Safeguards Regime of Euratom: A Regional Cornerstone of the Verification of Non-Proliferation Obligations in the European Union', in J. L. Black-Branch and D. Fleck (eds), *Nuclear Non-Proliferation in International Law, Volume II: Verification and Compliance*, The Hague: Asser Press, 2016, p. 155; and A. Lindroos, 'The Role of Euratom in the Non-Proliferation Regime', (1997) 8 *Finnish Yearbook of International Law*, p. 324.

856. European Commission, '50 Years of the Euratom Treaty', Memo/07/118, 26 March 2007 Brussels, p. 4. The international nuclear safeguards regime is established under the Treaty on the Non-Proliferation of Nuclear Weapons (1968) (NPT), London, Moscow and Washington, INFCIRC/140, under the responsibility of the IAEA. Under this international safeguards regime, the States are obliged to conclude safeguard agreements with the IAEA. The Euratom Community is not a party to the NPT, but meets the NPT requirements by concluding a safeguards agreement with IAEA in 1973, which meant that the Euratom Community's inspectors and IAEA inspectors work in tandem. In 1992 the IAEA and the Euratom Community concluded a New Partnership Approach, pursuant to which the Euratom Community's inspectors collect nuclear material accountancy information and then report it to the IAEA, but the Commission and the IAEA draw independent conclusions. For further information on this issue, *see*, *inter alia*, A. Södersten, *Euratom at the Crossroads*, Cheltenham, Northampton: Edward Elgar Publishing Limited, 2018, pp. 198–202 and 207–208; and R. Kobia, 'The EU and Non-Proliferation: Need for a Quantum Leap', (2008) 81 *Nuclear Law Bulletin*, p. 42. However, some authors take the view that the Euratom Community's safeguards system creates an additional level in the universal verification system. *See* A. Lindroos, 'The Role of Euratom in the Non-Proliferation Regime', (1997) 8 *Finnish Yearbook of International Law*, p. 334.

857. Article 81(3) and (4) of the Euratom Treaty.

858. Article 82(2) and (3) of the Euratom Treaty.

859. Article 258 TFEU provides that if the Commission considers that a Member State has failed to fulfil an obligation under the Treaties, it shall deliver a reasoned opinion on the matter after giving the State concerned the opportunity to submit its observations. Article 259 TFEU provides that before a Member State brings an action against another Member State for an alleged infringement of an obligation under the Treaties, it shall bring the matter before the Commission. The Commission shall deliver a reasoned opinion after each of the States concerned has been given the opportunity to submit its own case and its observations on the other party's case both orally and in writing.

860. Article 82(4) of the Euratom Treaty.

potential danger and hence the need for urgent action in the event of non-compliance.[861]

Third, the Commission's competence to impose sanctions on persons and undertakings in the Member States in the event of infringement of the obligations under Chapter 7 of the Euratom Treaty amounts to a unique quasi-judicial competence of the Euratom Community.[862] The Commission has a competence to impose a range of sanctions depending on the severity of the infringement: a warning; the withdrawal of special benefits such as financial or technical assistance; the placing of the undertaking for a period not exceeding four months under the administration of a person or board appointed by common accord of the Commission and the State having jurisdiction over the undertaking; and total or partial withdrawal of source materials or special fissile materials.[863] This ability to impose sanctions on the operator or on the Member State is unique among safeguards Treaties.[864]

To ensure that the Commission can utilise its powers to carry out inspections, identify infringements and impose sanctions, the Euratom Treaty provides the Euratom Community with additional competences. The Commission may require that the technical characteristics of an installation for the production, separation or other use of source materials or special fissile materials or for the processing of irradiated nuclear fuels be declared to the Commission, and it also has the competence to approve the techniques to be used for the chemical processing of irradiated materials.[865] In order to verify and ensure during the inspections that ores, source materials and special fissile materials are not diverted from their intended uses, the Commission has a competence to require that operating records be kept and produced in order to permit accounting for ores, source materials and special fissile materials used, produced or transported.[866] On this issue, the competence to determine the nature and the extent of the accounting system for ores, source materials and special fissile materials is allocated to the Commission, with the Council's approval.[867] In order to perform its duties, the Commission may also require any excess special fissile material to be deposited with the ESA or in other stores which are or can be supervised by the Commission.[868]

861. W. Kilb, 'The Nuclear Safeguards Regime of Euratom: A Regional Cornerstone of the Verification of Non-Proliferation Obligations in the European Union', in J. L. Black-Branch and D. Fleck, *Nuclear Non-Proliferation in International Law, Volume II: Verification and Compliance*, The Hague: Asser Press, 2016, p. 161.
862. *See, inter alia*, H. J. Hahn, 'Control under the Euratom Compact', (1958) 7 *American Journal of Comparative Law*, p. 28; and I. Cenevska, *The European Atomic Energy Community in the European Union Context: The 'Outsider' Within*, Leiden: Brill Nijhoff, 2016, p. 31.
863. Article 83(1) of the Euratom Treaty.
864. B. Patel and P. Chare, 'Fifty Years of Safeguards under the Euratom Treaty – A Regulatory Review', in G. Janssens-Maenhout (ed.), *Nuclear Safeguards and Non-Proliferation*, Luxembourg: Office for Official Publications of the European Communities, 2009, p. 102; J. Handrlica, 'Nuclear Law Revisited as an Academic Discipline', (2019) 12 *Journal of World Energy Law and Business*, p. 66.
865. Article 78(1) and (2) of the Euratom Treaty.
866. Article 79(1) of the Euratom Treaty.
867. Article 79(3) of the Euratom Treaty.
868. Article 80 of the Euratom Treaty.

Finally, the Commission may also make recommendations to Member States concerning laws or regulations which are designed to ensure compliance in their territories with the obligations arising under Chapter 7 of the Euratom Treaty.[869]

Analysis of the provisions of the Euratom Treaty in relation to safeguards shows that, in terms of horizontal division of competences, the Euratom Treaty provides for the almost absolute concentration of competences in one institution – the Commission.[870] The Commission is the institution entrusted with the authority to comprehensively verify and supervise the application of the safeguards requirements in the Euratom Community.[871] As distinct from the field of nuclear supply, the Euratom Treaty does not delegate operational functions to an agency or another institution and requires the Commission to assume responsibility for performing inspections and applying sanctions. However, as is the case in respect of nuclear supply,[872] the Euratom Treaty lays down a simplified amendment procedure that applies to the provisions in Chapter 7 of the Euratom Treaty. This procedure establishes that, where new circumstances so require, the safeguards provisions under Chapter 7 may, on the request of a Member State or the Commission, be adapted by the Council, acting unanimously on a proposal from the Commission and after consulting the EP.[873] This provision, in a similar manner to Article 76 of the Euratom Treaty, allows for ad hoc amendment by means of an internal Euratom Community procedure and does not require a standard amendment procedure of the primary legal act (which would, in turn, need to be ratified by the Member States).[874]

By way of conclusion to this analysis of the scope and content of the Euratom Community's competences in relation to nuclear safeguards under the Euratom Treaty, it may be stated that the main focus of the Euratom Community's competences is to ensure that ores, source materials and special fissile materials are not diverted from their originally intended uses. All the relevant horizontal competences are concentrated in one institution – the Commission. The content of the Euratom Community's competences in this area comprise three main competences of the Commission: inspections, infringement procedures and sanctions. The level of regulatory detail involved is appropriate to the Community's task of ensuring that ores, source materials and special fissile materials are not diverted from their intended use, thus creating a system of broad and unique Euratom Community competences in relation to safeguards.

869. Article 83(3) of the Euratom Treaty.
870. The Euratom safeguards regime is implemented by the Commission's Directorate-General for Energy, Directorate E – 'Euratom Safeguards'.
871. I. Cenevska, *The European Atomic Energy Community in the European Union Context: The 'Outsider' Within*, Leiden: Brill Nijhoff, 2016, p. 254.
872. *See* Article 76 of the Euratom Treaty and Chapter 6 of this study.
873. Article 85 of the Euratom Treaty.
874. D. Allen, 'The Euratom Treaty, Chapter VI: New Hope or False Dawn?', (1983) 20 *Common Market Law Review*, p. 475.

7.02 THE EXERCISE OF THE COMPETENCES

This section assesses the exercise of the Euratom Community's competences in relation to nuclear safeguards and the instruments through which these competences are exercised. In view of the scope and objectives of this study, analysis of the exercise of the Euratom Community's competences is limited to the secondary legislation in force.

Systematic analysis of the existing secondary legislation, adopted on the basis of one of the articles contained in Chapter 7 of the Euratom Treaty, shows that the competences in five articles out of nine in Chapter 7 are exercised through secondary legal acts.[875] The competences provided for in Articles 77, 78, 79 and 81 of the Euratom Treaty are exercised through the same secondary legal act: Commission Regulation (Euratom) No 302/2005.[876] This was adopted to implement the Commission's reporting requirements under the Additional Protocol of the International Atomic Energy Agency (IAEA).[877] The analysis of the exercise of the Euratom Community's competences in relation to safeguards accordingly starts with Commission Regulation (Euratom) No 302/2005, which lays down directly applicable provisions in the Member States.

Article 77 of the Euratom Treaty does not define the nuclear activities to which the safeguard provisions apply: it is worded as a requirement that the ores, source materials and special fissile materials are not diverted from their intended uses. On the one hand, this could imply that safeguard provisions apply to all nuclear activities where there is a risk that nuclear materials might be diverted from their intended use. On the other hand, it could mean that the Treaty focuses on the objective of the Euratom Community's competences in relation to nuclear safeguards, which is to delegate the definitions of scope to secondary legislation. Commission Regulation (Euratom) No 302/2005, which has Article 77 as one of its legal bases, defines the scope of application of Regulation (Euratom) No 302/2005 as covering the setting-up and operation of an installation for production, separation, reprocessing, storage or other use of source material or special fissile material. It also provides that end products used for non-nuclear purposes which incorporate nuclear materials that are in practice irrecoverable is beyond the scope of the Regulation.[878] Several points should be made in this regard.

First, Commission Regulation (Euratom) No 302/2005 does not explicitly exclude military nuclear materials from its scope. Article 84(3) of the Euratom Treaty states that safeguards may not extend to materials intended to meet defence requirements.

875. The competences provided for in Articles 77 to 79, 81 and 83 of the Euratom Treaty have been exercised through secondary legislation.
876. Commission Regulation (Euratom) No 302/2005 of 8 February 2005 on the application of Euratom safeguards, OJ L 54, 28.2.2005, pp. 1-71.
877. A. Södersten, *Euratom at the Crossroads*, Cheltenham, Northampton: Edward Elgar Publishing Limited, 2018, p. 204.
878. Article 1 of Commission Regulation (Euratom) No 302/2005.

Regulation (Euratom) No 302/2005 does not address this limitation of the competences[879] of the Euratom Community under Chapter 7 of the Euratom Treaty in its definition of scope. Furthermore, it states that a special safeguard procedures should be applied to some installations or parts thereof as well as to certain materials that are liable to be involved in the production cycle for defence needs.[880] The regulation also provides that certain articles of this regulation apply to installations or parts of installations which at certain times are operated exclusively with nuclear materials liable to be assigned to meet defence requirements but which at other times are operated exclusively with civil nuclear materials;[881] to installations or parts of installations to which access could be restricted for defence reasons but which produce, treat, separate, reprocess or use in any other way, simultaneously, both civil nuclear materials and nuclear materials assigned or liable to be assigned to meet defence requirements;[882] and to civil nuclear materials situated in the installations of parts of installations that have both civil and military operations.[883] Consequently, the Commission has interpreted the provisions of the Euratom Treaty as limiting its competences and as placing a prohibition on the application of safeguards to nuclear materials used in military operations, i.e., military nuclear materials, but not to military installations involving mixed civil and military materials. As a result, when implementing its competences under Chapter 7 of the Euratom Treaty, the Commission has to tread a fine line between its competence to ensure the application of safeguards to civil materials in military facilities, which falls under the scope of Euratom Community competences under Chapter 7 of the Euratom Treaty, and the application of safeguards to military materials in military facilities, which is excluded from the scope of the Euratom Community's competences under the safeguards provisions of the Euratom Treaty.[884]

Second, Article 77 of the Euratom Treaty includes ores in the scope of the Euratom Community's competences in relation to safeguards, but Commission Regulation (Euratom) No 302/2005 limits the application of the safeguard provisions to ores in a way that it excludes ores from the regulation's definition of scope, and from its

879. Article 84(3) of the Euratom Treaty has been interpreted both as a limitation on the scope of the Euratom Community's competences, as noted in Chapter 7 Section 01 of this study on the scope and content of safeguards, and as a derogation in relation to Member States' defence requirements. *See* I. Cenevska, *The European Atomic Energy Community in the European Union Context: The 'Outsider' Within*, Leiden: Brill Nijhoff, 2016, pp. 255 and 257.
880. Recital 8 of Commission Regulation (Euratom) No 302/2005.
881. Article 34(3)(a) of Commission Regulation (Euratom) No 302/2005. Article 3(1), Articles 4 and 6 of Commission Regulation (Euratom) No 302/2005 apply in respect of those installations.
882. Article 34(3)(b) of Commission Regulation (Euratom) No 302/2005. Article 3(1), Articles 4 and 6 of the same regulation apply to those installations, with exceptions for reasons of national security.
883. Article 34(3)(c) of Commission Regulation (Euratom) No 302/2005. Articles 2 and 5, Articles 7 to 32, Article 34(1) and (2), and Articles 35, 36 and 37 of Commission Regulation (Euratom) No 302/2005 apply in relation to those civil nuclear materials.
884. Even prior to the adoption of the secondary legislation currently in force, authors interpreted the Euratom Community's competences in relation to safeguards in terms of 'defence' and 'non-defence' materials. *See* D. D. Smith, 'The European Atomic Energy Community', (1970) 1 *California Western International Law Journal*, p. 45.

export, import and shipment requirements, and establishes special provisions for the production and handling of ores.[885]

Third, Chapter 7 of the Euratom Treaty does not specifically define nuclear waste as nuclear material to which safeguard provisions should be applied. Commission Regulation (Euratom) No 302/2005 provides for a broader exercise of the Euratom Community's competences than the explicit wording of Chapter 7 of the Euratom Treaty indicates, by applying certain safeguard requirements to nuclear material that is declared as retained or conditioned waste, to processing campaigns in respect of material that has previously been declared as retained or conditioned waste, and to transfers of conditioned waste.[886]

Commission Regulation (Euratom) No 302/2005 is based on four articles of the Euratom Treaty. This section assesses how the competences under each of these articles are exercised in the regulation.

Article 77 of the Euratom Treaty establishes general tasks for the Euratom Community's competences under Chapter 7 of the Euratom Treaty. Therefore, the Commission's obligation to ensure that ores, source materials and special fissile materials are not diverted from their intended uses may be considered as being exercised through Regulation (Euratom) No 302/2005 in its entirety. However, Article 6 of the regulation may be regarded as being of key importance in relation to the Commission's ability to exercise its competences under the Euratom Treaty. The reason for this is that it exercises competences under Article 77 of the Euratom Treaty by constituting the Commission's competence to adopt particular safeguard provisions for source materials and special materials, based on the characteristics of the installation. The Commission has, therefore, a competence to individualise the safeguard requirements, according to the installations' technical specifications, by adopting a decision. This means that the Commission can more effectively exercise its competences to ensure that source materials and special materials are not diverted from their original purpose. These decisions are addressed directly to a specific operator and are not published.[887]

The Euratom Community's competence to require declaration of technical characteristics under Article 78 of the Euratom Treaty is exercised under Article 3 of the Commission Regulation, which specifies the content of the basic technical characteristics, and Article 4, which defines time limits for the declaration of the basic technical characteristics. The regulation exercises the competence under Article 78 of the Euratom Treaty in a broader manner than the wording of the article indicates, as it also requires persons or undertakings extracting ores in the territory of a Member State to declare the basic technical characteristics of the ore extraction operations to the Commission.[888]

885. Articles 1, 3, 24 and 25 of Commission Regulation (Euratom) No 302/2005.
886. Articles 30 to 32 of Commission Regulation (Euratom) No 302/2005.
887. W. Kilb, 'The Nuclear Safeguards System of the European Atomic Energy Community (Euratom)', in C. Raetzke (ed.), *Nuclear Law in the EU and Beyond*, Baden-Baden: Nomos, 2014, p. 101.
888. Article 24(1) of Commission Regulation (Euratom) No 302/2005.

The Commission's competence to require accountancy in respect of ores, source materials and special fissile materials used or produced under Article 79 of the Euratom Treaty is exercised broadly in Commission Regulation (Euratom) No 302/2005, Articles 7 to 19 of which require persons and undertakings to maintain a system of accountancy and control.[889] This system must include, *inter alia*, accounting and operating records, information on the quantities, category, form and composition of these materials, their actual location and the particular safeguards obligation as provided for in Article 17, together with details of the recipient or shipper when nuclear materials are transferred.[890]

Regarding ores, the competences under Article 79 of the Euratom Treaty are exercised in Commission Regulation (Euratom) No 302/2005 by requiring any person or undertaking extracting ores to keep accounting records, indicating, *inter alia*, the quantities of the ore extracted, with the average uranium and thorium content, and the stock of extracted ore at the mine.[891] Article 79 of the Euratom Treaty also establishes the Commission's competence to require that operating records are kept for transport of source materials and special fissile materials. Articles 20 to 23 of Regulation (Euratom) No 302/2005 exercise this competence by laying down requirements for export, shipment, import and receipts of source materials and special fissile materials, and procedures that need to be followed in case of loss or delay during transfer, or change of date for packing and unpacking of nuclear materials. Article 25 of the regulation lays down separate provisions for ore shipment.

Analysis of the provisions of Commission Regulation (Euratom) No 302/2005 reveals that the competences established in Article 81 of the Euratom Treaty are exercised through this regulation in terms of its provisions requiring accounting and operating records to be made available to the Commission's inspectors in electronic form if they are kept in this form by the installation.[892]

Finally, it should be mentioned that the Commission has a competence under Regulation (Euratom) No 302/2005 to adopt recommendations on the application of this regulation.[893] The two legal instruments adopted on this basis and currently in

889. Some authors argue that the Community's control system has proved one of the more important and successful Euratom operations. *See, e.g.*, L. Scheinmann, 'Euratom: Nuclear Integration in Europe', (1967) 563 *International Conciliation*, p. 17.
890. Article 7(1) of Commission Regulation (Euratom) No 302/2005.
891. Article 24(2) of Commission Regulation (Euratom) No 302/2005.
892. Article 7(2) of Commission Regulation (Euratom) No 302/2005.
893. Article 37 of Commission Regulation (Euratom) No 302/2005.

force are Commission Recommendation 2009/120/Euratom,[894] and Commission Recommendation 2006/40/Euratom.[895]

In conclusion, it may be stated that Commission Regulation (Euratom) No 302/2005 exercises the Euratom Community's competences in relation to nuclear safeguards in a manner that makes the safeguards provisions laid down in the Euratom Treaty applicable to civil nuclear materials in military nuclear installations. The Euratom Community's competences are exercised in Regulation (Euratom) No 302/2005 in a way that creates a distinct separation as between the application of safeguards to source materials and special fissile materials on the one hand, and the application of safeguards to ores on the other. The competences in relation to both these areas are exercised in a broader manner than the wording of Chapter 7 of the Euratom Treaty indicates because the application of safeguards is expanded to cover certain nuclear waste. Commission Regulation (Euratom) No 302/2005 is based on four Euratom Treaty articles, but Article 77 of the Euratom Treaty is exercised through Regulation (Euratom) No 302/2005 in its entirety. Among the remaining three articles, Article 79 is exercised to the broadest extent.

The competences laid down in Article 77 of the Euratom Treaty are also exercised through Commission Regulation (Euratom) No 66/2006.[896] The decision to use a safeguards provision as a legal basis is, however, perhaps open to question because Commission Regulation (Euratom) No 66/2006 contains no provisions on exemptions from the application of the safeguards provisions under Chapter 7 of the Euratom Treaty.

As noted above,[897] Article 81 of the Euratom Treaty establishes the Commission's competence to carry out inspections in the Member States to ensure that nuclear materials are not diverted from their intended purposes, as required under Article 77 of the Euratom Treaty. Article 81 also empowers the Commission to apply to the President of the CJEU for an order to ensure that the inspection is carried out compulsorily if the carrying out of an inspection is opposed. The Decision of the Court of Justice 2012/671/EU concerning the judicial functions of the Vice President of the Court[898] exercises the Euratom Community's competences under Article 81 of the Euratom

894. Commission Recommendation 2009/120/Euratom of 11 February 2009 on the implementation of a nuclear material accountancy and control system by operators of nuclear installations, OJ L 41, 12.2.2009, pp. 17–23. This system must be capable of providing an accurate and timely account of the location and quantity of nuclear materials under its control and therefore be able to detect with high assurance in a timely fashion any losses or apparent losses. Some authors take the view that the system imposes responsibility on operators and may be considered as a line of defence against non-proliferation. *See, e.g.*, R. Kobia, 'The EU and Non-Proliferation: Need for a Quantum Leap', (2008) 81 *Nuclear Law Bulletin*, p. 42.

895. Commission Recommendation 2006/40/Euratom of 15 December 2005 on guidelines for the application of Regulation (Euratom) No 302/2005 on the application of Euratom safeguards, OJ L 28, 1.2.2006, pp. 1–85.

896. Commission Regulation (Euratom) No 66/2006. The legal bases of this regulation are Articles 74 and 77 of the Euratom Treaty and it is analysed in Chapter 6 of this study.

897. For more information, *see* Chapter 7 Section 01 regarding the scope and content of the Euratom Community's competences in respect of safeguards.

898. Decision of the Court of Justice 2012/671/EU of 23 October 2012 concerning the judicial functions of the Vice President of the Court, OJ L 300, 30.10.2012, p. 47.

Treaty by ruling that the Vice President of the Court takes the place of the President of the Court in the performance of the judicial functions referred to, *inter alia*, in Article 81 of the Euratom Treaty. There is no requirement to establish a suspected infringement prior to carrying out the safeguards inspections, which indicates that the Commission has a strong investigative competence.[899]

Under Article 83 of the Euratom Treaty, the Commission has a competence to adopt decisions on the imposition of sanctions, in the event of an infringement on the part of persons or undertakings of the obligations imposed on them under Chapter 7 of the Euratom Treaty. The Commission has exercised this competence on several occasions[900] and the Member States must ensure that the sanctions imposed are enforced.[901] When deciding on the sanction to be imposed, the Commission carries out an objective and a subjective analysis of the nature of the offences[902] on a case-by-case basis.

Systematic analysis of the Commission's decisions under Article 83 of the Euratom Treaty shows that the objective aspects include, *inter alia*, evaluation of whether the provisions breached by the person or undertaking comprise essential elements of Euratom Community legislation in relation to safeguards and the importance of the nuclear material.[903] The Commission has also determined that the quantity in terms of weight is a factor in determining the applicable sanction, as a certain quantity of enriched uranium could easily be further enriched to levels where it would be of strategic value.[904] In assessing the severity of the infringement, the Commission may also evaluate the objective specificities of the operation at hand.[905] In some cases, as part of the objective analysis, the Commission has underlined the particular importance of controlling exports of nuclear material, especially in cases where such material could be enriched to the level where it would be of strategic value.[906]

899. A. Södersten, *Euratom at the Crossroads*, Cheltenham, Northampton: Edward Elgar Publishing Limited, 2018, p. 204.
900. Commission Decision 90/413/Euratom of 1 August 1990 relating to a procedure in application of Article 83 of the Euratom Treaty, OJ L 209, 8.8.1990, pp. 27-30; Commission Decision 92/194/Euratom of 4 March 1992 relating to a procedure in application of Article 83 of the Euratom Treaty, OJ L 88, 3.4.1992, pp. 54-58; Commission Decision 94/955/Euratom: of 21 December 1994 relating to a procedure pursuant to Article 83 of the Euratom Treaty, OJ L 371, 31.12.1994, pp. 16-17; Commission Decision 96/671/Euratom of 13 November 1996 relating to a procedure in application of Article 83 of the Euratom Treaty, OJ L 313, 3.12.1996, pp. 20-24; Commission Decision 97/873/Euratom of 12 December 1997 relating to a procedure in application of Article 83 of the Euratom Treaty, OJ L 354, 30.12.1997, pp. 30-33; Commission Decision 2006/626/Euratom of 15 February 2006 pursuant to Article 83 of the Treaty establishing the European Atomic Energy Community, OJ L 255, 19.9.2006, pp. 5-6.
901. A. Södersten, *Euratom at the Crossroads*, Cheltenham, Northampton: Edward Elgar Publishing Limited, 2018, p. 205.
902. Commission Decision 92/194/Euratom; Commission Decision 94/955/Euratom; Commission Decision 96/671/Euratom; and Commission Decision 97/873/Euratom.
903. Commission Decision 94/955/Euratom; Commission Decision 96/671/Euratom; and Commission Decision 97/873/Euratom.
904. Commission Decision 90/413/Euratom.
905. Commission Decision 92/194/Euratom.
906. Commission Decision 90/413/Euratom and Commission Decision 97/873/Euratom.

The subjective aspects include evidence of an undertaking's intention to divert material for use for military purposes; the risk of recurrence of failures;[907] the undertaking's willingness to rectify the situation and comply with the legal requirements laid down in the safeguards provisions;[908] whether the undertaking is actually carrying out any activity involving nuclear material and whether it intends to continue operation of the installation;[909] and the presence of any possible ulterior motives behind the actions and undertaking's earlier attitude towards and awareness of safeguard issues.[910]

The tendencies that inform the Commission's choice of sanctions should also be mentioned here. The Commission has issued five warnings under Article 83(1)(a)[911] and has placed one undertaking under administration under Article 83(1)(c) of the Euratom Treaty.[912] In most cases the warning issued by the Commission was followed by a requirement to report to the Commission measures rectifying the identified failures that led to the infringement.[913] There have been cases where a warning is imposed on the understanding that the undertaking concerned demonstrates within a specified period that the implemented remedies have achieved the envisaged effects.[914] It should also be noted that when exercising its competence to apply sanctions under Article 83(1)(c) of the Euratom Treaty (i.e., placing the undertaking in question under administration), the Commission delegates power to an administration[915] to check, and if necessary, amend the internal regulations in relation to safeguards, and supervise their implementation and monitor their application.[916] Although this sanction is not the most draconian approach possible under Article 83 it is sometimes considered to be severe.[917]

The Court also exercised its competence under Article 83(2) on one occasion by making an order that the Commission's decision to impose sanctions be enforced forthwith, despite the undertaking involved having submitted an appeal.[918]

Under Article 83(3) of the Euratom Treaty the Commission has a competence to make any recommendations to Member States concerning laws or regulations which

907. Commission Decision 92/194/Euratom.
908. Commission Decision 94/955/Euratom.
909. Commission Decision 96/671/Euratom and Commission Decision 94/955/Euratom.
910. Commission Decision 97/873/Euratom.
911. Commission Decision 92/194/Euratom; Commission Decision 94/955/Euratom; Commission Decision 96/671/Euratom; Commission Decision 97/873/Euratom; and Commission Decision 2006/626/Euratom.
912. Commission Decision 90/413/Euratom.
913. For example, Commission Decision 97/873/Euratom and Commission Decision 96/671/Euratom.
914. For example, Article 2(3) of Commission Decision 2006/626/Euratom.
915. Administration in this context is a person or board appointed by common accord of the Commission and the State having jurisdiction over the undertaking. *See* Article 83(1)(c) of the Euratom Treaty.
916. Article 3 of Commission Decision 90/413/Euratom.
917. *See* W. Kilb, 'The European Atomic Energy Community and Its Primary and Secondary Law', in *International Nuclear Law: History, Evolution and Outlook, 10th Anniversary of the International School of Nuclear Law*, Paris: OECD, 2010, pp. 69–70.
918. Order of 7 December 1990 in *Advanced Nuclear Fuels v Commission*, C-308/90, ECLI: EU:C:1990:448.

are designed to ensure compliance in their territories with the obligations arising under Chapter 7 of the Euratom Treaty. Analysis of the secondary legislation currently in force shows that the Commission has exercised this competence on one occasion by recommending a Member State to adopt all necessary measures to ensure that all installations in that Member State for the production, separation or other use of source materials or special fissile materials or for the processing of irradiated nuclear fuels are declared to the Commission.[919]

By way of conclusion to the analysis of the exercise of the Euratom Community's competences under Chapter 7 of the Euratom Treaty, it may be stated that the competences provided for in four out of the five articles contained in Chapter 7 of the Euratom Treaty are exercised through Commission Regulation (Euratom) No 302/2005. Although these competences are exercised through one secondary legal act, the regulation exercises the competences of the Euratom Community in this field in a broader manner than the wording of the Euratom Treaty suggests, as it extends the applicability of the Euratom Treaty's safeguards provisions to civil nuclear materials in military nuclear installations and it expands the application of safeguards to certain nuclear waste. When exercising the Euratom Community's competences under Article 83 of the Euratom Treaty and applying sanctions, the Commission carries out its objective and subjective analysis on a case-by-case basis, which implies a broader exercise of the Euratom Community's competence than the wording of the Euratom Treaty indicates. Warnings are the sanction most often applied by the Commission.

7.03 THE CJEU's INTERPRETATION OF THE COMPETENCES

This section assesses whether and how the CJEU's case-law defines and elaborates on the Euratom Community's competence in relation to nuclear safeguards.

Quantitative analysis of the CJEU's case-law in relation to nuclear safeguards shows that the CJEU has not been very active in defining and delimiting the Euratom Community's competences under Chapter 7 of the Euratom Treaty. There have been two cases in which the Court has addressed the Euratom Community's competences in relation to nuclear safeguards under the Euratom Treaty. Before proceeding to the analysis of these cases, it should be mentioned that there is one additional case in which the Court did not specifically address the Euratom Community's competences in relation to safeguards, but established that the Euratom Treaty does not apply to uses of nuclear energy for military purposes.[920]

919. Commission Recommendation 94/956/Euratom of 21 December 1994 on the application of Euratom safeguards in Spain, OJ L 371, 31.12.1994, p. 18.

920. Judgment of 12 April 2005, *Commission v United Kingdom*, C-61/03, ECLI:EU:C:2005:210, paragraph. 44. Some authors consider, however, that there are grounds for questioning the Court's reasoning. *See, e.g.*, J. Grunwald, 'Peaceful Uses of Nuclear Energy under Euratom Law', in J. L. Black-Branch and D. Fleck (eds), *Nuclear Non-Proliferation in International Law, Volume III: Legal Aspects of the Use of Nuclear Energy for Peaceful Purposes*, The Hague: Asser Press, 2016, pp. 192–195. On Euratom Community's competences in respect of the military application of nuclear energy, *see*Chapter III Section C of this study.

In the first case, the Court interpreted the competences established in Article 2(e) of the Euratom Treaty as giving the Euratom Community the task of making certain, by means of appropriate supervision, that nuclear materials are not diverted to purposes other than those for which they are intended, without taking into account the nature of such diversions and the circumstances in which they might take place. The Court, therefore, dismissed the restrictive interpretations[921] of nuclear safeguards under the Euratom Treaty and took the view that the very concept of safeguards, which the Euratom Treaty uses to characterise the provisions of Chapter 7 of the Euratom Treaty, has a wider scope than the mere substitution of a different destination from that declared by a user of nuclear materials.[922] The Court also defined the Euratom Community's competences in relation to nuclear safeguards by ruling that the provisions of the Euratom Treaty designed to ensure that nuclear materials are not diverted to purposes other than those declared by their users are fundamental to the accomplishment of the Euratom Community's tasks, as laid down in Articles 1 and 2 of the Euratom Treaty. In the light of the Court's approach to this issue, it seems unjustifiable to argue, as some authors do, that the present-day version of the Euratom Community's safeguards regime has lost much of its significance.[923] On the contrary, the Euratom Community's safeguards regime is in a process of continuous improvement: it is heavily dependent on technology and its tools are subject to a continuous process of enhancement and modernisation.[924]

In the second case, the Court addressed compliance with the rules, overseen by the Commission pursuant to Articles 77, 79, 81 and 83 of the Euratom Treaty, as being essential elements of the safeguards regime. Consequently, the Court stated that deviation from those rules by an undertaking constitutes a serious infringement.[925] The Court also took the view that Article 83 of the Euratom Treaty ensures the effectiveness

921. On a restrictive interpretation, the security provisions laid down in the Treaty are nothing more than a check on 'conformity' or 'destination', that is to say, a check with a view to ensuring that the nuclear materials are not diverted, by the person in possession of them, to a purpose other than that which he or she declared. *See* Ruling of 14 November 1978, Ruling of the Court delivered pursuant to the third paragraph of Article 103 of the Euratom Treaty – Draft Convention of the International Atomic Energy Agency on the Physical Protection of Nuclear Materials, Facilities and Transports, Ruling 1/78, ECLI:EU:C:1978:202, paragraphs 19 and 20.

922. Regarding the Euratom Community's competences in relation to the physical protection of nuclear materials, the Court concluded that the concept of safeguards within the meaning of the Euratom Treaty is sufficiently comprehensive to include measures of physical protection. *See* Ruling of 14 November 1978, Ruling of the Court delivered pursuant to the third paragraph of Article 103 of the Euratom Treaty – Draft Convention of the International Atomic Energy Agency on the Physical Protection of Nuclear Materials, Facilities and Transports, Ruling 1/78, ECLI:EU:C:1978:202, paragraph 21.

923. *See* S. Wolf, 'Euratom Before the Court: A Political Theory of Legal Non-Integration', (2011) 15/10 *European Integration Online Papers*, p. 6.

924. S. Ciccarello and S. Lechner, 'Euratom Safeguards System', in L. Maiani, S. Abousahl and W. Plastino (eds), *International Cooperation for Enhancing Nuclear Safety, Security, Safeguards and Non-proliferation – 60 Years of IAEA and EURATOM*, Proceedings of the XX Edoardo Amaldi Conference Conference October 9–10, 2017, Accademia Nazionale dei Lincei, Rome, Italy: Springer-Verlag Berlin and Heidelberg GmbH & Co. K, 2018, p. 65.

925. Judgment of 21 January 1993, *Advanced Nuclear Fuels v Commission*, C-308/90, ECLI: EU:C:1993:23, paragraph 26.

of Chapter 7 of the Euratom Treaty by granting wide powers to the Commission to impose penalties, including those of a non-pecuniary nature. The Court accordingly concluded that the aim of Article 83 of the Euratom Treaty is in conformity with the intention of the authors of the Euratom Treaty to give the Commission the means necessary to carry out, in particular, the tasks of the Euratom Community laid down in Article 2(e) of the Euratom Treaty, namely to make certain that nuclear materials are not diverted to purposes other than those for which they are intended.[926] The Court ruled that the Commission has a competence to impose the sanctions provided for in Article 83 of the Euratom Treaty, without distinguishing between existing infringements and those that have ceased.[927]

In conclusion, although there has been limited case-law in the field of nuclear safeguards, the CJEU has defined the competences of the Commission under Chapter 7 of the Euratom Treaty as being fundamental to the accomplishment of the Euratom Community's tasks and wider in scope than the explicit wording of the Euratom Treaty might indicate.

7.04 FEATURES OF THE COMPETENCES

This section assesses the following features with a view to ensuring a basis for a comparative analysis: the level of detail of the provisions of the Euratom Treaty; the exercise of the competences as compared with the bare wording of the Euratom Treaty; and the existence of case-law and the effect of the Court's interpretation of the relevant provisions of primary and secondary legislation to the competences of the Euratom Community.

The level of detail of the provisions of the Euratom Treaty that establish the Euratom Community's competences in the field of nuclear safeguards is appropriate to the Community's task of ensuring that ores, source materials and special fissile materials are not diverted from their intended uses. The content of the Euratom Community's competences in this area can be categorised as the Commission's competence to execute inspections in the Member States, initiate infringement procedures and impose sanctions.

The Euratom Community's competences in relation to nuclear safeguards are exercised broader that the wording of the Euratom Treaty indicates because, *inter alia*, the safeguards provisions contained in the Euratom Treaty are applicable to civil nuclear materials in military nuclear installations and are expanded to cover certain nuclear waste.

926. Judgment of 21 January 1993, *Advanced Nuclear Fuels v Commission*, C-308/90, ECLI: EU:C:1993:23, paragraph 21.
927. Judgment of 21 January 1993, *Advanced Nuclear Fuels v Commission*, C-308/90, ECLI: EU:C:1993:23, paragraph 20.

The Court has delimited the Euratom Community's competences in relation to nuclear safeguards by ruling that the Commission's competences under Chapter 7 of the Euratom Treaty are fundamental to the accomplishment of the Euratom Community's tasks and by confirming that the Commission's competences under Chapter 7 of the Euratom Treaty are wider in scope than the explicit wording of the Euratom Treaty indicates.

CHAPTER 8

Property Ownership

- *The scope of the Euratom Community's competences in relation to property ownership is the exercise the right of ownership of all special fissile materials within the Euratom Community, while giving Member States, persons and undertakings unlimited right of use. The content of the Euratom Community's competences includes the ESA's competence to establish and manage the Euratom Community's Special Fissile Materials Account.*
- *The Euratom Community's competences under Chapter 8 of the Euratom Treaty have not been exercised through secondary legal acts, but the content of the competences indicate that direct application of those provisions would be viable.*
- *The CJEU has confirmed the Euratom Community's competences established under Chapter 8 of the Euratom Treaty and defined them in accordance with the wording of the Euratom Treaty. The Court has, however, used the terms to define special fissile materials inconsistently, which gives rise to a risk of confusion as to the limitations of the Euratom Community's competences in this area.*
- *The features of the Euratom Community's competences in relation to property ownership are as follows: the level of detail of the provisions of the Euratom Treaty that establish the Euratom Community's competences in relation to property ownership is too high in Article 89 of the Euratom Treaty, but appropriate in the other articles in Chapter 8 of the Euratom Treaty; the Euratom Community's competences under Chapter 8 of the Euratom Treaty have not been exercised through secondary legal acts; the CJEU's case-law has defined the Euratom Community's competences in relation to property ownership in accordance with the wording of the Euratom Treaty.*

8.01 THE SCOPE AND CONTENT OF THE COMPETENCES

This chapter assesses the scope and the content of the Euratom Community's competences in relation to property ownership under Chapter 8 of the Euratom Treaty.

The Euratom Treaty establishes the Euratom Community's competence and obligation to exercise a right of ownership in respect of all special fissile materials.[928] Under the provisions of Chapter 8 of the Euratom Treaty, the Euratom Community owns all special fissile materials that are produced or imported by a Member State, a person or an undertaking, and are subject to the safeguards under Chapter 7 of the Euratom Treaty.[929] This competence of the Euratom Community is considered to be unique and not comparable to anything observed in other legal systems,[930] and is a competence of a supranational character.[931] The provisions of Chapter 8 of the Euratom Treaty prevent private ownership of special fissile materials in the Euratom Community.[932] The Euratom Treaty connects the Euratom Community's competences in relation to nuclear safeguards with its right to own all special fissile materials within the Euratom Community, by limiting the right of ownership to special fissile materials that fall under the Euratom Treaty's safeguards regime.[933] This indicates that the Euratom Community's ownership of special fissile materials comes to an end when these materials are no longer subject to the safeguards regime provided for in Chapter 7 of the Euratom Treaty.[934]

The Euratom Treaty also defines the scope of the Euratom Community's ownership competences by providing that Member States, persons or undertakings have unlimited right of use and consumption of special fissile materials that have properly

928. Article 2(f) of the Euratom Treaty. The right of ownership is also a potentially powerful tool for the ESA to ensure the means of a common supply policy under Article 52 of the Euratom Treaty. *See* Chapter 6 of this study and W. Kilb, 'The Nuclear Safeguards Regime of Euratom: A Regional Cornerstone of the Verification of Non-Proliferation Obligations in the European Union', in J. L. Black-Branch and D. Fleck (eds), *Nuclear Non-Proliferation in International Law, Volume II: Verification and Compliance*, The Hague: Asser Press, 2016, p. 156.
929. Article 86 of the Euratom Treaty.
930. A. Bouquet, 'How Current Are Euratom Provisions on Nuclear Supply and Ownership in View of the European Union's Enlargement?', (2001) 68 *Nuclear Law Bulletin*, p. 27. A. Bouquet also identifies three different groups of doctrines regarding the concept of ownership under Chapter 8 of the Euratom Treaty: Euratom Community ownership as a private and public law concept to be interpreted in accordance with the different Member States' legal systems; Euratom Community ownership as a *sui generis* and essentially public law concept with real content, namely the addition of the Community's intervention rights, with some indirect private law consequences attached to it; and Euratom Community ownership as an empty shell that merely reconfirms the Euratom Community's existing intervention rights. *See* A. Bouquet, 'How Current Are Euratom Provisions on Nuclear Supply and Ownership in View of the European Union's Enlargement?', (2001) 68 *Nuclear Law Bulletin*, p. 33.
931. R. Efron and A. S. Nanes, 'The Common Market and Euratom Treaties: Supranationality and the Integration of Europe', (1957) 6 *International and Comparative Law Quarterly*, p. 682.
932. H. J. Hahn, 'Control under the Euratom Compact', (1958) 7 *American Journal of Comparative Law*, p. 43.
933. *See also* P. Mathijsen, 'Some Legal Aspects of Euratom', (1965–1966) 3 *Common Market Law Review*, p. 329.
934. The latter also implies that by releasing the special fissile materials from the Euratom Community's safeguards system, Article 84(3) of the Euratom Treaty, which establishes the limitations regarding safeguard application to materials intended to meet defence requirements, also releases that material from the Euratom Community's property ownership regime. *See* J. Grunwald, 'Peaceful Uses of Nuclear Energy under Euratom Law', in J. L. Black-Branch and D. Fleck (eds), *Nuclear Non-Proliferation in International Law, Volume III: Legal Aspects of the Use of Nuclear Energy for Peaceful Purposes*, The Hague: Asser Press, 2016, p. 197.

come into their possession,[935] and that ownership of all other assets, materials and objects, *inter alia*, ores and source materials,[936] is determined by the law of each Member State.[937] The Euratom Community's property ownership does not, however, entail its having the specific responsibilities of an owner in relation to such materials. This could be relevant, for example, for stolen material which is confiscated by the police and dealt with under national police and criminal law.[938] On the one hand, special fissile materials as defined under Article 197 of the Euratom Treaty, are subject to a special owner-user relationship, where extensive rights are left to the user.[939] On the other hand, as the Euratom Community's ownership competences apply only to special fissile materials,[940] the provisions of Chapter 8 of the Euratom Treaty divide the regulation of nuclear materials into two types of materials: special fissile materials; and ores and source materials.[941] This special owner-user relationship is sometimes considered to be a 'gentlemen's agreement' according to which the Euratom Community (via the Commission) does not press its property title as long as it is informed comprehensively about the movements of these materials within, into and from the Euratom Community.[942]

Systematic analysis of the ownership provisions under Chapter 8 of the Euratom Treaty raises the question of whether spent nuclear fuels, which are to be conditioned for direct disposal and which contain special fissile materials, fall under the Euratom Community's ownership competences. The Euratom Community's ownership ends when the safeguards regime ends.[943] Hence, the answer to this question should be

935. Article 87 of the Euratom Treaty. The possessor of the special fissile materials enjoys, therefore, the most extensive rights of use and consumption of those materials, which is considered to be a legal peculiarity of the Euratom Community. *See* P. Mathijsen, 'Some Legal Aspects of Euratom', (1965–1966) 3 *Common Market Law Review*, p. 336.
936. *See* Article 197 of the Euratom Treaty.
937. Article 91 of the Euratom Treaty.
938. J. Grunwald, 'Peaceful Uses of Nuclear Energy under Euratom Law', in J. L. Black-Branch and D. Fleck (eds), *Nuclear Non-Proliferation in International Law, Volume III: Legal Aspects of the Use of Nuclear Energy for Peaceful Purposes*, The Hague: Asser Press, 2016, p. 189.
939. W. Kilb, 'The Nuclear Safeguards Regime of Euratom: A Regional Cornerstone of the Verification of Non-Proliferation Obligations in the European Union', in J. L. Black-Branch and D. Fleck (eds), *Nuclear Non-Proliferation in International Law, Volume II: Verification and Compliance*, The Hague: Asser Press, 2016, p. 156; and A. Bouquet, 'How Current Are Euratom Provisions on Nuclear Supply and Ownership in View of the European Union's Enlargement?', (2001) 68 *Nuclear Law Bulletin*, p. 30.
940. Ores and source materials (natural and depleted uranium, thorium) are not subject to the ownership right. Fission products in nuclear waste are not in the category of special fissile materials either. *See* A. Bouquet, 'How Current Are Euratom Provisions on Nuclear Supply and Ownership in View of the European Union's Enlargement?', (2001) 68 *Nuclear Law Bulletin*, p. 27.
941. A. Lindroos, 'The Role of Euratom in the Non-Proliferation Regime', (1997) 8 *Finnish Yearbook of International Law*, p. 318.
942. P. Cornish, P. Van Ham and J. Krause (eds), *Europe and the Challenge of Proliferation*, Chaillot Papers 24, Paris: Institute for Security Studies of WEU, 1996, pp. 34–35; and A. Lindroos, 'The Role of Euratom in the Non-Proliferation Regime', (1997) 8 *Finnish Yearbook of International Law*, p. 319.
943. *See* A. Bouquet, 'How Current Are Euratom Provisions on Nuclear Supply and Ownership in View of the European Union's Enlargement?', (2001) 68 *Nuclear Law Bulletin*, p. 28. On this issue it should also be noted that Article 84(3) of the Euratom Treaty exempts special fissile materials imported into or produced in the Euratom Community with the intention of being

based on the safeguards condition: if spent fuel contains special fissile materials and falls under the Euratom Community's safeguards regime, it also falls under the Euratom Community's ownership regime. Although the Euratom Community has ownership of spent fuel that contains special fissile materials and falls under the Euratom safeguards regime, this ownership does not affect the spent nuclear fuel management regime established under the Euratom Community's competences contained in Chapter 3 of the Euratom Treaty.[944] Responsibility for safe management of spent fuel does not arise from ownership of the spent fuel, but from overall responsibility for any activity or facility related to the management of spent fuel and the Member State's' ultimate responsibility for management of the spent fuel and radioactive waste generated in that Member State.[945]

To ensure the Euratom Community's ownership of all special fissile materials, the ESA is required to establish and manage[946] a special account, in the name of the Community, known as the Special Fissile Materials Financial Account. This was envisaged to work on a credit-debit system, without any loss or gain to the Euratom Community as all loss or gain was to be borne by or accrue to the holder of the special fissile materials.[947] In other words, the Euratom Treaty provides that all the positive and negative variations in the value of these materials are vested in the party holding the right of use and consumption.[948] Comparative analysis of the six articles in Chapter 8 of the Euratom Treaty shows that Article 89 is more technical in nature than the others. In fact, the level of detail of the provisions governing the Special Fissile Materials Financial Account would be more appropriate in a secondary legal act. Apart from Article 89, the level of detail of the provisions of the Euratom Treaty is appropriate to the Euratom Community's task of exercising a right of ownership of special fissile materials in the Euratom Community.

As is the case in respect of nuclear supply and nuclear safeguards,[949] the provisions contained in Chapter 8 of the Euratom Treaty set out a simplified amendment procedure in the form of what is known as a renegotiation clause.[950] The Treaty provides that where new circumstances so require, the provisions relating to the Euratom Community's right of ownership under Chapter 8 of the Euratom Treaty may,

---

used to meet defence requirements from the application of the safeguards requirements. These materials are accordingly outside the scope of the Euratom Community's ownership competences. *See also* I. Cenevska, *The European Atomic Energy Community in the European Union Context: The 'Outsider' Within*, Leiden: Brill Nijhoff, 2016, p. 296.

944. *See also* Chapter 3 Section 02.A.3 of this study.
945. Articles 3(6), 7(1) and 4(1) of Council Directive 2011/70/Euratom.
946. Where the ESA undertakes transactions for its own account, it is, for the purposes of Chapter 8 of the Euratom Treaty, deemed to be an undertaking. *See* Article 89(4) of the Euratom Treaty.
947. Articles 88 and 89 of the Euratom Treaty. The credit-debit system implies that special fissile materials put at the disposal of a Member State, person or undertaking are credited to the Euratom Community and debited to that Member State, person or undertaking.
948. A. Bouquet, 'How Current Are Euratom Provisions on Nuclear Supply and Ownership in View of the European Union's Enlargement?', (2001) 68 *Nuclear Law Bulletin*, pp. 30–31.
949. *See* Articles 76 and 85 of the Euratom Treaty and Chapters 6 and 7 of this study.
950. H. J. Hahn, 'Control under the Euratom Compact', (1958) 7 *American Journal of Comparative Law*, p. 43.

at the request of a Member State or of the Commission, be adjusted by the Council, acting unanimously on a proposal from the Commission and after consulting the EP.[951]

In conclusion, the scope of the Euratom Community's competences in the field of property ownership focuses on exercising the right of ownership in respect of all special fissile materials within the Euratom Community, while giving the Member States, persons and undertakings unlimited right of use. The content of the Euratom Community's competences in this area lies in the ESA's competence to establish and manage the Euratom Community's Special Fissile Materials Financial Account. The level of detail of the Euratom Treaty provisions on this issue is appropriate to the Euratom Community's task of exercising the right of ownership of special fissile materials in the Euratom Community and creating a competence with a supranational character.

8.02 THE EXERCISE OF THE COMPETENCES

This section assesses the exercise of the Euratom Community's competences in relation to property ownership and the instruments through which this occurs.

Analysis of the existing secondary legislation under the Euratom Treaty shows that the articles contained in Chapter 8 of the Euratom Treaty do not provide the legal basis for any secondary legal acts. As has been established under the scope and content of the Euratom Community's competences in Chapter 8 of the Euratom Treaty,[952] Article 87 of the Euratom Treaty provides that Member States, persons and undertakings have an unlimited right of use and consumption of special fissile materials, and Articles 88 and 89 lay down the ESA's competences regarding the Special Fissile Materials Financial Account. The establishment of clear competences and the level of detail of the Treaty's provisions indicate that direct application of the provisions of Chapter 8 of the Euratom Treaty may be possible.[953]

8.03 THE CJEU's INTERPRETATION OF THE COMPETENCES

This section assesses whether and how the CJEU's case-law defines and delimits the Euratom Community's competence in relation to nuclear safeguards.

Analysis of the CJEU's case-law in relation to the Euratom Community's property ownership throws up two cases[954] in which the Court defines the Euratom Community's competences in this area.

951. Article 90 of the Euratom Treaty.
952. *See* Chapter 8 Section 01 of this study.
953. However, some authors consider that the lack of exercise of the Euratom Community's competences under Article 86 of the Euratom Treaty makes the exclusive ownership by the Euratom Community of the special fissile materials 'an empty shell'. *See* J. Handrlica, 'The Splendid Durability of the Provisional: A Tribute to Euratom', (2018) 14/14 *Croatian Yearbook of European Law & Policy*, p. 171.
954. The Euratom Community's competences in relation to property ownership were also mentioned in *Industrias Nucleares do Brasil and Siemens*, but the Court did not define or delimit them in that case. *See* judgment of 12 September 2006, *Industrias Nucleares do Brasil and Siemens*, Joined Cases C-123/04 and C-124/04, ECLI:EU:C:2006:542.

The Court has established that the system of property ownership under the Euratom Treaty signifies that, whatever the use to which nuclear materials are put, the Euratom Community remains the exclusive holder of the rights which form the essential content of the right of property. Regarding the right of use, the CJEU has confirmed that, under Article 87 of the Euratom Treaty, the right to use and consume the special fissile materials belongs to Member States, persons or undertakings when those materials have properly come into their possession.[955] The Court has also elaborated on the relation between the right of property and the right to use, by stating that in contrast to the right of use and consumption, which, for the purposes of economic exploitation, is divided between many different holders, the right of ownership of fissile materials is always concentrated in the hands of the Euratom Community. Moreover, the CJEU has confirmed that Article 87 of the Euratom Treaty establishes not only the right of use and consumption for Member States, persons and undertakings, but also a requirement to comply with the obligations under the Euratom Treaty including all matters relating to the rights of the ESA and safeguards regime.[956] In respect of the connection between different Euratom Community competences, the Court has ruled that the system of property ownership provided for under Article 2(f) and Articles 86 and 87 of the Euratom Treaty creates an integral part of the Euratom Community's competences and is closely connected with the Euratom Community's competences in the field of nuclear supply.[957]

Analysis of the available case-law concerning property ownership also shows that the Court has not been consistent in its use of terminology when referring to the Euratom Community's competences under the property ownership provisions in Chapter 8 of the Euratom Treaty. In both cases the CJEU used the term 'fuel' and 'nuclear materials' as synonyms for 'special fissile materials'.[958] It is clear, given the scope and content of the Euratom Community's competences in relation to property ownership, that the right of ownership and the right of use and consumption under Chapter 8 of the Euratom Treaty only applies to special fissile materials. The term 'nuclear materials' is used throughout the Euratom Treaty as generally covering special fissile materials, source materials and ores, as defined under Article 197 of the Euratom Treaty. Consequently, the fact that the CJEU refers to the Euratom Community's right of ownership of nuclear materials could be interpreted as the Court expanding the

955. Judgment of 4 June 2015, *Kernkraftwerke Lippe-Ems*, C-5/14, ECLI:EU:C:2015:354, paragraph 96.

956. Ruling of 14 November 1978, Ruling of the Court delivered pursuant to the third paragraph of Article 103 of the Euratom Treaty – Draft Convention of the International Atomic Energy Agency on the Physical Protection of Nuclear Materials, Facilities and Transports, Ruling 1/78, ECLI:EU:C:1978:202, paragraph 27.

957. Ruling of 14 November 1978, Ruling of the Court delivered pursuant to the third paragraph of Article 103 of the Euratom Treaty – Draft Convention of the International Atomic Energy Agency on the Physical Protection of Nuclear Materials, Facilities and Transports, Ruling 1/78, ECLI:EU:C:1978:202, paragraph 29.

958. *See* judgment of 4 June 2015, *Kernkraftwerke Lippe-Ems*, C-5/14, ECLI:EU:C:2015:354, paragraph 96; and Ruling of 14 November 1978, Ruling of the Court delivered pursuant to the third paragraph of Article 103 of the Euratom Treaty – Draft Convention of the International Atomic Energy Agency on the Physical Protection of Nuclear Materials, Facilities and Transports, Ruling 1/78, ECLI:EU:C:1978:202, paragraph 27.

Euratom Community's competences beyond the wording of Chapter 8 of the Euratom Treaty and accordingly poses a risk of confusion.[959]

In conclusion, there has been limited case-law in the field of property ownership, but the CJEU has confirmed the Euratom Community's ultimate competence to own all special fissile materials within the Euratom Community. The Court has also stated that Member States, persons or undertakings have a right to use special fissile materials subject to complying with the requirements established in relation to nuclear supply and safeguards. In this light, the Court has confirmed the Euratom Community's competences established under Chapter 8 of the Euratom Treaty and has defined them in accordance with the wording of the Treaty. The Court has, however, used terminology inconsistently, which, as noted above could pose a risk of confusion as to the limitations on the Euratom Community's competences in the field.

8.04 FEATURES OF THE COMPETENCES

This section assesses the following features with a view to ensuring a basis for a comparative analysis: the level of detail of the provisions of the Euratom Treaty; the exercise of the competences as compared with the bare wording of the Euratom Treaty; and the existence of case-law and the effect of the Court's interpretation of the relevant provisions of primary and secondary legislation to the competences of the Euratom Community.

The level of detail of the provisions of the Euratom Treaty that establish the Euratom Community's competences in relation to property ownership is too high in Article 89, but appropriate in the other articles contained in Chapter 8 of the Euratom Treaty, in respect of the Community's task of ensuring that the Euratom Community exercises the right of ownership of all special fissile materials within the Euratom Community, while giving Member States, persons and undertakings unlimited right of use. The content of the Euratom Community's competences in relation to property ownership lies in the ESA's competence to establish and manage the Euratom Community's Special Fissile Materials Financial Account.

The Euratom Community's competences in relation to property ownership under Chapter 8 of the Euratom Treaty have not been exercised through secondary legal acts, but their content is such that direct application of those provisions may be a possibility.

The Court has emphasised the Euratom Community's ultimate competence to own all special fissile materials in the Euratom Community and that Member States, persons or undertakings have a right of use regarding special fissile materials subject to complying with the requirements established in relation to supply and safeguards. Consequently, the Court has confirmed the Euratom Community's competences established under Chapter 8 of the Euratom Treaty and defined them in accordance with the wording of the Euratom Treaty.

959. The confusion is unnecessary as the Court uses the term 'special fissile materials' in its concluding remarks, which indicates that it does not interpret the Euratom Community's competences as going beyond ownership of special fissile materials, but uses terminology inconsistently.

CHAPTER 9

The Nuclear Common Market

- *The main scope of the Euratom Community's competences in relation to the nuclear common market under Chapter 9 of the Euratom Treaty is ensuring wide commercial outlets and access to the best technical facilities in the nuclear sector. The content of the Euratom Community's competences in this area comprises three main aspects: the creation of a common market for specialised materials and equipment and ensuring free movement of goods; ensuring the free movement of capital; and ensuring the free movement of workers within the Euratom Community. The level of detail of the provisions contained in the Euratom Treaty is appropriate to the Euratom Community's tasks in this area, but the wording of some of the provisions of Chapter 9 may limit the Euratom Community's competences to mainly ensuring that Member States fulfil their obligations.*
- *The Euratom Community's competences in the field of the nuclear common market under Articles 92 and 96 of the Euratom Treaty have been exercised in accordance with the Treaty wording. However, the choice of Article 98 as the legal basis for Commission recommendations is open to question. The Commission considers other provisions under Chapter 9 of the Euratom Treaty, which have not been exercised through secondary legislation, as directly applicable.*
- *The CJEU has defined the nuclear common market by finding parallels with the EU's general common market. The Court also clearly identified the differences between the Euratom Community's competences in relation to the nuclear common market and those in relation to nuclear supply policy.*
- *The features of the Euratom Community's competences in relation to the nuclear common market are as follows: appropriate level of regulatory detail given the Euratom Community's tasks under the Euratom Treaty; the Euratom Community's competences are exercised in accordance with the wording of the Euratom Treaty, except the Commission recommendations under Article 98 of the Euratom Treaty; the Court has defined the concept and purpose of the nuclear common market by comparing it with the general common market and has*

identified a significant difference as between the Euratom Community's competences in relation to the nuclear common market and those in relation to nuclear supply policy.

9.01 THE SCOPE AND CONTENT OF THE COMPETENCES

This section assesses the scope and the content of the Euratom Community's competences in relation to the nuclear common market under Chapter 9 of the Euratom Treaty.

The concept of a 'common market' was first realised in the Coal and Steel Community and may be best characterised as an institutional instrument of the common economic policies in specified sectors of economic activity for the purpose of accomplishing their harmonisation and progressive fusion.[960] The Euratom Treaty establishes the scope of the Euratom Community's competences in the nuclear common market. These competences comprise ensuring wide commercial outlets and access to the best technical facilities by the creation of a common market in specialised materials and equipment, by the free movement of capital for investments in the field of nuclear energy and by freedom of employment for specialists within the Euratom Community.[961]

Analysis of Chapter 9 of the Euratom Treaty shows that the Euratom Community's competences in the nuclear common market are established in six Treaty articles.[962] The content of the provisions of Article 2 and Chapter 9 of the Euratom Treaty leads one to conclude that the content of the Euratom Community's competences in relation to the nuclear common market comprises three aspects: the creation of a common market for specialised materials and equipment, i.e., free movement of goods; ensuring the free movement of capital; and ensuring the free movement of workers within the Euratom Community.

The Euratom Treaty defines the Euratom Community's competence to establish a specialised nuclear common market by specifying that freedom of movement of goods applies to certain goods and products specified in Annex IV of the Euratom Treaty.[963] In other words, Annex IV may be regarded as setting forth the definition of goods within the Euratom Community's nuclear common market.[964] Annex IV of the

960. J. G. Polach, *Euratom: Its Background, Issues and Economic Implications*, Dobbs Ferry, NY: Oceana Publications Inc., 1964, p. 39; and A. Moravcsik, *The Choice for Europe: Social Purpose and State Power from Messina to Maastricht*, Ithaca, NY: Cornell University Press, 1998, pp. 3 and 5.
961. Article 2(g) of the Euratom Treaty.
962. Chapter 9 of the Euratom Treaty originally consisted of nine articles, but Articles 94, 95 and 100 were repealed by Article 8 of the Amsterdam Treaty, OJ C 340, p. 73.
963. Article 92(1) of the Euratom Treaty.
964. This represents a significant difference from the general EU internal market, in respect of which there is no definition of goods in the TFEU. This may be explained by the fact that the nuclear common market is a specialised market limited to the nuclear field, which makes it easier to define the goods that may be sold on it. The CJEU has defined goods in the EU internal market as 'products which can be valued in money and which are capable, as such, of forming the

Euratom Treaty establishes a detailed end-list.[965] This implies that the nuclear common market for specifically defined types of goods cannot be broadened under the Euratom Treaty. Analysis of the content of Annex IV of the Euratom Treaty shows, however, that the level of specificity in defining goods within the nuclear common market is broad and varies significantly, i.e., from nuclear reactors in List A^2 to artificially separated stable isotopes in List B.

The Euratom Treaty confers a competence on the Euratom Community to ensure free movement of goods under the Treaty by requiring the Member States to prohibit all customs duties on imports and exports or charges having equivalent effect between themselves, and all quantitative restrictions on imports and exports.[966] Therefore, all restrictions on the import and export of nuclear goods within the Euratom Community must be eliminated and a common customs tariff must be set up.[967] The Euratom Community's competence to require the prohibition of customs duties or charges having equivalent effect does not cover the entirety of Annex IV of the Euratom Treaty. It is limited to products in List A^1 and A^2, and to products in List B if subject to a Common Customs Tariff and accompanied by a certificate issued by the Commission stating that they are intended to be used for nuclear purposes.[968]

The wording of the provisions of Chapter 9 of the Euratom Treaty on prohibitions of all quantitative restrictions on imports and exports of goods under Annex IV refers only to prohibitions on, for example, quotas on the amount of goods that may be

subject of commercial transactions'. See judgment of 10 December 1968, *Commission v Italy*, C-7/68, ECLI:EU:C:1968:51, p. 428.

965. Analysis of the lists in Annex IV of the Euratom Treaty shows that goods and products in the nuclear common market under the Euratom Treaty include, *inter alia*, nuclear fuels and materials; nuclear reactors; equipment for the separation of uranium isotopes; equipment specially designed for the chemical processing of radioactive material; vehicles specially designed for transport of highly radioactive substances; containers with lead radiation shielding for the transport or storage of radioactive material; remote-controlled mechanical manipulators specially designed for handling highly radioactive substances; reactor stimulators; liquid-vacuum and high-vacuum pumps; heat exchangers specially designed for nuclear power stations; specific radiation detection instruments, specially designed or adaptable, for the detection of measures of nuclear radiation; electrostatic generators, linear accelerators and other machines capable of imparting an energy greater than 1 MeV to nuclear particles; magnets specially designed and constructed for the above-mentioned machines and equipment; anti-radiation plate glass; airtight clothing affording protection against radiation of radioactive contamination. For further analysis of goods and products in the nuclear common market, see R. Ptasekaite, *The Euratom Treaty v. Treaties of the European Union: Limits of Competence and Interaction*, Swedish Radiation Safety Authority Report, SSM2011:32, Solna: SSM, 2011, pp. 74–75.
966. Article 93 of the Euratom Treaty. From 1 January 1959, customs barriers between Member States were abolished on all goods and products mentioned on the lists in Annex IV to the Euratom Treaty, subject in some cases to proof of a nuclear purpose. *See also* M. Gaudet, *Euratom*, London: Pergamon Press, 1959, p. 164.
967. The duties were temporarily suspended, thus creating a completely free flow of traffic for goods from outside the territories of the Member States. See P. Mathijsen, 'Some Legal Aspects of Euratom', (1965–1966) 3 *Common Market Law Review*, p. 334.
968. Article 93 of the Euratom Treaty also establishes an exemption regarding prohibition import and export duties or charges having equivalent effect for non-European territories under the jurisdiction of a Member State if they are of an exclusively fiscal nature. The rates of such duties and charges and the system governing them cannot, however, give rise to any discrimination between that State and the other Member States.

imported or exported, but not on measures having equivalent effect.[969] In the light of the CJEU's broad interpretation of measures having equivalent effect in the EU internal market,[970] the conclusion may be drawn that other measures that are capable of hindering directly or indirectly, actually or potentially intra-Community trade regarding goods under Annex IV of the Euratom Treaty, are not explicitly prohibited in the Euratom Community's nuclear common market. Consequently, the Euratom Community does not have a competence to prohibit the Member States from applying other restrictive measures, such as national regulatory requirements regarding radiation protection or nuclear safety aspects for goods covered by Annex IV of the Euratom Treaty. Furthermore, Article 93 of the Euratom Treaty states that the goods in List B of Annex IV are covered by the nuclear common market only if they are, *inter alia,* accompanied by a certificate confirming that they are intended to be used for nuclear purposes. The materials and technologies in List B do not have to be manufactured explicitly for a nuclear purpose, but fall under the concept of goods in respect of the nuclear common market only when used for a nuclear purpose. Goods in the nuclear common market are, therefore, materials and technologies that have a defined nuclear purpose.[971] Consequently, goods under List B, which are not used for nuclear purposes – for example, artificially separated stable isotopes used for medical purposes, or the production of goods that have deliberately incorporated radionuclides without being used in the nuclear field – do not fall within the scope of the nuclear common market of the Euratom Community.[972]

Annex IV of the Euratom Treaty includes special fissile materials, defined under Article 197 of the Treaty, within the ambit of goods in the nuclear common market.[973] Consequently, special fissile materials form a part of the nuclear common market. The interaction between the Euratom Community's competences under Chapter 9 of the Euratom Treaty and its competences under other provisions regulating special fissile materials in the Euratom Treaty (i.e., those contained in Chapters 6 to 8) are analysed here.[974]

969. Unlike the regulation of quantitative restrictions and measures of the equivalent effect in the EU internal market under Article 34 and Article 35 TFEU. Articles 34 and 35 TFEU are not applicable to the Euratom Community under Article 106a of the Euratom Treaty.
970. The CJEU has defined measures having equivalent effect under EU law as 'all trading rules enacted by Member States which are capable of hindering, directly or indirectly, actually or potentially, intra-Community trade are to be considered as measures having an effect equivalent to quantitative restrictions'. See judgment of 11 July 1974, *Dassonville*, C-8/74, ECLI: EU:C:1974:82, paragraph 5.
971. For example, even though a high-vacuum pump is a universal technical instrument that can also be used in the oil industry, if it is used in nuclear installations, it will fall under the goods of the nuclear common market.
972. *See also* R. Ptasekaite, *The Euratom Treaty v. Treaties of the European Union: Limits of Competence and Interaction*, Swedish Radiation Safety Authority Report, SSM2011:32, Solna: SSM, 2011, pp. 74–75.
973. For example, plutonium and uranium enriched in uranium-235 or uranium-233 are identified in List A[1] of Annex IV of the Euratom Treaty.
974. The focus here is on special fissile materials as the provisions regulating special fissile materials are contained in Chapters 6 to 9 of the Euratom Treaty. Certain aspects that are analysed below to a limited extent are also relevant to ores and source materials.

Special fissile materials form a part of the Euratom Community's common supply policy under Chapter 6 of the Euratom Treaty, which, *inter alia*, means that users have an obligation to periodically inform the ESA of the supplies they require and the producers of the offers they are able to make. The Euratom Community also has a right of option exercised by the ESA, meaning that every producer of special fissile materials is obliged to offer these nuclear materials to the ESA before they can be used, transferred or stored. Under Chapter 6 of the Euratom Treaty, the Euratom Community has competences in relation to the conclusion of supply contracts and price-setting.[975] Special fissile materials accordingly form a part of both the common supply policy and nuclear common market. This means that movement of special fissile materials is governed extensively under the Euratom Community's common supply policy. This extends to fixing the prices of special fissile materials, which are, however, free from all customs duties or charges having equivalent effect and all quantitative restrictions between Member States in the context of the Euratom Community's nuclear common market. On this point, it should also be noted that the list of 'products' under Chapter 9 and Annex IV of the Euratom Treaty is broader in scope than the concept of nuclear supplies under Article 197 of the Euratom Treaty, to which the regime laid down in Chapter 6 of the Euratom Treaty applies.[976]

Furthermore, the Euratom Community has a competence and an obligation to ensure that special fissile materials are not diverted from their originally intended purpose of use under the safeguards provisions. Movements of special fissile materials between Member States must be carried out free from all customs duties or charges having equivalent effect and all quantitative restrictions, and must also comply with the safeguards provisions under Chapter 7 of the Euratom Treaty, for example, by fulfilling the requirements on retention of operating records in respect of transport. Special fissile materials are also owned by the Euratom Community under Chapter 8 of the Euratom Treaty, and Member States have a right of use of such materials. Consequently, all special fissile materials in respect of which Member States are obliged to ensure free movement are owned by the Euratom Community.

Finally, regarding the analysis of the content of the Euratom Community's competences in relation to the creation of a specialised nuclear common market, it should be noted that the Council has a competence to amend all the lists in Annex IV of the Euratom Treaty at the request of the Commission or of a Member State, and acting on a proposal from the Commission.[977] This means that the Council has a competence to redefine the scope of the nuclear common market. The exact voting procedure in the Council, i.e., either simple or qualified majority, to make the amendments in Annex IV of the Euratom Treaty is, however, not specified in the Euratom Treaty.[978]

975. For further discussion of this issue, see the Chapter 6 Section 01 of this study on the scope and content of the Euratom Community's competences regarding nuclear supplies.
976. *See also* T. F. Cusack, 'A Tale of Two Treaties', (2003) 40 *Common Market Law Review*, p. 129.
977. Article 92(2) of the Euratom Treaty.
978. Unlike, e.g., Article 96 of the Euratom Treaty, which clearly states that the Council has a competence to issue directives for the application of Article 96 of the Euratom Treaty, after consulting the European Parliament, acting by a qualified majority on a proposal from the

The second aspect of the content of the Euratom Community's competences is ensuring the free movement of capital in the nuclear common market. The Euratom Treaty establishes the Euratom Community's competences in this area by stipulating that no restrictions based on nationality may be applied to natural or legal persons, whether public or private, under the jurisdiction of a Member State, where they desire to participate in the construction of nuclear installations of a scientific or industrial nature in the Euratom Community.[979] This provision ensures that capital that exists in one Member State and which can facilitate the development of the nuclear sector in another Member State of the Euratom Community can be moved freely and can be invested without discriminatory treatment. The reference to investments for participation in the construction of nuclear installations of a scientific or industrial nature make a connection with the Euratom Community's competences in the field of the promotion of research under Chapter 1 of the Euratom Treaty and with the competences that facilitate nuclear investments under Chapter 4 of the Euratom Treaty. It is a clear incentive to encourage natural and legal persons, both private and public, to participate in the development of the nuclear energy sector. The Euratom Treaty also confers a competence on the Commission to make recommendations to facilitate movements of capital intended to finance the industrial activities listed in Annex II of the Treaty.[980] As mentioned in Chapter 4 of this study in relation to the Euratom Community's competences in respect of investments, most of the activities listed in Annex II relate to the front end of the nuclear fuel cycle, with the exception of facilities for the industrial processing of radioactive waste. This also confirms that the purpose of the Commission's competence is to facilitate the development of the nuclear energy sector in the Euratom Community.[981]

The third aspect of the content of the Euratom Community's competences in relation to the nuclear common market is ensuring the free movement of employment within the Euratom Community. The Euratom Treaty confers a competence on the Euratom Community to require that Member States abolish all restrictions based on

---

Commission, which first requests the opinion of the Economic and Social Committee. This shows that the level of detail of the regulation of the Euratom Community's horizontal competences under Chapter 9 of the Euratom Treaty varies significantly.

979. Article 97 of the Euratom Treaty. This article confers competences on the Euratom Community in relation to the free movement of capital by making clear reference to the construction of nuclear installations in the Euratom Community. *See also* H. J. Hahn, 'Control under the Euratom Compact', (1958) 7 *American Journal of Comparative Law*, p. 43; and L. Scheinmann, 'Euratom: Nuclear Integration in Europe', (1967) 563 *International Conciliation*, p. 12. It is also possible to interpret these provisions as conferring competences on the Euratom Community in relation to freedom of establishment, and to interpret Article 99 of the Euratom Treaty as the only provision on free movement of capital. See A. Södersten, *Euratom at the Crossroads*, Cheltenham, Northampton: Edward Elgar Publishing Limited, 2018, pp. 116 and 126–127. However, this interpretation is more restrictive in terms of competences under the Euratom Treaty, particularly given that the Euratom Treaty clearly emphasises the importance of investment (Chapter 4 of the Euratom Treaty) and the role played by free movement of capital in ensuring that it occurs.

980. Article 99 of the Euratom Treaty.

981. These competences of the Commission are, however, limited to issuing recommendations, which, under Article 288 TFEU and Article 106a of the Euratom Treaty, have no binding force.

nationality affecting the right of nationals of any Member State to take skilled employment in the nuclear energy field.[982] On this point, it should be noted that the Euratom Treaty allows discriminatory treatment of skilled employment in the nuclear energy field based on public policy, public security or public health.[983] Consequently, the relevant provision of the Euratom Treaty is not drafted as a skilled individual's right to be considered for a certain position in the nuclear field, but as a requirement for Member States to abolish employment restrictions based purely on nationality. Furthermore, the Council has a competence to issue directives through which to exercise the Euratom Community's competences regarding free movement of employment under the Euratom Treaty.

Article 98 of the Euratom Treaty differs from the rest of the articles in Chapter 9 of Euratom Treaty and should be analysed separately from the Euratom Community's competences in respect of the free movement of goods, capital and employment. Under Article 98, the Euratom Community has a competence to require the Member States to take all necessary measures to facilitate the conclusion of insurance contracts covering nuclear risks. The Legal Study on Nuclear Third-Party Liability[984] contains a viability analysis and impact assessment in respect of five different options for the harmonisation of the nuclear liability regime in Europe.[985] Option E of the Legal Study analysed whether the wording of Article 98 of the Euratom Treaty regarding measures necessary to facilitate the conclusion of insurance contracts covering nuclear risks could be interpreted as covering nuclear liability issues.

On the one hand, Article 98 is limited in scope: it establishes the Euratom Community's competence in relation to nuclear insurance, but insurance contracts covering nuclear risks form only a part of the legal framework for nuclear liability. The principle of congruence of liability and coverage requires that an operator of a nuclear installation must maintain insurance or provide other financial security covering its liability for nuclear damage. The principle ensures that the amount of the operator's liability is always covered by an equal amount of money. In most cases the coverage is to be provided by the insurance industry. Other ways to provide coverage include pooling financial capacities to provide coverage jointly, the provision of coverage by

982. Article 96 of the Euratom Treaty.
983. The wording of the Article 96 of the Euratom Treaty on free movement of employment is similar to the provisions on free movement of workers under Article 45 TFEU, which require the abolition of any discrimination based on nationality between workers of the Member States as regards employment, and which are also subject to limitations justified on grounds of public policy, public security or public health.
984. Legal Study for the Accession of Euratom to the Paris Convention on Third Party Liability in the Field of Nuclear Energy, European Commission, Final Report TREN/CC/01-2005.
985. TREN/CC/01-2005, pp. 61–70. The options are as follows: Option A: Non-action. The current situation will persist, no unity of Community law; Option B: Accession of all twenty-seven Member States to the Paris Convention including all its Protocols: Unity assured but feasibility is questionable – many Member States would object; Option C: All Member States who are currently in the Vienna Convention accede to the Paris Convention, others not belonging to any convention stay out like before; Option D: The European Atomic Energy Community itself becomes a Party of the Paris Convention and its Protocols; Option E: The Euratom Community, with a view to harmonisation and better protection of its citizens, sets its own minimum compensation requirements via a directive based on Article 98 of Euratom Treaty. The levels would be oriented according to those of the Paris Convention and its Protocols.

the state, charging the operator a fee or even bank guarantees and the capital markets.[986] The important aspect of a nuclear liability regime is securing the finance capacity to cover possible damage. Insurance is one of the means by which this may be done, but interpreting the insurance provisions as covering the whole area of nuclear liability would require a significantly broader interpretation of Article 98 of the Euratom Treaty.

On the other hand, a more extensive interpretation of Article 98 of the Euratom Treaty is also possible. The obligation to take all measures necessary to facilitate the conclusion of insurance contracts covering nuclear risks under this article could also be interpreted as requiring Member States to, *inter alia*, create a nuclear liability framework that would, at the same time, facilitate the insurance of nuclear risks. The argument might be that the special legal framework for nuclear liability is itself a tool to facilitate the conclusion of insurance contracts covering nuclear risks.[987] This expansive interpretation would mean that Member States' obligations under Article 98 of the Euratom Treaty entail both the obligation to abolish any barriers with respect to the conclusion of insurance contracts to cover nuclear risks and to establish a legal framework for nuclear liability.[988] Keeping in mind the fact that insurance is the most common way of establishing a nuclear liability regime, the concept of insurance to cover nuclear risks could in this case be understood in a holistic sense and include all means of covering nuclear liability. The Commission has also interpreted the competences established under Article 98 broadly and stated that in the early years of the nuclear power industry, it was already recognised that the magnitude of damage that might be caused by a nuclear accident was such that insurance coverage to meet nuclear liability required international cooperation. This is not only illustrated by the two international regimes for nuclear third-party liability, which were developed in the early 1960s, but also by the inclusion of Article 98 in the Euratom Treaty.[989] It may, therefore, be argued that the Commission has leaned towards a broader interpretation of Article 98 to the effect that it covers a broad nuclear liability regime. Whether the Euratom Community has competence in relation to nuclear liability depends on the interpretation of the concept of insurance covering nuclear risks.

The deliberations on the coverage of nuclear liability under Article 98 should not, however, undermine the Euratom Community's competences in relation to nuclear insurance issues explicitly mentioned in the Euratom Treaty, i.e., that the Euratom

986. C. Stoiber, A. Baer, N. Pelzer and W. Tonhauser, *Handbook of Nuclear Law*, Vienna: International Atomic Energy Agency, 2003, pp. 114–115.
987. J. Handrlica, 'Harmonisation of Nuclear Liability in the European Union: Challenges, Options and Limits', (2009) 84 *Nuclear Law Bulletin*, p. 42.
988. J. Handrlica, 'Harmonisation of Nuclear Liability in the European Union: Challenges, Options and Limits', (2009) 84 *Nuclear Law Bulletin*, p. 43.
989. Written question No 3807/97 by Ilona Graenitz to the Commission (EU – level civil liability for nuclear power stations OJ C 158, 25 May 1998, p. 191). That was confirmed later by the Commissioner in Charge of Energy A. Piebalgs' statement that third party liability for nuclear damage does also fall within the scope of the Euratom Treaty. See A. Piebalgs (European Commissioner in Charge of Energy) 'Keynote Speech', in INLA/AIDN (ed.), *Nuclear Inter Jura 2007: Proceedings – Actes du Congrès, 1–4 Octobre 2007*, Bruxelles: Emilie Bruylant, 2008, p. 1073.

Community has competence to require Member States to ensure that nuclear insurance contracts are in place at national level. As this article does not identify specific types of nuclear risks, the conclusion can be drawn that the Euratom Community has a competence to require that there is an insurance contract for all types of risks posed by nuclear activities throughout the nuclear fuel cycle, i.e., not only nuclear power plants, but also nuclear waste and spent fuel management and storage facilities, fuel fabrication facilities, transport of nuclear materials, etc.

The level of regulatory detail of the Euratom Treaty on the establishment of the nuclear common market in the Euratom Community can be considered as appropriate to its task of ensuring wide commercial outlets and access to the best technical facilities in the nuclear sector. However, it should be noted that the provisions of Chapter 9 of the Euratom Treaty are mainly worded as obligations imposed on the Member States,[990] not as Euratom Community competences. These measures, which are intended to facilitate the pooling of the Euratom Community's human and material resources, are for the most part left in the hands of the Member States.[991] This indicates that the Euratom Community's role and competences in relation to the nuclear common market focus primarily on ensuring that Member States fulfil their obligations under Chapter 9 of the Euratom Treaty. Hence, in comparison with the wording of the Euratom Community's competences in relation, for example, to nuclear safeguards or supply policy,[992] the Community's competences concerning the nuclear common market seem to be weaker.

By way of conclusion of this analysis of the scope and content of the Euratom Community's competences in relation to the nuclear common market under the Euratom Treaty, it may be stated that the provisions under Chapter 9 of the Euratom Treaty cover three of the traditional freedoms of a common market:[993] free movement of goods, workers and capital.[994] The main scope of the Euratom Community's competences is ensuring wide commercial outlets and access to the best technical facilities in the nuclear sector. The content of the Euratom Community's competences in relation to the nuclear common market consists of three main aspects: creation of a common market for specialised materials and equipment and ensuring free movement of goods; ensuring the free movement of capital; and ensuring the free movement of employment within the Euratom Community. The level of regulatory detail in the

990. See Articles 93, 96 and 98 of the Euratom Treaty, and compare these provisions with Article 28 TFEU. The latter states that the Union shall comprise a customs union which shall cover all trade in goods and which shall involve the prohibition between Member States of customs duties on imports and exports and of all charges having equivalent effect, and the adoption of a common customs tariff in their relations with third countries. Article 28 TFEU clearly indicates the EU's exclusive competence in relation to the customs union under Article 3 TFEU.

991. M. Gaudet, *Euratom*, London: Pergamon Press, 1959, p. 164.

992. See Chapters 6 and 7 of this study.

993. On the traditional freedoms of a common market, see, *inter alia*, P. Craig and G. de Búrca, *EU Law: Text, Cases and Materials*, 5th edn, Oxford: Oxford University Press, 2011, p. 582.

994. Articles 28–37 and 45–66 TFEU establish four freedoms: free movement of goods (including duties, charges and taxes), workers, capital and services, together with freedom of establishment.

Euratom Treaty may be regarded as appropriate in the light of the Euratom Community's objectives in this area, but the wording of certain provisions of Chapter 9 of the Euratom Treaty may limit the Euratom Community's competences to mainly ensuring that Member States fulfil their obligations.

9.02 THE EXERCISE OF THE COMPETENCES

This section assesses the exercise of the Euratom Community's competences in relation to the nuclear common market and the instruments through which this occurs.

Analysis of the existing secondary legislation adopted under Chapter 9 of the Euratom Treaty shows that competences in three out of six of the articles contained in this Chapter serve as legal bases for secondary legal acts. The competences under Articles 93, 97 and 99 of the Euratom Treaty have not been exercised through secondary legislation. The Commission has, however, stated that Articles 93 and 97 are directly applicable.[995]

In Chapter 9 Section 01 of this study it is noted that Article 92 of the Euratom Treaty confers on the Council a competence to amend the list of goods and products under Annex IV of the Euratom Treaty, at the request of the Commission or of a Member State, acting on a proposal from the Commission. This competence has been exercised by the Council only once, in Regulation No 5 on the amendment of List B in Annex IV of the Euratom Treaty,[996] by deleting components and parts for nuclear reactors from List B, as nuclear reactors were already listed in List A^2 of Annex IV of the Euratom Treaty. The exercise of the Council's competences under Article 92 of the Euratom Treaty resulted in the prohibition of all customs duties on imports and exports or charges having equivalent effect, and all quantitative restrictions on imports and exports between Member States for both nuclear reactors and their parts and components. The amendment has merely clarified the list of goods and the Euratom Community's competences under Article 92 were exercised in accordance with the wording of the Euratom Treaty.

As also noted in Chapter 9 Section 01 of this study, Article 96 of the Euratom Treaty establishes the Euratom Community's competences in the field of free movement of workers. The Euratom Community has exercised this competence through secondary legislation on one occasion in the directive on freedom to take skilled employments in the field of nuclear energy.[997] The directive exercises the Euratom Community's competences by defining the concept of skilled employment in the field of nuclear energy as being employment in the field of nuclear energy which requires

995. See Commission Guide to the Community rules on open government procurement, OJ C 358, 31.12.1987, pp. 11–12; In this guidance document the Commission furthermore stated that Article 52 of the EEC Treaty on right of establishment (now Articles 49–55 TFEU) is also applicable to the nuclear field, insofar as they do not conflict with the provisions of the Euratom Treaty.
996. Regulation No 5 on amending of List B of Annex IV of the Euratom Treaty, OJ 7, 9.2.1959, p. 185.
997. Council Directive on freedom to take skilled employment in the field of nuclear energy, OJ 57, 9.7.1962, pp. 1650–1652.

specifically nuclear knowledge, the acquisition of which calls for special training or at least five months' practical work, and which relates, *inter alia*, to: nuclear energy research in the fields listed under Annex I of the Euratom Treaty; planning, designing or construction of nuclear installations or nuclear equipment or constituent parts of these installations or equipment; supervision, maintenance, repair or technical operation of nuclear installations and nuclear equipment; and protection against radiation. Furthermore, the directive establishes a list of types of skilled employment within the meaning of skilled employment in the field of nuclear energy.[998] The Euratom Community's competences under Article 96 of the Euratom Treaty are also exercised by aligning the rules on taking skilled employment in the field of nuclear energy to the rules governing freedom of movement for workers under EU legislation,[999] namely, by requiring that the conditions for granting authorisations required for any employment in the nuclear energy field are not less liberal than the conditions under EU legislation. The Euratom Community's competences under Article 96 of the Euratom Treaty are therefore exercised by specifying and defining the concepts established in the provisions of the Euratom Treaty. Consequently, the Euratom Community's competences under Article 96 of the Euratom Treaty are exercised in accordance with the wording of the Treaty.

Article 98 of the Euratom Treaty establishes a competence of the Euratom Community to require the Member States to take all measures necessary to facilitate the conclusion of insurance contracts covering nuclear risks. The Council has a competence to exercise the provisions of this article by issuing directives, acting by a qualified majority on a proposal from the Commission, which first requests the opinion of the Economic and Social Committee, and after consulting the EP. Even though it is the Council that has a horizontal competence to exercise competences laid down in Article 98 of the Euratom Treaty, the existing secondary legal acts based on Article 98 comprise two Commission recommendations to harmonise the legal framework for nuclear liability and financial security in the case of a nuclear incident.[1000] The Commission has stated that to ensure, *inter alia*, effective and uniform protection of victims and to eliminate the distortion of competition in the nuclear market resulting from unequal insurance burdens, there is a need for a system concerning civil liability and protection against damage that is appropriate to the specific nature of the nuclear risk posed and is as harmonised as possible.[1001] Therefore, both Commission Recommendations proposed the alignment of Member States' national provisions with those laid down in

998. Article 2 and Annex of Council Directive on freedom to take skilled employment in the field of nuclear energy.
999. Article 4 of Council Directive on freedom to take skilled employment in the field of nuclear energy. Article 4 refers to Articles 48 and 49 of the Treaty establishing the European Economic Community, which are now are Articles 45 to 48 TFEU.
1000. Commission Recommendation 65/42/Euratom of 28 October 1965 to the Member States on the harmonization of legislation applying the Paris Convention of 29 July 1960 and the Brussels Supplementary Convention of 31 January 1963, OJ 196, 18.11.1965, pp. 2995–2996; and Second Commission Recommendation 66/22/Euratom to the Member States on the harmonisation of legislation applying the Paris Convention of 29 July 1960, OJ 136, 25.7.1966, pp. 2553–2554.
1001. The recitals of Commission Recommendation 65/42/Euratom.

the 1960 Paris Convention on Third Party Liability in the Field of Nuclear Energy[1002] and the 1963 Brussels Convention Supplementary to the Paris Convention on Third Party Liability in the Field of Nuclear Energy.[1003] Systematic analysis of Article 160a of the Euratom Treaty and Article 292 TFEU[1004] leads one to conclude that the Commission's general competence to issue recommendations should clearly arise from the provisions of the primary legal act. It may be noted in this regard that the Euratom Treaty does not confer on the Commission the competence to issue recommendations under Article 98 of the Euratom Treaty. The Euratom Treaty establishes the Commission's competence to make recommendations to facilitate movements of capital intended to finance the industrial activities under Article 99 of the Treaty, but it is questionable whether the Commission Recommendations to harmonise the legal framework for nuclear liability and financial security in the event of a nuclear incident qualify for inclusion in this category. Consequently, these recommendations under Article 98 of the Euratom Treaty do not seem to have a proper legal basis.

The relevance of the Commission Recommendations referred to above significantly decreased after new Member States, which were Contracting Parties to another international nuclear liability convention (the 1963 Vienna Convention on Civil Liability for Nuclear Damage with a 1997 Protocol[1005]) joined the EU and the Euratom Community in the course of the 2004 and 2007 enlargements. This development gave rise to the European nuclear liability regime taking on a patchwork quality.[1006] The approach taken towards the regulation of nuclear liability has, however, recently shifted from the issue of competence under the Euratom Community towards the legal basis for the EU's competences in the field of external relations: Council decisions were adopted authorising the Member States to ratify or to accede to the 2004 Protocol

1002. The Paris Convention on Third Party Liability in the Field of Nuclear Energy of 29 July 1960, which was amended by the Additional Protocol of 28 January 1964 and by the Protocol of 16 November 1982, OECD, Paris, 1982.

1003. The Brussels Supplementary Convention of 31 January 1963 Supplementary to the Paris Convention of 29 July 1960, which was amended by the additional Protocol of 28 January 1964 and by the Protocol of 16 November 1982, OECD, Paris, 1982.

1004. Article 106a(1) of the Euratom Treaty states that horizontal provisions on legal acts of the EU under the TFEU are applicable to the Euratom Treaty. Under Article 292 TFEU, the Commission can adopt recommendations in specific cases provided for in the Treaties.

1005. The Vienna Convention on Civil Liability for Nuclear Damage, INFCIRC/500, IAEA, Vienna, 1996, which was amended by the Protocol to Amend the Vienna Convention on Civil Liability for Nuclear Damage, INFCIRC/566, IAEA, Vienna, 1998.

1006. For further discussion of the patchwork nature of the European nuclear liability regime, *see, e.g.*, P. Reyners, 'Liability Problems Associated with the Current Patchwork Nuclear Liability Regime Within the EU Member States', in N. Pelzer (ed.), *European Nuclear Liability Law in a Process of Change*, Baden-Baden: Nomos, 2010, pp. 93–104; J. Handrlica, 'Euratom Powers in the Field of Nuclear Liability Revised', (2010) 3/1 *International Journal of Nuclear Law*, pp. 1–18; J. Handrlica, 'Harmonisation of Nuclear Liability in the European Union: Challenges, Options and Limits', (2009) 84 *Nuclear Law Bulletin*, pp. 35–36; R. J. Heffron, S. F. Ashley and W. J. Nuttall, 'The Global Nuclear Liability Regime Post Fukushima Daiichi', (2016) 90 *Progress in Nuclear Energy*, pp. 4–5. On issues regarding international nuclear liability regime for transportable nuclear power plants, *see also*: J. Handrlica, 'Transportable Nuclear Power Plants: An Enigma of International Nuclear Liability Law', (2019) 6 *Journal of World Energy Law and Business*, pp. 1–15; and on the issues on nuclear liability and decommissioning, see: J. Handrlica, 'Nuclear Liability Conventions and Decommissioning: Exclusion Provisions Revisited', (2018) 11 *Journal of World Energy Law and Business*, pp. 196–208.

amending Paris Convention on Third Party Liability in the Field of Nuclear Energy[1007] and to the 1997 Protocol amending the Vienna Convention on Civil Liability for Nuclear Damage.[1008] Therefore, the relevance of Article 98 of the Euratom Treaty and the Euratom Community's competences in respect of nuclear liability have somewhat decreased.

Analysis of the exercise of the Euratom Community's competences in relation to the nuclear common market under Chapter 9 of the Euratom Treaty leads one to the conclusion that the Euratom Community's competences under Articles 92 and 96 of the Euratom Treaty have been exercised in accordance with the wording of the Treaty, as the secondary legal acts do not broaden the scope of the provisions of the Treaty but clarify and define them. The Commission does not, however, have an explicit competence to issue recommendations under Article 98 of the Euratom Treaty. The Commission has stated that the provisions of Articles 93 and 97 of the Euratom Treaty, which have not been exercised in secondary legislation, are directly applicable.

9.03 THE CJEU's INTERPRETATION OF THE COMPETENCES

This section assesses whether and how the CJEU's case-law defines and elaborates on the Euratom Community's competence in relation to the nuclear common market.

Analysis of the CJEU's case-law in relation to the Euratom Community's nuclear common market shows that there are two cases where the Court has addressed and defined the Euratom Community's competences in the field.

Regarding the concept and purpose of the nuclear common market in the Euratom Community, the Court has ruled that Article 93, together with the other provisions contained in Chapter 9 of the Euratom Treaty, constitute the application, in a highly specialised (nuclear) field, of the legal conceptions which form the basis of the structure of the general common market.[1009] In other words, the Court confirmed that the structure of the nuclear common market is based on the same legal concepts as the general common market.[1010] Some authors take the view that the Court has not

1007. Council Decision 2004/294/EC of 8 March 2004 authorising the Member States which are Contracting Parties to the Paris Convention of 29 July 1960 on Third Party Liability in the Field of Nuclear Energy to ratify, in the interest of the European Community, the Protocol amending that Convention, or to accede to it, OJ L 97, 1.4.2004, pp. 53–54. The legal basis for this Council Decision was Article 218 TFEU (previously Article 300 of the Treaty establishing the European Community).

1008. Council Decision 2013/434/EU of 15 July 2013 authorising certain Member States to ratify, or to accede to, the Protocol amending the Vienna Convention on Civil Liability for Nuclear Damage of 21 May 1963, in the interest of the European Union, and to make a declaration on the application of the relevant internal rules of Union law, OJ L 220, 17.8.2013, pp. 1–2. The legal basis for this Council Decision was, *inter alia*, Article 218 TFEU on international agreements.

1009. Judgment of 4 June 2015, *Kernkraftwerke Lippe-Ems*, C-5/14, ECLI:EU:C:2015:354, paragraph 86.

1010. A certain difference between the general common market and the nuclear common market may be identified, namely that the European Economic Community was based primarily on the existence of its common market, whereas in the Euratom Community, the nuclear common market is one of many instruments of atomic integration. See J. G. Polach, *Euratom:*

addressed the relationship between the EU Treaties and the Euratom Treaty.[1011] However, analysis of the available case-law in relation to the nuclear common market leads one to conclude that the CJEU elaborated on the comparative analysis between the general common market and nuclear common market in its statement that, like the EEC Treaty (which was then in force), the Euratom Treaty seeks to set up a homogeneous economic area in respect of the matters covered by it.[1012] In the same case the CJEU also took the view that the nuclear common market cannot be burdened with unnecessary barriers, and stated that the provisions of the Euratom Treaty relate to the liberalisation of transfers of nuclear materials and of specialised materials and equipment, without these movements being obstructed by barriers resulting directly or indirectly from national legislation on fiscal, commercial or technical matters.[1013]

The CJEU also made a distinction between the Euratom Community's competences in relation to nuclear supply and the Euratom Community's competences in respect of the nuclear common market. It defined the competences under Chapter 6 of the Euratom Treaty as an exclusive jurisdiction conferred on the Euratom Community with regard to nuclear supply; and the competences under Chapter 9 of the Euratom Treaty as the Euratom Community's general responsibility for the normal functioning of the nuclear common market.[1014] Consequently, the Court confirmed that the Euratom Community's competences in relation to the nuclear common market are weaker than its competences in respect of nuclear supply policy.

Finally, the Court has also addressed the issue of whether a duty introduced on nuclear fuel for production of electricity can constitute a charge having equivalent effect under Article 93 of the Euratom Treaty. It concluded that as the introduced duty was used for the commercial production of electricity, irrespective of the source of that fuel, and no distinction was made as regards the rate of taxation or the person liable for payment of the duty, the duty did not constitute a charge having equivalent effect to a customs duty within the meaning of Article 93(1).[1015] The Court also concluded that attainment of the Euratom Community's objective of establishing the conditions necessary for the speedy establishment and growth of nuclear industries, set out in Article 1(2) of the Euratom Treaty, does not have the effect of requiring Member States

Its Background, Issues and Economic Implications, Dobbs Ferry, N.Y: Oceana Publications Inc., 1964, p. 39; and A Moravcsik, *The Choice for Europe: Social Purpose and State Power from Messina to Maastricht*, Ithaca, NY: Cornell University Press, 1998, p. 4.

1011. *See, e.g.*, T. F. Cusack, 'A Tale of Two Treaties', (2003) 40 *Common Market Law Review*, p. 128.

1012. A Södersten correctly concludes that the Court interpreted the nuclear common market under a *lex specialis* approach. See A. Södersten, *Euratom at the Crossroads*, Cheltenham, Northampton: Edward Elgar Publishing Limited, 2018, p. 117.

1013. Ruling of 14 November 1978, Ruling of the Court delivered pursuant to the third paragraph of Article 103 of the Euratom Treaty – Draft Convention of the International Atomic Energy Agency on the Physical Protection of Nuclear Materials, Facilities and Transports, Ruling 1/78, ECLI:EU:C:1978:202, paragraph 15.

1014. Ruling of 14 November 1978, Ruling of the Court delivered pursuant to the third paragraph of Article 103 of the Euratom Treaty – Draft Convention of the International Atomic Energy Agency on the Physical Protection of Nuclear Materials, Facilities and Transports, Ruling 1/78, ECLI:EU:C:1978:202, paragraph 18.

1015. Judgment of 4 June 2015, *Kernkraftwerke Lippe-Ems*, C-5/14, ECLI:EU:C:2015:354, paragraphs 91 and 92.

to maintain or increase their level of use of nuclear fuel or of preventing them from taxing such use, which would make such use more costly and, therefore, less attractive. Consequently, Article 93, in conjunction with other articles of the Euratom Treaty, is to be interpreted as not precluding national legislation, which imposes a duty on the use of nuclear fuel for the commercial production of electricity.[1016]

Concluding the analysis of the CJEU's case-law in relation to the nuclear common market, it can be stated that the Court has defined the nuclear common market by finding parallels with the EU's general common market. The Court also clearly identified the differences between the Euratom Community's competences in relation to the nuclear common market and its competences in the field of nuclear supply. The parallel between the general common market and the nuclear common market is noted in Chapter 9 Section 01 of this study in the context of the analysis of the scope and content of the Euratom Community's competences in relation to the nuclear common market. The Court thus confirmed the Euratom Community's competences under Chapter 9 of the Euratom Treaty.

9.04 FEATURES OF THE COMPETENCES

This section assesses the following features with a view to ensuring a basis for comparative analysis: the level of detail of the provisions of the Euratom Treaty; the exercise of the competences as compared with the bare wording of the Euratom Treaty; and the existence of case-law and the effect of the Court's interpretation of the relevant provisions of primary and secondary legislation to the competences of the Euratom Community.

The level of detail of the provisions of the Euratom Treaty in relation to the nuclear common market is appropriate to the Community's task of ensuring wide commercial outlets and access to the best technical facilities in the nuclear sector. The wording of certain provisions contained in Chapter 9 of the Euratom Treaty may, however, limit the Euratom Community's competences mainly to ensuring that Member States fulfil their obligations.

The Euratom Community's competences in relation to the nuclear common market under Articles 92 and 96 of the Euratom Treaty have been exercised in accordance with the Treaty wording. The legal basis of the Commission Recommendations under Article 98 of the Euratom Treaty is, however, open to question. The Commission considers that Articles 93 and 97, which have not been exercised by secondary legislation, are directly applicable.

The Court has confirmed the Euratom Community's competences under Chapter 9 of the Euratom Treaty, by establishing a parallel between the nuclear common market and the general common market that stems from the fact that they are based on the same legal concepts. The Court also clearly identified the differences between the Euratom Community's competences in relation to the nuclear common market and its

1016. Judgment of 4 June 2015, *Kernkraftwerke Lippe-Ems*, C-5/14, ECLI:EU:C:2015:354, paragraphs 102 and 106.

competences in relation to nuclear supply policy, and confirmed that the Euratom Community's competences in respect of the nuclear common market are weaker than its competences in respect of nuclear supply policy.

Chapter 10

External Relations

- *The scope of the Euratom Community's competences in relation to external relations under the Euratom Treaty is defined through its competences as set out in the first nine chapters of the Euratom Treaty. The content of the Euratom Community's competences in this regard include: entering into external relations with third States, international organisations or nationals of a third state; approving draft agreements or contracts that Member States wish to conclude; and renegotiating certain agreements concluded by Member States before the date of their accession to the Euratom Community.*
- *The Euratom Community's competences laid down in Articles 101 and 103 of the Euratom Treaty have been exercised through secondary legislation. The competences under Article 101 are extensively exercised by concluding bilateral agreements with third States, by participating in multilateral projects and through accession to international conventions. The legal basis of Commission Recommendation (Euratom) 2016/538, which is the instrument through which the competences laid down in Article 103 of the Euratom Treaty are exercised, is open to question. However, this recommendation emphasises the importance of Article 103 of the Euratom Treaty in relation to compatibility assessments and addresses the division of competences between the Euratom Community and its Member States.*
- *The CJEU has defined the Euratom Community's competences by establishing that once an external relationship creates obligations that fall within the scope of the Euratom Community's competences, the competence to enter into such relations belongs exclusively to the Euratom Community. The CJEU has also indicated that the importance of Article 101 of the Euratom Treaty lies in its defining the Euratom Community's powers and jurisdiction in relation to external relations. The Court has also confirmed the role of Article 102 as providing the procedure for entering into external obligations with mixed competences, and has emphasised the importance of Article 103 as providing the Euratom Community with a supervisory competence.*

- *The features of the Euratom Community's competences in relation to external relations are as follows: the level of detail of the provisions of the Euratom Treaty is appropriate to the objective to enter into external relations with other countries and international organisations which foster progress in the peaceful uses of nuclear energy; the exercise of the Euratom Community's competences under Articles 101 and 103 of the Euratom Treaty is in accordance with the Treaty wording, with the possible exception of the provision of information to the Commission on agreements or contracts already in force under Article 103; in the few cases that the Court has heard in respect of this area, it has emphasised the importance of Articles 101 to 103 of the Euratom Treaty as defining the powers and jurisdiction of the Euratom Community in relation to external relations, and has delimited the Euratom Community's competences in this field.*

10.01 THE SCOPE AND CONTENT OF THE COMPETENCES

This section assesses the scope and content of the Euratom Community's competences in the field of external relations under Chapter 10 of the Euratom Treaty.

The Euratom Community has international legal personality under the Euratom Treaty.[1017] The Euratom Treaty confers a task on the Euratom Community to enter into external relations with other countries and international organisations which foster progress in the peaceful uses of nuclear energy.[1018] The purpose of Chapter 10 of the Euratom Treaty is sometimes characterised as safeguarding the interaction of national and supranational nuclear foreign policy.[1019] The scope of the Euratom Community's competences in this area may therefore be interpreted broadly, which means that the Euratom Community has a competence to enter into external relations in respect of all aspects that could foster progress in the peaceful use of nuclear energy. Provisions in Chapter 10 of the Euratom Treaty specify, however, that the Euratom Community's competence to enter into obligations by concluding agreements or contracts with a third state, an international organisation or a national of a third state, is applicable within the limits of the Euratom Community's powers and jurisdiction.[1020] In other words, the Euratom Community has a general competence to enter into agreements with third States or international organisations, concerning matters which fall within its internal competences.[1021] The provisions of Chapter 10 of the Euratom Treaty do not, therefore, bestow any new vertical competences on the Euratom Community, but

1017. Article 184 of the Euratom Treaty. *See also* H. de Waele, *Legal Dynamics of EU External Relations*, Antwerp: Springer, 2017, p. 4.
1018. Article 2(h) of the Euratom Treaty.
1019. H. J. Hahn, 'Control under the Euratom Compact', (1958) 7 *American Journal of Comparative Law*, p. 44.
1020. Article 101(1) of the Euratom Treaty.
1021. P. Mathijsen, 'Some Legal Aspects of Euratom', (1965–1966) 3 *Common Market Law Review*, p. 334; and T. F. Cusack, 'A Tale of Two Treaties', (2003) 40 *Common Market Law Review*, p. 140.

extend the existing competences under first nine chapters of the Euratom Treaty to an external dimension, i.e., in relation to third States, international organisations or nationals of a third state. This creates a parallel between the Euratom Community's internal and external powers.[1022] The scope of the Euratom Community's external competences is therefore defined through the Euratom Community's internal competences.[1023] Its internal competences in relation to the promotion of research, dissemination of information, health and safety, investments, Joint Undertakings, supplies, safeguards, property ownership and nuclear common market under the Euratom Treaty are within the scope of the Community's competences in external relations, when the Euratom Community enters into external obligations by concluding an agreement or a contracts a with a third state, international organisation or a national of a third state.

The Euratom Treaty also confers horizontal competences on the Council and the Commission in all phases of external relations, i.e., before, during and after the negotiation of the relevant agreements or contracts.[1024] The division of these horizontal competences between the Council and the Commission depends on whether the implementation of the agreements or contracts in question requires action by the Council and can be effected within the limits of the relevant budget. If a Council decision is needed and the agreement cannot be effected within the limits of the budget, the Council has a competence to give directives to the Commission for the negotiation of agreements and contracts, and the Commission has a competence to negotiate and conclude them. After that has been done, the Council has a competence to approve those agreements or contracts by a qualified majority. In other cases, the Commission has a competence both to negotiate and to conclude agreements and contracts without the Council's involvement, but is required to keep the Council informed.[1025] In respect of mixed participation in external relations - i.e., where both the Euratom Community and one or several Member States are parties to an agreement or a contract - the

1022. European Commission, '50 Years of the Euratom Treaty', Memo/07/118, 26 March 2007 Brussels, p. 1.

1023. EU law has developed a doctrine of parallelism, under which the exercise of an internal EU competence gives rise to an external EU competence. However, in this case the Court has ruled that the existence of an external EU competence precludes Member States from exercising an equivalent or overlapping competence (i.e., in this situation the EU has exclusive competence). *See, e.g.*, G. Conway, *EU Law*, London and New York: Routledge, 2015, p. 277.

1024. The Euratom Treaty does not confer any competences on the EP in respect of external relations under Chapter 10 of the Euratom Treaty. The EP has, therefore, adopted a Resolution on the role of the EP in the negotiation and ratification of Treaties of accession and of other Treaties and agreements between the European Community and third countries, OJ C 66, 15.3.1982, p. 68. It should also be noted that although Article 101 of the Euratom Treaty excludes the EP from involvement in international agreements under the Euratom Treaty, the EP is co-budgetary authority for all the expenditure which is based on the Euratom Treaty. See P. Barnes, 'Going forward into the past: the resurrection of the Euratom Treaty', European Union Studies Association (EUSA), Tenth Biennial International Conference, p. 12.

1025. Article 101(2) and (3) of the Euratom Treaty. Here a gentlemen's agreement has been reached between the two institutions, whereby in either case the Council is kept informed of negotiations and Commission action is basically sanctioned *a priori*. See L. Scheinmann, 'Euratom: Nuclear Integration in Europe', (1967) 563 *International Conciliation*, p. 18.

Euratom Treaty provides that the agreement or a contract cannot enter into force until the Commission has been notified by all Member States concerned that it has become applicable in accordance with the provisions of their respective national laws.[1026] This may entail such agreements being ratified by the Commission on behalf of the participant Member States or their collective confirmation by the Euratom Community and the Member States concerned.[1027]

Analysis of the provisions of Chapter 10 of the Euratom Treaty leads one to conclude that the content of the Euratom Community's competences in relation to external relations under this chapter may be defined through analysis of the Treaty requirements established for agreements or contracts signed by a Member State, a person or an undertaking[1028] in a Member State.[1029]

The main rule, as noted above, is that the Euratom Community has a competence to enter into external relations with a third state, an international organisation or a national of a third state, within its scope of its competences under the Euratom Treaty. This also implies a renegotiation clause. In other words, when Member States have concluded agreements with third States providing for cooperation in the field of nuclear energy before the date of their accession to the Euratom Community, these are to be renegotiated jointly with the Commission to ensure that the rights and obligations arising out of such agreements are, as far as possible, assumed by the Euratom Community. A new agreement arising from these renegotiations needs the consent of the Member State or Member States concerned[1030] and approval by the Council, acting by a qualified majority.[1031]

The Euratom Community, via the Commission, also has a competence to require that the Member States notify their draft agreements or contracts with third States, international organisations or nationals of a third state, if the content in those agreements or contracts concerns matters within the Euratom Community's competences. The Commission also has a competence to comment on the proposed agreement or contract, within one month of receipt of notification if it takes the view that the agreement or contract in question may impede the application of the Euratom Treaty.[1032] Although this competence is worded as a notification, a Member State

1026. Article 102 of the Euratom Treaty.
1027. H. J. Hahn, 'Control under the Euratom Compact', (1958) 7 *American Journal of Comparative Law*, p. 44.
1028. Under Article 196 of the Euratom Treaty, a person means any natural person who pursues all or any of his activities in the territories of Member States within the field specified in the relevant chapter of the Euratom Treaty; and an undertaking means any undertaking or institution which pursues all or any of its activities in the territories of Member States within the field specified in the relevant chapter of the Euratom Treaty, whatever its public or private legal status.
1029. It remains important to identify the content of these Euratom Community's competences under the Euratom Treaty due to the possible accession of new Member States to the Euratom Community.
1030. The need for the consent of the Member State here is considered to restrict the supranational features of the Euratom Community's competences. See R. Efron and A. S. Nanes, 'The Common Market and Euratom Treaties: Supranationality and the Integration of Europe', (1957) 6 *International and Comparative Law Quarterly*, p. 682.
1031. Article 106 of the Euratom Treaty.
1032. Article 103(1) and (2) of the Euratom Treaty.

cannot conclude the proposed agreement or contract until it has satisfied the objections of the Commission or complied with a ruling of the CJEU, adjudicating urgently upon an application from the Member State, on the compatibility of the proposed clauses with the provisions of the Euratom Treaty.[1033] Consequently, this mandatory scrutiny procedure gives a competence to the Commission to check *ex ante* whether draft agreements or contracts which the Member States intend to conclude are compatible with the Euratom Treaty.[1034]

Regarding agreements and contracts signed by a person or undertaking of a Member State, the Euratom Treaty establishes specific provisions, stating that if such agreement or contract has been concluded after Member State's date of accession to the Euratom Community[1035] – no person or undertaking can invoke this agreement or contract in order to evade obligations imposed by the Euratom Treaty.[1036] This could be interpreted to mean that an agreement or contract between a third state, international organisation or national of a third state and a person or undertaking from a Member State can be valid when signed after the date of accession of that Member State to the Euratom Community, if it does not interfere with the obligations under the Euratom Treaty.

The Euratom Treaty also provides that the Commission has a competence to request Member States of the Euratom Community to notify to it agreements or contracts signed by the Member States under Article 103 of the Euratom Treaty, and agreements and contracts signed by persons or undertakings in the Member State's jurisdiction. In addition to its competences to evaluate agreements and contracts signed by the Member States under Article 103 of the Euratom Treaty, the CJEU also has a competence to evaluate and determine the compatibility of agreements or contracts signed by persons or undertakings with the provisions of Euratom Treaty.[1037] These provisions establish the supremacy of the Euratom Treaty over any agreement concluded by a Member State which contains provisions incompatible with the Euratom Treaty or which impede its application.[1038]

The Euratom Treaty also contains a protection clause in respect of agreements or contracts signed by Member States, persons or undertakings and concluded before the Member State's date of accession to the Euratom Community[1039] which means that the provisions of the Euratom Treaty cannot be invoked to prevent the implementation of such agreements or contracts if they have been communicated to the Commission no later than thirty days following accession. If an agreement or contract has been

1033. Article 103(3) of the Euratom Treaty. An application may be made to the CJEU at any time after the Member State has received the Commission's comments.
1034. J. Grunwald, 'Peaceful Uses of Nuclear Energy under Euratom Law', in J. L. Black-Branch and D. Fleck (eds), *Nuclear Non-Proliferation in International Law, Volume III: Legal Aspects of the Use of Nuclear Energy for Peaceful Purposes*, The Hague: Asser Press, 2016, p. 191.
1035. Or 1 January 1958, which is the Euratom Treaty's date of entry into force.
1036. Article 104(1) of the Euratom Treaty.
1037. Article 104(2) and (3) of the Euratom Treaty.
1038. R. Efron and A. S. Nanes, 'The Common Market and Euratom Treaties: Supranationality and the Integration of Europe', (1957) 6 *International and Comparative Law Quarterly*, p. 681.
1039. Or the date of the Euratom Treaty's entry into force.

concluded by a person or an undertaking with a third state, an international organisation or a national of a third state, and signed between the signature of the instrument of the Member State's accession and the date of its accession to the Euratom Community,[1040] such an agreement or contract cannot be invoked as grounds for failure to implement the Euratom Treaty if one of the decisive reasons on the part of either of the parties in concluding the agreement or contract was an intention to evade the provisions of the Euratom Treaty.[1041]

Before concluding the analysis of the scope and content of the Euratom Community's competences in relation to external relations under the Euratom Treaty, it should be noted that the Euratom Treaty has explicitly regulated certain Euratom Community competences in respect of external relations with international organisations, apart from the provisions contained in Chapter 10 of the Euratom Treaty. The Euratom Treaty confers on the Commission the competence to ensure the maintenance of all appropriate relations with the organs of the United Nations, of its specialised agencies and of the World Trade Organization. The Commission also has a competence to maintain relations as appropriate with all international organisations.[1042] In addition, the Euratom Community has a competence to establish close cooperation with the Organization for Economic Cooperation and Development.[1043] Finally, the Euratom Community has a competence to conclude with international organisations agreements establishing an association involving reciprocal rights and obligations, common actions and special procedures. These agreements are to be concluded by the Council, acting unanimously after consulting the EP.[1044] The provisions outlined above add further elements to the Euratom Community's external policy[1045] and the interaction between them and the provisions contained in Chapter 10 of the Euratom Treaty are analysed here.

The Euratom Community's competences under Chapter 10 of the Euratom Treaty differ significantly in their legal consequences from the provisions under Title V ('General Provisions') of the Euratom Treaty. Article 101 of the Euratom Treaty confers a competence on the Euratom Community to enter into obligations by concluding agreements or contracts, *inter alia*, with international organisations, implying the creation of legal obligations for the Euratom Community through such agreements or contracts. The Euratom Community's competences under Articles 199 and 201 of the Euratom Treaty entail maintaining relations and establishing close cooperation with certain specific international organisations, but do not explicitly create specific legal obligations for the Euratom Community. This indicates a lighter approach to external relations in respect of established international organisations. Article 206 of the Euratom Treaty refers to agreements that may require amendment of the Euratom

1040. Or between the date of signature of the Euratom Treaty (25 March 1957) and its entry into force.
1041. Article 105 of the Euratom Treaty.
1042. Article 199 of the Euratom Treaty.
1043. Article 201 of the Euratom Treaty.
1044. Article 206 of the Euratom Treaty.
1045. M. Gaudet, *Euratom*, London: Pergamon Press, 1959, p. 173.

Treaty. These agreements are beyond the scope of the Euratom Community's competences under Chapter 10 of the Euratom Treaty, as Article 101 requires external relations to be within the limits of the Euratom Community's powers and jurisdiction. Therefore, the competences laid down in Article 206 go beyond the legal framework of external relations under Chapter 10 of the Euratom Treaty. This opens up the possibility of agreements that go beyond the Euratom Community's current competences being concluded with international organisations on the basis that the Council takes a unanimous decision and the necessary amendments are adopted under the procedure laid down in Articles 48(2) and (5) TFEU. Consequently, Articles 199, 201 and 206 of the Euratom Treaty establish Euratom Community competences in respect of external relations with international organisations, which differ, in terms of their legal consequences, from the Euratom Community's competences under Chapter 10 of the Euratom Treaty.

In conclusion, the scope of the Euratom Community's competences in respect of external relations under Chapter 10 of the Euratom Treaty is defined through the Euratom Community's competences under the first nine chapters of the Euratom Treaty. The content of the Euratom Community's competences regarding external relations indicates that the Euratom Community has competence to enter into external relations with third States, international organisations or nationals of a third state, and includes its competence to renegotiate agreements between Member States and third States on nuclear energy cooperation where these agreements were concluded before the date of Member State's accession to the Euratom Community. The Euratom Community, via the Commission, also has a competence to approve all draft agreements or contracts that Member States wish to sign with a third state, an international organisation or a national of a third state. The Euratom Treaty also confers priority on the Euratom Community over agreements or contracts signed by a person or undertaking with a third state, an international organisation or a national of a third state, and concluded after entry into force of the Euratom Treaty: such agreements or contracts cannot interfere with obligations under the Euratom Treaty or be invoked to evade obligations imposed by the Euratom Treaty. Finally, the Euratom Community still protects agreements or contracts signed by a Member State, a person or an undertaking and concluded before the date of the Euratom Treaty's entry into force: these are to be implemented if communicated to the Commission no later than thirty days after the Euratom Treaty's entry into force. No such protection is provided in respect of agreements or contracts if a person or undertaking has concluded such an agreement or contract with the intention of evading the provisions of the Euratom Treaty. Some authors consider that the content of the Euratom Community's competences under Chapter 10 of the Euratom Treaty finds comparable counterparts only in the constitutions of federal States.[1046] The level of detail of the provisions of the Euratom Treaty that establish the Euratom Community's competences in relation to external relations is appropriate to the objective of entering into external relations with third countries

1046. H. J. Hahn, 'Control under the Euratom Compact', (1958) 7 *American Journal of Comparative Law*, p. 45.

and international organisations which foster progress in the peaceful use of nuclear energy.

10.02 THE EXERCISE OF THE COMPETENCES

This section assesses the exercise of the Euratom Community's competences in relation to external relations under Chapter 10 of the Euratom Treaty and the instruments through which this occurs.

Analysis of the currently in force secondary legislation that was adopted on the basis of one of the articles contained in Chapter 10 of the Euratom Treaty reveals that competences under two articles in this chapter have been exercised by the Euratom Community.[1047] This secondary legislation is based on Articles 101 and 103.[1048]

The competence under Article 101 of the Euratom Treaty to enter into obligations by concluding agreements or contracts with a third state, an international organisation or a national of a third state, within the limits of the Euratom Community's powers and jurisdiction, is an extensively exercised Euratom Community competence. During the last two decades the Euratom Community's competences under Article 101 have been exercised through a total of ninety-seven secondary legal acts, as follows: twenty-nine Council decisions[1049] and twenty-seven Commission decisions that have a legal basis in the Euratom Treaty[1050] and forty-one Council and Commission decisions that have a dual EU and Euratom legal basis.[1051] The Euratom Community has exercised its

1047. The Euratom Community's competences under Article 102 and Articles 104 to 106 of the Euratom Treaty have not been exercised through secondary legislation.

1048. Analysis of the exercise of the Euratom Community's competences under Articles 199, 201 and 206 of the Euratom Treaty are beyond the scope of this study. However, since they are mentioned in Chapter 10 Section 01 regarding the analysis of scope and content of the Euratom Community's competences in the field of external relations, it is worth noting that, of these three articles, only the Euratom Community's competences under Article 199 of the Euratom Treaty have been exercised. This was done through Commission Decision 2010/398/Euratom of 15 July 2010 on the conclusion of a Memorandum of Understanding between the European Commission and the International Atomic Energy Agency concerning the EURDEP (European Radiological Data Exchange Platform), OJ L 182, 16.7.2010, pp. 15–17.

1049. Council Decisions, No: 2001/411/Euratom; 2001/761/Euratom; 2003/744/Euratom; 2004/755/Euratom; 2005/84/Euratom; 2007/513/Euratom; 2007/614/Euratom; 2010/487/Euratom; 2010/488/Euratom; 2011/186/Euratom; 2011/334/Euratom; 2013/4/Euratom; 20 14/317/Euratom; 2014/315/Euratom; 2014/495/Euratom; 2014/493/Euratom; 2014/670/Euratom; 2014/954/Euratom; 2015/1892; 2015/1993; 2015/1990; 2015/2227; 2015/2228; 2016/829; 2016/852; 2016/2116; 2017/76; 2018/386.

1050. Commission Decisions, No: 2001/412/Euratom; 2001/762/Euratom; 2002/924/Euratom; 2004/282/Euratom; 2004/491/Euratom; 2005/419/Euratom; 2005/845/Euratom; 2005/844/Euratom; 2006/635/Euratom; 2006/890/Euratom; 2006/943/Euratom; 2007/58/Euratom; 2008/72/Euratom; 2008/99/EC,Euratom; 2009/25/Euratom; 2012/55/Euratom; 2013/363/Euratom; 2013/408/Euratom; 2015/C 364/04; 2015/C 385/03; 2016/C 52/03; 2016/C 52/04; 2016/C 52/05; 2016/C 52/06; C/2016/7207; 2016/C 467/06; 2017/251; C/2017/5303.

1051. Council and Commission Decisions on a dual EU and Euratom legal basis: 2000/682/EC,ECSC,Euratom; 2000/683/EC,ECSC,Euratom; 2000/684/EC,ECSC,Euratom; 2002/309/EC,Euratom; 2003/462/EC; 2004/112/EC,Euratom; 2004/239/EC,Euratom; 2005/192/EC,Euratom; 2005/205/EC,Euratom; 2005/252/EC,Euratom; 2005/459/

competences in respect of external relations under Article 101 of the Euratom Treaty in three different ways.

First, it has done so by concluding bilateral agreements with third States. During the last two decades the Euratom Community[1052] has concluded bilateral agreements under Article 101 with the Kyrgyz Republic,[1053] Bosnia and Herzegovina,[1054] Turkmenistan,[1055] Tajikistan,[1056] Kosovo,[1057] Macedonia,[1058] Serbia,[1059] Moldova,[1060] Georgia,[1061] Montenegro,[1062] Albania,[1063] Uzbekistan,[1064] South Africa[1065] and Australia.[1066]

EC,Euratom; 2006/365/EC,Euratom; 2006/457/EC,Euratom; 2006/455/EC,Euratom; 2006/453/EC,Euratom; 2006/536/EC,Euratom; 2006/538/EC,Euratom; 2006/710/EC,Euratom; 2006/712/EC,Euratom; 2007/502/EC,Euratom; 2007/541/EC,Euratom; 2007/644/EC,Euratom; 2007/681/EC,Euratom; 2007/834/EC,Euratom; 2008/429/EC,Euratom; 2008/430/EC,Euratom; 2008/438/EC,Euratom; 2009/50/EC,Euratom; 2009/81/EC,Euratom; 2009/82/EC,Euratom; 2009/153/EC,Euratom; 2009/331/EC,Euratom; 2009/332/EC,Euratom; 2009/816/EC,Euratom; 2009/989/EC,Euratom; 2009/990/EC,Euratom; 2010/224/EU,Euratom; 2013/489/EU,Euratom; 2013/490/EU,Euratom; 2015/54; 2015/55; 2015/60; 2015/998.

1052. Solely or together with the EU. Bilateral agreements which only have a dual legal basis, i.e., where the Euratom Community has not concluded any specific agreement under the Euratom Treaty, but is a part of the broader cooperation agreement, have been concluded with Azerbaijan (Council and Commission Decision 2006/453/EC,Euratom and Council and Commission Decision 2009/816/EC,Euratom), Armenia (Council and Commission Decision 2005/252/EC,Euratom and Council and Commission Decision 2008/429/EC,Euratom) and Croatia (Council and Commission Decision 2005/205/EC,Euratom and Council and Commission Decision 2009/153/EC,Euratom. These decisions remain in force, but became non-applicable following Croatia's accession to the EU and the Euratom Community in 2013. See Article 2 of the Treaty on the accession of the Republic of Croatia to the European Union, OJ L 112, 24.4.2012, pp. 10–110.

1053. Council and Commission Decision 2006/712/EC,Euratom of 25 September 2006 on the conclusion of the Protocol to the Partnership and Cooperation Agreement establishing a partnership between the European Communities and their Member States, of the one part, and the Republic of Kyrgyzstan, of the other part, OJ L 303, 1.11.2006, pp. 13–13; Council and Commission Decision 2009/82/EC,Euratom of 18 December 2008 on the conclusion of the Protocol to the Partnership and Cooperation Agreement between the European Communities and their Member States, of the one part, and the Kyrgyz Republic, of the other part, OJ L 26, 30.1.2009, p. 5; Council Decision (Euratom) 2018/386 of 16 October 2017 approving the conclusion, by the European Commission, on behalf of the European Atomic Energy Community, of the Protocol to the Partnership and Cooperation Agreement establishing a partnership between the European Communities and their Member States, of the one part, and the Kyrgyz Republic, of the other part, OJ L 69, 13.3.2018, p. 8.

1054. Council and Commission Decision (EU, Euratom) 2015/998 of 21 April 2015 on the conclusion of the Stabilisation and Association Agreement between the European Communities and their Member States, of the one part, and Bosnia and Herzegovina, of the other part, OJ L 164, 30.6.2015, pp. 548–549; Commission Decision (2016/C 467/06) of 9 December 2016 on the conclusion, on behalf of the European Atomic Energy Community, of the Protocol to the Stabilisation and Association Agreement between the European Communities and their Member States, on the one part, and Bosnia and Herzegovina, of the other part, OJ C 467, 15.12.2016, pp. 16–17; Council Decision (Euratom) 2017/76 of 21 November 2016 approving the conclusion, by the European Commission, on behalf of the European Atomic Energy Community, of the Protocol to the Stabilisation and Association Agreement between the European Communities and their Member States, of the one part, and Bosnia and Herzegovina, of the other part, OJ L 12, 17.1.2017, pp. 22–23.

1055. Council Decision 2011/186/Euratom of 14 June 2010 approving the conclusion, by the European Commission on behalf of the European Atomic Energy Community, of the Interim Agreement on trade and trade-related matters between the European Community, the

European Coal and Steel Community and the European Atomic Energy Community, of the one part, and Turkmenistan, of the other part, OJ L 80, 26.3.2011, p. 1; Council Decision (Euratom) 2016/852 of 12 May 2016 approving the conclusion, by the European Commission, on behalf of the European Atomic Energy Community, of a Protocol to the Partnership and Cooperation Agreement establishing a partnership between the European Communities and their Member States, of the one part, and Turkmenistan, of the other part, OJ L 142, 31.5.2016, pp. 1–2.

1056. Council decision 2004/755/Euratom of 11 October 2004 approving the conclusion by the Commission, on behalf of the European Atomic Energy Community, of the Interim Agreement on trade and trade-related matters between the European Community and the European Atomic Energy Community, of the one part, and the Republic of Tajikistan, of the other part, OJ L 340, 16.11.2004, p. 21; Decision of the Council and of the Commission 2009/989/EC,Euratom of 17 November 2009 on the conclusion of a Partnership and Cooperation Agreement establishing a partnership between the European Communities and their Member States, of the one part, and the Republic of Tajikistan, of the other part, OJ L 350, 29.12.2009, pp. 1–2; Council and Commission Decision 2009/990/EC,Euratom of 17 November 2009 on the conclusion of the Protocol to the Partnership and Cooperation Agreement between the European Communities and their Member States, of the one part, and the Republic of Tajikistan, of the other part, OJ L 350, 29.12.2009, p. 52; Council Decision (Euratom) 2016/829 of 12 May 2016 approving the conclusion, by the European Commission, on behalf of the European Atomic Energy Community, of a Protocol to the Partnership and Cooperation Agreement establishing a partnership between the European Communities and their Member States, of the one part, and the Republic of Tajikistan, of the other part, OJ L 140, 27.5.2016, pp. 3–4.

1057. Council Decision (Euratom) 2015/1993 of 22 October 2015 approving the conclusion, by the European Commission, on behalf of the European Atomic Energy Community, of the Stabilisation and Association Agreement between the European Union and the European Atomic Energy Community, of the one part, and of Kosovo, of the other part, OJ L 290, 6.11.2015, pp. 14–15; Commission Decision (2015/C 364/04) of 26 October 2015 on the conclusion of the Stabilisation and Association Agreement between the European Union and the European Atomic Energy Community, of the one part, and of Kosovo, of the other part, OJ C 364, 4.11.2015, pp. 4–5.

1058. Council and Commission Decision 2004/239/EC,Euratom of 23 February 2004 concerning the conclusion of the Stabilisation and Association Agreement between the European Communities and their Member States, of the one part, and the former Yugoslav Republic of Macedonia, of the other part, OJ L 84, 20.3.2004, pp. 1–2; Council and Commission Decision 2005/192/EC,Euratom of 21 February 2005 on the conclusion of the Protocol to the Stabilisation and Association Agreement between the European Communities and their Member States, of the one part, and the former Yugoslav Republic of Macedonia, of the other part, OJ L 63, 10.3.2005, pp. 21–22; Council and Commission Decision 2008/438/EC,Euratom of 14 May 2008 on the conclusion of the Protocol to the Stabilisation and Association Agreement between the European Communities and their Member States, of the one part, and the former Yugoslav Republic of Macedonia, of the other part, OJ L 155, 13.6.2008, pp. 15–16; Council Decision (Euratom) 2015/1892 of 18 February 2014 approving the conclusion, by the European Commission, on behalf of the European Atomic Energy Community, of the Protocol to the Stabilisation and Association Agreement between the European Communities and their Member States, of the one part, and the former Yugoslav Republic of Macedonia, of the other part, to take account of the accession of the Republic of Croatia to the European Union, OJ L 279, 23.10.2015, p. 3; Commission Decision (2016/C 52/03) of 8 February 2016 on the conclusion, on behalf of the European Atomic Energy Community, of the Protocol to the Stabilisation and Association Agreement between the European Communities and their Member States, on the one part, and the former Yugoslav Republic of Macedonia, of the other part, to take account of the accession of the Republic of Croatia to the European Union, OJ C 52, 11.2.2016, pp. 3–4.

1059. Council and Commission Decision 2013/490/EU,Euratom of 22 July 2013 on the conclusion of the Stabilisation and Association Agreement between the European Communities and their Member States, of the one part, and the Republic of Serbia, of the other part, OJ L 278,

18.10.2013, pp. 14–15; Council Decision 2014/518/Euratom of 14 April 2014 approving the conclusion, by the European Commission, on behalf of the European Atomic Energy Community, of the Protocol to the Stabilisation and Association Agreement between the European Communities and their Member States, of the one part, OJ L 233, 6.8.2014, p. 20; Commission Decision (2016/C 52/06) of 8 February 2016 on the conclusion, on behalf of the European Atomic Energy Community, of the Protocol to the Stabilisation and Association Agreement between the European Communities and their Member States, on the one part, and the Republic of Serbia, of the other part, OJ C 52, 11.2.2016, pp. 9–10.

1060. Council and Commission Decision 2000/684/EC,ECSC,Euratom of 12 October 2000 on the conclusion of the Protocol to the Partnership and Cooperation Agreement establishing a partnership between the European Communities and their Member States, of the one part, and the Republic of Moldova, of the other part, OJ L 283, 9.11.2000, p. 36; Council and Commission Decision 2006/536/EC,Euratom of 21 February 2005 on the conclusion of the Protocol to the Partnership and Cooperation Agreement establishing a partnership between the European Communities and their Member States, of the one part, and the Republic of Moldova, of the other part, OJ L 224, 16.8.2006, p. 14; Council and Commission Decision 2007/681/EC,Euratom of 9 October 2007 concerning the conclusion of the Protocol to the Partnership and Cooperation Agreement (PCA) between the European Communities and their Member States, of the one part, and the Republic of Moldova, of the other part, OJ L 281, 25.10.2007, pp. 23–24; Council Decision 2014/493/Euratom of 16 June 2014 approving the conclusion, by the European Commission, on behalf of the European Atomic Energy Community, of the Association Agreement between the European Union and the European Atomic Energy Community and their Member States, of the one part, and the Republic of Moldova, of the other part, OJ L 260, 30.8.2014, pp. 739–740.

1061. Council and Commission Decision 2006/455/EC,Euratom of 21 February 2005 on the conclusion of the Protocol to the Partnership and Cooperation Agreement establishing a partnership between the European Communities and their Member States, of the one part, and Georgia, of the other part, to take account of the accession of the Czech Republic, the Republic of Estonia, the Republic of Cyprus, the Republic of Latvia, the Republic of Lithuania, the Republic of Hungary, the Republic of Malta, the Republic of Poland, the Republic of Slovenia and the Slovak Republic to the European Union, OJ L 185, 6.7.2006, p. 14; Council and Commission Decision 2008/430/EC,Euratom of 26 May 2008 on the conclusion of the Protocol to the Partnership and Cooperation Agreement between the European Communities and their Member States, of the one part, and Georgia, of the other part, to take account of the accession of the Republic of Bulgaria and Romania to the European Union, OJ L 151, 11.6.2008, p. 35; Council Decision 2014/495/Euratom of 16 June 2014 approving the conclusion, by the European Commission, on behalf of the European Atomic Energy Community, of the Association Agreement between the European Union and the European Atomic Energy Community and their Member States, of the one part, and Georgia, of the other part, OJ L 261, 30.8.2014, pp. 744–745.

1062. Council and Commission Decision 2010/224/EU,Euratom of 29 March 2010 on the conclusion of the Stabilisation and Association Agreement between the European Communities and their Member States, of the one part, and the Republic of Montenegro, of the other part, OJ L 108, 29.4.2010, pp. 1–2; Council Decision 2014/315/Euratom of 22 October 2013 approving the conclusion, by the European Commission, on behalf of the European Atomic Energy Community, of the Protocol to the Stabilisation and Association Agreement between the European Communities and their Member States, of the one part, and the Republic of Montenegro, of the other part, OJ L 165, 4.6.2014, pp. 1–2; Commission Decision (2016/C 52/04) of 8 February 2016 on the conclusion, on behalf of the European Atomic Energy Community, of the Protocol to the Stabilisation and Association Agreement between the European Communities and their Member States, on the one part, and the Republic of Montenegro of the other part, to take account of the accession of the Republic of Croatia to the European Union, OJ C 52, 11.2.2016, pp. 5–6.

1063. Council and Commission Decision 2009/331/EC,Euratom of 26 February 2009 on the conclusion of the Protocol to the Stabilisation and Association Agreement between the European Communities and their Member States, of the one part, and the Republic of Albania, of the other part, OJ L 107, 28.4.2009, p. 164; Council and Commission Decision

Some of these bilateral agreements have focused on cooperation in specific fields under the Euratom Treaty. The Euratom Community has concluded cooperation agreements with Kazakhstan in relation to nuclear safety[1067] and controlled nuclear fusion,[1068] which have been supplemented by the broader Agreement for cooperation in the peaceful uses of nuclear energy[1069] and the Partnership and Cooperation Agreement.[1070] The Agreement for cooperation with South Korea focuses on fusion energy

2009/332/EC,Euratom of 26 February 2009 concerning the conclusion of the Stabilisation and Association Agreement between the European Communities and their Member States, of the one part, and the Republic of Albania, of the other part, OJ L 107, 28.4.2009, p. 165; Council Decision 2014/317/Euratom of 15 November 2013 approving the conclusion, by the European Commission, on behalf of the European Atomic Energy Community, of the Protocol to the Stabilisation and Association Agreement between the European Communities and their Member States, of the one part, and the Republic of Albania, of the other part, OJ L 165, 4.6.2014, p. 5; Commission Decision (2016/C 52/05) of 8 February 2016 on the conclusion, on behalf of the European Atomic Energy Community, of the Protocol to the Stabilisation and Association Agreement between the European Communities and their Member States, on the one part, and the Republic of Albania, of the other part, OJ C 52, 11.2.2016, pp. 7–8.

1064. Council Decision 2003/744/Euratom of 22 September 2003 approving the conclusion by the Commission of an Agreement for cooperation in the peaceful uses of nuclear energy between the European Atomic Energy Community (Euratom) and the Government of the Republic of Uzbekistan, OJ L 269, 21.10.2003, p. 8; Council and Commission Decision 2005/459/EC,Euratom of 3 October 2005 on the conclusion of the Protocol to the Partnership and Cooperation Agreement establishing a partnership between the European Communities and their Member States, of the one part, and the Republic of Uzbekistan, of the other part, OJ L 185, 6.7.2006, p. 27; Council and Commission Decision 2009/50/EC,Euratom of 18 December 2008 on the conclusion of the Protocol to the Partnership and Cooperation Agreement between the European Communities and their Member States, of the one part, and the Republic of Uzbekistan, of the other part, OJ L 21, 24.1.2009, pp. 41–42.

1065. Commission Decision 2013/408/Euratom of 31 July 2012 on the conclusion of the Agreement for Cooperation in the Peaceful Uses of Nuclear Energy between the European Atomic Energy Community and the Government of the Republic of South Africa, OJ L 204, 31.7.2013, p. 2.

1066. Commission Decision 2012/55/Euratom of 2 March 2011 on the conclusion of the Agreement for cooperation in the peaceful uses of nuclear energy between the European Atomic Energy Community and the Government of Australia, OJ L 29, 1.2.2012, p. 3.

1067. Commission Decision 2004/282/Euratom of 29 March 1999 concerning the conclusion of a cooperation Agreement between the European Atomic Energy Community and the Republic of Kazakhstan in the field of nuclear safety, OJ L 89, 26.3.2004, p. 36.

1068. Commission Decision 2005/419/Euratom of 27 November 2002 on the conclusion of a Cooperation Agreement between the European Atomic Energy Community and the Government of the Republic of Kazakhstan in the field of controlled nuclear fusion, OJ L 143, 7.6.2005, p. 27.

1069. Commission Decision 2009/25/Euratom of 4 December 2006 on the conclusion of the Agreement for co-operation in the peaceful uses of nuclear energy between the European Atomic Energy Community and the Government of the Republic of Kazakhstan, OJ L 10, 15.1.2009, p. 15.

1070. Council and Commission Decision 2006/710/EC,Euratom of 25 September 2006 on the conclusion of the Protocol to the Partnership and Cooperation Agreement establishing a partnership between the European Communities and their Member States, of the one part, and the Republic of Kazakhstan, of the other part, OJ L 303, 1.11.2006, p. 7; Council and Commission Decision 2009/81/EC,Euratom of 18 December 2008 on the conclusion of the Protocol to the Partnership and Cooperation Agreement between the European Communities and their Member States, of the one part, and the Republic of Kazakhstan, of the other part, OJ L 26, 30.1.2009, p. 4.

research,[1071] but there is also a more general Agreement between the Euratom Community and the Korean Peninsula Energy Development Organisation (KEDO).[1072] The Cooperation Agreement between the Euratom Community and the Government of Japan concerns peaceful uses of nuclear energy in general,[1073] but the Euratom Community has also concluded an Agreement for the Joint Implementation of the Broader Approach Activities in the Field of Fusion Energy Research.[1074] Fusion energy research is also the focus of the Euratom Community's cooperation agreements with the US,[1075] Brazil[1076] and India.[1077] In addition to the Protocol to the Partnership and Cooperation Agreement between the EU and Russia,[1078] the Euratom Community has concluded two cooperation agreements with Russia in relation, respectively, to nuclear

1071. Council Decision 2011/334/Euratom of 21 November 2006 approving the conclusion, by the Commission, of the Agreement for cooperation between the European Atomic Energy Community represented by the Commission of the European Communities and the Government of the Republic of Korea in the field of fusion energy research, OJ L 154, 11.6.2011, p. 1.
1072. Commission Decision 2013/363/Euratom of 17 May 2013 on the conclusion of the Agreement between the European Atomic Energy Community (Euratom) and the Korean Peninsula Energy Development Organisation (KEDO), OJ L 188, 9.7.2013, p. 1.
1073. Commission Decision 2007/58/Euratom of 28 August 2006 concerning the conclusion of an Agreement between the Government of Japan and the European Atomic Energy Community for co-operation in the peaceful uses of nuclear energy, OJ L 32, 6.2.2007, p. 64.
1074. Council Decision 2007/614/Euratom of 30 January 2007 concerning the conclusion, by the Commission, of the Agreement between the European Atomic Energy Community and the Government of Japan for the Joint Implementation of the Broader Approach Activities in the Field of Fusion Energy Research, OJ L 246, 21.9.2007, pp. 32–33.
1075. Council Decision 2001/411/Euratom of 8 March 2001 approving the conclusion, by the Commission, of the Agreement for cooperation between the European Atomic Energy Community represented by the Commission and the Department of Energy of the United States of America in the field of fusion energy research and development, OJ L 148, 1.6.2001, p. 78; Commission Decision, 2001/412/Euratom, of 21 March 2001 concerning the conclusion of the Agreement for cooperation between the European Atomic Energy Community represented by the Commission and the Department of Energy of the United States of America in the field of fusion energy research and development, OJ L 148, 1.6.2001, p. 79.
1076. Council Decision 2010/488/Euratom of 16 November 2009 approving the conclusion, by the Commission, of the Agreement for cooperation between the European Atomic Energy Community and the Government of the Federative Republic of Brazil in the field of fusion energy research, OJ L 242, 15.9.2010, p. 33.
1077. Council Decision 2010/487/Euratom of 9 October 2009 on the conclusion, by the Commission, of the Agreement for cooperation between the European Atomic Energy Community and the Government of the Republic of India in the field of fusion energy research, OJ L 242, 15.9.2010, p. 25.
1078. Council and Commission Decision 2000/682/EC,ECSC,Euratom of 12 October 2000 on the conclusion of the Protocol to the Partnership and Cooperation Agreement establishing a partnership between the European Communities and their Member States, of the one part, and the Russian Federation, of the other part, OJ L 283, 9.11.2000, p. 18; Council and Commission Decision 2006/457/EC,Euratom of 21 February 2005 on the conclusion of the Protocol to the Partnership and Cooperation Agreement establishing a partnership between the European Communities and their Member States, of the one part, and the Russian Federation, of the other part, OJ L 185, 6.7.2006, p. 21; Council and Commission Decision 2007/541/EC,Euratom of 28 June 2007 on the conclusion of the Protocol to the Partnership and Cooperation Agreement establishing a partnership between the European Communities and their Member States, of the one part, and the Russian Federation, of the other part, OJ L 200, 1.8.2007, pp. 44–45.

safety and controlled nuclear fusion.[1079] It has also established the Framework Agreement and its Protocol on a Multilateral Nuclear Environmental Programme in the Russian Federation.[1080] Similar bilateral relations have been established between the Euratom Community and Ukraine: the Protocol to the Partnership and Cooperation Agreement establishing a partnership between the EU and Ukraine,[1081] and the conclusion of two cooperation agreements between the Euratom Community and Ukraine in respect of nuclear safety and controlled nuclear fusion,[1082] together with the Agreement for Co-operation in the Peaceful Uses of Nuclear Energy,[1083] and the Association Agreement.[1084] The EU and the Euratom Community has also concluded the Agreement on the Scientific and Technological Cooperation with Switzerland,[1085]

1079. Council Decision 2001/761/Euratom of 27 September 2001 authorising the conclusion by the Commission of two Cooperation Agreements between the European Autonomic Energy Community and the Government of the Russian Federation in the fields of nuclear safety and controlled nuclear fusion, OJ L 287, 31.10.2001, pp. 21–22; and Commission Decision 2001/762/Euratom of 28 September 2001 on the conclusion of two cooperation agreements between the European Atomic Energy Community and the Russian Federation in the field of nuclear safety and in the field of controlled nuclear fusion, OJ L 287, 31.10.2001, p. 23.

1080. Council Decision 2003/462/EC,Euratom of 19 May 2003 on the signing on behalf of the European Community and provisional application of a Framework Agreement on a Multilateral Nuclear Environmental Programme in the Russian Federation and its Protocol on Claims, Legal Proceedings and Indemnification and approving the conclusion by the Commission on behalf of the European Atomic Energy Community of the above-mentioned Agreement and its Protocol, OJ L 155, 24.6.2003, pp. 35–36; Commission Decision 2006/890/Euratom of 4 December 2006 concerning the conclusion on behalf of the European Atomic Energy Community of a Framework Agreement on a Multilateral Nuclear Environmental Programme in the Russian Federation and of the Protocol on Claims, Legal Proceedings and Indemnification to the Framework Agreement on a Multilateral Nuclear Environmental Programme in the Russian Federation, OJ L 343, 8.12.2006, pp. 85–86.

1081. Council and Commission Decision 2000/683/EC,ECSC,Euratom of 12 October 2000 on the conclusion of the Protocol to the Partnership and Cooperation Agreement establishing a partnership between the European Communities and their Member States, of the one part, and Ukraine, of the other part, OJ L 283, 9.11.2000, p. 27; Council and Commission Decision 2006/538/EC,Euratom of 24 January 2006 on the conclusion of the Protocol to the Partnership and Cooperation Agreement between the European Communities and their Member States, of the one part, and Ukraine, of the other part (PCA), OJ L 224, 16.8.2006, p. 21; Council and Commission Decision 2007/644/EC,Euratom of 18 September 2007 concerning the conclusion of the Protocol to the Partnership and Cooperation Agreement (PCA) between the European Communities and their Member States, of the one part, and Ukraine, of the other part, OJ L 261, 6.10.2007, p. 25.

1082. Commission Decision 2002/924/Euratom of 23 July 1999 on the conclusion of two cooperation agreements between the European Atomic Energy Community and the Cabinet of Ministers of Ukraine in the field of nuclear safety and in the field of controlled nuclear fusion, OJ L 322, 27.11.2002, pp. 32–46.

1083. Commission Decision 2006/635/Euratom of 4 April 2006 on the conclusion, by way of signature, of an Agreement for Co-operation in the Peaceful Uses of Nuclear Energy between the European Atomic Energy Community (Euratom) and the Cabinet of Ministers of Ukraine, OJ L 261, 22.9.2006, p. 26.

1084. Council Decision 2014/670/Euratom of 23 June 2014 approving the conclusion, by the European Commission, on behalf of the European Atomic Energy Community, of the Association Agreement between the European Union and the European Atomic Energy Community and their Member States, of the one part, and Ukraine, of the other part, OJ L 278, 20.9.2014, pp. 8–9.

1085. Decision of the Council and of the Commission 2002/309/EC,Euratom as regards the Agreement on Scientific and Technological Cooperation, of 4 April 2002 on the conclusion of

and this has been developed into a multilateral agreement continuing the International Science and Technology Centre under the Euratom Treaty.[1086] Bilateral agreements between the Euratom Community and Switzerland have also been concluded in respect of Switzerland's membership of the European Joint Undertaking for ITER and the Development of Fusion Energy, and the field of nuclear research.[1087] It should be noted here that the Euratom Community has also concluded two trilateral agreements. The parties to the first of these are the Euratom Community, the IAEA and the UK; while the parties to the second are the Euratom Community, the IAEA and France. Both agreements concern safeguards in connection with the Treaty for the Prohibition of Nuclear Weapons in Latin America and the Caribbean.[1088]

---

seven Agreements with the Swiss Confederation, OJ L 114, 30.4.2002, pp. 1–5; Council and Commission Decision 2004/112/EC,Euratom of 22 December 2003 on the signature on behalf of the European Community and of the European Atomic Energy Community of the Agreement on Scientific and Technological Cooperation between the European Community and the European Atomic Energy Community, of the one part, and the Swiss Confederation, of the other part, OJ L 32, 5.2.2004, p. 22; Decision of the Council and of the Commission 2006/365/EC,Euratom of 15 May 2006 on the conclusion on behalf of the European Community and of the European Atomic Energy Community of the Agreement on Scientific and Technological Cooperation between the European Community and the European Atomic Energy Community, of the one part, and the Swiss Confederation, of the other part, OJ L 135, 23.5.2006, p. 13; Decision of the Council and of the Commission 2007/502/EC,Euratom of 25 June 2007 on the signing, on behalf of the European Community and the European Atomic Energy Community, and provisional application of the Agreement on Scientific and Technological Cooperation between the European Community and the European Atomic Energy Community, of the one part, and the Swiss Confederation, of the other part, OJ L 189, 20.7.2007, pp. 24–25.

1086. Council Decision (Euratom) 2015/1990 of 26 October 2015 approving the conclusion, by the European Commission, on behalf of the European Atomic Energy Community, of the Agreement continuing the International Science and Technology Centre, OJ L 290, 6.11.2015, p. 8; Commission Decision (Euratom) 2017/251 of 2 June 2016 on the conclusion on behalf of the European Atomic Energy Community, of the Agreement continuing the International Science and Technology Centre between the European Union and Euratom acting as one Party and Georgia, Japan, the Kingdom of Norway, the Kyrgyz Republic, the Republic of Armenia, the Republic of Kazakhstan, the Republic of Korea, the Republic of Tajikistan and the United States of America, OJ L 37, 14.2.2017, pp. 17–18.

1087. Commission Decision 2008/72/Euratom of 22 November 2007 on the conclusion of Agreements in the form of Exchange of Letters between the European Atomic Energy Community (Euratom) and the Swiss Confederation (Switzerland) on the application of the ITER Agreement, the Agreement on Privileges and Immunities for ITER and the Broader Approach Agreement to the territory of Switzerland and on Switzerland's membership in the European Joint Undertaking for ITER and the Development of Fusion Energy, OJ L 20, 24.1.2008, pp. 11–12; Council Decision 2014/954/Euratom of 4 December 2014 approving the conclusion by the European Commission, on behalf of the European Atomic Energy Community, of the Agreement for scientific and technological cooperation between the European Union and European Atomic Energy Community and the Swiss Confederation associating the Swiss Confederation to Horizon 2020 – the Framework Programme for Research and Innovation and the Research and Training Programme of the European Atomic Energy Community complementing Horizon 2020, and regulating the Swiss Confederation's participation in the ITER activities carried out by Fusion for Energy, OJ L 370, 30.12.2014, pp. 19–20.

1088. Council Decision (Euratom) 2015/2227 of 10 November 2015 approving the conclusion, by the European Commission, of the amendments to Protocols 1 and 2 to the Agreement between the United Kingdom, the European Atomic Energy Community and the International Atomic Energy Agency for the Application of Safeguards in Connection with the Treaty for the Prohibition of Nuclear Weapons in Latin America and the Caribbean, OJ L 317, 3.12.2015, pp.

Consequently, over the last two decades, the Euratom Community via the Council and/or the Commission has exercised its competences to enter into obligations, within the limits of its powers and jurisdiction, under Article 101 of the Euratom Treaty by concluding agreements with twenty-six third States, both in the overarching field of nuclear energy cooperation and in specific fields of, *inter alia*, nuclear safety and fusion energy research.

Second, the Euratom Community has exercised its competences under Article 101 of the Euratom Treaty by participating in multilateral projects under the purview of the Euratom Treaty. The Euratom Community is part of the ITER International Fusion Energy Organization for the Joint Implementation of the ITER Project[1089] and participates in the International Collaboration on Research and Development of Generation IV nuclear energy systems.[1090]

Third, the Euratom Community has exercised its external competences under Article 101 of the Euratom Treaty through accession to international Conventions under the auspices of the IAEA in relation to nuclear safety and nuclear security. It has been established that the scope and content of the Euratom Community's competences under Chapter 10 of the Euratom Treaty give the Euratom Community competence to enter into obligations in respect of external relations only within the limits of its internal powers and jurisdiction. When acceding to international Treaties, the Euratom Community is required to submit a Declaration of Competences, which identifies the Euratom Community's competences by referring to specific articles in the relevant international Treaty that are applicable to the Euratom Community.[1091]

9–10; and Council Decision (Euratom) 2015/2228 of 10 November 2015 approving the conclusion, by the European Commission, of the amendments to Protocols 1 and 2 to the Agreement between the French Republic, the European Atomic Energy Community and the International Atomic Energy Agency for the Application of Safeguards in Connection with the Treaty for the Prohibition of Nuclear Weapons in Latin America and the Caribbean, OJ L 317, 3.12.2015, pp. 11–12.

1089. Commission Decision 2006/943/Euratom of 17 November 2006 on Provisional Application of the Agreement on the Establishment of the ITER International Fusion Energy Organization for the Joint Implementation of the ITER Project and of the Agreement on Privileges and Immunities of the ITER International Fusion Energy Organization for the Joint Implementation of the ITER Project, OJ L 358, 16.12.2006, pp. 60–61. The ITER International Fusion Energy Organisation has headquarters in St Paul-lès-Durance (Bouches-du-Rhône) (France) and has full responsibility for constructing, operating, exploiting and deactivating the ITER facilities. As established in Chapter 1 Section 02 and Chapter 4 Section .02 of this study, the Euratom Community has exercised its competences in the field of Joint Undertakings under Chapter 4 of the Euratom Treaty by establishing the European Joint Undertaking for ITER – Fusion for Energy, under Council Decision 2007/198/Euratom, OJ L 90, 30.3.2007, pp. 58–72.

1090. Council Decision (Euratom) 2016/2116 of 12 February 2016 approving the conclusion by the European Commission, on behalf of the European Atomic Energy Community, of the Agreement extending the Framework Agreement for International Collaboration on Research and Development of Generation IV nuclear energy systems, OJ L 329, 3.12.2016, pp. 1–2.

1091. Article 30(4)(iii) of the Convention on Nuclear Safety; Article 39(4)(iii) of the Joint Convention on the Safety of Spent Fuel Management and on the Safety of Radioactive Waste Management; Article 12(5)(c) of the Convention on Early Notification of a Nuclear Accident; Article 14(5)(c) of the Convention on Assistance in the case of a Nuclear Accident or Radiological Emergency; Article 18(4) of the Convention on the Physical Protection of Nuclear Material.

Under Commission Decision 1999/819/Euratom the Euratom Community acceded to the Convention on Nuclear Safety.[1092] The Declaration made by the Euratom Community at the time of its accession was based on a Council Decision, which was partially annulled by the CJEU.[1093] After the Court's delimitation of the Euratom Community's competences in respect of nuclear safety under Chapter 3 of the Euratom Treaty, the Commission adopted Decision 2004/491/Euratom amending Commission Decision 1999/819/Euratom of 16 November 1999 concerning the accession to the 1994 Convention on Nuclear Safety.[1094] The Euratom Community has declared that Articles 1 to 5, 7 and 14 to 35 of the Nuclear Safety Convention apply to the Euratom Community and that the Euratom Community possesses competences, shared with its Member States, in the fields covered by Articles 7 and 14 to 19 of the Nuclear Safety Convention, as provided for in Article 2(b) and the relevant articles of Chapter 3 of the Euratom Treaty.[1095]

The Euratom Community has also acceded to the Joint Convention on the Safety of Spent Fuel Management and on the Safety of Radioactive Waste Management.[1096] The Euratom Community has declared that Articles 1 to 16, 18, 19, 21 and 24 to 44 of the Joint Convention apply to it, and it possesses competences, shared with the Member States, in the fields covered by Articles 4, 6 to 11, 13 to 16, 19 and 24 to 28 of the Joint Convention as provided for in Article 2(b) and the relevant articles of Chapter 3 (on Health and Safety) of the Euratom Treaty.[1097]

On acceding to the Convention on Early Notification of a Nuclear Accident,[1098] and to the Convention on Assistance in the case of a Nuclear Accident or Radiological Emergency,[1099] the Euratom Community's declaration of competences was more general: it stated that the Euratom Community possessed competences, shared with its

1092. Commission Decision 1999/819/Euratom of 16 November 1999 concerning the accession to the 1994 Convention on Nuclear Safety by the European Atomic Energy Community (Euratom), OJ L 318, 11.12.1999, p. 20.
1093. The Court concluded that the Euratom Community's declaration failed to state that the Euratom Community has competences in the fields covered by Articles 7 and 14, Article 16(1) and (3) and Articles 17 to 19 of the Nuclear Safety Convention, see judgment of 10 December 2002, *Commission v Council*, C-29/99, ECLI:EU:C:2002:734. The analysis of the CJEU's delimitation of competences in the field of nuclear safety is provided in Chapter 3 (Health and Safety) of this study.
1094. Commission Decision 2004/491/Euratom of 29 April 2004 amending Commission Decision 1999/819/Euratom of 16 November 1999 concerning the accession to the 1994 Convention on Nuclear Safety by the European Atomic Energy Community (Euratom) with regard to the Declaration attached thereto, OJ L 172, 6.5.2004, pp. 7–8.
1095. Article 1 of Commission Decision 2004/491/Euratom.
1096. Council Decision 2005/84/Euratom of 24 January 2005 approving the accession of the European Atomic Energy Community to the Joint Convention on the Safety of Spent Fuel Management and on the Safety of Radioactive Waste Management, OJ L 30, 3.2.2005, pp. 10–11.
1097. Annex to Council Decision 2005/84/Euratom.
1098. Commission Decision 2005/844/Euratom of 25 November 2005 concerning the accession of the European Atomic Energy Community to the Convention on Early Notification of a Nuclear Accident, OJ L 314, 30.11.2005, p. 21.
1099. Commission Decision 2005/845/Euratom of 25 November 2005 concerning the accession of the European Atomic Energy Community to the Convention on Assistance in the case of a Nuclear Accident or Radiological Emergency, OJ L 314, 30.11.2005, p. 27.

Member States, in respect of assistance in the event of a radiological emergency and in respect of the notification of radiological emergencies, to the extent provided by Article 2(b) and the relevant provisions of Chapter 3 of the Euratom Treaty.[1100] Although no references to specific articles were made in the Declarations of Competences regarding these two conventions, it is a clear confirmation that the Euratom Community has competences, by dint of various provisions of these conventions, in relation to radiological emergencies.

The Euratom Community is also party to the amended Convention on the Physical Protection of Nuclear Material and Nuclear Facilities (the CPPNM).[1101] Unlike other IAEA conventions mentioned above, the CPPNM required the Euratom Community to communicate a declaration indicating which articles of this Convention do not apply to it.[1102] The Euratom Community declared that Articles 8 to 13 and 14(2) and (3) of the CPPNM do not apply to the Community. Furthermore, pursuant to Article 17(3) of that Convention, the Euratom Community has also declared that since only States may be parties in cases before the International Court of Justice, the Euratom Community is bound only by the arbitration procedure laid down in Article 17(2) of this Convention.[1103]

Analysis above shows that the Euratom Community's exercise of its competences through accession to international conventions and submission of declaration of competences require the Community to evaluate the extent to which its internal and external competences accord.

Concluding the analysis of exercise of the Euratom Community's competences under Article 101 of the Euratom Treaty, it can be stated that the Euratom Community's competences in this field have been extensively exercised, if measured on a quantitative basis. Regarding the content, the Euratom Community has exercised its competences under Article 101 of the Euratom Treaty in three different ways: by concluding bilateral agreements with third States, by participating in multilateral projects under the purview of the Euratom Treaty, and through accession to international conventions under the auspices of the IAEA in respect of nuclear safety and nuclear security, which allows the Community to evaluate its internal competences in the external domain. Article 101 of the Euratom Treaty establishes the Euratom Community's competence to enter into obligations by concluding agreements or contracts with a third state, an international organisation or a national of a third state. Consequently, it can be

1100. Declaration referred to in Article 12(5)(c) of the Convention on Early Notification of a Nuclear Accident in Commission Decision 2005/844/Euratom and Declaration referred to in Article 14(5)(c) of the Convention on Assistance in the case of a Nuclear Accident or Radiological Emergency in Commission Decision 2005/845/Euratom.

1101. Council Decision 2007/513/Euratom of 10 July 2007 approving the accession of the European Atomic Energy Community to the amended Convention on the Physical Protection of Nuclear Material and Nuclear Facilities, OJ L 190, 21.7.2007, pp. 12–14; and Commission Decision 2008/99/EC, Euratom of 19 December 2007 concerning the accession of the European Atomic Energy Community to the Convention on the Physical Protection of Nuclear Material and Nuclear Facilities, OJ L 34, 8.2.2008, pp. 3–18.

1102. Article 18(4)(c) of the CPPNM.

1103. Declaration by the European Atomic Energy Community according to Articles 18(4) and 17(3) of the CPPNM in Council Decision 2007/513/Euratom.

concluded that the Euratom Community has exercised its competences under Article 101 of the Euratom Treaty in accordance with the wording of the primary legal act.

It has been established that the scope and content of the Euratom Community's competences under Article 103 of the Euratom Treaty include the competence for the Euratom Community via the Commission to approve all draft agreements or contracts that Member States wish to sign with third States, international organisations or nationals of a third state. Commission Recommendation (Euratom) 2016/538 on the application of Article 103 of the Euratom Treaty[1104] is the only secondary legal act that exercises the Euratom Community's competences under Article 103 of the Euratom Treaty.

The legal basis of Commission Recommendation (Euratom) 2016/538 should be analysed. It comprises Articles 103 and 106a (through which Article 292 TFEU applies to the Euratom Treaty). The competences under Article 103 of the Euratom Treaty do not include the Commission's power to issue recommendations. Article 106a of the Euratom Treaty refers to Article 292 TFEU, which explicitly state that the Commission shall adopt recommendations in specific cases provided for in the Treaties. As Article 103 of the Euratom Treaty does not provide the Commission with a competence in this regard, the legal basis of Commission Recommendation (Euratom) 2016/538 is open to question.

In the context of Article 103 of the Euratom Treaty, Commission Recommendation (Euratom) 2016/538 lays down an interpretation of the division of competences between the Euratom Community and the Member States, by stating that in accordance with the Euratom Treaty, Member States retain, under the conditions provided for in the Euratom Treaty, their Treaty-making capacity as actors on the international scene and, consequently, have the right to conclude, at any time, bilateral agreements with third countries that concern matters within the purview of the Euratom Treaty. The Commission identified the central role of Article 103 of the Euratom Treaty in reconciling the need to ensure the unity and primacy of Euratom Community law with Member States' freedom of action in conducting their external relations in the nuclear field.[1105] The Commission also pointed out that the compatibility assessment under Article 103 of the Euratom Treaty applies not only to the Euratom Treaty, but also to secondary legislation adopted on its basis. This assessment does not, however, extend to the compatibility of the draft agreement or contract with the provisions of the TFEU.[1106]

In addition, Commission Recommendation (Euratom) 2016/538 exercises the Euratom Community's competences under Article 103 of the Euratom Treaty by clarifying the concept of a draft agreement or contract within the meaning of Article 103

1104. Commission Recommendation (Euratom) 2016/538 of 4 April 2016 on the application of Article 103 of the Euratom Treaty, OJ L 89, 6.4.2016, pp. 20–24.
1105. Recitals 4 and 5 of Commission Recommendation (Euratom) 2016/538.
1106. Recital 7 of Commission Recommendation (Euratom) 2016/538. Under Article 3(2) TFEU the EU has an exclusive competence to conclude international agreements, when its conclusion is provided for in a legislative act of the Union or is necessary to enable the Union to exercise its internal competence. Consequently, an assessment of the kind required under Article 103 of the Euratom Treaty is not required.

of the Euratom Treaty, i.e., it is agreement negotiated by a Member State on matters within the purview of the Euratom Treaty and includes amending existing agreement or contract between one or more Member States and a third state, an international organisation or a national of a third state concerning matters within the purview of the Euratom Treaty. The Recommendation also states that agreements or contracts concerning the supply or the processing, conversion or shaping of ores, source materials or special fissile materials which are to be notified to the ESA should not be notified to the Commission under Article 103 of the Euratom Treaty.[1107] This clarifies the distinction between the Euratom Community's competences under Chapters 6 (nuclear supply) and 10 (external relations) of the Euratom Treaty in respect of agreements and contracts.

Finally, the Recommendation also provides certain guidance to the Member States. First, how Member States should act towards the Commission with regard to their intended agreement or contract prior the notification stage: the Commission encourages Member States to submit their notifications pursuant to Article 103 of the Euratom Treaty after an agreement has been reached between the parties on the main elements of the draft agreement or contract, but before it is concluded.[1108] Second, it provides guidance on the content of the notification under Article 103 of the Euratom Treaty. Third, it defines the decisive aspects of the agreement or contract that determine its compliance with the Euratom Treaty: the draft agreements or contracts cannot contain clauses that conflict with provisions in Chapter 3 of the Euratom Treaty on Health and Safety, especially the basic principles of spent nuclear fuel and radioactive waste management, which are further defined in Directive 2011/70/Euratom, or with the Euratom Community's competences under the following chapters of the Euratom Treaty: Chapter 6 (on Euratom nuclear supply policy and diversification of supplies); Chapter 7 (on safeguards requirements); Chapter 8 (on ownership of special fissile materials); Chapter 9 and Annex IV (on the nuclear common market); such agreements or contracts must also be compliant with any other secondary legislation through which the Euratom Community's competences are exercised. Fourth, it gives guidance that the Commission's comments to the Member State concerned will be structured with the reference to specific chapter of the Euratom Treaty. Fifth, the Recommendation also clarifies that in respect of the follow-up on the Commission's assessment, the fact that the Commission does not find any elements that impede the application of the Euratom Treaty under notification procedure in Article 103 of the Euratom Treaty does not exclude the possibility that the implementation of that agreement or contract may give rise to an infringement of Euratom law. Sixth and final, the Recommendation also indicates that the Commission should be furnished, at its request, with information relating to the implementation or interpretation of agreements or contracts in force.[1109] Article 103 of the Euratom Treaty makes

1107. Paragraph 1 of Commission Recommendation (Euratom) 2016/538.
1108. Part I, paragraphs 2–4 of Commission Recommendation (Euratom) 2016/538. A Member State may also inform the Commission at an early stage of its intention to enter into negotiations with a third State, an international organisation or a national of a third State and then keep the Commission updated on an ongoing basis on the progress of negotiations.
1109. Parts II to IV of Commission Recommendation (Euratom) 2016/538.

explicit reference only to draft agreements or contracts before their conclusion. Consequently, this recommendation on the provision of information to the Commission concerning the implementation or interpretation of agreements or contracts that are in force could be regarded as amounting to a broader exercise of the Euratom Community's competences under Article 103 of the Euratom Treaty than the wording of the Euratom Treaty would tend to indicate.[1110]

By way of summary in respect of the exercise of the Euratom Community's competences under Article 103 of the Euratom Treaty, it can be concluded that, despite its questionable legal basis, Commission Recommendation (Euratom) 2016/538 provides guidance on the division of competences between the Euratom Community and the Member States. Furthermore, it emphasises the importance of Article 103 of the Euratom Treaty, which provides for a compatibility assessment, in reconciling the need to ensure the unity and primacy of Euratom Community law with Member States' freedom to conduct their external relations in the nuclear field. Commission Recommendation (Euratom) 2016/538 also exercises the competence of the Euratom Community in relation to compatibility assessments by specifying, *inter alia*, the point during the negotiations process at which the notification should be submitted to the Commission; the key aspects of the Euratom Treaty that must be taken into account in order for the draft agreements or contracts to be compatible with the Treaty; and finally that the Commission also recommends Member States to provide information relating to the implementation or interpretation of agreements or contracts in force. The Euratom Community's competences under Article 103 of the Euratom Treaty are, therefore, exercised in accordance with the wording of the Treaty. One possible exception to this is that the recommendation to provide information on agreements or contracts already in force could be regarded as the Euratom Community exercising its competences under Article 103 of the Euratom Treaty in a manner that goes beyond the Treaty wording.

By way of conclusion in respect of the analysis of the exercise of the Euratom Community's external relations competences under Chapter 10 of the Euratom Treaty, it can be stated that only the competences laid down in Articles 101 and 103 have been exercised through secondary legislation. The competences provided for in Article 101 of the Euratom Treaty are extensively exercised by concluding bilateral agreements with third States, by participating in multilateral projects under the purview of the Euratom Treaty, and through accession to international conventions under the auspices of the IAEA in respect of nuclear safety and security. The Euratom Community has exercised its competences under Article 101 of the Euratom Treaty in accordance with the Treaty wording. However, the legal basis of the secondary legal act exercising the Euratom Community's competences laid down in Article 103 of the Euratom Treaty is open to question.

1110. It should be borne in mind, however, that the secondary legal act exercising the Euratom Community's competences under Article 103 of the Euratom Treaty – Commission Recommendation (Euratom) 2016/538 – is a recommendation. Under Article 106a of the Euratom Treaty and Article 288 TFEU, recommendations do not create legally binding obligations.

10.03 THE CJEU'S INTERPRETATION OF THE COMPETENCES

This section assesses the CJEU's case-law in relation to the Euratom Community's competences concerning external relations under Chapter 10 of the Euratom Treaty and considers how the CJEU has defined and elaborated on these competences.

Quantitative analysis of the CJEU's case-law in respect of external relations under the Euratom Treaty shows that the Court has addressed the Euratom Community's competences under Chapter 10 of the Euratom Treaty in three cases.[1111]

The CJEU has identified and confirmed the importance of Articles 101 and 103 of the Euratom Treaty by stating that the former defines the powers and jurisdiction of the Euratom Community in respect of external relations, while the latter provides for a Euratom Community supervisory procedure allowing for preliminary examination of the compatibility of such agreements with the Euratom Treaty.[1112]

The Court has also addressed the division of horizontal competences in respect of external relations under Chapter 10 of the Euratom Treaty. The Court has interpreted the provisions of Article 101 of the Euratom Treaty and ruled that the legal effect of the Council's approval of accession to an international convention, in accordance with the second paragraph of Article 101 of the Euratom Treaty, is to authorise the Commission to join that convention within the framework established by the Council decision.[1113] The CJEU also ruled that the Council decision approving accession to an international convention must enable the Commission to comply with international law, which implies that the Council is obliged under the Euratom Community law to attach a complete declaration of competences to its decision approving accession to the international convention.[1114]

The Court has compared the Commission's competences to conclude agreements under Article 101 of the Euratom Treaty with the Commission's competence to conclude agreements under EU law.[1115] It has ruled that the Article 101 procedure differs greatly from the regulation of external competences under EU law, and expressed the view that, since the EEC and the Euratom Treaties were negotiated simultaneously and signed on the same day, it follows that if those negotiating the two

1111. Judgment of 10 December 2002, *Commission v Council*, C-29/99, ECLI:EU:C:2002:734; Ruling of 14 November 1978, Ruling of the Court delivered pursuant to the third paragraph of Article 103 of the Euratom Treaty – Draft Convention of the International Atomic Energy Agency on the Physical Protection of Nuclear Materials, Facilities and Transports, Ruling 1/78, ECLI: EU:C:1978:202; Judgment of 9 August 1994, *France v Commission*, C-327/91, ECLI: EU:C:1994:305.

1112. Ruling of 14 November 1978, Ruling of the Court delivered pursuant to the third paragraph of Article 103 of the Euratom Treaty – Draft Convention of the International Atomic Energy Agency on the Physical Protection of Nuclear Materials, Facilities and Transports, Ruling 1/78, ECLI:EU:C:1978:202, paragraphs 2 and 3.

1113. Judgment of 10 December 2002, *Commission v Council*, C-29/99, ECLI:EU:C:2002:734, paragraph 67.

1114. Judgment of 30 March 1995, *Parliament v Council*, C-65/93, ECLI:EU:C:1995:91, paragraph 23; judgment of 10 December 2002, *Commission v Council*, C-29/99, ECLI:EU:C:2002:734, paragraphs 69 and 71.

1115. Judgment of 9 August 1994, *France v Commission*, C-327/91, ECLI:EU:C:1994:305, paragraph 37.

Treaties had intended to grant the Commission the same powers, they would have done so expressly.[1116] Consequently, the Court implied that the Euratom Community's external competences should not be compared with the external competences established under the EU law.

For some time, there was some ambiguity as to whether the provisions of Chapter 10 of the Euratom Treaty imply that all external nuclear relations of the Member States would be absorbed by the Euratom Community's competences or whether Member States would retain a certain degree of capacity to enter into third-party agreements.[1117] In terms of the balance between the Euratom Community's competences in respect of external relations and those of the Member States, the Court has finally established that to the extent to which jurisdiction and powers have been conferred on the Euratom Community under the Euratom Treaty, the Member States, whether acting individually or collectively, are no longer allowed to impose on the Euratom Community obligations to which conditions are attached as to the exercise of prerogatives of the Euratom Community. The Member States are not to intervene in the exercise of those prerogatives because in accordance with the division of powers laid down in Article 101 of the Treaty that right is conferred upon the common institutions alone.[1118] In other words, the Court ruled that once an external action – in this case, a draft of a convention – can create obligations that would fall within the scope of the Euratom Community's vertical competences, the competence to enter into such external relation belongs to the Euratom Community. The Court also confirmed that in circumstances where the draft of the convention includes fields that fall within the scope of the Euratom Community's competences as well as those that fall within the scope of Member State national competences, Article 102 of the Euratom Treaty provides a procedure under which such obligations may be entered into by the Euratom Community in association with the Member States. The Court clarified that, in such cases, agreements or contracts of this kind are to be concluded in accordance with the ordinary procedure laid down in the second paragraph of Article 101 of the Euratom Treaty. However, in compliance with the specific requirements contained in Article 102, these agreements or contracts are not to enter into force until the Commission has been notified by all the Member States concerned that those agreements or contracts have become applicable in accordance with the provisions of their respective national laws.[1119] The Court also stated that once this draft convention has entered into force, the Euratom Community

1116. Judgment of 9 August 1994, *France v Commission*, C-327/91, ECLI:EU:C:1994:305, paragraphs 38 and 39.

1117. See L. Scheinmann, 'Euratom: Nuclear Integration in Europe', (1967) 563 *International Conciliation*, p. 19; and D. D. Smith, 'The European Atomic Energy Community', (1970) 1 *California Western International Law Journal*, p. 36.

1118. Ruling of 14 November 1978, Ruling of the Court delivered pursuant to the third paragraph of Article 103 of the Euratom Treaty – Draft Convention of the International Atomic Energy Agency on the Physical Protection of Nuclear Materials, Facilities and Transports, Ruling 1/78, ECLI:EU:C:1978:202, paragraphs 32 and 33.

1119. Ruling of 14 November 1978, Ruling of the Court delivered pursuant to the third paragraph of Article 103 of the Euratom Treaty – Draft Convention of the International Atomic Energy Agency on the Physical Protection of Nuclear Materials, Facilities and Transports, Ruling 1/78, ECLI:EU:C:1978:202, paragraph 34.

must ensure that obligations are fulfilled in the context of its institutional system in accordance with the distribution of vertical competences between the Community and its Member States.[1120]

In conclusion, the CJEU has heard few cases concerning external relations under Chapter 10 of the Euratom Treaty, but has specified that the importance of Article 101 of the Euratom Treaty lies in its defining the Euratom Community powers and jurisdiction in respect of external relations, and that these competences should not be compared with external competences established under the EU law. Furthermore, the Court has confirmed the role of Article 102 in laying down the procedure for entering into external obligations with mixed competences (i.e., Euratom Community competences and Member State national competences), and has emphasised the importance of Article 103 in providing the Euratom Community with a supervisory procedure allowing for the preliminary examination of the compatibility of external agreements or contracts with the requirements of the Euratom Treaty. Most importantly, the CJEU has delimited the Euratom Community's competences by establishing that once a potential external relationship can create obligations that fall within the scope of the Euratom Community's competences, the competence to enter into such external relation belongs to the Euratom Community.

10.04 FEATURES OF THE COMPETENCES

This section assesses the following features with a view to ensuring a basis for a comparative analysis: the level of detail of the provisions of the Euratom Treaty; the exercise of the competences as compared with the bare wording of the Euratom Treaty; and the existence of case-law and the effect of the Court's interpretation of the relevant provisions of primary and secondary legislation to the competences of the Euratom Community.

The level of detail of the provisions of the Euratom Treaty that establish the Euratom Community's competences concerning external relations is appropriate to the objective of entering into external relations with other countries and international organisations that foster progress in the peaceful uses of nuclear energy.

The scope of the Euratom Community's competences in respect of external relations under Chapter 10 of the Euratom Treaty is defined through the Euratom Community's competences as laid down in the first nine chapters of the Euratom Treaty. The content of the Euratom Community's competences includes competence to enter into external relations with third States, international organisations or nationals of a third state; to approve draft agreements or contracts that Member States wish to conclude; and to renegotiate agreements concluded by Member States before the date of their accession to the Euratom Community.

1120. Ruling of 14 November 1978, Ruling of the Court delivered pursuant to the third paragraph of Article 103 of the Euratom Treaty – Draft Convention of the International Atomic Energy Agency on the Physical Protection of Nuclear Materials, Facilities and Transports, Ruling 1/78, ECLI:EU:C:1978:202, paragraph 36 and point 2 in the final conclusions of the ruling.

The Euratom Community has exercised its external relations competences under Chapter 10 by concluding bilateral agreements with third States, participating in multilateral projects under the purview of the Euratom Treaty, and acceding to international conventions. Its competences under Articles 101 of the Euratom Treaty are exercised in accordance with the wording of the Treaty, but the legal basis of the secondary legal act exercising the Euratom Community's competences laid down in Article 103 of the Euratom Treaty is open to question.

The CJEU has emphasised the importance of Articles 101 to 103 of the Euratom Treaty as defining the Euratom Community's powers and jurisdiction concerning external relations, specifying the procedure for entering into external obligations with mixed competences, and establishing a supervisory preliminary examination procedure for draft agreements or contracts. The CJEU has interpreted the Euratom Community's competences by ruling that where an external relationship creates obligations that fall under its competences, the Euratom Community has competence to enter into this external relationship. The Court also established that the Euratom Community's competences in respect of external relations are not comparable with external competences established under the EU law.

Conclusions of This Study

I CLASSIFICATION OF THE EURATOM COMMUNITY'S COMPETENCES UNDER THE EURATOM TREATY

The analysis of the Euratom Community's competences, based on the method of evaluation of specific Euratom Community competences established in Chapter II Section C of this study, has led to the identification of certain features in each of the Community's areas of competence under the Euratom Treaty. These comprise the level of regulatory detail of the competences in the primary legal act and their scope and content; the extent to which these competences have been exercised as compared with the wording used in respect of them in the Euratom Treaty; and the Court's interpretation of the scope and nature of these competences. These features allow for systematic grouping of the Euratom Community's competences[1121] and analysis of the effect that stagnation of the Euratom Treaty has had on the overall *acquis* of the Euratom Community.

II REGULATION OF THE EURATOM COMMUNITY'S COMPETENCES UNDER THE EURATOM TREATY

The analysis of the scope, content and the level of detail of the Euratom Community's competences under the Euratom Treaty set out above shows that these competences

1121. Some authors have categorised the Euratom Community's competences as being exclusive or shared. For example, A. Södersten has concluded that the Euratom Community has exclusive powers in respect of ownership, dissemination of information and safeguards. In certain other areas, competence is shared with the Member States. In yet other areas, the Euratom Community's powers are limited to coordinating or supplementing Member States' actions (e.g., in relation to investment). See A. Södersten, *Euratom at the Crossroads*, Cheltenham, Northampton: Edward Elgar Publishing Limited, 2018, pp. 228–229. However, as the classification of competences under the EU is not applicable to the Euratom Treaty, this study focuses on the features of competences from the perspective of the Euratom Community, without evaluating their effect on the balance of competences between the Euratom Community and the Member States and defining them as exclusive or shared.

can be classified based on the legislative amendment procedure and on the level of regulatory detail involved in relation to the Euratom Community's tasks.[1122]

Based on the regulation of the legislative amendment procedure, the Euratom Community's competences can be divided into two groups: those that fall under the ordinary revision procedure set out in the TEU, and those for which a special amendment procedure is established in the Euratom Treaty.

The regular amendment procedure of the Euratom Treaty is laid down in Article 106a(1) of the Treaty and Article 48(2) to (5) TEU. Article 76(1) of the Euratom Treaty establishes the Euratom Community's competence to amend the provisions of Chapter 6 of the Euratom Treaty by means of a special amendment procedure, if unforeseen circumstances create a general supply shortage. The provisions of Chapter 6 can be amended by the Council acting unanimously on a proposal from the Commission and after consulting the EP. Article 85 of the Euratom Treaty lays down a simplified amendment procedure in respect of the provisions of Chapter 7 of the Euratom Treaty. It provides that where new circumstances so require the safeguards procedures under Chapter 7 of the Euratom Treaty may, at the request of a Member State or of the Commission, be adapted by the Council, acting unanimously on a proposal from the Commission and after consulting the EP. In a similar manner to the procedures adopted in respect of supplies and safeguards, Article 90 of the Euratom Treaty establishes a simplified amendment procedure for the provisions laid down in Chapter 8 of the Euratom Treaty if new circumstances so require. This article makes it possible, at the request of a Member State or of the Commission, for the Council to adjust the provisions regulating the Euratom Community's right of ownership under Chapter 8 of the Euratom Treaty. In this regard the Council must act unanimously on a proposal from the Commission and after consulting the EP. The differences between the amendment procedure under Articles 76, 85 and 90 of the Euratom Treaty and the ordinary revision procedure under Article 49 TEU are substantial: unlike Article 48(4) TEU, the Euratom Treaty does not require, *inter alia*, a convention, the involvement of the European Council in the revisions procedure, or the Member States' ratification of the amendments for them enter into force.

The existence of the special Euratom Treaty amendment provisions in relation to supplies, safeguards and property ownership shows that the founding Member States of the Euratom Community regarded these three competence areas as being of great importance and saw a need for them to be able to change and evolve, depending on the dynamics of the nuclear industry in the Euratom Community. This feature of the Euratom Treaty makes it impervious to radical change and adaptable to newly arising circumstances, and is sometimes referred to as the Euratom Treaty's 'ability to learn'.[1123] Consequently, these competences combined ensure the flexibility of the

1122. The Euratom Community's objectives and tasks are identified in Chapter III Section A of this study.

1123. N. P. Serrano, 'Wakening the Serpent: Reflections on the Possible Modification of the Euratom Treaty', (2006) 1/1 *International Journal of Nuclear Law*, pp. 13–14; I. Cenevska, *The European Atomic Energy Community in the European Union Context: The 'Outsider' Within*, Leiden: Brill Nijhoff, 2016, p. 70. Some authors consider the special amendment procedure in these three chapters of the Euratom Treaty to be a sign of the provisional character of the

Euratom Treaty, and show the importance of and priority given to the Euratom Community's competences under Chapters 6, 7 and 8 of the Euratom Treaty.

Based on the level of regulatory detail of the competences under the Euratom Treaty, in relation to the Euratom Community's tasks, three groups of competences can be identified: those in respect of which the level of regulatory detail under the Euratom Treaty is fully appropriate to the tasks of the Euratom Community under Article 2 of the Euratom Treaty; those in respect of which the level of regulatory detail is generally appropriate, but where certain improvements may be recommended; and those in respect of which the level of regulatory detail may be considered too detailed. This classification does not focus on the level of regulatory detail under the Euratom Treaty per se, but identifies the relationship between the level of detail of the provisions in the Euratom Treaty and the tasks of Euratom Community in given areas under the Euratom Treaty.

The first category of competences, where the level of regulatory detail is fully appropriate to the Community's tasks, contains those established in respect of the following: research under Chapter 1 of the Euratom Treaty; investments under Chapter 4; Joint Undertakings under Chapter 5; nuclear supply under Chapter 6; safeguards under Chapter 7; and external relations under Chapter 10.

Research was singled out as one of the main areas of integration in the Euratom Treaty.[1124] The regulatory framework under Chapter 1 of the Euratom Treaty is appropriate to fulfil the task of promoting the development of the nuclear energy sector and research in the broader field of radiation protection in the Euratom Community, as it establishes the purpose and length of the research programme, the budgetary provisions to finance it and requirements relating to the reporting and implementation of the research programme.

The objectives of the Euratom Community's competences under Chapters 4 and 5 of the Euratom Treaty are similar as they both seek to provide the incentives needed to develop nuclear energy in the Euratom Community.[1125] Under Chapter 4 of the Euratom Treaty, the Euratom Community has a competence not only to collect and analyse information, but also to publish illustrative programmes and require persons and undertakings to inform the Euratom Community of their investments both in the front end and back end of the nuclear fuel cycle. The Commission has also established that the Euratom Community's competences in respect of investments under Chapter 4 of the Euratom Treaty cannot be undermined by the Commission's competences relating to state aid control under the TFEU.[1126] Consequently, the level of regulatory

Euratom Treaty and the peculiar nature of the Euratom Community. See J. Handrlica, 'The Splendid Durability of the Provisional: A Tribute to Euratom', (2018) 14/14 *Croatian Yearbook of European Law & Policy*, pp. 167 and 169.

1124. J. G. Polach, *Euratom: Its Background, Issues and Economic Implications*, Dobbs Ferry, NY: Oceana Publications Inc., 1964, p. 139.

1125. Communication from the Commission to the Council and the European Parliament, '50 Years of the Euratom Treaty', Brussels, 20.3.2007, pp. 3–4.

1126. Paragraphs 276 to 278 of Commission Decision (EU) 2017/2112 of 6 March 2017 on the measure/aid scheme/State aid SA.38454 – 2015/C (ex 2015/N) which Hungary is planning to implement for supporting the development of two new nuclear reactors at Paks II nuclear power station, C/2017/1486, OJ L 317, 1.12.2017, pp. 45–118, at p. 102.

detail under Chapter 4 of the Euratom Treaty is fully appropriate to the Euratom Community's task of stimulating investment actions by persons and undertakings that facilitate coordinated development of investments in the nuclear field in the Euratom Community.[1127] The purpose of the Euratom Community's competences under Chapter 5 of the Euratom Treaty is to encourage ventures in the form of Joint Undertakings in the Euratom Community. The level of detail of the regulation laid down is appropriate to fulfil this task because Chapter 5 sets out a legislative procedure for establishing Joint Undertakings in the Euratom Community and gives Joint Undertakings certain privileges due to their fundamental importance to the nuclear industry in the Community. For example, a project can be at least partially financed by the Euratom Community and receive exemption from all direct taxes, customs duties and charges having equivalent effect.[1128] These privileges are especially important in cases where private initiatives are not able to meet, in sufficient quantity and at the necessary speed, the need for industrial equipment within the Euratom Community.[1129]

The level of regulatory detail in Chapter 6 of the Euratom Treaty is high, given that this is a primary legal act, but this detailed regulation fulfils the tasks of the Euratom Community in terms of ensuring regular and equitable access to nuclear supplies.[1130] Twenty-five articles in Chapter 6 of the Euratom Treaty establish a detailed regulatory system for the common nuclear supply policy. This covers equal access to sources of supply; prohibition of a privileged position for, and discrimination between, users; a right of option in respect of nuclear supplies; and establishment of the Euratom Supply Agency. The provisions set out in Chapter 6 also confer competences upon the Euratom Community throughout the nuclear supply chain. These relate to such varied matters as prospecting for minerals, production and processing of nuclear supplies, concluding contracts, setting prices, exporting, importing and transferring supplies, storage and stocking of supplies and disposal of nuclear supplies outside the Euratom Community. The purpose of this detailed regulation is to ensure that all users in the Euratom Community receive a regular and equitable supply of nuclear fuels. The scope of the Euratom Community's competences does not extend to the creation of a common nuclear supply market,[1131] but concerns the establishment of a common nuclear supply policy, which ensures a regular and equitable supply of ores, source materials and special fissile materials.[1132]

The objective of the Euratom Community's competences under Chapter 7 of the Euratom Treaty is to ensure that ores, source materials and special fissile materials are not diverted from their originally intended uses. A safeguards system capable of accounting for the movement and stocks of nuclear material is an essential element of

1127. Article 2(c) of the Euratom Treaty.
1128. Articles 46(2), 47(4) and 48(1), and Annex III, of the Euratom Treaty.
1129. M. Gaudet, *Euratom*, London: Pergamon Press 1959, pp. 166–167.
1130. Article 2(d) of the Euratom Treaty.
1131. Some authors generalise the scope of the Euratom Community's competences as creating a nuclear common market for trade in nuclear ores and materials within the EU. See P. Barnes, 'Nuclear Safety for Nuclear Electricity – The Search for a Solid Legal Basis for Nuclear Safety in an Enlarged EU', (2003) 45 *Managerial Law*, p. 9.
1132. As defined in Article 197 of the Euratom Treaty.

that endeavour.[1133] The provisions of Chapter 7 establish a three-tier system of competences – comprising inspections, infringement procedures and sanctions – which constitutes the content of the Euratom Community's competences in respect of nuclear safeguards and ensures that the task of ensuring the effective functioning of the safeguards system can be fulfilled.[1134] The level of detail of these provisions is therefore appropriate to Euratom Community's tasks under Chapter 7.

The objective of the Euratom Community's competences under Chapter 10 is to establish relations with other countries and international organisations that will foster progress in the peaceful uses of nuclear energy. The Euratom Community has international legal personality[1135] and the provisions of Chapter 10 establish a system of competences that ensure that the Euratom Community can enter into external relations with other countries and international organisations, renegotiate certain agreements concluded by the Member States and approve all draft agreements and contracts that Member States wish to sign. The level of detail of the provisions of the Euratom Treaty that establish the Euratom Community's competences concerning external relations is thus appropriate to fulfil this task.

The second category of competences are characterised by a level of regulatory detail that can in general be considered as appropriate in respect of the tasks of the Euratom Community, but where some need for improvement in the level of regulatory detail can be identified. This category includes Euratom Community competences in respect of health and safety established under Chapter 3 of the Euratom Treaty, competences in respect of property ownership under Chapter 8, and competences in respect of the nuclear common market under Chapter 9.

The Euratom Community's competences under Chapter 3 of the Euratom Treaty structurally cover two main aspects: establishing and updating basic safety standards in accordance with the existing scientific knowledge; and ensuring the compliance to these standards.[1136] The level of detail of the provisions of the Euratom Treaty that establish the Euratom Community's competences in respect of health and safety is relatively low in relation to the nature of the Community's task of protecting the health of workers and the general public against the dangers arising from ionising radiation. Chapter 3 of this study, on health and safety, notes that radiation protection is an overarching field of legislation that covers regulation of nuclear safety, safe management of radioactive waste and spent nuclear fuel and emergency preparedness and

1133. B. Patel and P. Chare, 'Fifty Years of Safeguards under the Euratom Treaty – A Regulatory Review', in G. Janssens-Maenhout (ed.), *Nuclear Safeguards and Non-Proliferation*, Luxembourg: Office for Official Publications of the European Communities, 2009, p. 95.

1134. Some authors view the system of safeguards as having four separate legal dimensions, see Chapter 7 Section 01 of this study and W. Kilb, 'The Nuclear Safeguards System of the European Atomic Energy Community (Euratom)', in C. Raetzke (ed.), *Nuclear Law in the EU and Beyond*, Baden-Baden: Nomos, 2014, pp. 98–111. The Euratom Community's safeguards regime is sometimes called a supranational system, with no police force: see H. W. Schleicher, 'Nuclear Safeguards in the European Community: A Regional Approach', (1980) 22 *IAEA Bulletin*, p. 46; or a regime of stringent and incisive 'conformity control': see H. J. Hahn, 'Control under the Euratom Compact', (1958) 7 *American Journal of Comparative Law*, p. 39.

1135. Article 184 of the Euratom Treaty.

1136. Articles 2, 30 and 33 to 38 of the Euratom Treaty.

response.[1137] Consequently, it could be concluded that the level of regulatory detail involved would fulfil the tasks of the Euratom Community in respect of health and safety more appropriately if the Euratom Treaty contained specific and more detailed provisions on nuclear safety, safe management of radioactive waste and spent nuclear fuel and emergency preparedness and response.

The purpose of the provisions of Chapter 8 of the Euratom Treaty is ensure the Euratom Community's right of ownership over all special fissile materials in the Euratom Community.[1138] Article 89 of the Euratom Treaty is detailed and technical and thus differs from other six articles in this chapter. The provisions relating to the Euratom Community's Special Fissile Materials Account under Article 89 would therefore be more suitable in a secondary legal act. Consequently, the level of detail of the provisions of the Euratom Treaty that establish the Euratom Community's competences in respect of property ownership is too high in Article 89, but appropriate in the other articles in Chapter 8 of the Euratom Treaty in relation to ensuring that the Euratom Community exercises the right of ownership of all special fissile materials in the Euratom Community, while affording unlimited rights of use to the Member States, persons and undertakings.[1139]

The provisions of Chapter 9 of the Euratom Treaty establish three of the traditional common market freedoms – the free movement of goods, workers and capital – to ensure wide commercial outlets and access to the best technical facilities in the nuclear sector. However, as opposed to the regulation of the customs union under the TFEU, the provisions of Chapter 9 of the Euratom Treaty are mainly worded as obligations of the Member States, not as Euratom Community competences.[1140] Measures intended to facilitate the pooling of the human and material resources of the Euratom Community are for the most part left to the competences of the Member States. This implies that the Euratom Community's role and competences in relation to the nuclear common market focus on seeking to ensure, on a passive basis, that Member States fulfil their obligations under Chapter 9. Furthermore, the content of Article 98 of the Euratom Treaty has ramifications for discussion of the Euratom

1137. See concluding remarks in Chapter 3 Section 02 of this study on the exercise of the Euratom Community's competences regarding health and safety.

1138. Article 2(f) of the Euratom Treaty. The right of ownership is also a potentially powerful tool for the ESA to ensure the means of maintaining a common supply policy under Article 52 of the Euratom Treaty. See Chapter 6 of this study and W. Kilb, 'The Nuclear Safeguards Regime of Euratom: A Regional Cornerstone of the Verification of Non-Proliferation Obligations in the European Union', in J. L. Black-Branch and D. Fleck (eds), *Nuclear Non-Proliferation in International Law, Volume II: Verification and Compliance*, The Hague: Asser Press, 2016, p. 156.

1139. Article 87 of the Euratom Treaty. The possessor of the special fissile materials enjoys, therefore, the most extensive rights of use and consumption of those material, which is considered to be a characteristic legal aspect of the Euratom Community. See P. Mathijsen, 'Some Legal Aspects of Euratom', (1965–1966) 3 *Common Market Law Review*, p. 336.

1140. See Articles 93, 96 and 98 of the Euratom Treaty. Compare, e.g., with Article 28 TFEU, which states that the Union shall comprise a customs union which shall cover all trade in goods and which shall involve the prohibition between Member States of customs duties on imports and exports and of all charges having equivalent effect, and the adoption of a common customs tariff in their relations with third countries. Article 3 TFEU clearly indicates the exclusive competence of the EU in relation to the customs union.

Community's competences in relation to nuclear liability and allows the patchwork European nuclear liability regime to continue.[1141] Consequently, the level of detail of the provisions of the Euratom Treaty that establish the Euratom Community's competences in relation to the nuclear common market is considered as being appropriate in relation to the Euratom Community's tasks under Chapter 9, but could be improved by clearer definition and establishment of the Euratom Community's competences in the field.

In the third category of competences, with a level of regulatory detail that could be considered too high in comparison to the tasks of the Euratom Community, are the competences in respect of the dissemination of information under Chapter 2 of the Euratom Treaty. The main purpose of the Euratom Community's competences under Chapter 2 is to ensure the dissemination of technical information in the Euratom Community.[1142] The Euratom Community's competences in this regard are broad and the provisions of the Euratom Treaty in this area have a high level of detail. The Euratom Community not only has a competence to disseminate the information that it owns or has rights of disposal in respect of, but also has wide powers to obtain such information by using amicable agreements, compulsory notifications, arbitration or compulsory powers. The Euratom Community's competences in the field are established in eighteen articles of the Euratom Treaty. These provide a detailed level of regulation and, in some cases, establish procedures and time frames, which are usually to be found in secondary legislation and not in a primary legal act. Although this detailed approach to regulation may have represented a means of ensuring the appropriate handling of such information from the very beginning of the Euratom Community's existence, with no immediate need for secondary legislation, the appropriateness of such detailed regulation in the primary legal act is, however, open to question. In order to fulfil the Euratom Community's tasks concerning the dissemination of information in a satisfactory manner, it would have been sufficed to establish general principles of dissemination of information in the primary legal act and delegate horizontal competences to the institutions to adopt secondary legislation that would appropriately exercise these competences. The level of detail of the provision of Chapter 2 of the Euratom Treaty is therefore too high in relation to the Euratom Community's tasks in respect of dissemination of information.

The classification of the Euratom Community's competences outlined above indicates that six out of ten chapters of the Euratom Treaty have a level of regulatory detail that is fully appropriate in view of the tasks and objectives at hand, and that three chapters have some aspects in respect of which certain improvements in the level of

1141. P. Reyners, 'Liability Problems Associated with the Current Patchwork Nuclear Liability Regime within the EU Member States', in N. Pelzer (ed.), *European Nuclear Liability Law in a Process of Change*, Baden-Baden: Nomos, 2010, pp. 93–104; J. Handrlica, 'Euratom Powers in the Field of Nuclear Liability Revised', (2010) 3/1 *International Journal of Nuclear Law*, pp. 1–18; J. Handrlica, 'Harmonisation of Nuclear Liability in the European Union: Challenges, Options and Limits', (2009) 84 *Nuclear Law Bulletin*, pp. 35–36; R. J. Heffron, S. F. Ashley, W. J. Nuttall, 'The Global Nuclear Liability Regime Post Fukushima Daiichi', (2016) 90 *Progress in Nuclear Energy*, pp. 4–5.

1142. Article 2(a) of the Euratom Treaty.

regulatory detail can be identified. The conclusion is that the level of regulatory detail regarding the Euratom Community's competences under the Euratom Treaty is mostly appropriate to the tasks and objectives of the Community. Despite the stagnancy of the Euratom Treaty and the fact that the substantive law of the Euratom Treaty has never undergone amendment from the adoption of this primary legal act, the regulation of the Euratom Community's competences under the Euratom Treaty is nonetheless appropriate in relation to the Euratom Community's tasks in specific fields and continues to ensure appropriate functioning of the Euratom Community.

III EXERCISE OF THE EURATOM COMMUNITY'S COMPETENCES IN SECONDARY LEGISLATION

Two analytical approaches to competences can be applied based on the exercise of the Euratom Community's competences. The first of these involves the analysis of the quantitative aspects of exercise of the Euratom Community's competences by evaluating how many articles in each competence area of the Euratom Community have been a legal basis for secondary legal acts and the number of secondary legal acts in each of these competence areas. The second involves evaluating whether these secondary legal acts exercise the Euratom Community's competences in accordance with the wording of those competences in the Euratom Treaty.

Based on the quantitative elements of exercise of Euratom Community competences under the Euratom Treaty, two distinct groups of competences can be identified: those that are exercised to a great extent through secondary legal acts, and those that are exercised to a limited extent through secondary legal acts. Euratom Community competences that do not belong in either of these groups may be regarded as having been exercised, in quantitative terms, to an extent that is generally appropriate and does not lead to identification of characteristics that are relevant to this study.

The group characterised by a high level of exercise includes the Euratom Community's competences in respect of health and safety under Chapter 3 of the Euratom Treaty and in respect of external relations under Chapter 10 of the Euratom Treaty. The competences established in most of articles under Chapter 3 of the Euratom Treaty are exercised through various types of secondary legal acts: regulations, directives, decisions, recommendations and opinions. Articles 31 and 32 of the Euratom Treaty, which establish procedure for the adoption and revision of basic safety standards, have been the legal basis for eight secondary legal acts. These may in turn be divided into four fields of regulation: radiation protection, nuclear safety, safe management of radioactive waste and spent nuclear fuel and emergency preparedness and response.[1143] Article 37 of the Euratom Treaty requires the Member States to

1143. Radiation protection: Council Directive 2013/59/Euratom; Council Directive 2013/51/Euratom; Council Regulation (Euratom) No 1493/93; nuclear safety of nuclear installations: Council Directive 2009/71/Euratom; and Council Directive 2014/87/Euratom; the safe management of radioactive waste and spent nuclear fuel: Council Directive 2011/70/Euratom; Council Directive 2006/117/Euratom; and emergency preparedness and response: Council Regulation (Euratom) 2016/52; and Council Decision 87/600/Euratom.

provide the Commission with such general data relating to any plan for the disposal of radioactive waste which will make it possible for the Commission to determine whether the implementation of such plan is liable to result in the radioactive contamination of the water, soil or airspace of another Member State. Quantitative analysis shows that Article 37 of the Euratom Treaty is exercised through the Commission's recommendation on the application of Article 37 of the Euratom Treaty[1144] and more than 180 Commission opinions on Member States' radioactive waste disposal plans that have been notified to the Commission under the provisions of Article 37.

The Euratom Community's competences in respect of external relations have been exercised through secondary legislation that has either Article 101 or Article 103 of the Euratom Treaty as a legal basis. Quantitative analysis of the secondary legislation under Article 101 of the Euratom Treaty shows that the Euratom Community's competence to enter into obligations by concluding bilateral agreements with third States, by participating in multilateral projects under the purview of the Euratom Treaty, and through accession to international conventions under the auspices of the IAEA, is an extensively exercised competence of the Euratom Community. As identified in Chapter 10 of this study, during the last two decades, the Euratom Community has exercised its competences under Article 101 of the Euratom Treaty through a total of ninety-seven secondary legal acts: twenty-nine Council decisions, twenty-seven Commission decisions and forty-one Council and Commission decisions that have a dual EU and Euratom legal basis.

The group of competences that have been exercised to a limited extent through secondary legislation includes the Euratom Community's competences in respect of dissemination of information under Chapter 2 of the Euratom Treaty, Joint Undertakings under Chapter 5, nuclear supplies under Chapter 6 and property ownership under Chapter 8 of the Euratom Treaty. The quantitative element of exercise of the Euratom Community's competences in respect of dissemination of information under Chapter 2 and nuclear supply under Chapter 6 of the Euratom Treaty is similar. Both fields are characterised by a high number of articles that regulate these competences under the Euratom Treaty, but relatively few articles that have been used as a legal basis for secondary legislation. Of a total of eighteen articles that establish the Euratom Community's competences in relation to dissemination of information, competences under three articles – Articles 18, 24 and 25 – have been exercised through secondary legislation. The exercise of the Euratom Community's competences under Chapter 2 of the Euratom Treaty can therefore be identified as having been carried out to a limited extent. The Euratom Community's competences in respect of nuclear supply are established in twenty-five articles under Chapter 6 of the Euratom Treaty, but only five articles in this chapter have been used as a legal basis for secondary legislation: Articles 52, 53, 54, 60 and 74 of the Euratom Treaty. The competences under the majority of the articles in Chapter 6 of the Euratom Treaty have not been exercised by the Euratom Community, and, in quantitative terms, the exercise of the Euratom Community's

1144. Commission Recommendation 2010/635/Euratom. *See also* Chapter 3 Section 3.02.B of this study.

competences in respect of nuclear supply is therefore limited. The Euratom Community's competences in respect of Joint Undertakings under Chapter 5 are regulated by seven articles in the Euratom Treaty, but have only been exercised through one secondary legal act, which has Articles 47 and 48 of the Euratom Treaty as a legal basis: Decision 2007/198/Euratom, establishing the ITER Joint Undertaking for research and the promotion of fusion energy and its future exploitation. The Euratom Community's competences in respect of property ownership under Chapter 8 of the Euratom Treaty are last in the group of competences that have been exercised to a limited extent. Systematic analysis of the existing secondary legislation shows that no secondary legal acts have articles contained in Chapter 8 of the Euratom Treaty as their legal basis. Consequently, the Euratom Community's competences in respect of property ownership have not been exercised. Chapter 8 establishes the Euratom Community's right of ownership of all special fissile materials in the Euratom Community, while giving the Member States, persons and undertakings unlimited right of use. The content of the competences may thus imply that there is scope for direct application of these provisions.

The Euratom Community competences that have been, in quantitative terms, exercised to an extent that is generally appropriate and does not lead to identification of characteristics that are relevant to this study include competences in respect of research under Chapter 1 of the Euratom Treaty, investments under Chapter 4, safeguards under Chapter 7 and the nuclear common market under Chapter 9. It should be mentioned, that the Commission has considered two articles contained in Chapter 9 of the Euratom Treaty[1145] to be directly applicable.[1146]

The classification, based on the quantitative elements of the exercise of the Euratom Community's competences under the Euratom Treaty, permits two conclusions. First, the extent to which the Euratom Community's competences have been exercised indicates the significance of regulation under the Euratom Treaty: competences in respect of health and safety under Chapter 3 of the Euratom Treaty and external relations under Chapter 10 have been exercised to a high extent and therefore have high priority in the Euratom Community. Second, the consequences of the Euratom Community not exercising its competences under the Euratom Treaty vary. In some cases – such as in respect of the provisions of Chapter 8 – the high level of detail utilised in regulating competences in the primary legal act may indicate the possibility of direct application of the provisions of the Euratom Treaty without the need for secondary legislation. In other cases – such as Article 15 of the Euratom Treaty – this may mean breach of the Commission's obligations under the Euratom Treaty.

The second analytical approach to the exercise of the Euratom Community's competences evaluates whether secondary legal acts in force exercise these competences in accordance with the way in which they are drafted in the Euratom Treaty. On this basis, three groups of Euratom Community competences can be identified: competences that are exercised narrower than the wording of the Euratom Treaty; competences that are exercised in accordance with the wording of the Euratom Treaty;

1145. Articles 93 and 97 of the Euratom Treaty.
1146. See Chapter 9 Section 02 of this study.

and competences that are exercised more broadly than the wording of the Euratom Treaty would indicate. The lack of secondary legal acts in respect of property ownership under Chapter 8 of the Euratom Treaty makes it difficult to allocate this regulatory field to one of these three groups.

The Euratom Community's competences in respect of the dissemination of information under Chapter 2 of the Euratom Treaty and competences in respect of investments under Chapter 4 have one common feature: both delegate certain obligations to the Commission that have not been exercised properly. Article 15 of Chapter 2 of the Euratom Treaty explicitly requires the Commission to establish a procedure by which Member States, persons and undertakings may exchange provisional or final results of their research, insofar as these results have not been acquired by the Community. This procedure has not been formally established by the Commission as there is no secondary legislation based on Article 15 of the Euratom Treaty. Therefore, it can be stated that the Commission is not exercising its obligations established under the Euratom Treaty and that these Euratom Community competences are being exercised in a narrower way than the wording of the Euratom Treaty indicates. Article 40 of Chapter 4 of the Euratom Treaty states that the Commission has a competence and an obligation to periodically publish an illustrative nuclear programme, especially indicating nuclear energy production targets and all the types of investments required to achieve them. However, the content of the latest PINC Nuclear Illustrative Programme[1147] shows that the Commission is not fulfilling its obligation under Article 40 of the Euratom Treaty to include nuclear energy production targets in a nuclear illustrative programme. It may therefore be stated that the Euratom Community exercises its competences under Article 40 of the Euratom Treaty in a narrower manner than the wording of the Treaty indicates.

The Euratom Community's competences in respect of the overall field of investments under Chapter 4 of the Euratom Treaty, Joint Undertakings under Chapter 5, the nuclear common market under Chapter 9 and external relations under Chapter 10 belong to the group of competences which have been exercised in accordance with the wording of the Euratom Treaty.

Taking into consideration the exception laid down in Article 40 of the Euratom Treaty mentioned above, the Euratom Community's competences in respect of investment are generally exercised in accordance with the wording of the provisions of Chapter 4 of the Euratom Treaty. The secondary legal acts that have Article 41 of the Euratom Treaty as a legal basis do not broaden the scope of the provisions in the primary legal act, but implement them. The fact that exercise of these competences is time-limited is a salient attribute of the exercise of the Euratom Community's competences in the field of Joint Undertakings under Chapter 5 of the Euratom Treaty.[1148] The

1147. Communication from the Commission on Nuclear Illustrative Programme presented under Article 40 of the Euratom Treaty – Final (after opinion of EESC) COM(2017) 237 final. This was the first Communication from the Commission on Nuclear Illustrative Programme after the Fukushima Daiichi accident in March 2011. The previous one was presented in 2008.

1148. All Joint Undertakings are established for a limited period of time. The ITER Joint Undertaking was established for a period of thirty-five years starting from April 2007. See Article 1(1) of Council Decision 2007/198/Euratom.

Euratom Community's competences under Chapter 5 are currently exercised through Council Decision 2007/198/Euratom, which establishes the ITER Joint Undertaking. The Euratom Community exercises its competences in accordance with the wording of the Euratom Treaty, *inter alia*, by establishing the Euratom Community as one of the members of the ITER Joint Undertaking and by making significant financial contributions to the ITER Project. Consequently, the exercise of the Euratom Community's competences under Chapter 5 of the Euratom Treaty is focused on research and the promotion of fusion energy and its future exploitation. The Euratom Community's competences under Articles 92 and 96 of Chapter 9 of the Euratom Treaty have been exercised in accordance with wording of the Euratom Treaty: the secondary legal acts do not expand on the scope of the provisions, but clarify them and give them further definition. For example, Regulation No 5 on the amendment of List B in Annex IV of the Euratom Treaty,[1149] which exercises the competences laid down in Article 92 of the Euratom Treaty, clarified the provisions of the Euratom Treaty by deleting components and parts for nuclear reactors from List B of the Euratom Treaty, as nuclear reactors were already to be found in List A2 of the Treaty. The Directive on freedom to take skilled employments in the field of nuclear energy,[1150] exercising the Euratom Community's competences under Article 96 of the Euratom Treaty, has defined the concept of skilled employment in the nuclear energy field,[1151] and aligned the rules on taking skilled employment with those governing freedom of movement for workers under EU legislation, by requiring that the conditions for granting authorisations required for any employment in the nuclear energy field are not less liberal than those laid down under EU law.[1152] The Euratom Community's competences in respect of external relations under Chapter 10 of the Euratom Treaty have been extensively exercised by concluding bilateral agreements with third States, by participating in multilateral projects under the purview of the Euratom Treaty, and through accession to international conventions. The provisions of Articles 101 and 103 of the Euratom Treaty lay down the basis for these Euratom Community competences and they are therefore exercised in accordance with the wording of the Treaty.

The group of competences that are exercised broader than the wording of the Euratom Treaty includes the Euratom Community's competences in respect of research under Chapter 1 of the Euratom Treaty, health and safety under Chapter 3, supply under Chapter 6 and safeguards under Chapter 7.

The Euratom Community's competences in respect of research under Chapter 1 of the Euratom Treaty have been exercised more broadly than the strict wording of the

1149. Regulation No 5 on amending of List B of Annex IV of the Euratom Treaty.
1150. Council Directive on freedom to take skilled employment in the field of nuclear energy.
1151. Article 2 and Annex of Council Directive on freedom to take skilled employment in the field of nuclear energy.
1152. Article 4 of Council Directive on freedom to take skilled employment in the field of nuclear energy. Article 4 refers to Articles 48 and 49 of the Treaty establishing the European Economic Community, which are now are Articles 45 to 48 TFEU.

Euratom Treaty indicates in the following ways: the Euratom Community's competences cover not only fission, but also fusion research;[1153] the exercise of competences under Article 7 of the Euratom Treaty establishes a link to the EU's research activities both by referring to Horizon 2020 and by defining the JRC's research functions within the scope of the Euratom Treaty as well as in other research areas that fall within the scope of the EU's competences.[1154]

The exercise of the Euratom Community's competences in respect of health and safety under Chapter 3 of the Euratom Treaty is also carried out in a significantly broader manner than the wording of the Euratom Treaty indicates. Articles 31 and 32 of the Euratom Treaty are the legal basis of the Euratom Community's broad competences. Although the Euratom Treaty does not explicitly mention the operational safety of nuclear power plants, radioactive waste storage or the development of disposal facilities,[1155] a comprehensive analysis of the relevant secondary legal acts indicates that the Euratom Community's competences under Chapter 3 of the Treaty extend to four different regulatory areas: radiation protection, nuclear safety, safe management of radioactive waste and spent fuel and emergency preparedness and response. This creates a system of regulation in the field of health and safety under the Euratom Treaty. The extensive exercise of the Euratom Community's competences under Article 37 of the Euratom Treaty shows that the Commission has broad competences concerning the content of notifications to be submitted by the Member States. The obligation to notify applies in respect of any planned disposal or accidental release of radioactive substances, including plans for disposal of spent nuclear fuels;[1156] the concept of disposal is broadened to include storage of radioactive waste and spent nuclear fuel;[1157]

1153. Article 3(2)(e) of Council Regulation (Euratom) No 2018/1563. Fusion research is not mentioned in the list of research fields set out in Annex I, or in any other provisions, of the Euratom Treaty.

1154. Recitals 5, 27 and 32 of Council Regulation (Euratom) No 2018/1563 indicate that the Euratom Programme contributes to achieving the objectives of the Horizon 2020 Framework Programme for Research, and that achieving the Euratom Programme's objectives in relevant areas requires support for cross-cutting activities that occur both within the Euratom Programme and jointly with the activities of the Horizon 2020 Framework Programme, and participation in the Euratom Programme and dissemination of research results should be subject to the rules applicable to the Horizon 2020 Framework Programme. Under Article 6 of Council Regulation (Euratom) No 2018/1563, the Commission may entrust the implementation of indirect action under the Euratom Programme to bodies created under, or referred to in, the Horizon 2020 Framework Programme and there may be activities that cut across the indirect actions set out in both Euratom Research Programme and Horizon 2020, under Article 8 of Council Regulation (Euratom) No 2018/1563. Furthermore, the Commission is required to identify the cross-cutting activities between the Euratom Programme and Horizon 2020 in the work programme for the implementation of the indirect actions and the multi-annual work programme for direct actions of the JRC, under Article 11 of Council Regulation (Euratom) No 2018/1563.

1155. P. M. Barnes, 'Nuclear Safety for Nuclear Electricity – The Search for a Solid Legal Basis for Nuclear Safety in an Enlarged European Union', (2003) 45 *Managerial Law*, p. 129.

1156. Article 2(11) of Council Directive 2011/70/Euratom and paragraph 1 of Commission Recommendation 2010/635/Euratom.

1157. The Commission has established that disposal of radioactive waste within the meaning of Article 37 of the Treaty covers any planned or accidental release of radioactive substances associated with, *inter alia*, the operation of nuclear reactors, the reprocessing of irradiated nuclear fuel, the mining and enrichment of uranium, the fabrication of nuclear fuel, the

and the concept of general data is given a broad interpretation that extends to technical aspects of Member States' disposal plans.[1158]

Exercise of the Euratom Community's competences in relation to nuclear supply under Article 53 of Chapter 6 of the Euratom Treaty is broader than the wording of the Treaty indicates because it allows Euratom Community users to negotiate with producers of their choice and denies the existence of a 'Community preference' for nuclear supplies under the Euratom Treaty.[1159] The exercise of these competences under Chapter 6 also broadens the wording of the Euratom Treaty by separating the ESA's exclusive right to conclude contracts, established under Article 52 of the Euratom Treaty, from the right to negotiate contracts; with the exception of contracts for special fissile materials, which should be both negotiated and concluded by the ESA.[1160] The exercise of the Euratom Community's competences under Chapter 6 of the Euratom Treaty also expands on the principles of common supply policy, by emphasising the importance of diversification of nuclear supplies,[1161] which is not established in the provisions of the Euratom Treaty.

The Euratom Community's competences in respect of nuclear safeguards under Chapter 7 of the Euratom Treaty are in some respects exercised more broadly than the wording of the Euratom Treaty indicates, as it expands the Commission's competences in relation to safeguards to cover military installations with mixed civil and military materials.[1162] It has been established that although the provisions of the Euratom Treaty do not provide a clear answer as to whether the Euratom Community has competences in relation to the military application of nuclear energy, the CJEU has ruled that activities falling within the military sphere are outside the scope of the

---

storage of irradiated nuclear fuel, the handling and processing of artificial radioactive substances on an industrial scale, the dismantling of nuclear reactors, mixed-oxide fuel fabrication plants and reprocessing plants and the predisposal management, i.e., including storage of radioactive waste arising from these operations. See paragraph 1 of Commission Recommendation 2010/635/Euratom.

1158. Requirements imposed on the Member States include the submission of technical aspect on installations, such as annual discharges foreseen; origins of the radioactive effluents, their composition and physicochemical forms; and management of these effluents, methods and paths of release. See points 3.2 and 4.2 in Annexes I to IV of Commission Recommendation 2010/635/Euratom.

1159. Rules of the Supply Agency of the European Atomic Energy Community of 5 May 1960 determining the manner in which demand is to be balanced against the supply of ores, source materials and special fissile materials; Regulation of the Supply Agency of the European Atomic Energy Community amending the rules of the Supply Agency of 5 May 1960 determining the manner in which demand is to be balanced against the supply of ores, source materials and special fissile materials; and recitals 8, 10 and 12 of Commission Decision 93/428/Euratom.

1160. Article 5 bis of the Rules of the Supply Agency of the Euratom Community.

1161. In Commission Decision 94/285/Euratom the Commission exercises its competences under Article 53 of the Euratom Treaty by confirming the importance of diversification of supplies in the Euratom Community's common supply policy and the ESA's role.

1162. Article 34(3)(a) of Commission Regulation (Euratom) No 302/2005 provides that certain articles of Commission Regulation (Euratom) No 302/2005 apply to installations or parts of installations which at certain times are operated exclusively with nuclear materials liable to be assigned to meet defence requirements but which at other times are operated exclusively with civil nuclear materials. Article 3(1), Articles 4 and 6 of Commission Regulation (Euratom) No 302/2005 are applicable to those installations.

Euratom Treaty, and the Euratom Community does not have a general competence concerning military nuclear activities.[1163] This means that, when implementing its competences under Chapter 7 of the Euratom Treaty, the Commission has to strike a fine balance between its competence to ensure the application of safeguards to civil materials in military facilities, which falls within the scope of the Euratom Community's competences under Chapter 7, and the application of safeguards to military materials in military facilities, which is excluded from the scope of the Euratom Community's competences in respect of safeguards under the provisions of the Euratom Treaty. In addition, the Commission has exercised its competences in a broader manner than the wording in Chapter 7 of the Euratom Treaty indicates, by applying certain safeguards requirements to nuclear waste.[1164] Consequently, the Euratom Community's competences in respect of nuclear safeguards are exercised in a broader manner than the wording of the Euratom Treaty indicates.

The categorisation based on how the exercise of Euratom Community's competences corresponds to the wording of the primary legal act allows for the following conclusions. First, certain of the Commission's competences established by the Euratom Treaty have not been properly exercised by the Commission. Consequently, there is a need for the Commission to address this, either by exercising them appropriately or by explaining why this is not necessary in order to fulfil the Euratom Community's objectives and tasks under the Euratom Treaty. Second, the broad exercise of the Euratom Community's competences in respect of research, health and safety, nuclear supply and safeguards show the relevance of these competences to the European nuclear energy sector. Although the substantive law contained in the Euratom Treaty has never undergone amendment, the Euratom Community's competences in these fields have remained relevant as a result of continuous updates by means of secondary legal acts. In conclusion, in a similar manner to the conclusions reached concerning the level of regulatory detail, the broader exercise of certain of the Euratom Community's competences achieved through the use of secondary legislation shows that, despite the stagnation of the Euratom Treaty, the effective exercise of these competences has ensured the appropriate functioning of the Euratom Community.

IV THE CJEU'S INTERPRETATION OF THE EURATOM COMMUNITY'S COMPETENCES UNDER THE EURATOM TREATY

Based on the role of the CJEU in defining and delimiting the Euratom Community's competences, three groups of competences can be identified: competences that involve a high level of case-law and an active role of the Court; competences where the Court has played a confirming role in its case-law; and competences involving a low level of case-law.

1163. Judgment of 12 April 2005, *Commission v United Kingdom*, C-61/03, ECLI:EU:C:2005:210, paragraphs 32, 33 and 36.
1164. Articles 30 to 32 of Commission Regulation (Euratom) No 302/2005.

The CJEU has played an active and important role in three areas of Euratom Community competence: health and safety under Chapter 3 of the Euratom Treaty, nuclear supply under Chapter 6 and external relations under Chapter 10.

The CJEU has interpreted the provisions of the Euratom Treaty in respect of health and safety in nine cases and established that the Euratom Community has broad competences to fulfil the objectives of Chapter 3 of the Euratom Treaty.[1165] In defining the Euratom Community's competences, the Court has repeatedly taken an approach to the scope and purpose of Chapter 3 that involves giving its provisions a broad interpretation in order to ensure that they have practical effect, form a coherent whole and confer wide competences on the Commission in the field.[1166] The CJEU has also addressed the issue of whether the basic safety standards established under the Euratom Treaty have harmonising effect in the Euratom Community – i.e., whether Member States can adopt more stringent requirements in relation to radiation protection than those established by the Euratom Community – and has concluded that the uniformity of the safety standards is assured through the minimum basic safety standards and not through a harmonised basic safety standard.[1167] Furthermore, the CJEU has expanded the Euratom Community's competences in respect of health and safety to cover all types of ionising radiation, and has ruled that the purpose of Articles 30 and 31 of the Euratom Treaty is to ensure consistent and effective protection of the health of the general public against the dangers arising from ionising radiation, whatever their source.[1168] The Court has also confirmed the Euratom Community's competences in respect of emergency preparedness and response[1169] and defined the Euratom Community's competences in respect of nuclear safety, which was for a long

1165. The CJEU has defined and delimited the Euratom Community's competences in respect of health and safety under Chapter 3 of the Euratom Treaty in nine cases. Some authors are of the opinion that, over the last few decades, the CJEU has not dealt with substantive Euratom law in many cases and that most of the cases it has heard have been similar and rather unspectacular actions initiated by the Commission for a declaration that a Member State has failed to fulfil its obligations under certain Euratom directives. See S. Wolf, 'Euratom, the European Court of Justice and the Limits of Nuclear Integration in Europe', (2011) 12/8 *German Law Journal*, p. 1639. Other authors consider that the consequences of, e.g., *ČEZ*, C-115/08, are far-reaching because in such cases the Court strengthened the position of the European Atomic Energy Community (EAEC) in respect of nuclear safety. See W.-G. Schärf, 'The Temelín-Judgement of the European Court of Justice', (2010) 85 *Nuclear Law Bulletin*, p. 79.

1166. Judgment of 12 February 2015, *Parliament v Council*, C-48/14, ECLI:EU:C:2015:91, paragraph 35; judgment of 10 December 2002, 78, *Commission v Council*, C-29/99, ECLI:EU:C:2002:734, paragraphs 78 and 79; judgment of 27 October 2009, *ČEZ*, C-115/08, ECLI:EU:C:2009:660, paragraph 100; Case 187/87, *Land de Sarre v Ministre de l'Industrie*, ECLI:EU:C:1988:439, paragraph 11; judgment of 27 October 2009, *ČEZ*, C-115/08, ECLI:EU:C:2009:660, paragraphs 119 and 124.

1167. Judgment of 25 November 1992, *Commission v Belgium*, C-376/90, ECLI:EU:C:1992:457, paragraphs 19 and 27; judgment of 27 October 2009, *ČEZ*, C-115/08, ECLI:EU:C:2009:660, paragraphs 135 and 141; judgment of 4 October 1991, *Parliament v Council*, C-70/88, ECLI:EU:C:1991:373, paragraph 17.

1168. Judgment of 4 October 1991, *Parliament v Council*, C-70/88, ECLI:EU:C:1991:373, paragraphs 13 and 14; judgment of 27 October 2009, *ČEZ*, C-115/08, ECLI:EU:C:2009:660, paragraph 112.

1169. Judgment of 10 December 2002, *Commission v Council*, C-29/99, ECLI:EU:C:2002:734, paragraph 97.

time considered to be an inherent national competence of the Member States.[1170] The CJEU has stated that the Euratom Community's competences under Articles 30 and 32 of the Euratom Treaty include legislative competence to establish an authorisation system for nuclear installations, which must be applied by the Member States, but does not grant the Euratom Community competence to authorise the construction or operation of nuclear installations.[1171] This broad interpretation has resulted in secondary legal acts exercising the Euratom Community's competences in the fields of nuclear safety and the safe management of radioactive waste and spent fuel, and broader and more detailed regulation of measures for emergency preparedness and response at Euratom Community level.

The CJEU has also been active in interpreting the Euratom Community's competences under Chapter 6 of the Euratom Treaty. The Court has confirmed the relevance and mandatory nature of the Euratom Community's competences in respect of nuclear supply by emphasising the precise and binding manner of the Euratom Community's exclusive competences in this area.[1172] The Court has addressed the issue of the validity of these provisions by ruling that the fact that market conditions have made it less necessary to use the supply mechanisms laid down in the Euratom Treaty does not suffice to deprive those provisions of their mandatory character.[1173] In several cases, the Court has elaborated on the competences and role of the ESA in respect of nuclear supply. It has concluded that the ESA plays an essential role in the common supply policy and that it has broad discretion when exercising its competences in relation to decisions involving economic, commercial and nuclear policy. This discretion involves a right of option in relation to ores, source materials and special fissile materials produced in the territories of Member States, and an exclusive right to conclude contracts relating to the supply of ores, source materials and special fissile materials coming from both inside or outside the Euratom Community.[1174] The Court has addressed the issue of 'Community preference' in relation to nuclear supplies produced inside the Euratom Community and has ruled that the Euratom Treaty does not contain

1170. I. Cenevska, *The European Atomic Energy Community in the European Union Context: The 'Outsider' Within*, Leiden: Brill Nijhoff, 2016, p. 54.
1171. Judgment of 10 December 2002, *Commission v Council*, C-29/99, ECLI:EU:C:2002:734, paragraphs 82 and 89; judgment of 27 October 2009, *ČEZ*, C-115/08, ECLI:EU:C:2009:660, paragraph 102.
1172. Ruling of 14 November 1978, Ruling of the Court delivered pursuant to the third paragraph of Article 103 of the Euratom Treaty – Draft Convention of the International Atomic Energy Agency on the Physical Protection of Nuclear Materials, Facilities and Transports, Ruling 1/78, ECLI:EU:C:1978:202, paragraph 14; Judgment of 15 September 1995, *ENU v Commission*, Joined Cases T-458/93 and T-523/93, ECLI:EU:T:1995:165, paragraph 56.
1173. Judgment of 14 December 1971, *Commission v France*, C-7/71, ECLI:EU:C:1971:121, paragraphs 41 and 43; judgment of 15 September 1995, *ENU v Commission*, Joined Cases T-458/93 and T-523/93, ECLI:EU:T:1995:165, paragraph 56.
1174. Judgment of 11 March 1997, *ENU v Commission*, C-357/95 P, ECLI:EU:C:1997:144, paragraphs 6 and 45; judgment of 15 September 1995, *ENU v Commission*, joined cases T-458/93 and T-523/93, ECLI:EU:T:1995:165, paragraph 57; judgment of 22 April 1999, *Kernkraftwerke Lippe-Ems v Commission*, C-161/97 P, ECLI:EU:C:1999:193, paragraph 63; judgment of 25 February 1997, *Kernkraftwerke Lippe-Ems v Commission*, Joined Cases T-149/94 and T-181/94, ECLI:EU:T:1997:21, paragraphs 85 and 90.

any provisions that guarantee, expressly or implicitly, preferential treatment of production coming from the Euratom Community. The Court's view in this regard has been that showing a systematic Community preference for producers of nuclear ores would run counter to the objectives of the Euratom Treaty.[1175] This confirms that the Euratom Community does not need to intervene in relation to situations of oversupply in the Euratom Community. In addition, the Court has interpreted the Euratom Community's competences under Chapter 6 of the Euratom Treaty broadly by emphasising the principle of geographical diversification of supplies, which is not mentioned in the provisions of the Euratom Treaty. The CJEU has accordingly established that the geographical origin of the materials to be supplied is one of the principal elements of a supply contract and has concluded that in order to ensure the geographical diversification of external sources of supply, the Euratom Community has a competence to bar certain imports of supplies that would reduce such diversification, using its exclusive right to conclude contracts for the supply of nuclear fuels, in accordance with the Euratom Treaty.[1176] Finally, in addition to the valid, binding and exclusive nature of the Euratom Community's competences under Chapter 6 of the Euratom Treaty, the Court has ruled that until a decision is taken under Article 76 of the Euratom Treaty either to make the existing rules permanent, or to replace them with new rules, the provisions of Chapter 6 of the Euratom Treaty are to be maintained on a temporary basis.[1177]

The Court has heard few cases concerning the Euratom Community's competences in respect of external relations under Chapter 10 of the Euratom Treaty. However, the interpretative guidance that it has given in respect of the Euratom Community's competences in this area has been significant for a number of reasons. First, the Court has carried out a comparative analysis between the Euratom Community's external competences and those of the EU, and established that procedure provided for in Article 101 of the Euratom Treaty differs from the regulation of external competences under the EU law. It accordingly concluded that the Euratom Community's external competences should not be regarded as being comparable to those established in EU law.[1178] Second, the Court defined the balance between the Euratom Community's competences and the Member States' national competences in respect of external relations. It established that to the extent to which jurisdiction and powers have been conferred on the Euratom Community under the Euratom Treaty, the Member States are no longer allowed to act individually or collectively in a way which

1175. Judgment of 15 September 1995, *ENU v Commission*, Joined Cases T-458/93 and T-523/93, ECLI:EU:T:1995:165, paragraphs 64 and 65; judgment of 11 March 1997, *ENU v Commission*, C-357/95 P, ECLI:EU:C:1997:144, paragraph 46.
1176. Judgment of 22 April 1999, *Kernkraftwerke Lippe-Ems v Commission*, C-161/97 P, ECLI:EU:C:1999:193, paragraphs 62, 67 and 110; judgment of 25 February 1997, *Kernkraftwerke Lippe-Ems v Commission*, Joined Cases T-149/94 and T-181/94, ECLI:EU:T:1997:21, paragraphs 35 and 92; judgment of 15 September 1995, *ENU v Commission*, Joined Cases T-458/93 and T-523/93, ECLI:EU:T:1995:165, paragraph 68.
1177. Judgment of 14 December 1971, *Commission v France*, C7-71, ECLI:EU:C:1971:121, paragraphs 22, 26 and 28.
1178. Judgment of 9 August 1994, *France v Commission*, C-327/91, ECLI:EU:C:1994:305, paragraphs 37–39.

imposes conditions on the exercise of prerogatives of the Euratom Community.[1179] Consequently, the CJEU delimited the Euratom Community's competences, by establishing that once an external relationship creates obligations that fall within the scope of the Euratom Community's competences, the power to enter into this external relationship belongs to the Community.

Common features of the second group of competences include fewer cases having been heard by the CJEU, and the Court's focus in those cases being primarily on confirming the Euratom Community's competences as established in the provisions of the Euratom Treaty. This group comprises competences in respect of investments under Chapter 4 of the Euratom Treaty, Joint Undertakings under Chapter 5, safeguards under Chapter 7, property ownership under Chapter 8 and the nuclear common market under Chapter 9.

In respect of investments under Chapter 4 of the Euratom Treaty, the CJEU has confirmed that competences under Chapter 4 of the Euratom Treaty have the objective of promoting or coordinating investments in nuclear field.[1180] The Court has also confirmed the Euratom Community's competences as they are established in the Euratom Treaty, i.e., by opposing the Commission's broad interpretation of the provisions of the Treaty and by concluding that the Commission does not have the implicit competence to adopt a regulation establishing procedures for the examination of investment projects under Chapter 4.[1181] In respect of Chapter 5 of the Euratom Treaty, the CJEU has confirmed that the Joint Undertaking established by the Council under Chapter 5 is not an institution of the Euratom Community and does not form part of the Euratom Community.[1182] Regarding the Euratom Community's competences in relation both to safeguards under Chapter 7 of the Euratom Treaty and property ownership under Chapter 8, the CJEU has emphasised the important role of these competences under the Euratom Treaty. In respect of safeguards, the Court has underlined their broad purpose in the context of achieving the Euratom Community's objectives and tasks[1183] and has stressed the importance of the Commission's competences to impose sanctions to ensure compliance with the provisions of Chapter 7.[1184] Regarding property ownership, the Court has emphasised the Euratom Community's ultimate competence to own all special fissile materials in the Euratom Community, and the right of use in relation to special fissile materials held by Member States,

1179. Ruling of 14 November 1978, Ruling of the Court delivered pursuant to the third paragraph of Article 103 of the Euratom Treaty – Draft Convention of the International Atomic Energy Agency on the Physical Protection of Nuclear Materials, Facilities and Transports, Ruling 1/78, ECLI:EU:C:1978:202, paragraphs 32 and 33.

1180. Judgment of 6 September 2012, *Parliament v Council*, C-490/10, ECLI:EU:C:2012:525, paragraph 84.

1181. Judgment of 17 September 2007, *France v Commission*, T-240/04, ECLI:EU:T:2007:290.

1182. Order of 16 December 1994, *Altmann and Others v Commission*, Case T-177/94, ECLI:EU:T:1994:314, paragraphs 38 and 44.

1183. Ruling of 14 November 1978, Ruling of the Court delivered pursuant to the third paragraph of Article 103 of the Euratom Treaty – Draft Convention of the International Atomic Energy Agency on the Physical Protection of Nuclear Materials, Facilities and Transports, Ruling 1/78, ECLI:EU:C:1978:202, paragraphs 19 to 21.

1184. Judgment of 21 January 1993, *Advanced Nuclear Fuels v Commission*, C-308/90, ECLI:EU:C:1993:23, paragraphs 20, 21 and 26.

persons or undertakings, under a prerequisite that they comply with the requirements established in relation to nuclear supply and safeguards in the Treaty.[1185] In other words, the Court has confirmed the Euratom Community's competences in respect of nuclear safeguards and property ownership, as they are defined under the Euratom Treaty. The Court has also defined the Euratom Community's competences under Chapter 9 of the Euratom Treaty, by confirming that the structure of the nuclear common market is based on the same legal concepts as the general common market,[1186] and that the Euratom Community's competences in respect of the nuclear common market are weaker than its competences in respect of nuclear supply policy,[1187] which marks a clear difference between these two regulatory fields under the Euratom Treaty.

The group of competences in respect of which there has been a low level of CJEU case-law include the Euratom Community's competences in respect of research under Chapter 1 of the Euratom Treaty and dissemination of information under Chapter 2. The cases that have been heard by the Court in respect of research have principally focused on the Euratom Community's horizontal competences. The CJEU has interpreted the provisions of Chapter 1 of the Euratom Treaty twice, but the case-law did not have a significant effect on interpretation of the Euratom Community's competences in respect of research under the Euratom Treaty.[1188] In relation to the dissemination of information, the CJEU has once referred to existence of Articles 24 to 28 of the Euratom Treaty when determining the Euratom Treaty's application to military activities. The Court has not interpreted the provisions of Chapter 2 of the Euratom Treaty and has not therefore influenced the Euratom Community's competences under Chapter 2 of the Euratom Treaty.

The classification, based on how active the CJEU has been in interpreting and defining the Euratom Community's competences, is essential in understanding the relevance of the Euratom Community's competences under the Euratom Treaty. The substantive law of the Euratom Treaty has never been changed, and analysis of the role of the Court allows one to identify the regulatory fields in which the Euratom Community's competences have evolved based on the interpretative approaches taken by the Court, as well as those in which the Euratom Community's competences have remained unchanged. In conclusion, the stagnation of the Euratom Treaty has not

1185. Judgment of 4 June 2015, *Kernkraftwerke Lippe-Ems*, C-5/14, ECLI:EU:C:2015:354, paragraph 96; Ruling of 14 November 1978, Ruling of the Court delivered pursuant to the third paragraph of Article 103 of the Euratom Treaty – Draft Convention of the International Atomic Energy Agency on the Physical Protection of Nuclear Materials, Facilities and Transports, Ruling 1/78, ECLI:EU:C:1978:202, paragraph 27.
1186. Judgment of 4 June 2015, *Kernkraftwerke Lippe-Ems*, C-5/14, ECLI:EU:C:2015:354, paragraph 86.
1187. Ruling of 14 November 1978, Ruling of the Court delivered pursuant to the third paragraph of Article 103 of the Euratom Treaty – Draft Convention of the International Atomic Energy Agency on the Physical Protection of Nuclear Materials, Facilities and Transports, Ruling 1/78, ECLI:EU:C:1978:202, paragraph 18.
1188. Judgment of 24 October 1989, *Commission v Council*, C-16/88, ECLI:EU:C:1989:397; Judgment of 20 October 1977, *Jänsch v Commission*, C-5/76, ECLI:EU:C:1977:163.

hindered the evolution of the Euratom Community's competences, particularly in respect of health and safety, supply and external relations.

V EVALUATION OF THE STAGNATION OF THE EURATOM TREATY

The Euratom Treaty was adopted more than sixty years ago. While the EEC has evolved through decades into the legal entity of the EU, the Euratom Community and the substantive law contained in the Euratom Treaty has never been amended. Stagnation of primary substantive law is a key legal feature that distinguishes the Euratom Treaty from the EU Treaties.[1189] Due to the need for consensus in decision-making and the political sensitivity of the issue, it thus appears unlikely that the substantive law of the Euratom Treaty will be subject to major reform in the short or mid-term.[1190] Therefore, an overarching objective of this study has been to analyse and evaluate the effects of the stagnation of this primary legal act on the overall legal system of the Euratom Community, based on the features of the Euratom Community's competences: their the scope and content, their exercise and the CJEU's role in respect of them. The purpose of the final section of this study is to determine whether the Euratom Treaty can be regarded as a living Treaty and how its stagnation has affected the Euratom Community's *acquis*.

The analysis of the scope and content of the Euratom Community's competences has shown that the Euratom Treaty comprises provisions establishing a simplified Treaty amendment procedure, which can be applied if new circumstances so require. The existence of such provisions in a primary legal act shows that the Euratom Treaty has incorporated flexibilities to be able to adapt to changing circumstances in a timely manner. The existence of special Euratom Treaty amendment provisions in respect of supply, safeguards and property ownership shows that the founders of the Euratom Community regarded it as being of great importance that the Euratom Community's competences have capabilities of changing, evolving and adjusting to the changing dynamics of the European nuclear industry – an attribute that may be characterised as the Euratom Treaty's 'ability to learn'.[1191] The regulation of the Euratom Community's competences also demonstrates that the level of regulatory detail they entail is, on the whole, in line with the Euratom Community's objectives and tasks in respect of the areas of regulation under Title 2 of the Euratom Treaty. Only the Euratom Community's competences in respect of dissemination of information under Chapter 2 of the Euratom Treaty may be considered to be excessively detailed in view of the Euratom

1189. Some authors define this feature as the Euratom Treaty's immunity to any amendments or changes. See J. Handrlica, 'The Splendid Durability of the Provisional: A Tribute to Euratom', (2018) 14/14 *Croatian Yearbook of European Law & Policy*, p. 163.
1190. W. Kilb, 'The European Atomic Energy Community and Its Primary and Secondary Law', in *International Nuclear Law: History, Evolution and Outlook, 10th Anniversary of the International School of Nuclear Law*, Paris: OECD, 2010, p. 85.
1191. N. P. Serrano, 'Wakening the Serpent: Reflections on the Possible Modification of the Euratom Treaty', (2006) 1/1 *International Journal of Nuclear Law*, pp. 13–14; I. Cenevska, *The European Atomic Energy Community in the European Union Context: The 'Outsider' Within*, Leiden: Brill Nijhoff, 2016, p. 70.

Community's tasks in this regard.[1192] Despite the stagnancy of the Euratom Treaty and the fact that the substantive law of the Euratom Treaty has never undergone amendment from the adoption of this primary legal act, the regulation of the Euratom Community's competences under the Euratom Treaty is nonetheless appropriate to the tasks established in respect of the Euratom Community and hence continues to ensure the appropriate functioning of the Euratom Community. Both the Euratom Treaty's ability to learn and adapt to the changing circumstances, and the wording of the Treaty, which remains appropriate to fulfil the Euratom Community's objectives and tasks, permit the conclusion that the Euratom Treaty has not been hindered by the stagnation of the substantive law and may be considered as a living Treaty.

The evaluation of the regulation of competences in the primary legal act is an important indicator in assessing the stagnation of the Euratom Treaty, but the exercise of the Euratom Community's competences through secondary legislation, the CJEU's role in defining and delimiting the Euratom Community's competences, and the correlation between these two features, are the cornerstones in determining the implications of the stagnation of the Euratom Treaty.

Both the quantitative and the qualitative aspects of exercise of the Euratom Community's competences through secondary legislation are significant when evaluating the effects of stagnation of primary law. Active and broad exercise of the Euratom Community's competences in certain fields is indicative of the importance of those fields, which means in turn that the provisions of the Euratom Treaty relating to them are also of significance. The Euratom Community's competences are primarily exercised, both in quantitative and qualitative terms, through secondary legislation, which either exercises these competences in accordance with the wording of the Euratom Treaty or in a broader manner. The highest level of exercise – both in quantitative and qualitative terms – and the broadest exercise of the Community's competences in relation to the wording of the Euratom Treaty is in the field of health and safety. The overall lowest level of exercise is in the field of dissemination of information, in which the level of exercise is low in quantitative terms and the competences are exercised in the secondary legal acts in a narrower manner than the wording of the Euratom Treaty indicates.

The same tendencies can be seen in relation to the CJEU's role in defining and delimiting the Euratom Community's competences. Health and safety, nuclear supply policy and external relations are the areas in which the Court has been most active in expanding the Euratom Community's competences. This indicates the importance of these areas in the European nuclear sector and the relevance of the Euratom Treaty's provisions in these fields. The CJEU has been most passive in relation to research and dissemination of information, and its case-law in these areas has not affected the Euratom Community's competences.

The interconnection between the exercise of the Euratom Community's competences and the CJEU's case-law reveals the continuously high relevance of the Euratom Community's competences in some fields and its low relevance, with no adaptation to

1192. Article 2(a) of the Euratom Treaty.

changing circumstances, in others. This study has shown that the Court' case-law concerning health and safety has led to a broadening of the Euratom Community's competences by expanding them to cover nuclear safety and instilling a degree of flexibility to regulate the level of harmonisation in secondary legislation. Furthermore, the Court has confirmed the Euratom Community's competences in respect of emergency preparedness and response. The active role played by the CJEU has had a great effect on the secondary legislation, as it has led to adoption of directives covering nuclear safety, the safe management of radioactive waste and spent fuel, as well as more detailed regulation of emergency preparedness and response. The field of health and safety offers proof of the Euratom Treaty being a living Treaty, since the need to adapt to changing circumstances and to respond to the need for better regulation concerning protection from the hazardous effects of ionising radiation has transformed the general wordings of Articles 31 and 32 of the Euratom Treaty into a systematic legal framework for health and safety.

External relations under Chapter 10 constitutes another field that demonstrates the dynamic aspects of the Euratom Treaty. The handful of articles that this chapter contains have evolved into extensive exercise of the Euratom Community's competences through the conclusion of bilateral agreements, participation in multilateral projects and accession to international conventions. The CJEU has played an important role here by continuously evaluating whether and how the Euratom Community's internal competences and external powers match, and by determining whether the Euratom Community has competences to enter into external obligations, based on its internal competences.

Nuclear safeguards may also be mentioned in this context. Chapter 7 of the Euratom Treaty lays down clear Euratom Community functions: to carry out inspections, initiate infringement procedures and impose sanctions. However, these competences have been exercised in a broader manner than the wording of the Euratom Treaty indicates, by making safeguards provisions applicable to civil materials in military installations. The Court has confirmed that the Euratom Community's competences are wider than the wording of the Euratom Treaty indicates, which also confirms that the stagnation of these provisions has not affected the development of the legal framework of the Euratom Community in respect of safeguards.

In conclusion, in these three fields, the stagnation of the Euratom Treaty has had no significant effect on the development of the legal framework of the Euratom Community.

In certain areas of competence under the Euratom Treaty – particularly investment, Joint Undertakings and the nuclear common market – the Euratom Community's legal framework has not evolved as has been the case in respect of health and safety or external relations, but in respect of which the balance between the exercise of competences and the case-law leads one to conclude that the stagnation of the Euratom Treaty has not had a major effect on the Euratom Community's *acquis*. In these three areas, the Euratom Community's competences have generally been exercised in accordance with the wording of the Euratom Treaty[1193] and the case-law relating to them has primarily focused on confirming the Euratom Community's competences as established in the Euratom Treaty. On the one hand, the Euratom Community's competences in respect of research have been exercised broadly through secondary legal acts, but there is very limited case-law in relation to them. On the other hand, while the Euratom Community's competences in respect of supply have been exercised to a limited extent, the Court has been active in defining and delimiting them in its case-law.

At this point it is worth revisiting the notion highlighted in the introduction of this study that some authors have implied that the provisions governing nuclear supply under Chapter 6 of the Euratom Treaty are obsolete.[1194] The analysis set out in this study shows that it does not suffice purely to assess the exercise of a certain competence in order to determine the relevance or obsoleteness of the Euratom Treaty's provisions. Instead, it is necessary to take a systematic approach in which all three elements of a competence are evaluated: its regulation, its exercise and its interpretation in case-law. Consequently, as the CJEU has been active in defining and confirming the importance of Euratom Community's competences in respect of common nuclear supply policy, the conclusion that these provisions are obsolete may be considered doubtful. The Euratom Community's competences in respect of property ownership under Chapter 8 of the Euratom Treaty have not been exercised through secondary legal acts, but their content indicates scope for direct application of these provisions. Indeed, the Court has confirmed and emphasised that these competences constitute the ultimate power to own all special fissile materials in the Euratom Community.

In conclusion, these three areas of competence have shown adaptability in the face of the stagnation of the Euratom Treaty. In the case of research, this has occurred through secondary legal acts, and in the cases of supply and property ownership it has occurred as a result of the Court's interpretative approach.

The Euratom Community's competences in respect of dissemination of information have been characterised in this study by a too high level of regulatory detail given the Euratom Treaty's tasks in this area, by a low level of exercise and scant case-law. This combination of features leads one to the conclusion that the Euratom Community's competences in this area have been most affected by the stagnation of the Euratom Treaty. The relevance of the provisions of Chapter 2 of the Euratom Treaty in preventing restrictive practices from impeding the free flow of nuclear information has decreased over time, and the lack of secondary legislation and case-law through which to interpret these provisions has made it difficult for this regulatory field to survive the changing conditions affecting the European nuclear sector. In the absence of the possibility to utilise a simplified amendment procedure, these provisions are frozen in

1193. Except for Articles 40 and 98 of the Euratom Treaty, which have been exercised in a narrower manner than the wording of the Euratom Treaty indicates. For further discussion of this issue, see Chapter 4 Section 02 on investments and Chapter 9 Section 02 on the nuclear common market.
1194. See Chapter I Section A of this study on origin and stagnation of the Euratom Treaty.

time, and thus stand as evidence of stagnation not only of the Euratom Treaty, but also of the entire field of dissemination of information in the Euratom Community.

Through systematic analysis of the scope, content and exercise of specific substantive Euratom Community competences under Title II of the Euratom Treaty, and of the case-law concerning them, this study has identified the risks of generalisation when evaluating the relevance or obsoleteness of the provisions of the Euratom Treaty and the need for a systematic approach when evaluating the effects of stagnation of the Euratom Treaty on the *acquis* of the Euratom Community.

The overall conclusion of the study is that, except for the dissemination of information, the stagnation of the Euratom Treaty and the fact that the substantive law contained in this primary legal act has never undergone amendment has not had a significant effect on the Euratom Community's system of competences. Some authors argue that the Euratom Treaty is in need of 'rejuvenation',[1195] but this study has established that, in general, the Euratom Community and its competences have stood the test of time.[1196] Over the years these competences have evolved and adapted through secondary legal acts and the case-law of the CJEU to the changing circumstances and shifting role of nuclear energy within European energy policy.

1195. I. Cenevska, *The European Atomic Energy Community in the European Union Context: The 'Outsider' Within*, Leiden: Brill Nijhoff, 2016, p. 31.

1196. J. Grunwald, 'Peaceful Uses of Nuclear Energy under Euratom Law', in J. L. Black-Branch and D. Fleck (eds), *Nuclear Non-Proliferation in International Law, Volume III: Legal Aspects of the Use of Nuclear Energy for Peaceful Purposes*, The Hague: Asser Press, 2016, p. 211. N. P. Serrano labels the Euratom Community as a 'serpent'. See N. P. Serrano, 'Wakening the Serpent: Reflections on the Possible Modification of the Euratom Treaty', (2006) 1/1 *International Journal of Nuclear Law*. P. M. Barnes defines the Euratom Community as a 'phoenix'. See P. M. Barnes, 'The Resurrection of the Euratom Treaty: Contributing to the Legal and Constitutional Framework for Secure, Competitive and Sustainable Energy in the European Union', in T. Etty and H. Somsen (eds), *The Yearbook of European Environmental Law*, Volume 8, Oxford: Oxford University Press, 2008. One might agree with J. Handrlica that the Euratom Community is a 'true chameleon'. See J. Handrlica, 'The Splendid Durability of the Provisional: A Tribute to Euratom', (2018) 14/14 *Croatian Yearbook of European Law & Policy*.

Glossary

Competence	The ability or capacity of a natural, legal person or institution to do something that is legally binding or has some legally valid effect.[1197]
EU Treaties	The Treaty of the European Union and the Treaty on the Functioning of the European Union.[1198]
Euratom Treaty	The Treaty establishing the European Atomic Energy Community.[1199]
Euratom Community	The European Atomic Energy Community.
Nuclear fuel cycle	All operations associated with the production of nuclear energy.[1200]
Radiation protection	Protection of people from the harmful effects of exposure to ionising radiation, including the means for achieving this, and the means for preventing accidents and for mitigating the consequences of accidents if they do occur.[1201]

1197. G. Conway, *EU Law*, London and New York: Routledge, 2015, p. 259.
1198. Consolidated version of the Treaty on the Functioning of the European Union, OJ C 326, 26.10.2012, pp. 47-390.
1199. Consolidated version of the Treaty establishing the European Atomic Energy Community, OJ C 327, 26.10.2012, pp. 1-107.
1200. International Atomic Energy Agency, *IAEA Safety Glossary. Terminology Used in Nuclear Safety and Radiation Protection*, Vienna: IAEA, 2016, p. 114.
1201. International Atomic Energy Agency, *IAEA Safety Glossary. Terminology Used in Nuclear Safety and Radiation Protection*, Vienna: IAEA, 2016, pp. 131-132.

Bibliography

Books and Reports

Azoulai L. (ed.), The Question of Competence in the European Union, Oxford: Oxford University Press, 2014.

Azoulai L., 'Introduction: The Question of Competence', in L. Azoulai (ed.), The Question of Competence in the European Union, Oxford: Oxford University Press, 2014.

Barnes P. M. and Leverkusen B., The Politics of Nuclear Energy in the European Union. Framing the Discourse: Actors, Positions and Dynamics, Opladen, Berlin and Toronto: Budrich Publishers, 2018.

Barnes P. M., 'The Resurrection of the Euratom Treaty: Contributing to the Legal and Constitutional Framework for Secure, Competitive and Sustainable Energy in the European Union', in T. Etty and H. Somsen (eds), The Yearbook of European Environmental Law, Volume 8, Oxford: Oxford University Press, 2008.

Bouquet A., 'Which Competition Rules for Nuclear Energy in a (Progressively) Liberalised European Market Environment?', in INLA/AIDN (ed.) Nuclear Inter Jura 2007: Proceedings - Actes du Congrès, 1-4 Octobre 2007, Bruxelles: Emilie Bruylant, 2008.

Bruckner T., Bashmakov I. A., Mulugetta Y., Chum H., de la Vega Navarro A., Edmonds J., Faaij A., Fungtammasan B., Garg A., Hertwich E., Honnery D., Infield D., Kainuma M., Khennas S., Kim S., Nimir H. B., Riahi K., Strachan N., Wiser R. and Zhang X., '2014: Energy Systems', in: Climate Change 2014: Mitigation of Climate Change. Contribution of Working Group III to the Fifth Assessment Report of the Intergovernmental Panel on Climate Change, United Kingdom and New York: Cambridge University Press, 2014.

Cenevska I., The European Atomic Energy Community in the European Union Context: The 'Outsider' Within, Leiden: Brill Nijhoff, 2016.

Ciccarello S. and Lechner S., 'Euratom Safeguards System', in L. Maiani, S. Abousahl and W. Plastino (eds), 'International Cooperation for Enhancing Nuclear Safety, Security, Safeguards and Non-proliferation–60 Years of IAEA and EURATOM',

Proceedings of the XX Edoardo Amaldi Conference October 9–10, 2017, Accademia Nazionale dei Lincei, Rome, Italy: Springer-Verlag Berlin and Heidelberg GmbH & Co. K, 2018.

Conway G., EU Law, London and New York: Routledge, 2015.

Cornish P., Van Ham P. and Krause J. (eds) 'Europe and the Challenge of Proliferation', Chaillot Papers 24, Paris: Institute for Security Studies of WEU, 1996.

Craig P. and de Búrca G., EU Law: Text, Cases and Materials, 5th edn, Oxford: Oxford University Press, 2011.

Craig P., 'Competence and Member State Autonomy: Causality, Consequence and Legitimacy', in H.-W. Micklitz and B. De Witte (eds), The European Court of Justice and the Autonomy of the Member States, Antwerp: Intersentia, 2012.

de Waele H., Legal Dynamics of EU External Relations, Antwerp: Springer, 2017.

Gaudet M., Euratom, London: Pergamon Press 1959.

Garzaniti L., 'Competition Law in the Nuclear Sector', in INLA/AIDN (ed.), Nuclear Inter Jura 2007: Proceedings - Actes du Congrès, 1–4 Octobre 2007, Bruxelles: Emilie Bruylant, 2008.

Groussat X. and Bogojević S., 'Subsidiarity as a Procedural Safeguard of Federalism', in L. Azoulai (ed.), The Question of Competence in the European Union, Oxford: Oxford University Press, 2014.

Grunwald J., 'Peaceful Uses of Nuclear Energy under Euratom Law', in J. L. Black-Branch and D. Fleck (eds), Nuclear Non-Proliferation in International Law, Volume III: Legal Aspects of the Use of Nuclear Energy for Peaceful Purposes, The Hague: Asser Press, 2016.

Guzzetti L., A Brief History of European Union Research Policy, Brussels: OOPEC, 1995.

Handrlica J., 'Between the Public and Private Responsibility for the Management of Spent Nuclear Fuel and Radioactive Waste in EU', in B. Delvaux, M. Hunt and K. Talus (eds), *EU Energy Law and Policy Issues*, Volume 4, Cambridge – Antwerp – Portland: Intersentia, 2014.

Heffron R. J., Deconstructing Energy Law and Policy: The Case of Nuclear Energy, Edinburgh: Edinburgh University Press, 2015.

International Atomic Energy Agency, IAEA Safety Glossary. Terminology Used in Nuclear Safety and Radiation Protection, Vienna: IAEA, 2016.

International Energy Agency, Nuclear Power in a Clean Energy System, Paris: IEA, May 2019.

Intergovernmental Panel on Climate Change, Global Warming of 1.5 °C, An IPCC Special Report on the impacts of global warming of 1.5°C above pre-industrial levels and related global greenhouse gas emission pathways, in the context of strengthening the global response to the threat of climate change, sustainable development, and efforts to eradicate poverty, IPCC: in Press, 2019.

Kilb W., 'The European Atomic Energy Community and its Primary and Secondary Law', in International Nuclear Law: History, Evolution and Outlook, 10th Anniversary of the International School of Nuclear Law, Paris: OECD/NEA, 2010.

Kilb W., 'The Nuclear Safeguards Regime of Euratom: A Regional Cornerstone of the Verification of Non-Proliferation Obligations in the European Union', in J. L.

Black-Branch and D. Fleck (eds), Nuclear Non-Proliferation in International Law, Volume II: Verification and Compliance, the Hague: Asser Press, 2016.

Kilb W., 'The Nuclear Safeguards System of the European Atomic Energy Community (Euratom)', in C. Raetzke (ed.), Nuclear Law in the EU and Beyond, Baden-Baden: Nomos, 2014.

Krämer L., EU Environmental Law, London: Sweet & Maxwell, 2011.

Kramish A., The Peaceful Atom in Foreign Policy, New York: Harper & Row/Council on Foreign Relations, 1963.

Larik J., Worldly Ambitions: Foreign Policy Objectives in European Constitutional Law, Florence: EUI, 2013.

Millet F.-X., 'The Respect for National Constitutional Identity in the European Legal Space: An Approach to Federalism as Constitutionalism', in L Azoulai (ed.), The Question of Competence in the European Union, Oxford: Oxford University Press, 2014.

Monnet J., Mémoires, Paris: Fayard, 1976.

Moravcsik A., The Choice for Europe: Social Purpose and State Power from Messina to Maastricht, Ithaca, NY: Cornell University Press, 1998.

Patel B. and Chare P., 'Fifty Years of Safeguards under the Euratom Treaty – A Regulatory Review', in G. Janssens-Maenhout (ed.), Nuclear Safeguards and Non-Proliferation, Luxembourg: Office for Official Publications of the European Communities, 2009.

Pescatore P., The Law of Integration: Emergence of a New Phenomenon in International Relations, Based on the Experience of the European Communities, Leiden: Sijthoof, 1974.

Piebalgs A. (European Commissioner in Charge of Energy) 'Keynote Speech', in INLA/AIDN (ed.), Nuclear Inter Jura 2007: Proceedings – Actes du Congrès, 1–4 Octobre 2007, Bruxelles: Emilie Bruylant, 2008.

Polach J. G., Euratom: Its Background, Issues and Economic Implications, Dobbs Ferry, NY: Oceana Publications Inc., 1964.

Ptasekaite R., 'Competition Law and Nuclear Regulation: European Perspective', in B. Delvaux, M. Hunt and K. Talus (eds), EU Energy Law and Policy Issues, Volume 4, Cambridge – Antwerp – Portland: Intersentia, 2014.

Ptasekaite R., 'Continuous Improvement of Nuclear Safety', in C. Raetzke (ed.), Nuclear Law and Beyond, Baden-Baden: Nomos, 2014.

Ptasekaite R., 'The Euratom Treaty v. Treaties of the European Union: Limits of Competence and Interaction', Swedish Radiation Safety Authority Report SSM2011:32, Solna: SSM, 2011.

Report by Working group III on Legal Certainty in International Nuclear Trade, in Lamm V. (ed.), Nuclear Inter Jura 2001: Proceedings of the 15th Nuclear Inter Jura Congress 'Nuclear Law under the Sign of Safety and Confidence', Budapest: Archaeolingua, 2002.

Reyners P., 'Liability Problems Associated with the Current Patchwork Nuclear Liability Regime within the EU Member States', in N. Pelzer (ed.), European Nuclear Liability Law in a Process of Change, Baden-Baden: Nomos, 2010.

Schütze R., From Dual to Cooperative Federalism: The Changing Structure of European Law, Oxford: Oxford University Press, 2009.

Stoiber C., Baer A., Pelzer N. and Tonhauser W., Handbook of Nuclear Law, Vienna: International Atomic Energy Agency, 2003.

Södersten A., Euratom at the Crossroads, Cheltenham, Northampton: Edward Elgar Publishing Limited, 2018.

The OECD Nuclear Energy Agency, 'Nuclear New Build: Insights into Financing and Project Management', No. 7195, Paris: OECD/NEA, 2015.

Timmermans C., 'ECJ Doctrines on Competences', in L. Azoulai (ed.), The Question of Competence in the European Union, Oxford: Oxford University Press, 2014.

von Bogdandy A. and Bast J., 'The Federal Order of Competences', in A. von Bogdandy and J. Bast (eds), Principles of European Constitutional Law, Oxford: Hart Publishing, 2011.

Weatherill S., 'The Constitutional Context of (Ever-Wider) Policy-Making', in E. Jones, A. Menon, and S. Weatherill (eds), The Oxford Handbook of the European Union, Oxford: Oxford University Press, 2012.

Articles, Working Papers Etc.

Allen D., 'The Euratom Treaty, Chapter VI: New Hope Or False Dawn?', (1983) 20 Common Market Law Review.

Barnes P. M., 'Nuclear Safety for Nuclear Electricity – The Search for a Solid Legal Basis for Nuclear Safety in an Enlarged European Union', (2003) 45 Managerial Law.

Bermann G. A., 'Taking Subsidiarity Seriously: Federalism in the European Community and the United States', (1994) 94 Colombia Law Review.

Blohm-Hieber U., 'The Radioactive Waste Directive: A Necessary Step in the Management of Spent Fuel and Radioactive Waste in the European Union', (2011) 88 Nuclear Law Bulletin.

Bouquet A., 'How Current Are Euratom Provisions on Nuclear Supply and Ownership in View of the European Union's Enlargement?', (2001) 68 Nuclear Law Bulletin.

Cameron P. D., 'The Revival of Nuclear Power: An Analysis of the Legal Implications', (2007) 19/1 Journal of Environmental Law.

Cenevska I., 'Protection of the Health of Workers and the General Public under the Euratom Treaty and the EU Environmental Policy – The Ratio between Human Health Protection and Environmental Protection', (2012) 21 European Energy and Environmental Law Review.

Cenevska I., 'The European Parliament and the European Atomic Energy Community: A Legitimacy Crisis?', (2010) 35/3 European Law Review.

Char N. L. and Csik B. J., 'Nuclear Power Development: History and Outlook', (1987) 29/3 IAEA Bulletin.

Circolo A., Hamulak O., 'Euratom and Brexit: Could the United Kingdom Maintain One Foot in the European Union? Current Scenarios and Future Prospects of British Withdrawal from the EAEC', (2018) 18/2 International and Comparative Law Review.

Conway G., 'Conflicts of Competence Norms in EU Law and the Legal Reasoning of the ECJ', (2010) 11/9 German Law Journal.

Cusack T. F., 'A Tale of Two Treaties', (2003) 40 Common Market Law Review.

Dashwood A., 'The Limits of European Community Powers', (1996) 21/2 European Law Review.

Drupady I. M., 'Emerging Nuclear Vendors in the Newcomer Export Market: Strategic Considerations', (2019) 12 Journal of World Energy Law and Business.

Efron R. and Nanes A. S., 'The Common Market and Euratom Treaties: Supranationality and the Integration of Europe', (1957) 6 International and Comparative Law Quarterly.

Emmerechts S., 'Environmental Law and Nuclear Law: A Growing Symbiosis', (2008) 82 Nuclear Law Bulletin.

'Energy Files. Brexit Implications for the Energy Sector – State of Play', (2017) 7/2 European Energy Journal.

Erhag T., 'Är kärnavfall ett bekymmer för EU eller medlemsstaterna? – om kärnavfallsfrågan och principen om nationellt ansvar i EG-fördraget och Euratomfördraget', (2007) 7/1 CERGU Working Papers Series.

Hahn H. J., 'Control under the Euratom Compact', (1958) 7 American Journal of Comparative Law.

Hahn H. J., 'Euratom: The Conception of an International Personality', (1958) 71/6 Harvard Law Review.

Handrlica J., 'Euratom Powers in the Field of Nuclear Liability Revised', (2010) 3/1 International Journal of Nuclear Law.

Handrlica J., 'From the Front Lines of International Nuclear Law: Looking Back at the 'Nuclear Inter Jura' Congress, held in Abu Dhabi, United Arab Emirates', (2019) 12 Journal of World Energy Law and Business.

Handrlica J., 'Harmonisation of Nuclear Liability in the European Union: Challenges, Options and Limits', (2009) 84 Nuclear Law Bulletin.

Handrlica J., 'Nuclear Law Revisited as an Academic Discipline', (2019) 12 Journal of World Energy Law and Business.

Handrlica J., 'Nuclear Liability Conventions and Decommissioning: Exclusion Provisions Revisited', (2018) 11 Journal of World Energy Law and Business.

Handrlica J., 'The Politics of Nuclear Energy in the European Union. Framing the Discourse: Actors, Positions and Dynamics', (2019) 37/4 Journal of Energy & Natural Resources Law.

Handrlica J., 'The Splendid Durability of the Provisional: A Tribute to Euratom', (2018) 14/14 Croatian Yearbook of European Law & Policy.

Handrlica J., 'Transportable Nuclear Power Plants: An Enigma of International Nuclear Liability Law', (2019) 6 Journal of World Energy Law and Business.

Hay P. H., 'Patent Aspects of Domestic Law, EURATOM, and the International Atomic Energy Agency', (1958) 56/5 Michigan Law Review.

Heffron R. J. and Talus K., 'The Development of Energy Law in the 21st Century: A Paradigm Shift?', (2016) 9 Journal of World Energy Law and Business.

Heffron R. J., Ashley S. F. and Nuttall W. J., 'The Global Nuclear Liability Regime Post Fukushima Daiichi', (2016) 90 Progress in Nuclear Energy.

Knapp V. and Pevec D., 'Promises and Limitations of Nuclear Fission Energy in Combating Climate Change', (2018) 120 Energy Policy.

Kobia R., 'The EU and Non-Proliferation: Need for a Quantum Leap', (2008) 81 Nuclear Law Bulletin.

Koutrakos P., 'Case C-29/99 Commission v Council (re: Nuclear Safety Convention)', (2004) 41 Common Market Law Review.

Lamm V., 'Reflections on the Development of International Nuclear Law', (2017) 99 Nuclear law Bulletin.

Lauterpacht E., 'Aspects of the Administration of International Justice', (1991) 9 Hersch Lauterpacht Memorial Lectures Series.

Lierman S. and Veuchelen L., 'The Optimisation Approach of ALARA in Nuclear Practice: An Early Application of the Precautionary Principle? Scientific Uncertainty Versus Legal Uncertainty and Its Role in Tort Law', (2006) 15/4 European Environmental Law Review.

Lindroos A., 'The Role of Euratom in the Non-Proliferation Regime', (1997) 8 Finnish Yearbook of International Law.

Lucet F. P., 'Conditions and Possibilities for Financing New Nuclear Power Plants', (2019) 12 Journal of World Energy Law and Business.

Mallard G., 'Can the Euratom Treaty Inspire the Middle East? The Political Promises of Regional Nuclear Communities', (2018) 15/3 Non-proliferation Review.

Mathijsen P., 'Problems Connected with the Creation of Euratom', (1961) 26/3 Law and Contemporary Problems.

Mathijsen P., 'Some Legal Aspects of Euratom', (1965–1966) 3 Common Market Law Review.

Meuwese A. and Popelier P., 'Legal Implications of Better Regulation: A Special Issue', (2011) 17 European Public Law.

Molodstova E., 'Nuclear Energy and Environmental Protection: Responses of International Law', (1994) 12/1 Pace Environmental Law Review.

Nanes A., 'The Evolution of Euratom', (1957–1958) 13/1 International Journal.

Prechal S., 'Competence Creep and General Principles of Law', (2010) 3/1 Review of European Administrative Law.

Ptasekaite R., 'The Role of the Regulator: Nuclear Safety and Nuclear Safety Culture', (2013) 1 Nuclear Law and Policy.

Schärf W.-G., 'The Temelín-Judgement of the European Court of Justice', (2010) 85 Nuclear Law Bulletin.

Scheinmann L., 'Euratom: Nuclear Integration in Europe', (1967) 563 International Conciliation.

Schleicher H. W., 'Nuclear Safeguards in the European Community: A Regional Approach', (1980) 22 IAEA Bulletin.

Schutze R., 'Lisbon and the Federal Order of Competences: A Prospective Analysis', (2008) 33/5 European Law Review.

Serrano N. P., 'Wakening the Serpent: Reflections on the Possible Modification of the Euratom Treaty', (2006) 1/1 International Journal of Nuclear Law.

Smith D. D., 'The European Atomic Energy Community (Euratom): The Limits of Supranationalism', (1970) 1 California Western International Law Journal.

Sousa Ferro M., 'Competition Law and the Nuclear Sector: An EU Outlook', (2010) 86 Nuclear Law Bulletin.

Spaak T., 'Norms That Confer Competence', (2003) 16/1 Ratio Juris.

Steiger H., 'An Evaluation of Legal Development on a Regional Basis: The Search for European Unity', (1961) 22 Ohio State Law Journal.

Södersten A., 'Brexit, Euratom and Nuclear Proliferation', (2016) 98 Nuclear Law Bulletin.

Södersten A., 'The EU and Nuclear Safety: Challenges Old and New', (2012) 10 SIEPS European Policy Analysis.

Tromans S. Q.C., 'State Support for Nuclear New Build', (2019) 12 Journal of World Energy Law and Business.

True C., 'The Euratom Community Treaty's Prospects at the Start of the New Millennium', (2006) 1/1 International Journal of Nuclear Law.

Weiss L., 'Reliable Energy Supply and Nonproliferation', (2009) 16/2 Nonproliferation Review.

Williams L. G., 'Nuclear Safety and Nuclear Security Regulatory Challenges Facing a Country Embarking on a Nuclear Power Programme', (2019) 12 Journal of World Energy Law and Business.

Wolf S., 'Euratom Before the Court: A Political Theory of Legal Non-Integration', (2011) 15/10 European Integration Online Papers.

Wolf S., 'Euratom, the European Court of Justice, and the Limits of Nuclear Integration in Europe', (2011) 12/8 German Law Journal.

Wood I. and Broom R., 'Newcomer Countries, Welcome to the "Nuclear Club" but Before You Join, Plan Ahead and Take Example from Those Before You; Issues Relating to Construction Contracts in Countries Developing New Build Nuclear Power Plants', (2019) 12 Journal of World Energy Law and Business.

News, Web Pages and Internet Sources

Barnes P., 'Going Forward into the Past: The Resurrection of the Euratom Treaty', European Union Studies Association (EUSA), Tenth Biennial International Conference.

Commission Press Release, Commission decides on reserves for nuclear power plant decommissioning, IP/01/1799, 11 December 2001.

EU Press Release, Commission authorises aid for nuclear electricity sector, IP/90/267, 3 March 1990.

Sousa Ferro M., European Nuclear Law (10 July 2012), available at SSRN: https://ssrn.com/abstract=2103202 or http://dx.doi.org/10.2139/ssrn.2103202.

EU Law, Cases, Regulatory Decisions

Cases and Regulatory Decisions

EU Primary and Secondary Law

Council Decision 1999/64/Euratom of 22 December 1998 concerning the Fifth Framework Programme of the European Atomic Energy Community (Euratom) for research and training activities (1998 to 2002), OJ L 26, 1.2.1999, 51

Council Regulation (Euratom) No 1074/1999 of 25 May 1999 concerning investigations conducted by the European Anti-Fraud Office (OCAF), OJ L 136, 31.5.1999, 39, 41, 42

Council Regulation (Euratom) No 2587/1999 of 2 December 1999 defining the investment projects to be communicated to the Commission in accordance with Article 41 of the Treaty establishing the European Atomic Energy Community, OJ L 315, 9.12.1999, 118, 120

Commission Regulation (EC) No 1209/2000 of 8 June 2000 determining procedures for effecting the communications prescribed under Article 41 of the Treaty establishing the European Atomic Energy Community, OJ L 138, 9.6.2000, 118, 119

Commission Recommendation 2000/473/Euratom of 8 June 2000 on the application of Article 36 of the Euratom Treaty concerning the monitoring of the levels of radioactivity in the environment for the purpose of assessing the exposure of the population as a whole (notified under document number C(2000) 1299), OJ L 191, 27.7.2000, 86

Council and Commission Decision 2000/682/EC, ECSC, Euratom of 12 October 2000 on the conclusion of the Protocol to the Partnership and Cooperation Agreement establishing a partnership between the European Communities and their Member States, of the one part, and the Russian Federation, of the other part, OJ L 283, 9.11.2000, 210, 215

Council and Commission Decision 2000/683/EC, ECSC, Euratom of 12 October 2000 on the conclusion of the Protocol to the Partnership and Cooperation Agreement establishing a partnership between the European Communities and their Member States, of the one part, and Ukraine, of the other part, OJ L 283, 9.11.2000, 210, 216

Council and Commission Decision 2000/684/EC, ECSC, Euratom of 12 October 2000 on the conclusion of the Protocol to the Partnership and Cooperation Agreement establishing a partnership between the European Communities and their Member States, of the one part, and the Republic of Moldova, of the other part, OJ L 283, 9.11.2000, 210, 213

Council Decisions 2001/411/Euratom of 8 March 2001 approving the conclusion, by the Commission, of the Agreement for cooperation between the European Atomic Energy Community represented by the Commission and the Department of Energy of the United States of America in the field of fusion energy research and development, OJ L 148, 1.6.2001, 210, 215

Commission Decision 2001/412/Euratom of 21 March 2001 concerning the conclusion of the Agreement for cooperation between the European Atomic Energy Community represented by the Commission and the Department of Energy of the United States of America in the field of fusion energy research and development (notified under document number C(2001) 735), OJ L 148, 1.6.2001, 210, 215

Council Decision 2001/761/Euratom of 27 September 2001 authorising the conclusion by the Commission of two Cooperation Agreements between the European

Autonomic Energy Community and the Government of the Russian Federation in the fields of nuclear safety and controlled nuclear fusion, OJ L 287, 31.10.2001, 210, 216

Commission Decision 2001/762/Euratom of 28 September 2001 on the conclusion of two cooperation agreements between the European Atomic Energy Community and the Russian Federation in the field of nuclear safety and in the field of controlled nuclear fusion (notified under document number C(2001) 2901), OJ L 287, 31.10.2001, 210, 216

Council Decision (EC/Euratom) No 2001/792 of 23 October 2001 establishing a Community mechanism to facilitate reinforced cooperation in civil protection assistance interventions, OJ L 297, 15.11.2001, 39

Commission Recommendation of 20 December 2001 on the protection of the public against exposure to radon in drinking water supplies (notified under document number C(2001) 4580), OJ L 344, 28.12.2001, 85

Decision of the Council and of the Commission 2002/309/EC,Euratom as regards the Agreement on Scientific and Technological Cooperation, of 4 April 2002 on the conclusion of seven Agreements with the Swiss Confederation, OJ L 114, 30.4.2002,216–217

Council Decision 2002/668/Euratom of 3 June 2002 concerning the sixth framework programme of the European Atomic Energy Community (Euratom) for nuclear research and training activities, also contributing to the creation of the European Research Area (2002 to 2006), OJ L 232, 29.8.2002, 51

Commission Decision 2002/924/Euratom of 23 July 1999 on the conclusion of two cooperation agreements between the European Atomic Energy Community and the Cabinet of Ministers of Ukraine in the field of nuclear safety and in the field of controlled nuclear fusion (notified under document number C(1999) 2405), OJ L 322, 27.11.2002, 210, 216

Council Decision 2003/462/EC of 19 May 2003 on the signing on behalf of the European Community and provisional application of a Framework Agreement on a Multilateral Nuclear Environmental Programme in the Russian Federation and its Protocol on Claims, Legal Proceedings and Indemnification and approving the conclusion by the Commission on behalf of the European Atomic Energy Community of the abovementioned Agreement and its Protocol, OJ L 155, 24.6.2003, 210, 216

Council Regulation (EC, Euratom) No 1700/2003 of 22 September 2003 amending Regulation (EEC, Euratom) No 354/83 concerning the opening to the public of the historical archives of the European Economic Community and the European Atomic Energy Community, OJ L 243, 27.9.2003, 39

Council Decision 2003/744/Euratom of 22 September 2003 approving the conclusion by the Commission of an Agreement for cooperation in the peaceful uses of nuclear energy between the European Atomic Energy Community (Euratom) and the Government of the Republic of Uzbekistan, OJ L 269, 21.10.2003, 210, 214

Commission Recommendation 2004/2/Euratom of 18 December 2003 on standardised information on radioactive airborne and liquid discharges into the environment from nuclear power reactors and reprocessing plants in normal operation, OJ L 2, 6.1.2004, 86

Council and Commission Decision 2004/112/EC,Euratom of 22 December 2003 on the signature on behalf of the European Community and of the European Atomic Energy Community of the Agreement on Scientific and Technological Cooperation between the European Community and the European Atomic Energy Community, of the one part, and the Swiss Confederation, of the other part, OJ L 32, 5.2.2004, 210, 217

Council and Commission Decision 2004/239/EC,Euratom of 23 February 2004 concerning the conclusion of the Stabilisation and Association Agreement between the European Communities and their Member States, of the one part, and the former Yugoslav Republic of Macedonia, of the other part, OJ L 84, 20.3.2004, 210, 212

Commission Decision 2004/282/Euratom of 29 March 1999 concerning the conclusion of a cooperation Agreement between the European Atomic Energy Community and the Republic of Kazakhstan in the field of nuclear safety, OJ L 89, 26.3.2004, 210, 214

Council Decision 2004/294/EC of 8 March 2004 authorising the Member States which are Contracting Parties to the Paris Convention of 29 July 1960 on Third Party Liability in the Field of Nuclear Energy to ratify, in the interest of the European Community, the Protocol amending that Convention, or to accede to it, OJ L 97, 1.4.2004, 199

Commission Decision 2004/491/Euratom of 29 April 2004 amending Commission Decision 1999/819/Euratom of 16 November 1999 concerning the accession to the 1994 Convention on Nuclear Safety by the European Atomic Energy Community (Euratom) with regard to the Declaration attached thereto, OJ L 172, 6.5.2004, 210, 219

Council Decision 2004/755/Euratom of 11 October 2004 approving the conclusion by the Commission, on behalf of the European Atomic Energy Community, of the Interim Agreement on trade and trade-related matters between the European Community and the European Atomic Energy Community, of the one part, and the Republic of Tajikistan, of the other part, OJ L 340, 16.11.2004, 210, 212

Council Decision 2005/84/Euratom of 24 January 2005 approving the accession of the European Atomic Energy Community to the 'Joint Convention on the Safety of Spent Fuel Management and on the Safety of Radioactive Waste Management', OJ L 30, 3.2.2005, 210, 219

Commission Regulation (Euratom) No 302/2005 of 8 February 2005 on the application of Euratom safeguards, OJ L 54, 28.2.2005, 167, 168, 169, 170, 171, 174, 242, 243

Council and Commission Decision 2005/192/EC, Euratom of 21 February 2005 on the conclusion of the Protocol to the Stabilisation and Association Agreement between the European Communities and their Member States, of the one part, and the former Yugoslav Republic of Macedonia, of the other part, to take account of the accession of the Czech Republic, the Republic of Estonia, the Republic of Cyprus, the Republic of Latvia, the Republic of Lithuania, the Republic of Hungary, the Republic of Malta, the Republic of Poland, the Republic

Energy Organization for the Joint Implementation of the ITER Project and of the Agreement on Privileges and Immunities of the ITER International Fusion Energy Organization for the Joint Implementation of the ITER Project (notified under document number C(2006) 5557, OJ L 358, 16.12.2006, 210, 218

Council Decision 2006/970/Euratom of 18 December 2006 Concerning the Seventh Framework Programme of the European Atomic Energy Community (Euratom) for nuclear research and training activities (2007 to 2011), OJ L 400, 30.12.2006, 51

Commission Decision 2007/58/Euratom of 28 August 2006 concerning the conclusion of an Agreement between the Government of Japan and the European Atomic Energy Community for co-operation in the peaceful uses of nuclear energy, OJ L 32, 6.2.2007, 210, 215

Council Decision 2007/198/Euratom of 27 March 2007 establishing the European Joint Undertaking for ITER and the Development of Fusion Energy and conferring advantages upon it, OJ L 90, 30.3.2007, 55, 56, 123, 125, 126, 127, 128, 129, 130, 133, 218, 238, 239, 240

Decision of the Council and of the Commission 2007/502/EC,Euratom of 25 June 2007 on the signing, on behalf of the European Community and the European Atomic Energy Community, and provisional application of the Agreement on Scientific and Technological Cooperation between the European Community and the European Atomic Energy Community, of the one part, and the Swiss Confederation, of the other part, OJ L 189, 20.7.2007, 211, 217

Council Decision 2007/513/Euratom of 10 July 2007 approving the accession of the European Atomic Energy Community to the amended Convention on the Physical Protection of Nuclear Material and Nuclear Facilities - Declaration by the European Atomic Energy Community according to Articles 18(4) and 17(3) of the CPPNM, OJ L 190, 21.7.2007, 210, 220

Council and Commission Decision 2007/541/EC,Euratom of 28 June 2007 on the conclusion of the Protocol to the Partnership and Cooperation Agreement establishing a partnership between the EuropeaCommunities and their Member States, of the one part, and the Russian Federation, of the other part, to take account of the accession of the Republic of Bulgaria and Romania to the European Union, OJ L 200, 1.8.2007, 211, 215

Council Decision 2007/614/Euratom of 30 January 2007 concerning the conclusion, by the Commission, of the Agreement between the European Atomic Energy Community and the Government of Japan for the Joint Implementation of the Broader Approach Activities in the Field of Fusion Energy Research, OJ L 246, 21.9.2007, 210, 215

Council and Commission Decision 2007/644/EC,Euratom of 18 September 2007 concerning the conclusion of the Protocol to the Partnership and Cooperation Agreement (PCA) between the European Communities and their Member States, of the one part, and Ukraine, of the other part, on accession of the Republic of Bulgaria and Romania to the PCA, OJ L 261, 6.10.2007, 211, 216

Council and Commission Decision 2007/681/EC,Euratom of 9 October 2007 concerning the conclusion of the Protocol to the Partnership and Cooperation Agreement

(PCA) between the European Communities and their Member States, of the one part, and the Republic of Moldova, of the other part, on accession of the Republic of Bulgaria and Romania to the PCA, OJ L 281, 25.10.2007, 211, 213

Decision of the Council and of the Commission 2007/834/EC,Euratom of 22 November 2007 on the position to be taken by the Communities in the Governing Board of the International Science and Technology Centre as regards the accession of the Swiss Confederation to the Agreement establishing an International Science and Technology Centre between the United States of America, Japan, the Russian Federation and, acting as one Party, the European Atomic Energy Community and the European Economic Community, OJ L 330, 15.12.2007, 211

Commission Decision 2008/72/Euratom of 22 November 2007 on the conclusion of Agreements in the form of Exchange of Letters between the European Atomic Energy Community (Euratom) and the Swiss Confederation (Switzerland) on the application of the ITER Agreement, the Agreement on Privileges and Immunities for ITER and the Broader Approach Agreement to the territory of Switzerland and on Switzerland's membership in the European Joint Undertaking for ITER and the Development of Fusion Energy, OJ L 20, 24.1.2008, 210, 217

Commission Decision 2008/99/EC,Euratom of 19 December 2007 concerning the accession of the European Atomic Energy Community to the Convention on the Physical Protection of Nuclear Material and Nuclear Facilities, OJ L 34, 8.2.2008, 210, 220

Council Decision 2008/114/EC,Euratom of 12 February 2008 establishing Statutes for the Euratom Supply Agency, OJ L 41, 15.2.2008, 148, 149, 150

Council and Commission Decision 2008/429/EC,Euratom of 26 May 2008 on the conclusion of the Protocol to the Partnership and Cooperation Agreement between the European Communities and their Member States, of the one part, and the Republic of Armenia, of the other part, to take account of the accession of the Republic of Bulgaria and Romania to the European Union, OJ L 151, 11.6.2008, 211

Council and Commission Decision 2008/430/EC,Euratom of 26 May 2008 on the conclusion of the Protocol to the Partnership and Cooperation Agreement between the European Communities and their Member States, of the one part, and Georgia, of the other part, to take account of the accession of the Republic of Bulgaria and Romania to the European Union, OJ L 151, 11.6.2008, 211, 213

Council and Commission Decision 2008/438/EC,Euratom of 14 May 2008 on the conclusion of the Protocol to the Stabilisation and Association Agreement between the European Communities and their Member States, of the one part, and the former Yugoslav Republic of Macedonia, of the other part, to take account of the accession of the Republic of Bulgaria and Romania to the European Union, OJ L 155, 13.6.2008, 211, 212

Commission Decision 2009/25/Euratom of 4 December 2006 on the conclusion of the Agreement for co-operation in the peaceful uses of nuclear energy between the European Atomic Energy Community and the Government of the Republic of Kazakhstan, OJ L 10, 15.1.2009, 210, 214

European Union and European Atomic Energy Community and the Swiss Confederation associating the Swiss Confederation to Horizon 2020 — the Framework Programme for Research and Innovation and the Research and Training Programme of the European Atomic Energy Community complementing Horizon 2020, and regulating the Swiss Confederation's participation in the ITER activities carried out by Fusion for Energy, OJ L 370, 30.12.2014, 210, 217

Council and Commission Decision (EU, Euratom) 2015/54 of 17 November 2014 on the position to be taken on behalf of the European Union and the European Atomic Energy Community within the Association Council established by the Association Agreement between the European Union and the European Atomic Energy Community and their Member States, of the one part, and Georgia, of the other part, as regards the adoption of decisions of the Association Council on the Rules of Procedure of the Association Council and those of the Association Committee and of Sub-Committees, the establishment of two Sub-Committees, and the delegation of certain powers by the Association Council to the Association Committee in Trade configuration, OJ L 9, 15.1.2015, 211

Council and Commission Decision (EU, Euratom) 2015/55 of 17 November 2014 on the position to be taken on behalf of the European Union and the European Atomic Energy Community within the Association Council established by the Association Agreement between the European Union and the European Atomic Energy Community and their Member States, of the one part, and the Republic of Moldova, of the other part, as regards the adoption of decisions of the Association Council on the Rules of Procedure of the Association Council and those of the Association Committee and of Sub-Committees, the establishment of two Sub-Committees and the delegation of certain powers by the Association Council to the Association Committee in Trade configuration, OJ L 9, 15.1.2015, 211

Council and Commission Decision (EU, Euratom) 2015/60 of 15 December 2014 on the position to be taken on behalf of the European Union and the European Atomic Energy Community within the Association Council established by the Association Agreement between the European Union and the European Atomic Energy Community and their Member States, of the one part, and Ukraine, of the other part, as regards the adoption of decisions of the Association Council on the Rules of Procedure of the Association Council and those of the Association Committee and of Sub-Committees, the establishment of two Sub-Committees, and the delegation of certain powers by the Association Council to the Association Committee in Trade configuration, OJ L 10, 16.1.2015, 211

Council Decision (Euratom) 2015/224 of 10 February 2015 amending Decision 2007/198/Euratom establishing the European Joint Undertaking for ITER and the Development of Fusion Energy and conferring advantages upon it, OJ L 37, 13.2.2015, 125, 126

Council and Commission Decision (EU, Euratom) 2015/998 of 21 April 2015 on the conclusion of the Stabilisation and Association Agreement between the European Communities and their Member States, of the one part, and Bosnia and Herzegovina, of the other part, OJ L 164, 30.6.2015, 211

Council Regulation (EU) 2015/1589 of 13 July 2015 laying down detailed rules for the application of Article 108 of the Treaty on the Functioning of the European Union, OJ L 248, 24.9.2015, 148

Council Decision (EU) 2015/1892 of 18 February 2014 approving the conclusion, by the European Commission, on behalf of the European Atomic Energy Community, of the Protocol to the Stabilisation and Association Agreement between the European Communities and their Member States, of the one part, and the former Yugoslav Republic of Macedonia, of the other part, to take account of the accession of the Republic of Croatia to the European Union, OJ L 279, 23.10.2015, 210, 212

Commission Decision 2015/C 364/04 of 26 October 2015 on the conclusion of the Stabilisation and Association Agreement between the European Union and the European Atomic Energy Community, of the one part, and of Kosovo, of the other part, OJ C 364, 4.11.2015, 210, 212

Council Decision (Euratom) 2015/1990 of 26 October 2015 approving the conclusion, by the European Commission, on behalf of the European Atomic Energy Community, of the Agreement continuing the International Science and Technology Center, OJ L 290, 6.11.2015, 210, 217

Council Decision (EU) 2015/1993 of 22 October 2015 approving the conclusion, by the European Commission, on behalf of the European Atomic Energy Community, of the Stabilisation and Association Agreement between the European Union and the European Atomic Energy Community, of the one part, and of Kosovo, of the other part, OJ L 290, 6.11.2015, 210, 212

Commission Decision 2015/C 385/03 of 3 November 2015 establishing the position to be taken on behalf of the European Atomic Energy Community within the Stabilisation and Association Council established by the Stabilisation and Association Agreement between the European Communities and their Member States, of the one part, and Bosnia and Herzegovina, of the other part, concerning a Decision of the Stabilisation and Association Council adopting its rules of procedure, OJ C 385, 19.11.2015, 210

Council Decision (Euratom) of 10 November 2015 approving the conclusion, by the European Commission, of the amendments to Protocols 1 and 2 to the Agreement between the United Kingdom, the European Atomic Energy Community and the International Atomic Energy Agency for the Application of Safeguards in Connection with the Treaty for the Prohibition of Nuclear Weapons in Latin America and the Caribbean, OJ L 317, 3.12.2015, 210, 217–218

Council Decision (Euratom) 2015/2228 of 10 November 2015 approving the conclusion, by the European Commission, of the amendments to Protocols 1 and 2 to the Agreement between the French Republic, the European Atomic Energy Community and the International Atomic Energy Agency for the Application of Safeguards in Connection with the Treaty for the Prohibition of Nuclear Weapons in Latin America and the Caribbean, OJ L 317, 3.12.2015, 210, 218

Council Regulation (Euratom) 2016/52 of 15 January 2016 laying down maximum permitted levels of radioactive contamination of food and feed following a nuclear accident or any other case of radiological emergency, and repealing

Regulation (Euratom) No 3954/87 and Commission Regulations (Euratom) No 944/89 and (Euratom) No 770/90, OJ L 13, 20.1.2016, 87, 97, 98, 236

Commission Decision 2016/C 52/03 of 8 February 2016 on the conclusion, on behalf of the European Atomic Energy Community, of the Protocol to the Stabilisation and Association Agreement between the European Communities and their Member States, on the one part, and the former Yugoslav Republic of Macedonia, of the other part, to take account of the accession of the Republic of Croatia to the European Union, OJ C 52, 11.2.2016, 210, 212

Commission Decision 2016/C 52/04 of 8 February 2016 on the conclusion, on behalf of the European Atomic Energy Community, of the Protocol to the Stabilisation and Association Agreement between the European Communities and their Member States, on the one part, and the Republic of Montenegro of the other part, to take account of the accession of the Republic of Croatia to the European Union, OJ C 52, 11.2.2016, 210, 213

Commission Decision 2016/C 52/05 of 8 February 2016 on the conclusion, on behalf of the European Atomic Energy Community, of the Protocol to the Stabilisation and Association Agreement between the European Communities and their Member States, on the one part, and the Republic of Albania, of the other part, to take account of the accession of the Republic of Croatia to the European Union, OJ C 52, 11.2.2016, 210, 214

Commission Decision 2016/C 52/06 of 8 February 2016 on the conclusion, on behalf of the European Atomic Energy Community, of the Protocol to the Stabilisation and Association Agreement between the European Communities and their Member States, on the one part, and the Republic of Serbia, of the other part, to take account of the accession of the Republic of Croatia to the European Union, OJ C 52, 11.2.2016, 210, 213

Commission Recommendation (Euratom) 2016/538 of 4 April 2016 on the application of Article 103 of the Euratom Treaty, OJ L 89, 6.4.2016, 203, 221, 222, 223

Council Decision (Euratom) 2016/829 of 12 May 2016 approving the conclusion, by the European Commission, on behalf of the European Atomic Energy Community, of a Protocol to the Partnership and Cooperation Agreement establishing a partnership between the European Communities and their Member States, of the one part, and the Republic of Tajikistan, of the other part, to take account of the accession of the Republic of Croatia to the European Union, OJ L 140, 27.5.2016, 210, 212

Council Decision (Euratom) 2016/852 of 12 May 2016 approving the conclusion, by the European Commission, on behalf of the European Atomic Energy Community, of a Protocol to the Partnership and Cooperation Agreement establishing a partnership between the European Communities and their Member States, of the one part, and Turkmenistan, of the other part, to take account of the accession of the Republic of Bulgaria, the Czech Republic, the Republic of Estonia, the Republic of Croatia, the Republic of Cyprus, the Republic of Latvia, the Republic of Lithuania, Hungary, the Republic of Malta, the Republic of Poland, Romania, the Republic of Slovenia and the Slovak Republic to the European Union, OJ L 142, 31.5.2016, 210, 212

EU Documents and Communications

European Commission, '50 Years of the Euratom Treaty', Memo/07/118, 26 March 2007 Brussels, 3, 46, 80, 84, 85, 124, 139, 164, 205

European Parliament Report on the proposal for a Council Directive (Euratom) setting up a Community framework for nuclear safety of nuclear installations (Hökmark Report) A6-0236/2009, 31, 84

European Parliament, Committee on Industry, Research and Energy, Rapporteur: E. Maldeikis, Report on Assessing Euratom: 50 years of European nuclear energy policy, A6-0129/2007, 31

European Parliament, Report on the proposal for a Council Directive (Euratom) setting up a Community framework for nuclear safety of nuclear installations, A6-0236/2009, 31, 84

JRC Implementation Review 2017: In the context of the interim evaluation of the Horizon 2020 Programme, July 2017, European Commission Joint Research Centre (JRC), Adviser for Evaluation and Scientific Integrity Brussels, 59

JRC, The European Commission's science and knowledge service: 60 stories for the 60th anniversary, Brussels 2017, 59

Laeken Declaration of December 15, 2001 on the Future of the European Union, DOC/01/18, 17

Legal Study for the Accession of Euratom to the Paris Convention on Third Party Liability in the Field of Nuclear Energy, European Commission, Final Report TREN/CC/01-2005, 193

Report from the Commission on Subsidiarity and Proportionality COM (2012)373 final, 19

Report from the Commission to the European Parliament, the Council and the European Economic and Social Committee, Interim evaluation of the Euratom Research and Training Programme 2014–2018, COM(2017) 697 final, 62, 63

Report on Assessing Euratom: 50 years of European nuclear energy policy, European Parliament, Committee on Industry, Research and Energy, Rapporteur: E. Maldeikis, A6-0129/2007, 30, 31

The Commission of the European Communities, Action Plan 'Simplifying and improving the regulatory environment', COM (2002) 278 final, 19

The Commission of the European Communities, Green Paper: A European Strategy for Sustainable, Competitive and Secure Energy, COM (2006) 105 final, 1

The European Commission, Proposal for a Council Regulation establishing a European Instrument for Nuclear Safety complementing the Neighbourhood, Development and International Cooperation Instrument on the basis of the Euratom Treaty, COM(2018) 462, 14.6.2018, 40

The European Commission's science and knowledge service: JRC Strategy 2030, adopted in the spring of 2016, 62

The European Parliament Directorate-General for Research/ M. O´Driscoll and G. Lake, The European Parliament and the Euratom Treaty: past, present and future, Energy Research Series, Working Paper ENER 114 EN, EUROPEAN PARLIAMENT L-2929 Luxembourg, 3

International Legal Acts and Documents

Index

ENERGY AND ENVIRONMENTAL LAW & POLICY SERIES

1. Stephen J. Turner, *A Substantive Environmental Right: An Examination of the Legal Obligations of Decision-makers towards the Environment*, 2009 (ISBN 978-90-411-2815-7).
2. Helle Tegner Anker, Birgitte Egelund Olsen & Anita Rønne (eds), *Legal Systems and Wind Energy: A Comparative Perspective*, 2009 (ISBN 978-90-411-2831-7).
3. David Langlet, *Prior Informed Consent and Hazardous Trade: Regulating Trade in Hazardous Goods at the Intersection of Sovereignty, Free Trade and Environmental Protection*, 2009 (ISBN 978-90-411-2821-8).
4. Louis J. Kotzé and Alexander R. Paterson (eds), *The Role of the Judiciary in Environmental Governance: Comparative Perspectives*, 2009 (ISBN 978-90-411-2708-2).
5. Tuula Honkonen, *The Common but Differentiated Responsibility Principle in Multilateral Environmental Agreement's: Regulatory and Policy Aspects*, 2009 (ISBN 978-90-411-3153-9).
6. Barbara Pozzo (ed.), *The Implementation of the Seveso Directives in an Enlarged Europe: A Look into the Past and a challenge for the Future*, 2009 (ISBN 978-90-411-2854-6).
7. Henrik M. Inadomi, *Independent Power Projects in Developing Countries: Legal Investment Protection and Consequences for Development*, 2010 (ISBN 978-90-411-3178-2).
8. Nahid Islam, *The Law of Non-Navigational Uses of International Watercourses: Options for Regional Regime-Building in Asia*, 2010 (ISBN 978-90-411-3196-6).
9. Yasuhiro Shigeta, *International Judicial Control of Environmental Protection: Standard Setting, Compliance Control and the Development of International Environmental Law by the International Judiciary*, 2010 (ISBN 978-90-411-3151-5).
10. Katleen Janssen, *The Availability of Spatial and Environmental Data in the European Union: At the Crossroads between Public and Economic Interests*, 2010 (ISBN 978-90-411-3287-1).
11. Henrik Bjørnebye, *Investing in EU Energy Security: Exploring the Regulatory Approach to Tomorrow's Electricity Production*, 2010 (ISBN 978-90-411-3118-8).
12. Véronique Bruggeman, *Compensating catastrophe victims: A Comparative Law and Economics Approach*, 2010 (ISBN 978-90-411-3263-5).
13. Michael G. Faure, Han Lixin & Shan Hongjun, *Maritime Pollution Liability and Policy: China, Europe and the US*, 2010 (ISBN 978-90-411-2869-0).

14. Anton Ming-Zhi Gao, *Regulating Gas Liberalization: A Comparative Study on Unbundling and Open Access Regimes in the US, Europe, Japan, South Korea and Taiwan*, 2010 (ISBN 978-90-411-3347-2).
15. Mustafa Erkan, *International Energy Investment Law: Stability through Contractual Clauses*, 2011 (ISBN 978-90-411-3411-0).
16. Levente Borzsa´k, *The Impact of Environmental Concerns on the Public Enforcement Mechanism under EU law: Environmental protection in the 25th hour*, 2011 (ISBN 978-90-411-3408-0).
17. Tarcísio Hardman Reis, *Compensation for Environmental Damages under International Law: The Role of the International Judge*, 2011 (ISBN 978-90-411-3437-0).
18. Kim Talus, *Vertical Natural Gas Transportation Capacity, Upstream Commodity Contracts and EU Competition Law*, 2011 (ISBN 978-90-411-3407-3).
19. WangHui, *Civil Liability for Marine Oil Pollution Damage: A Comparative and Economic Study of the International, US and Chinese Compensation Regime*, 2011 (ISBN 978-90-411-3672-5).
20. Chowdhury Ishrak Ahmed Siddiky, *Cross-Border Pipeline Arrangements: What Would a Single Regulatory Framework Look Like?*, 2012 (ISBN 978-90-411-3844-6).
21. Rozeta Karova, *Liberalization of Electricity Markets and Public Service Obligations in the Energy Community*, 2012 (ISBN 978-90-411-3849-1).
22. Sandra Cassotta, *Environmental Damage and Liability Problems in a Multilevel Context: The Case of the Environmental Liability Directive*, 2012 (ISBN 978-90-411-3830-9).
23. Mark Wilde, *Civil Liability for Environmental Damage: Comparative Analysis of Law and Policy in Europe and US*, 2013 (ISBN 978-90-411-3233-8).
24. Bernard Taverne, *Petroleum, Industry and Governments: A Study of the Involvement of Industry and Governments in Exploring for and Producing Petroleum*, 2013 (ISBN 978-90-411-4563-5).
25. Anton Ming-Zhi Gao & Chien Te Fan (eds), *Legal Issues of Renewable Energy in the Asia Region: Recent Developments in a Post-Fukushima and Post-Kyoto Protocol Era*, 2014 (ISBN 978-90-411-4856-8).
26. Sabina Manea, *The Instrumentalization of Property: Legal Interests in the EU Emissions Trading System*, 2014 (ISBN 978-90-411-5420-0).
27. Joseph A. Tolorunse, *Protection of Property Rights in Discovered Petroleum Reservoirs*, 2014 (ISBN 978-90-411-5604-4).
28. Katelijn Van Hende, *Offshore Wind in the European Union: Towards Integrated Management of Our Marine Waters*, 2015 (ISBN 978-90-411-5613-6).
29. Ken'ichi Matsumoto & Anton Ming-Zhi Gao (eds), *Economic Instruments to Combat Climate Change in Asian Countries*, 2015 (ISBN 978-90-411-5408-8).

30. Eduardo G. Pereira & Damilola S. Olawuyi (eds), *Practical Considerations to Negotiate an Enforceable Joint Operating Agreement under Civil Law Jurisdictions*, Second Edition, 2020 (ISBN 978-94-035-0664-7).
31. Ying Shen, *China's Way to Carbon Emissions Reduction: The Choice of Regulatory Instruments and Its Legal Challenges*, 2015 (ISBN 978-90-411-6049-2).
32. Roy Andrew Partain, *Environmental Hazards from Offshore Methane Hydrate Operations: Civil Liability and Regulations for Efficient Governance*, 2017 (ISBN 978-90-411-8730-7).
33. Anton Ming-Zhi Gao & Chien-Te Fan (eds), *The Development of a Comprehensive Legal Framework for the Promotion of Offshore Wind Power: The Lessons from Europe and Pacific Asia*, 2017 (ISBN 978-90-411-8397-2).
34. Tade Oyewunmi, *Regulating Gas Supply to Power Markets: Transnational Approaches to Competitiveness and Security of Supply*, 2018 (ISBN 978-90-411-9869-3).
35. Huseyin Cagri Corlu, *Application of Anti-manipulation Law to EU Wholesale Energy Markets and Its Interplay with EU Competition Law*, 2018 (ISBN 978-90-411-9603-3).
36. Kaisa Huhta, *Capacity Mechanisms in EU Energy Law: Ensuring Security of Supply in the Energy Transition*, 2019 (ISBN 978-94-035-1451-2).
37. Maria João C. Pereira Rolim, *Reconciling Energy, the Environment and Sustainable Development: The Role of Law and Regulation*, 2019 (ISBN 978-94-035-1461-1).
38. Eduardo G. Pereira, Alexandra Wawryk, Heike Trischmann, Catherine Banet & Keith B. Hall (eds), *The Regulation of Decommissioning, Abandonment and Reuse Initiatives in the Oil and Gas Industry: From Obligation to Opportunities*, 2020 (ISBN 978-94-035-0693-7).
39. Rasa Engstedt, *Handbook on European Nuclear Law: Competences of the Euratom Community under the Euratom Treaty*, 2021 (ISBN 978-94-035-2830-4).

www.ingramcontent.com/pod-product-compliance
Lightning Source LLC
Chambersburg PA
CBHW071240230926
51849CB00001B/173
* 9 7 8 9 4 0 3 5 2 8 3 0 4 *